COLIN WILSON was hailed as a prodigy on publication of *The Outsider* in 1956. He has since become one of the world's leading criminologists and true crime authors, as well as a distinguished broadcaster and journalist.

By the same author:

Encyclopedia of Murder
A Criminal History of Mankind
Written in Blood: A History of Forensic Detection
The Mammoth Book of True Crime
Beyond the Occult: Twenty Years Research into the Paranormal
The Corpse Garden
The Mammoth Encyclopedia of Unsolved Mysteries

The World's Greatest True Crime Stories

Edited by
Colin Wilson, Ian Schott,
Ed Shedd, Damon Wilson and
Rowan Wilson

Magpie Books, London

Constable & Robinson Ltd
3 The Lanchesters
162 Fulham Palace Road
London W6 9ER

This edition published by Magpie Books,
an imprint of Constable & Robinson Ltd 2004

This collection first published in the UK as
Colin Wilson's World Famous Crimes by Robinson Publishing Ltd 1995

First published as *World Famous Gangsters*, *World Famous Robberies*,
World Famous Swindles and Hoaxes and *World Famous Scandals*
all copyright © Magpie Books 1994

Collected edition copyright © Constable & Robinson Ltd 1995, 2004

A copy of the British Library Cataloguing in
Publication Data is available from the British Library

ISBN 1-84119-858-7

Printed and bound in the EU

CONTENTS

PART 2
**WORLD FAMOUS ROBBERIES by Colin Wilson, with
  Damon and Rowan Wilson**

PART 1: WORLD FAMOUS GANGSTERS

THE SICILIAN DONS

Sicily is a parched, mountainous and pitiless country. Despite its small size, it possesses a peculiar sense of remoteness; it is full of wild, empty places, for hundreds of years the haunt of the infamous Sicilian bandits (these, often mafiosi on the run, were still customarily holding up vehicles in the 1960s). Apart from one or two cities favoured by the tourists, the morose and introverted island is covered by dull, crumbling towns, into which the rural population has traditionally huddled for mutual protection from the elements and from brigands.

It is an innately feudal society, and though the Sicilian princes and their houses have passed away, the Mafia has long since filled that power vacuum, and the Mafia dons have bought up the estates of the impotent aristocrats.

No one knows where the name "Mafia" originates. Sicilians say that when Sicily was occupied by the French in 1282, a young Sicilian woman was raped by a French soldier on her wedding day. Her distraught mother ran through the streets shouting *"Ma fia! Ma fia!"* (my daughter, my daughter). The Sicilians immediately rose up and massacred their French oppressors. It is also said that the name "Mafia" derives from a similar word in Arabic, which means "place of refuge".

But the Mafia, the very existence of which has been frequently denied, not only by its members but by prominent politicians, has been an integral part of southern Italian culture for centuries. For two thousand years the peasants of Sicily and southern Italy struggled against bitter poverty, rapacious landlords, and endured constant changes of master as a consequence of territorial battles between princes; Sicily has been invaded no less than six times.

It was an anarchistic world, in need of order. But the law was the oppressor of the peasants, not their defence. As a consequence, a system of underground government evolved, run by men outside the law. These were often violent and committed criminals, but to the peasants their word was their bond, and they could be expected to arbitrate in local disputes, protect the people from outside marauders, preserve the integrity of the local culture and intercede with the nominal rulers of the land. Such a man, who had to be strong enough to avenge any insult to himself and his friends, took the title of *un uomo d'onore*, a man of honour, or *un uomo di rispetto*, a man of respect. They became the Mafia, the most closed and ruthless of secret societies.

Though the Mafia has long been driven by the pursuit of wealth, it has continued to rely for its support on this tradition of "honour". In addition, certain traits in the Sicilian character make it wholly suited to the temperament required of mafiosi. As an isolated race, the Sicilians have clung to the ties of blood and soil with a savage ferocity, in a fashion both atavistic and tribal; indeed some of their customs are echoed in the remote tribes of Africa and Asia.

When the Italians emigrated to America, the men of honour went with them, and were initially a useful defence against an often hostile American society. They protected the Italian communities, ran the lotteries, dealt with the authorities and offered loans. The Italians were ambivalent about the Mafia, or, as it was also known, *amici nostri*, meaning "our friends" (*cosa nostra*, another branch of the Mafia, literally means "the things we have in common"). They venerated these paternal criminals, while praying that their children would never enter into this strange, violent world, the detritus of which they would come across in the shape of unrecognizable corpses strewn over the local wastelands. Many families noticed, when burying some aged and withered relative, how heavy the coffin was. They would know that alongside their grandmother in the coffin lay some victim of a Mafia dispute, whom the undertaker had been asked to squeeze in.

The Sicilian tradition of the *vendetta* – a fight to the death between clans until honour is satisfied – is a mainstay of the Mafia mentality. Vendettas have made for some of the bloodiest episodes in the island's history. The worst vendetta of them all took place in the neighbourhood of the poor, dusty towns of Bagheria and Monreale between 1872 and 1878.

The two Mafia clans involved were the Fratuzzi and the Stoppaglieri, who were both active in the same area but had hitherto kept hostilities to a minimum. Then, in 1872, Giuseppe Lipari, a member of the Fratuzzi clan, committed what in Mafia parlance is called *infamità* by denouncing a member of the Stoppaglieri to the police. The Stoppaglieri duly sent word to the Fratuzzi that they should, in time honoured fashion, execute Lipari. This they failed to do, and a vendetta was born. Within months all the close relations of the original disputants had been killed, and the more remote kin were being compelled to participate in the tit-for-tat murders. When everybody who was officially a Fratuzzi or a Stoppaglieri was dead, the entire population began fearfully rummaging through its ancestry to find out if they too had some distant blood links which would compel them to participate in the round of killings. Within a few years, a man walking down the street would find himself approached by a withered old crone swathed in black mourning who would inform him that he

They say that there is nothing personal about a proper Mafia execution. These are the words of Nick Gentile, an American mafioso from Sicily, discussing the ethics of eliminating an uncontrollable young hood from his native country: "There was nothing we could do about him so he had to be rubbed out. We embalmed the body and sent it back to his people in Sicily. His folks were poor – they didn't have anything – so we put a diamond ring on his finger, the way they'd see it the moment they opened the casket. I guess we did the right thing. We figured otherwise that he'd end up in the electric chair or the gas chamber. That way they wouldn't even get his body back." The Sicilians regard the retrieval of the body after a murder to be of the greatest importance. For vengeance must be sworn "in the presence of the corpse". If the body cannot be found, the anger of the relatives has no ritual outlet. Hence the most perfidious of crimes are kidnappings in which the victim disappears altogether.

Even in this century, some towns have been decimated by prolonged vendettas. The Mafia stronghold of Corleone, a tiny sullen town set in an unforgiving rocky landscape, experienced no less than 153 murders in the years between 1944 and 1948. Most of the bodies were never recovered. The town of Favara suffered 150 Mafia-vendetta killings in a single year; between 1914 and 1924 only one male inhabitant died of natural causes in old age (residents were not sure whether to be proud or not of this absurd statistic). Mass emigration to escape involvement in vendettas resulted in Sicily losing one-tenth of its adult population between 1953 and 1961; some towns became virtually uninhabited.

might not be aware, but he was now the surviving head of the Fratuzzi or Stoppaglieri clan, and was therefore in state of ritual vendetta.

In vain, many distant relatives of the decimated clans tried to emigrate, or conceal themselves; the area was becoming depopulated and reverting to wilderness. But the inheritors of the vendetta were always tracked down and forced to continue the feud, though the original ground for it had long since been forgotten. By 1878, the supply of able-bodied men was almost exhausted, and boys were being pressed into service. On one occasion a child was informed that in the absence of living seniors, he was now a clan leader, and, presented with a loaded blunderbuss, he was escorted to a point where he might attempt an ambush.

In the end, one of the few surviving Fratuzzi, a man called Salvatore D'Amico, who had lost all his family and was sick of the slaughter, offered his own life to end it. He went to the police and, in a repetition of the events that sparked the feud, informed on the Stoppaglieri, thus giving his own clan a ritual means to end the vendetta. The Fratuzzi understood D'Amico's noble intent; this time they made no mistake and duly killed him, displaying his body so that the Stoppaglieri might see that after six years and the blood of several hundred people the infamità had finally been paid for. Thus the vendetta was halted.

Another tradition of the Sicilian Mafia is that of *omertà*. Omertà is a complex notion. At one level it simply means "manliness", but at another it is to do with silence and self-

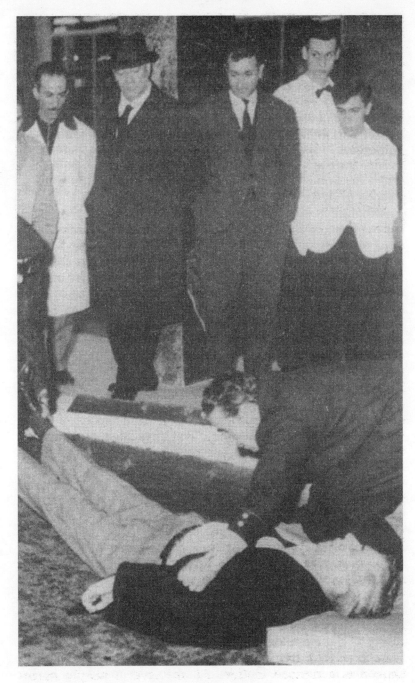

The end of a gangster – Charles 'Lucky' Luciano

restraint. When the police would come across a seriously wounded mafioso and ask him to identify his attacker, the reply would traditionally be couched in the followed terms: "If I die, may God forgive me, as I forgive the one who did this. If I manage to pull through, I know how to settle my own accounts." Such a response displays omertà. If wronged, a true man of honour will not wreak his vengeance in a rash, bloody act, or betray his anger; he will certainly not tell the authorities. Instead he will wait, for years if necessary, to avenge himself in the coldest way possible, often striking when he seems to be on excellent terms with the man he intends to destroy.

Although it stands outside Christian morality, the uncorrupted form of the feudal Mafia that survives in Sicily has a strict morality of its own. Mafiosi don't see themselves as petty criminals, but as lawgivers; they do not steal from the community, but take what is rightfully theirs in return for offering their continued protection. Killing is a pragmatic and at times inevitable action; a punishment.

The position of strength that the Mafia has achieved in this century, as it progressed from a federation of outlaws into a consolidated money-making machine, is largely the work of two formidable dons: Don Vito Cascio Ferro and Don Calogero Vizzini. These men struck the deals that brought the Mafia out of the shadows into the abandoned palaces of Sicily's lost aristocrats, and into the town halls.

In the early part of the century, Don Vito Cascio Ferro was for twenty-five years the undisputed master of Sicily. In his youth he had emigrated to America, where he had become a leader of the "Black Hand", an amalgamation of fugitive mafiosi and members of the Naples-based *Camorra*. While in America, he picked up a taste for smart expensive clothes and on his return to Sicily sported dashing, anachronistic garb: frock coat, wide-brimmed fedora, pleated shirt and flowing cravat. While other Mafia dons still dressed like surly peasants, Don Vito cut a sartorial swath through Sicilian society. He became an honoured guest at the salons of Palermo, opened exhibitions, romped with Dukes and Duchesses, frequented theatres, bought himself a phonograph and even took a hot-air balloon flight to demonstrate his interest in scientific advancement. Society women trembled with a strange passion when they spoke his name, and Don Vito had to reprimand his barber severely for selling off his hair cuttings as sacred amulets.

In the nineteenth century it was the Mafia, casting itself as a supporter of the popular leader Garibaldi, that whipped up the Sicilians into the violent frenzy that finally broke the shackles of the Bourbon state. When, before the turn of the century, democratic elections were held in Sicily, the Mafia took control of the political machinery and gradually drew apart from the people, blatantly compelling them at gunpoint to elect the Mafia's own chosen creatures. With political power assured, Don Vito was free to develop the system of *pizzi*. *Pizzo* refers to the beak of a small bird, and Don Vito adopted this term as a euphemism for racketeering, describing Mafia tolls and levies as "wetting the beak" – taking his cut.

Don Vito organized beak-wetting at the expense of the farmers, whose produce the Mafia bought dirt cheap and then sold at vast profits in the markets (where only those who had paid a levy were allowed to own a stall, and all prices were fixed by the Mafia). The Mafia also wet its beak in the meat, beer, and fish industries; in the sulphur mines, salt mines, building industry and cemeteries. It also took up a large portion of the tobacco smuggling racket and cornered the market in stolen Roman artifacts. The owners of country houses and estates were invited to employ mafiosi as guards against the otherwise inevitable arson attack. The Mafia sold and managed the monopolies in every area of trade; even beggars were obliged to pay for their right to occupy a prominent pitch.

The Mafia effectively replaced the police force as the arbiters of law and order and thereby established one of its most consistent sources of income: the recovery of stolen property. If a horse, mule, jewel or, latterly, motor-car was stolen, the victim would be approached by a mafioso who would offer to recover the lost object for a commission of up to thirty-three per cent of its value. If the commission was agreed upon, the object would be virtually guaranteed to reappear without delay. The original thief would be compelled to sell the object back to the mafioso at a small price (but would be grateful to escape with his life) and the mafioso would profit at the expense of both parties. It was a popular service; the police charged nothing but could only recover stolen property in one case out of ten. The Mafia might be expensive, but was successful ninety per cent of the time.

This happy state of affairs continued until Mussolini and the Fascists came to power. Although the Mafia had contributed to the Fascists' funds (an insurance policy; besides, Fascism was preferable to any form of Communism), Mussolini was wholly distrustful of the Mafia, realizing that its members habitually turned on their allies. More importantly, the power of the Mafia presented a direct challenge to the arrogance of his authority. Il Duce made a most unhappy trip to Sicily in 1924. He saw that the Fascist administrators were powerless in the face of the Mafia, that the police could obtain no witnesses to any crime, and that the Mafia-elected deputies to Parliament devoted their time exclusively to composing speeches denying the existence of their criminal masters.

Some of the rackets Don Vito established were quite fantastic. The Mafia imposed a tax on lovers, so that a young man going to court a girl who sat – as was the custom – behind a barred window, had to pay what was known as "the price of a candle" to guarantee his safety. The Mafia also exploited the financial opportunities offered by religion. It controlled the standing committees of the various cults of the Sicilian saints (the committees had access to the funds raised in the saint's name), and had a virtual monopoly on the manufacture of devotional candles. Later the organization began manufacturing religious artifacts, producing holy statues, medallions and even relics by the thousand; one Italian newspaper reported that there were in existence seventeen embalmed arms attributed to St Andrew, thirteen to St Stephen and twelve to St Philip. There were also no less than sixty fingers said to belong to St John the Baptist and forty "Heads of St Julian". All these had been manufactured and sold by the Sicilian Mafia, who discovered a vast market for these bogus relics in the United States. In areas where there was no saint and no holy relic to be prostituted, a convenient "miracle" would be arranged – the appearance of the Madonna to a child for example – to bring the pilgrims flocking in, who would buy their passage on Mafia-run coaches and stay in Mafia-owned guesthouses. The cult of Padre Pio, the "stigmatized" monk of San Giovanni Rotondo, who supposedly bore wounds similar to Christ's, was one such scam. The Mafia created this peculiar attraction, and fleeced the faithful, who journeyed hundreds of miles to see this monk, of a fortune. It even sold acres of bandages asserting that they were soaked in the monk's miraculous blood (in 1960 it was analysed and revealed to be the blood of chickens).

On a tour of the island, Mussolini suddenly announced that he wished to visit the grubby town of Piana dei Greci, then run by a Mafia potentate named Don Ciccio Cuccia – an ugly man noted for his acute vanity. Since it was an unscheduled visit, the police had no time to make elaborate security arrangements, and they realized that the only guarantee of Mussolini's safety was to suggest that he ride in Don Ciccio's car. When Mussolini sat next to Don Ciccio, with the police motorcycle escort lined up on either side, Ciccio turned to Il Duce and asked him why he was bothering to surround himself with police; "Nothing to worry about so long as you're with me . . ." he gloated. It was then that Mussolini understood that he had no power in Sicily.

On his return to Italy, the furious Mussolini immediately declared war on the Mafia and assigned Prefect Cesare Mori to the task of extermination. Mori was a stupid, pompous and cruel man. Given *carte blanche*, he measured success solely in terms of numbers arrested and confessions extracted; his onslaught naturally provided an unprecedented opportunity for the settling of old clan feuds. Hundreds of anonymous denunciations poured in; thousands were arrested on the basis of rumour and vindictive gossip and shipped off to penal colonies. Mori would frequently descend on a village and arrest the whole male population. After a while, the people worked out that the only way of pacifying this vain monster was to erect a banner on his approach to the village, bearing the words "HAIL CAESAR".

In 1927, Mussolini proudly announced to the Fascist Parliament that his heroic colleague, Prefect Mori, had won the battle against the Mafia. In reality, it had been a bloody but ineffectual campaign. Most of the important "Men of Honour" had either made their escape or gone underground, or disguised their loyalties by joining the Fascist Party; they would be back. But at least many of the Mafia dons had been deprived of their quasi-feudal authority, and for the next few years – until the Allied invasion of Sicily – the peasants were better off than they had ever been.

One Man of Honour that Mori had managed to arrest was Don Vito Cascio Ferro. Charged with smuggling (on bogus evidence), the old don spent most of his trial disdainfully ignoring the proceedings of the court, becoming animated only when his defence counsel pleaded for leniency. "That," barked Don Vito, "is in conflict with my principles and offensive to my authority."

Prefect Mori reintroduced the use of the *cassetta*, a traditional tool of the Inquisition, to extort confessions. A small, low-standing box, it was used as a platform across which a torture victim could be painfully spread-eagled. Brine was then poured over his body and he was scourged; if he failed to confess, he was then forced to drink gallons of sea-water. Next his fingernails would be removed, then slivers of skin. If he still persisted in claiming innocence, his genitals would be crushed.

Asked if he had anything to say before he was sentenced, Don Vito stood up and, after carefully considering his position, said: "Gentlemen, since you have been unable to obtain proof of any of my numerous crimes, you have been reduced to condemning me for the only one I have never committed."

He had indeed over the years been charged with sixty-nine major crimes, twenty of which were killings, but no case was ever sustained. He only ever admitted to one murder, that of Jack Petrosino, an American detective whose researches into the Mafia had brought him to Italy in 1909. Don Vito, dining one evening with an influential politician, suddenly announced that he had to return home to attend to an important matter. He would borrow the politician's carriage and return immediately. He was driven into Palermo where he shot Petrosino, and then returned to his dinner. The politician happily swore that Don Vito had never left his house.

Locked up in the Ucciardone prison, Don Vito was the most beneficent of men, preoccupying himself with the welfare of his fellow inmates, who made his bed and cleaned his cell (thereafter something of a shrine, and only given to prisoners of equal honour). He even hired and fired the prison warders. He did not complete his sentence, but died of a heart attack. His death made Don Calogero Vizzini the acknowledged head of the Mafia and it was "Don Calò" who would engineer its resurgence.

The son of a peasant farmer, Calogero Vizzini was born in the small, shabby Sicilian town of Villalba in 1877. His family had some prestige locally, not only because they had the rare distinction of owning a few grim acres of barren land, but because Calogero's uncle was a bishop, and his brother the parish priest of Villalba – important considerations in a place where the church shares power with the police and the Mafia.

Young Calò was not a good student, and remained an

illiterate all his life, perversely flaunting his ignorance and parochial bigotry. His first brush with the law came at the age of seventeen, when he was charged, unsuccessfully, with criminal assault. It seems that he took a fancy to the pretty daughter of a neighbouring family, the Solazzo clan. Though he had no intention of marrying her, he nonetheless forbade her to have dealings with any other man. When his honour in this affair was threatened by the girl's association with a rising young magistrate, Calogero and his gang burst in on the courting couple and beat the unfortunate suitor senseless. He nearly died, and the girl remained a spinster all her life.

At eighteen, Calogero went into business escorting grain shipments from peasant farmers across the remote, bandit-infested countryside to the flour mills. He did well, having struck a bargain with one of the most notorious of Sicilian bandits, Paolo Varsalona, who ran an extremely elusive band of brigands. Far from living their lives as roaming outlaws and making themselves an identifiable prey for the authorities, Varsalona's men maintained the outward appearance of re-spectability; they lived in the towns and pursued the traditional lives of peasants. At his call they would assemble, commit whatever crime was on the agenda, and then melt back into the workaday world. Calogero was so impressed with the bandit that he spent a number of formative years in Varsalona's gang, before they were finally caught in a police trap. Calogero was acquitted of murder on the grounds of "insufficiency of proof", and having made a sufficient impression on the necessary figures, was formally invited to become a member of the "Honoured Society" – the Mafia.

At the age of twenty-five, Calogero took the title of *zu*, meaning "uncle", and by the outbreak of the First World War was head of the Mafia in the Province of Caltanissetta. During the war he made a fortune from selling broken-winded and clapped out nags to the Italian cavalry; he also charged the farmers of his region to guarantee that their fit horses were not requisitioned.

Shortly afterwards, faced with claims that the army had become the country's largest receiver of stolen goods, the Italian authorities sought to put Calogero on trial. His inevi-table acquittal brought him further prestige as the scope of his enormous influence was seen; he was allowed to take the title of "don" and so became, after Don Vito Cascio, the second most important member of the Sicilian Mafia.

When Mori's purges took place, Don Calò (as he was universally known) was sentenced to five years, but he had fostered good relations with a young Fascist administrator, and was quietly released a few days after he entered prison.

The years between Mori and the Allied landings in Sicily were a time of retrenchment for the Mafia. But from the early days of the Second World War, it was clear to the Mafia that there was much to be gained from co-operating with the Americans and the British. Firstly, the eviction of Mussolini and the end of domination by Rome (many mafiosi dreamed of Sicily becoming, if not an independent state, then a colony of the US or Britain); and secondly, the suppression of Communism, which threatened the feudal stranglehold of the Mafia. Furthermore, an invasion and the ensuing power vacuum would provide the necessary opportunity for the Mafia to reassert itself. Indeed, it was to be expected that the Allies would need the services of the Mafia, and would willingly make concessions in return for assistance in taking first Sicily, then Italy itself.

The full history of the Allied involvement with the Mafia has never been disclosed, but that it happened is no secret. Sadly, in some ways it is the US that is responsible for the dreadful Mafia rule that has so traumatized post-war Italy.

It seems fairly certain that the initial connection was made through the don of all dons, "Lucky" Luciano, who was imprisoned in America at the outbreak of the Second World War. He was released at the cessation of hostilities and deported to Italy, and it is believed that the price of his release was that the Mafia assist the American authorities in a number of areas. One such area was the surveillance of suspected Nazi agents and insurgents in America's docks, another was the invasion of Sicily. From Luciano the message was passed to Don Calò, and it all came to pass as planned.

When, on 10 July 1943, the Allies landed on the south coast of Sicily and began to push northwards, their forces were divided into two bodies. The British and Canadian troops ploughed up the east coast – in theory the easier invasion route – and encountered a poorly equipped and inexperienced enemy who nevertheless fought back well, compelling the battle-hardened British troops to a tough, five-week campaign. The Americans, on the other hand, were allocated the mountainous terrain of central and western Sicily, which appeared on paper to be a much more arduous task. Surprisingly, they obtained their objectives at startling speed, reaching the north coast with barely a casualty.

The key point in the Italo-German defence of the route was a series of fortified positions near the towns of Villalba and Mussomeli, commanding the route along which the Americans had to come. Here, under the command of Colonel Salemi, a man noted for his courage, the Italians and Germans gathered together a substantial force of artillery, tanks, anti-tank guns and foot soldiers. Though Salemi had no illusions as to the probable outcome of any battle, he knew that, given the strength of his position, he would make the Americans fight a long and bloody battle; he might be able to halt their advance for weeks.

But Villalba, as one will recall, was the home town of Don Calò, the beloved Mafia potentate of all Sicily. A few days after the Allies landed, American planes could be seen dropping strange packages into the town, which, it was later disclosed by a man who saw Don Calò unwrap one, contained yellow silk handkerchiefs embroidered with the letter "L". This stood for Luciano. It was a pre-arranged signal. On 20 July three American tanks made a dash into Villalba, flying yellow handkerchiefs, and bore away the invaluable Don Calò, who then went to join the US Army as guide and passport to bloodless conquest. It is reported that the meeting between the Americans and the don took place in utter silence; he knew precisely what the agreement was.

The following morning, Colonel Salemi awoke to discover that two-thirds of his troops had deserted. They had been approached in the night by mafiosi who had courteously informed them of the hopelessness of their position and given them civilian clothes in which to escape. Salemi himself was them ambushed and held in the Town Hall of Mussomeli by the Mafia. The Americans strolled through without firing a shot. Don Calò returned to Villalba to be greeted by cries of "Long live the Allies; long live the Mafia!". He was elected Mayor of the town and was thereafter accompanied by a guard of "anti-fascists" armed by special permission of the Allied Military Government.

He subsequently cornered the trade in olive oil, and divided his time between this lucrative area of the black market and controlling the post-war direction of Sicilian politics. The fall of the Fascists brought thirty-two alternative political parties into existence; the Mafia threw its weight behind the Separatist

Party (later it would consider the Christian Democrats most suitable for its purpose). Don Calò considered it absolutely necessary that all left-wing parties be suppressed. When the socialist Popular Front asked permission to hold a rally in Villalba, they were most surprised to find the don warm to the idea. On 16 September 1944, as Girolamo Li Causi, the left-wing leader, began to address the crowd gathered in the town square of Villalba, the Mafia opened fire and wounded Li Causi and thirteen others.

Worse was to come. In 1945, the Separatists decided that an armed rising was necessary to guarantee their power, so Don Calò brokered a deal between them and the most famous of all Sicilian bandits, Salvatore Giuliano, who for many years had opposed the Mafia, but was to end up as its pliant tool. Giuliano offered, for a large sum, to attack the carabineri outposts and precipitate the anarchy necessary for an uprising. But the Separatists had big plans: they raised a volunteer force, and dispatched it to join up with the bandits. Under Giuliano's command, this force was to await the chosen moment and then commence all-out insurgency. The order never came. Eventually the bandits left the volunteer army, which dwindled to fifty-eight men. The volunteers were then attacked by Italian military forces (sanctioned by the Allies) of 5000 men accompanied by tanks and artillery. It was an extraordinary battle. The Separatists were dug-in on a hill, and their assailants, though out-numbering them fifty to one, exhibited the most remarkable caution. The fight went on for over a day, and apocalyptic reports of it filled the press. When it was over, each side had lost only six men and most of the surviving Separatists had escaped.

Don Calò abandoned his support for the lost Separatist cause, but Giuliano continued to rage around the countryside, well equipped with weapons and explosives of American origin, shooting, robbing and blowing up all non-patriotic elements. The authorities made no serious effort to eliminate him: he was too useful a loose cannon. His violence had the effect of quelling peasant unrest.

Giuliano's moment of infamy came on 1 May 1947, the day of the elections to the Regional Parliament. Sicily was to be allowed independent status within the Italian state, and, since the Separatist movement was now defunct, the Church, the landlords, the Mafia and the Allies put their weight behind the Christian Democrats; the other parties supported the principle of land-reform, and were therefore considered dangerously left-wing.

For decades the people of the neighbouring towns of Piana dei Greci and San Giuseppe Jato had held a rally on May Day, at the mountain pass of Porta della Finestra. Quite apart from any political significance, it was a holiday, and the feast of Santa Crocefissa. But despite the Mafia's warnings, there was an increasingly upbeat Communist movement among the peasants, and they wound their way to the high mountain pass in a cheerful mood, singing and waving banners. It was a brilliant, quiet morning. By 9.30 a.m. there were over 2000 of the poor and oppressed gathered at Porta della Finestra. They would listen to some speeches and then enjoy themselves, eating and drinking the day away. At 10 a.m., the leader of the Popular Front took the stand to make the first speech. Fifteen minutes later, as he opened his mouth, a seventy-year-old woman in the crowd fell over, shot dead. Behind her lay a thirteen-year-old girl, half her face blown away. Old men tumbled over, their intestines spilling out. Concealed in the rocks above the crowd, Giuliano's men were carrying out a massacre. Ten minutes later, it was all over. There were eleven killed outright and fifty-five others wounded, some of whom died later.

Shortly afterwards, three young men and a local prostitute who were on their way up to the meeting saw a strange sight: twelve armed men in American uniforms, and one in a white raincoat, came scrambling down the mountainside. The onlookers concealed themselves. They had just seen Giuliano and his band returning from their bloody work. His actions were wholly successful: the Popular Front had a disastrous election.

For the next two years, Giuliano was a popular man among the landlords, the Mafia, and (however distasteful it was) the occupying American forces; there would be no Communism in Sicily. But Giuliano finally outlived his usefulness, and became an embarrassment to his former allies. The police could not catch him, or find witnesses to testify against him. But they finally managed to buy the treasonable services of his lieutenant, Pisciotta. For fifty million lire he agreed to kill the bandit king. At 3.19 on the morning of 5 July 1950, Pisciotta shot Giuliano twice in the chest as he lay sleeping in a safe house in the town of Castelvetrano. The police then hastily hauled the dead bandit out of bed, dressed him, took him outside and sprayed him with machine-gun fire to try and conceal Pisciotta's treachery, so that he might live to enjoy his reward. Unfortunately, the corpse refused to bleed dramatically enough, and they were obliged to slit the throat of a chicken and pour its contents all over Giuliano.

Don Calò was relieved to see the bandit die. Latterly, his power had been so great that when he was disowned by his Christian Democrat supporters, Giuliano had openly threatened to abduct and kill its backers, including Don Calò. The latter, having helped create this monster, was reduced to hiding from him and travelled concealed in the backs of vegetable lorries. A year after the bandit died, Don Calò also went to the grave, though somewhat more peacefully.

Inclined to over-indulge and take little exercise, he had grown sluggish and corpulent. While travelling to Villalba one day, he asked that his car be stopped so that he could assume a comfortable supine position on the verge. Lying there, his vast belly pointing skywards, he sighed deeply, murmured "How beautiful life is!" and promptly expired. His funeral was a state occasion attended by all of significance, and his plaque in the church at Villalba declares, without irony, his many virtues; he was chaste, temperate, forbearing, tireless in his defence of the weak and, above all, a gentleman.

FROM "LUCKY" TO GOTTI: A MISCELLANY OF AMERICAN MAFIOSI

The American Mafia, the most powerful criminal organization in the world, owes its present strength to the pioneering efforts of Charles "Lucky" Luciano, who in the first half of this century transformed a collection of feuding extortionists and racketeers into a multi-billion dollar corporation.

He was born Salvatore Lucania in East Harlem, New York, into a large and poor family; his father was a construction worker and his mother supplemented their meagre income by taking in laundry. At the age of fifteen, he was thrown out of the house by his father who despaired at his son's drift into crime; not even the severest of beatings seemed to inhibit him. His mother continued to adore him, and smuggled jars of her home-made pasta sauce (the one thing he missed) to her errant son.

He rented his own apartment and formed his own *borgata*: a gang of young, street-wise criminals. Many of the New York Mafia's foremost members began their careers in Luciano's *borgata*: Frank Costello, Gaetano "Three Fingers Brown" Lucchese, Albert Anastasia and Vito Genovese.

For fear of shaming his family name, the embryonic mobster changed his surname from Lucania to Luciano. He also decided he hated being called Salvatore, as it was often shortened to "Sal", and re-christened himself Charles; he later acquired his nickname "Lucky" by surviving an assassination attempt by knife. Lucky stood head and shoulders above his confederates; he possessed extraordinary business acumen and a capacity for organization. By the age of eighteen he was a czar of petty crime and was formulating plans for a nation-wide confederacy of hoodlums. He even made the unprecedented move of forming an alliance with two Jewish mobsters, Meyer Lansky and Benjamin "Bugsy" Siegel, from the Lower East Side.

Within a few years, Lucky went to work for the don of the "amici", the boss of the Mafia, Giuseppe "Joe the Boss" Masseria, who insisted on patronizing Lucky by calling him *bambino*. Masseria, who was rampantly anti-semitic, hated Siegel and Lansky and insisted that Lucky "get rid of those fucking hebes". Lucky detested Masseria and had the pleasure of arranging for him to be murdered on the orders of Salvatore Maranzano, who succeeded him to the throne of power. Masseria was shot in a restaurant where he thought he was joining Lucky for a plate of pasta. Lucky got up mid-way through the meal and went to the toilet; while he was in there the restaurant was raked with gunfire.

Maranzano, an elegant figure, was something of a Sicilian traditionalist, and Lucky, while having nothing personal against him, could see that there was little prospect of the man instigating any of the modern business plans that Lucky had his heart set on. Maranzano read Roman history for inspiration, whilst Lucky dreamed of a modern empire of crime, sheltered by accountants and lawyers. Lucky had to take the throne by force: in September 1931 Maranzano and his supporters died, on an occasion that was thereafter remembered as "The Night of the Sicilian Vespers". Four men, disguised as members of the Internal Revenue, visited Maranzano and knifed him to death; some forty of his associates were also murdered. At the age of thirty-four, Lucky Luciano was the head of the New York Mafia, which he eventually welded into the most powerful criminal organization ever known.

He was finally brought down by the efforts of a determined District Attorney, Thomas E. Dewey, who nailed him on charges of running a prostitution ring; but Lucky's luxurious sojourn in New York's Clinton State prison set the tone for

From its earliest days in America, much of the Mafia's wealth was founded upon illegal gambling rackets, the most basic of which was the "numbers" game that predominated in the black ghettos. Tickets, costing between twenty-five cents and a dollar, were sold at barber shops and candy stores. It was a simple variety of lottery: the participant would select up to three digits from one to ten, with odds thus ranging from ten to one to a thousand to one. The winning number was determined by the last three digits of an established daily number that could not in theory be fixed, such as the circulation of a newspaper or the day's sale of US Treasury stocks. The profit was the difference between tickets sold and winnings paid out. With no tax and low overheads the income could be vast.

incarcerated mafiosi. He had a private cell with an electric stove, curtains over the cell door and a pet canary. Dressed in a tailor-made prison uniform of silk shirt and highly polished shoes, he was guarded round the clock by paid bodyguards, and held formal audiences in the prison exercise yard, bestowing favours like a monarch.

Perhaps his greatest achievement – for it enabled the uninterrupted pursuit of illicit wealth – was the peace he forged between the Mafia clans. But as the network of organized crime expanded, his position – that of *capo di tutti i capi* (the boss of all bosses) – became an increasingly attractive post.

When he was sent to prison, the Second World War had started, and the Mafia was approached by the US Government for assistance at home and abroad. They wanted the cooperation of the Sicilian Mafia in the event of Allied landings and they also wanted the Mafia to provide the eyes and ears for a counter-intelligence operation along the New York waterfront, to balk anticipated acts of sabotage by German and Italian agents. The Mafia agreed; its secret pay-off was to be the release of Lucky Luciano, to which the Government acquiesced on condition that he was returned to Italy.

On 9 February 1946, Luciano was transported from his upstate New York prison cell to Brooklyn where he was to be put on an ocean-liner with a one-way ticket to Italy. The entire high command of the New York Mafia turned out to see Lucky off: Albert Anastasia, Vito Genovese, Joseph Profaci, Joseph Bonanno, Frank Costello and Joe Adonis. Also present were two fast-rising mobsters, Carlo Gambino and Thomas Lucchese.

Lucky stayed put in Rome for a while, but then began to creep back towards the US and turned up in Cuba, run by the corrupt Batista, where the Mafia had invested heavily in casinos and hotels. But he was too close for the comfort of the US authorities, and they encouraged the Cubans to return him to Italy. In January 1962, Lucky Luciano went to the Naples airport to await the arrival of an American film producer interested in making a film based on the gangster's life. To general consternation, he dropped dead of a heart attack in the airport lounge.

Lucky had been concerned that in his absence the Mafia would begin to tear itself apart. No sooner was his ship out of the harbour than his worst fears came true. The arrogant Vito Genovese was not only making a pitch for the position of "capo di tutti i capi", but was also demanding that the Mafia move into the rapidly expanding narcotics market, and wanted to see the fruitful partnership that Lucky had formed with the Jewish mobsters broken. His demands found little favour with Frank Costello, the Mafia don of Manhattan, who had been one of those closest to Lucky and who commanded great influence and respect, both inside and outside the Mafia. Costello was known as the "prime minister of the underworld" for his skill in defusing potentially explosive disputes. He was an affable and cautious man who detested violence, and had assiduously courted police and politicians so that New York's authorities turned a blind eye to Mafia activities, so long as they stayed clear of drugs and kept the violence internal and to a minimum. Moreover, he liked the Jews and appreciated their business acumen. The Mafia had learned much from them, particularly the importance of maintaining a quasi-legality in its activities, infiltrating legitimate businesses wherever possible.

Costello made an enemy in Genovese, who in turn found an ally in Anastasia. Their resentment – and ambition – festered, and in 1957 they decided to make a play for power. On 2 May Costello was attacked in the lobby of his hotel by a notoriously stupid hood, an ex-boxer called Vincent "the Chin" Gigante. He shot Costello at point-blank range in the head. He hit him squarely in the temple, but, miraculously, the bullet pierced only the skin, made a complete circuit of the head under the surface, and finally re-emerged at its entry point. The Chin was unaware of this: he left Costello for dead. Costello told the

John Gotti goes on trial on charges of orchestrating the slaying of Castellano as well as other racketeering charges

police that he had no idea who would want to kill a dull businessman such as himself, and immediately made plans to retire. He had got the message, and died peacefully twenty years later.

Anastasia was a wholly deranged individual and the failure of the attempt on Costello sent him off the deep end. He became paranoid that he would be killed in retribution, and took steps to eliminate anyone he thought posed a physical threat to him. It was a blood-bath. As his violence and demands for power increased, it was decided that something must be done. Finally one of his capi, Carlo Gambino, arranged for the elimination of Albert Anastasia, nominally on the grounds that he had been charging a $40,000 fee for entry into his Mafia family – an unforgivable lapse in traditional protocol. Gambino turned to the most infamous killers around, the Gallo brothers: "Crazy Joe", "Kid Twist" and "Kid Blast". In October 1957 they walked into a barber's in a Manhattan hotel, where Anastasia was having his morning shave, and, while a towel was over his head, blew his brains out.

Gambino died peacefully in 1976, and his son-in-law Paul Castellano, also from the Gambino family, became "capo di tutti i capi". Castellano was a man very much in the mould of Carlo Gambino. He was diplomatic by instinct and liked a quiet life, unlike Gambino's long-time lieutenant, Aniello Dellacroce, the mentor of John Gotti, future head of the Gambino clan and Mafia don in the making.

Aniello Dellacroce (which literally means, in Sicilian Italian, "little lamb of the cross") was Gambino's number two for many years. His unadulterated sadism provided an admirable foil for the smooth charms of the don. Born in Italy, Dellacroce drifted into crime while still a boy and by his late teens was a Mafia hood specializing in strong-arm work and killing, for which he had a considerable gift, and which he obviously enjoyed. He

---

Salvatore "Sally" De Vita was a most unusual hood. An incredibly ugly man, he was the only known Mafia transvestite, and spent much of his time off duty trying to disguise himself as a woman. He wore blonde wigs, rouge, mascara, lipstick and a padded bra, and owned wardrobes full of stunning designer dresses, mostly stolen. But it was unwise to tease him excessively: he invariably carried a loaded pistol in his Gucci handbag.

would fix his bulging eyes on his victim and, in carefully modulated tones, would tell the man exactly how he was going to die; first he would shoot him in the knees, then in the stomach, and, after pausing to savour the pain he had inflicted, he would occasionally consent to administering a *coup de grâce* in the head. When an enforcer for the vicious hood Alberto Anastasia, Dellacroce had been delegated to "manage" his casinos. He would punish bent dealers and croupiers by smashing their hands with a sledgehammer.

Once, upon finding the corpse of one of his victims, police were convinced it had been decapitated. Pathologists later found the remains of the head beaten into the chest cavity.

Carlo Gambino, the figure said to have inspired Brando's portrayal of Don Corleone in *The Godfather*, arrived in America as a twenty-two-year-old stowaway in 1924. He was a loyal Mafia member from the start, a waterfront hood, a leading capo and finally a brilliant strategist who took control of the entire Mafia. His business intelligence was second to none. During Prohibition he managed to corner the market in distilled alcohol, buying at fifteen dollars per tin and selling at fifty. During the Second World War he set up a huge black market racket using forged ration stamps, netting himself millions of dollars. He took the Mafia further into the twilight world of quasi-legality, where the profit from illegal activities could be laundered and invested legally to create yet more money. Under him, the Mafia consolidated its grip on the unions, some of whom were happy to let their pension funds be invested at his discretion. A modest, soft-spoken man, Gambino was the subject of police investigations for forty years, but his last stint in prison was in 1937. They never pinned anything on him after that: it was impossible to find anyone insane enough to testify against this endearing, kind old gentleman. When police came to question him at his unassuming Brooklyn house they could always count on being received courteously and offered some of Mrs Gambino's excellent homemade cookies. But while he detested flashiness and unnecessary violence in business, as a Mafia disciplinarian Gambino was utterly ruthless, and countless numbers died on his whispered orders. One man who attempted to seduce wives of imprisoned mafiosi was subjected, on Gambino's orders, to the most horrible death, being slowly fed while alive into a large meat grinder, feet first.

Another corpse could only be identified by teeth found inside its stomach. Curiously, when travelling incognito, Dellacroce liked to dress up as a catholic priest.

Dellacroce – and, under him, Gotti – made millions for the Mafia from dealing in heroin. Publicly, the Mafia has always forbidden its members to deal in drugs, upon penalty of death. It has given the impression that gambling, protection rackets and large-scale swindles were the foundation of its wealth, and that its activities have become increasingly legal. One reason to discourage its members from dealing in narcotics is the long sentence the crime carries. Faced with forty years in prison, a criminal can be tempted to turn informer in exchange for immunity.

But in reality, the Mafia has from its first days in America been involved with narcotics. There is too much money to be made, too easily: a kilo of the opium base for heroin costs $12,000 at its source in the Middle East or Southeast Asia. After being processed and cut with other substances until it is only three and a half per cent heroin, the same kilo will fetch two million dollars on the streets.

Mafia bosses generally stayed carefully in the background, and avoided being seen to be involved in the trade. Instead, the Mafia would normally operate in association with some other branch of organized crime. Since the mid-1950s, the Mafia has controlled the American heroin trade at a discreet distance. It reorganized the supply line, linking up with the powerful Corsican heroin dealers, and established processing laboratories in Sicily staffed with French drug chemists. The "French Connection" was created and the Mafia flooded the streets of urban America with high-quality "smack". The number of heroin addicts in the United States rose from fifty thousand in the 1950s to something near half a million.

The son of poor immigrants from Southern Italy, John Gotti was born in New York in 1940. Brought up in East Harlem and Brooklyn, he quickly became known for his volcanic temper. He seemed to be in a constant rage, and was uncontrollable at school, though he was by no means unintelligent and had an IQ of around 140. A born leader, he soon attracted a group of equally wild companions and formed a "borgata".

After his father, John Gotti, moved his family to the violent waterfront district of Brooklyn and then the even meaner streets of East New York, Gotti joined a tough gang, the "Fulton Rockaway Boys". They ran minor extortion rackets,

stole and hijacked, organized a little illegal gambling (taking
care in all of these not to intrude on Mafia territory), and, above
all, fought territorial battles with other gangs for the right to
parade up and down their grim home turf.

Gotti was soon leader of the "borgata". Quite apart from his
canniness and naked aggression he stood out for his appalling
taste in clothing: he wore anything, so long as it was loud,
colourful and stolen. Purple suits were a favourite. He attracted
the attention of Carmine "Charley Wagons" Fatico, an associate
of the late Alberto Anastasia. Although only seventeen, Gotti
quickly proved his worth as a strong man, performing one or
two spectacular beatings, and became one of the 120 men Fatico
had working for him. Fatico had a well-established organization,
which grossed him around thirty million dollars annually. The
money came from hijacking, illegal gambling and loan-sharking,
but Fatico had a special line in gay bars. Homosexuality was still
illegal in America, and Fatico's discreet string of private gay
clubs, where exotic stage acts could be seen by men prepared to
pay exotic prices for admission and drinks, was highly lucrative.
Ironically, it would be at one of his bars, the Stonewall Inn, that
gay men in 1969 began the gay rights movement.

Throughout his early years Gotti was in and out of prison,
principally on charges of theft and hijacking. His time in jail
gave him the opportunity to meet a whole host of mafiosi, who,
in turn, remembered the explosive and capable young man.
When Carmine Fatico began to ail, Gotti was put in charge of
the outfit, and along with a number of other middle-ranking
hoods he successfully organized a lucrative narcotics channel
into New York. He went to great lengths to ensure that
Castellano was not aware of the narcotics trade; he even
publicly banished one of his crew on the grounds that he
was a drugs dealer. By 1979 Gotti, although little more than
a Mafia soldier, was already rumoured to be Dellacroce's
chosen successor as underboss of the Gambino clan, a remarkable rate of progress since he had only been "made" (formally
initiated into the Mafia) two years beforehand.

Gotti's principal weakness was gambling. He could blow
$30,000 a day on betting and at one point in the 1982 American
football season Gotti had lost a quarter of a million dollars. He
and his brother ran an illegal casino in Little Italy. Gotti could
not resist betting against his own house and on one night lost
$55,000.

Dellacroce died of cancer in 1985. At the same time, Gotti's

In 1980 Gotti's already unstable temperament was heightened by personal tragedy: his twelve-year-old son Frank was accidentally run over by one of his neighbours, a man called John Favara. Favara was utterly distraught, but his expressions of remorse and sympathy met with angry silence. Later, his car was stolen, and "murderer" scrawled across it. He found a black-edged picture of the dead boy in his mail-box. Rumours began circulating that he was about to be killed. He decided to move, but on the very day that he sold his house, three men in a van rolled up to his work-place. He pulled a gun, but his shots went wild. Bludgeoned insensible, he was thrown into the back of the van and never seen again.

narcotics network had been uncovered by the police and he and several other Mafia members were facing trial. Castellano, furious at the heroin-trafficking, had come to regard Gotti as a substantial embarrassment. It was only a matter of time before he had him killed. With his protector Dellacroce gone, Gotti felt exposed and decided to strike first. He rapidly established the necessary support for his actions throughout the Mafia membership, alternately seducing and threatening, and convinced many that the ageing Castellano was too afflicted by conscience and needed replacing.

On 16 December 1985, Castellano arrived outside Sparks Restaurant in New York. Getting out of his chauffeur-driven car, he encountered three men in identical overcoats and fur hats. They fired six shots into his body. He died instantly. The men then shot his chauffeur dead and melted away. Gotti did not attend his funeral.

By Christmas 1985, John Gotti was head of the most powerful criminal organization in the world. In April 1992, he was convicted of murder and racketeering, and sentenced to life without parole. His case is currently under appeal.

Castellano's funeral was a modest affair, unlike most Mafia funerals. The standard for these events was set in 1928 by the spectacular last rites of Brooklyn mobster Frank Uale, who was shot to death. There were two hundred cars in his funeral procession, thirty-eight of which carried the flowers, and several thousand mourners. He was buried in a casket of silver and nickel, costing $15,000; the whole occasion cost $200,000.

MURDER INCORPORATED

Just before the First World War, the overcrowded population of the predominantly Jewish quarter of the Lower East Side in New York's Manhattan and the Italian neighbourhoods of Little Italy and East Harlem began to overflow and move eastwards, across the East River and into the vast interior plains of Brooklyn. Here for generations the quiet villages of Williamsburg, Brownsville and East New York had existed in a rural torpor which was soon dispelled. With the immigrants came organized crime, and by 1930 the Italian Mafia and the Jewish mobs were flourishing alongside one another. Though they had often fought, they were, for the most part, content to come to mutually beneficial arrangements in the pursuit of profit.

The Italian Mafia concentrated on its conventional interests, primarily loan-sharking and illegal gambling, while the Jewish mobsters derived their wealth from extortion, principally targeting the small garment manufacturers. Many of these had fled over the river in order to escape from the Garment Center in Manhattan, which had for years been under the control of mobsters like Louis "Lepke" Buchalter, who was used by the manufacturers to break strikes, and then found that he could make money by charging the manufacturers for his protection.

The manufacturers who fled across the river did not elude Buchalter for long. He came after them, but in Brooklyn he found that seven local punks were already attempting to run a protection racket involving clothing manufacturers. Buchalter was deeply offended at this intrusion into his private territory, and accordingly made plans to have them eliminated. But the killing of the seven posed problems. While he was blessed with strong-arm men who could be relied on to break heads effectively, Buchalter was short of talented, discreet killers who could perform their task efficiently, without upsetting the authorities and leaving a trail of bloody footprints that would lead the police to his door.

To solve this problem, Buchalter opened negotiations with the Mafia, represented by its rising star in Brooklyn, Albert Anastasia, a capo from the waterfront rackets. Buchalter proposed that the Italians and the Jews should pool their talents and create a combined force of Italian and Jewish professional killers, who would work – for a price – for both individuals and organized crime syndicates. Anastasia accepted, and Murder Incorporated was born.

The organization fused murder with corporate methods. Buchalter was president and Anastasia chief executive officer, and they had a staff of selected, smart killers, who were put on annual $12,000 retainers. There were strict corporate rules: murder was only to be committed for "business reasons", and "civilians" were not to be harmed in the course of the hit.

The policy on each job submitted was jointly agreed by president and chief executive, who rationally and coldly considered the ramifications of requests for killing within the sphere of organized crime. If they accepted the job, the execution was assigned to a team of assassins.

The organization's star killer was Abraham "Kid Twist" Reles. Fat, five foot two inches tall, with thick lips, a flat, broken nose and gangling arms, Reles derived his nickname from his habit of munching boxfuls of chocolate candy twists.

By the mid-1930s, Louis Buchalter was extorting nearly fifty million dollars a year from the New York garment manufacturers in return for guaranteeing that there would be no disruption of labour. He had nearly 250 vicious hoods in his employment, including the infamous Jacob Shapiro, his chief lieutenant, who walked around with lead window-sash weights in his pockets with which he used to smash in the skulls of manufacturers and union leaders unwilling to cooperate.

He specialized in the use of the ice-pick, which he jammed into his victim's heart. Reles showed no mercy, and when people saw him walking down the street they were inclined to cross to the opposite pavement. Everybody knew that Reles had once openly killed two black men without any provocation: one of them had worked at a car wash and failed to spot a small smudge on the front fender of Reles' car, the other had worked at a parking lot and had failed to move fast enough when Reles ordered him to fetch his Cadillac.

It will never be known how many people Murder Incorporated killed during the peak years of business, between 1935 and 1939. Some estimates are as high as 300, but only about a dozen or so murders – including that of Arthur "Dutch Schultz" Fleigenheimer – have actually been laid at its door. Its "employees" swaggered around the streets of Brooklyn, untroubled by the police, who generally avoided them. There were nearly 200 "employees", because, apart from the elite killers, there were "fingermen" who charted the movements of prospective victims, "wheelmen" who stole the cars used in the hits and "evaporators" who tidied up after the crime and ensured that the body of the victim disappeared.

Murder Incorporated might still be terrorizing America, were it not for the arrest of the erratic Abe Reles. The lethal Kid Twist was forever committing non-sanctioned murders, casual killings over and above his Murder Incorporated quota. The police picked him up for one of these; the evidence was indisputable, and Reles faced the electric chair. In return for immunity from prosecution, Kid Twist agreed to turn stool-pigeon and tell everything he knew about Murder Incorporated. His sensational revelations allowed the police to crush

---

Each assignment was called a "contract", a euphemism which rapidly passed into common usage, along with "hit", the Murder Incorporated official parlance for the actual killing. The killers retained by Murder Incorporated were the cream of New York's hit-men. Among them were Vito "Chicken Head" Gurino, who earned his nickname because he perfected his aim by blasting the heads off live chickens, and Frank "The Dasher" Abbanando, so called because once, when his gun misfired during a hit and the victim pursued him around a building, Abbanando was faster, and succeeded in lapping him; he came up behind his pursuer and shot him in the back of the head.

Anastasia (left) walks out of the federal Court on 23rd May 1955

the organization, and Louis Buchalter went to the electric chair.

But Reles never lived to enjoy the new life the authorities had promised him. After spilling the beans on Murder Incorporated, he began to blab about the Mafia, and mentioned specific people, including Albert Anastasia, to the Brooklyn District Attorney, William O'Dwyer. Too late he learned that O'Dwyer had allegedly gone straight out and sold the glad news of Reles' revelations to Anastasia. The Mafia boss paid the corrupt attorney $100,000 for the silencing of Kid Twist.

On 11 November 1941, Kid Twist mysteriously fell from the seventh-floor window of a Coney Island hotel, where he was being concealed by the District Attorney's office under a twenty-four hour guard. Although the murder case remains officially unsolved to this day, it was alleged that O'Dwyer or Anastasia arranged for two or three corrupt police officers to defenestrate the stool-pigeon before he said any more.

The death ended any further investigation into Murder Incorporated, but Reles remained a legendary figure in New York. Throughout Brooklyn, gangsters would raise their glasses and say: "Here's to Abe Reles, a great canary. He could sing, but he couldn't fly."

Albert Anastasia, the Mafia's "King of Brooklyn", was also known as "The Mad Hatter" or "The Executioner". A homicidal maniac with a violent temper, he liked killing for the sake of killing and ordered deaths on the slightest pretext. After reading in the newspaper that a local citizen had recognized the famous bank robber Willie Smith and turned him in to the police, Anastasia ordered that this conscientious citizen be immediately killed. "I hate a rat," he said, "no matter who he is." He liked to have murder victims hideously tortured before their death and when unable to participate himself he insisted that every detail of the torture be later recounted to him; he particularly relished it when they begged for mercy. He lived like an emperor near New York Harbour in New Jersey, in a vast house surrounded by a seven-foot barbed-wire fence, a pack of Dobermans and a permanent bodyguard. His money came from the waterfront rackets: extortion, theft, gambling, loan-sharking and kick-backs. The 40,000 longshoremen who worked in the port were all under his thumb. Also, his brother "Tough Tony" was president of the biggest union and he was thought to have the entire roll-call of local police and politicians on his payroll.

"BUGSY" SIEGEL: CASANOVA MOBSTER

Benjamin "Bugsy" Siegel (he hated being called Bugsy, a name he acquired in his early mob days) was the most suave and charming of criminals. Intelligent, cosmopolitan, Jewish and handsome, he effortlessly infiltrated American society. The titled loved him, and he enjoyed the trust of the most hard-bitten and cynical of businessmen. To movie stars he was tangible proof of the reality of the romantic hoods they played. Many, such as Cary Grant, were close friends though sometimes they became frightened as to where their friendship with this man might take them. Siegel once told Del Webb that he had personally killed twelve men. When Webb's face betrayed his fear, Siegel looked at him and laughed.

"There's no chance that you'll get killed," he told him. "We only kill each other."

Benjamin Siegel was born on 28 February 1906 in the Jewish Williamsburg district of Brooklyn, then a labyrinth of crowded tenements, street pedlars, delicatessens and synagogues. He left home without finishing school, and joined a band of other juvenile delinquents who prowled the East Side in Manhattan at night. His first crime was a stick-up in a loan company office, and he was soon "rolling" drunks, committing burglaries and vigorously participating in the perpetual, violent gang wars.

On one foray he met another young hood, George Ranft, who later changed his name to Raft and became the Hollywood star. Siegel and Raft became the closest of buddies. Many years later, when Raft was a national celebrity, his aging mother saw him being escorted into a cinema by an honorary guard of four policemen. So accustomed was she to thinking of her son as a criminal that her first reaction was to shout "Run, Georgie, run!"

From Siegel's earliest days he became known for his love of horse-play and his sheer effrontery towards the police. Later, when a major player in crime, he would still amuse himself by leaning out of the windows of hotels and dropping water-bombs on the heads of the snooping police.

By rights, Siegel should have remained a petty crook and tearaway, just one of the other thousands of struggling street bums from the Jewish and Italian ghettos. But during the days of Prohibition – there was never a single edict more favourable to organized crime – he made the transition from punk to swaggering gangster.

During this era the Lower East Side was dominated by two ruthless mobs: the Italians – the Mafia – led by Lucky Luciano, Vito Genovese and Albert Anastasia, and the Jewish mob, headed by Louis Buchalter and Jacob Shapiro, known as the "Gold Dust Twins". It was as part of this group that Siegel encountered Meyer Lansky, his long-time associate. Together they split away and formed the "Bug-Meyer Mob".

Little hard evidence of the extent of his early criminal activities survives, though his mob had a fearful reputation. He was regularly picked up by the police for such offences as possessing concealed weapons, and at the age of nineteen was accused of rape by a local girl. When the case came to court, the witnesses had mysteriously vanished. The only conviction he ever suffered was for illegal gambling, when he was picked up by the police during a raid on a Miami hotel. Even then he gave a false name and was fined only $100.

Furthermore, as Siegel ascended the hierarchy of crime, his file at New York Police Department, which should have bulged with the records of his arrests and various suspected offences, grew perversely thinner. Over the years, this smartest of gangsters managed to wipe his past record clean, arranging, by legal and illegal means, to have past offences deleted, pictures withheld and charge sheets appropriated. The only official memento of his early career now remaining to the New York Police is a solitary mugshot.

Still in his twenties, Siegel already had a suite at the Waldorf-Astoria, two floors below his mentor, Lucky Luciano. He wore coats with velvet collars, handmade shirts and sharp, pointed and highly glossed shoes. He had a special line in hats and favoured a snap-brim, a style he had picked up from the Broadway columnist, Mark Hellinger, one of the first of many friends in show-business. Broadway was a great melting-pot for the legal and illegal sectors of society. Criminals, celebrities, politicians, magnates, actors and actresses – anyone who was news – mingled and networked at the same parties and the same restaurants and clubs. They dressed alike, and thought alike. They were drawn by the same things: the craving for success, recognition and the good life that money could buy. More than one major movie or Broadway show was financed by the proceeds from speakeasies, extortion and murder.

The Siegel-Meyer mob hauled liquor and supplied armed convoys for other groups trucking it between New York and Philadelphia. The gang also had a wholesale liquor business of their own and operated a string of illicit stills and a smuggling network. They were in business for money, and though they happily committed robberies, hijackings and murders these were less for profit than to assert their identity and discourage any major competitors in the truly lucrative field of bootlegging. Siegel's earnings were near the one million dollar mark. He once told a friend that, had he not taken a beating in the Wall Street crash, he would have happily gone "legit".

Like any high profile gangster he had his enemies and his life was always at risk, and in these early years Siegel was constantly on the move, shifting between his apartment on Eighty-fifth Street, the Waldorf, his headquarters near Lewis Street on the Lower East Side, and the various hideouts and offices of his criminal associates. He kept his family – his wife Esta and his two daughters – tucked out of sight in an expensive house in Scarsdale. In the early 1930s, Bugsy survived a number of attempts on his life: his car was shot up by machine-gun fire, and a bomb was placed in a room in which he was hosting a meeting of senior mobsters (he escaped with minor injuries, and apparently was able to slip unseen out of the hospital to avenge himself on the would-be assassin, before returning to his sick bed – a perfect alibi).

Siegel, like many Jewish mobsters, preferred to settle disagreements by negotiation, but would not hesitate to order the execution of problematic individuals. In 1934 Joey and Louis "Pretty" Amberg, minor drug pedlars and extortionists from Brownsville, who had already demanded a cut of a fee charged by Siegel's gang for a piece of strong arm strike-breaking in their territory, exasperated his patience when they killed one of his henchmen. Joey was called into Bugsy's office, forced to confess and then summarily shot; Louis was finely diced with an axe.

When Prohibition came to an end, the Mafia and their associates – and Siegel was still an ally – needed to replace their lost income. They began to look more closely at the previously minor areas of narcotics, prostitution, casinos, union enforcement and even wholesale murder for the right money (Murder Incorporated was one result). They also looked to expand westwards, into California.

In 1936 Bugsy Siegel moved to California. California seemed a territory ripe for crime and Bugsy didn't want to stay in New York and end up dead on the streets, nor did he enjoy the company of fellow gangsters. He always thought a little more of himself, and craved respectability. For Siegel, Hollywood was a natural home: here people could re-invent their pasts freely, and a little urbanity, good looks and a lot of money bought acceptance. Furthermore, he had a weakness for actresses, and had recently formed an association with Ketti Gallian, a French starlet. He was to spend $50,000 vainly trying to launch her career in movies.

Siegel settled down in Beverly Hills, living in a house rented from the famous singer, Lawrence Tibbet. He styled himself a "sportsman" and bon viveur, and joined the exclusive Hillcrest Country Club. His daughters attended the best private school and he socialized with George Raft, Jean Harlow and Clark Gable. Jean Harlow had a particular affection for Bugsy and was thought to have been the godmother of his daughter Millicent. Siegel also made the acquaintance of the million-airess and socialite Countess Dorothy Dendice Taylor DiFrasso. Tired of her marriage, and jaded with her fortune, this buxom and frosty eyed woman frequently visited her mansion in Beverly Hills, where she organized elaborate entertainment – such as bare fist boxing – for her celebrity guests. She had an unhappy affair with Gary Cooper, and was casting around for something a little out of the ordinary, when she was introduced to Siegel. Within days, the semi-literate gangster from New York, driven by an enormous need for social acceptance, was in her bed. He was literally sleeping his way to the top.

Siegel still had "business" interests in New York, mainly protection rackets, from which he derived a steady income. But

Benjamin "Bugsy" Siegel

with his taste for the glamorous life, the cost of the mansion he was building, the education of his family and the endless string of girlfriends to be discreetly maintained, he always needed more. He was also a compulsive gambler who could spend $2,000–$5,000 a day on football and horses. But for the moment, he was on a winning streak.

He had interests in pieces of property in California, which brought in a little, but his first major coup was to invest heavily – with money borrowed from unfortunate friends like George Raft – in a series of off-shore, floating casinos: gambling ships, which stood outside the state's jurisdiction. He made a small fortune, but Raft, who was always in money troubles and had been virtually forced to invest in the ship, never saw a cent of profit. Indeed he was lucky to get his original stake back: his $20,000 was returned to him in tiny instalments over a period of months. Bugsy might have been extravagant, but he was never unduly generous.

Siegel, the most assiduous social climber of his day, kept lists of people he wished to meet – and bed – and even managed to inveigle his way into the house of Jack Warner, the movie mogul, quite against Warner's wishes. Siegel managed to conceal his criminal association from his new Californian neighbours, but a reporter on the *Los Angeles Examiner* received a tip-off from a mysterious informant and a front-page exposé followed; Bugsy found that his local reputation was taking a dip. He decided to spend some time away and, leaving his family behind, he took off with the Countess DiFrasso to Italy and thence all over Europe. Initially, the reason for the trip was to try and sell the patent of a new explosive, "Atomite", which he had interested the Countess in, to Mussolini. The Countess, feeling that she should be seen to be travelling with someone of her own class, bestowed a bogus baronetcy on Bugsy, who enjoyed going under the title Bart Siegel, English aristocrat. The explosive was another expensive disaster for the Countess, and they had to cut short their stay in Rome because Siegel, seeing that Goering and Goebbels were also paying a visit, decided that one or both of them needed killing. Whatever his crimes, Siegel always possessed a healthy attitude towards Nazis, and to his dying day regretted that he had not killed Goebbels when he had had the opportunity.

Returning to California, Siegel found himself pitched into the roughest waters he had hitherto experienced.

Harry Greenberg was a minor mob member of Polish

parentage, who was also an illegal immigrant. Deported by the American authorities, he jumped ship and found his way back to California, where he started threatening to talk to the police about the mob unless a lot of money was forthcoming. Siegel was called upon by his New York associates – men like Albert Anastasia and Buchalter – to help them to shut the mouth of the fat, overwrought Greenberg before he blabbed. Greenberg was located by a hood named Whitey Krakower, and assassins were imported from the East. But, for some unknown reason, Siegel himself – perhaps because he needed to reassert his authority in the underworld – decided to participate directly in the killing. In November 1939, Greenberg was gunned down outside his apartment. The naïve Krakower then began to talk freely about Siegel's involvement in the killing, and in July 1940 he too was found shot dead. Bugsy did not like bad publicity.

Then Abe "Kid Twist" Reles was arrested. When he turned stool-pigeon, he implicated Bugsy in the Greenberg murder, and the police felt fairly certain that they could also get him on the death of Whitey. Siegel was arrested and held in a County jail awaiting trial. This made little difference to his lifestyle. He

---

The Countess DiFrasso was in love with Siegel and in 1938 bankrolled one of his more extravagant schemes: the search for a legendary ninety-million-dollar treasure supposedly buried on an island off Costa Rica. Equipped with a treasure map supplied by an old soak called Bill Bowbeer, the couple assembled an extraordinary entourage of fellow speculators, chartered a boat and set off for Cocos Island, where, Siegel told the company, concealed in a cave was this fabulous treasure. After several weeks of sailing, the motley crew of socialites and crooks reached the deserted, inhospitable island. Its shore was rocky, and the land was covered by thick jungle and creepers. They spent ten horrible days looking for the gold; few on board had actually expected to find anything, but it quickly became apparent that Siegel had been in deadly earnest. His temper rose rapidly as the fruitless search continued. They dug everywhere in temperatures approaching ninety degrees, eaten alive by mosquitoes and plagued by tropical sickness. The Countess retreated to the boat and sat in the shade, drinking champagne and wilting. Finally, having dynamited large portions of the island, the furious Siegel was forced to abandon the search. The expedition cost the Duchess at least $50,000.

was idolized by other inmates, who would queue up to polish
his shoes. He had a specially made uniform, which another
inmate regularly pressed, and he was able to order his meals
from outside; roast pheasant was a particular favourite. It was
election year, and Siegel was a vociferous supporter of the
Democrat President, Roosevelt; he was allowed to wear a
Roosevelt badge on his prison uniform. Social life presented
no problems. On the pretext of visiting his dentist or conferring
with his lawyer, Siegel was able to make countless trips outside
prison, much to the consternation of the police, who believed
they'd put him in the can and instead would come across him
holding court in clubs, restaurants and movie-theatres.

In December 1940, the District Attorney dropped the charges
against Siegel. The authorities now thought they had little
evidence against him, but it was also murmured that Siegel
had made one or two useful contributions to the re-election
funds of certain people, and that, furthermore, the New York
authorities didn't want to risk putting Reles in the witness
stand against Siegel; they wanted to keep him alive to testify
against the big New York mafiosi.

Bugsy walked free, with all the glamour the whiff of crime
bestowed, but without the taint of a conviction. He was
considered even more desirable, and he was further sought
after by the ladies. The Hollywood stars invited this poisonous
but charming curiosity to their houses, and even the local police
developed an affection for him, often giving him lifts back from
the race track, their sirens wailing as they escorted the cosseted

Bugsy Siegel was supremely vain. A fanatic on the subject of
physical fitness and virility, he smoked and drank little, worked-
out in the boxing ring and spent every afternoon in the gym,
where he held many of his business meetings. At night-time he
rubbed beauty cream into his face and put on an elastic chin strap
to keep his features from sagging. Unless he was out on the town
he went to bed at 10 p.m., having spent an hour or so struggling
with a self-improvement book (he was continually trying to
extend his vocabulary and lose the New York accent that
betrayed his origins). He had a horror of going bald, and nobody
was allowed to mention his receding hairline. Anyone with a full
head of hair would be aware of his jealous gaze and he once paid
an associate who had a full complement of hair $2500 to allow
him to cut a mass of it off.

gangster home. Later, when the police thought they had more evidence against him, he was re-arrested, but the untimely death of Kid Twist ensured his release.

At some point in 1941 Siegel met Virginia Hill. Hill, the daughter of poor, small-town folk from Alabama, had slept her way across America and Mexico, marrying at least twice, and breaking a host of hearts. She had no regard for thrift, and spent the considerable sums of money admirers lavished on her on lingerie and parties. One man, Joe Epstein, a good-natured and short-sighted accountant from Chicago with lucrative connections to a gambling syndicate, used to send her weekly packets containing wads of thousand dollar bills; he continued to do so for years. Hill was very beautiful: her auburn hair and grey eyes – and her extravagant and generous personality – could reduce the most rational of men to cringing sexual supplicants. She and Siegel were a natural pairing. When he came calling for her – as he did every day – she would bath in Chanel No. 5. Her kid brother, Chick, whom she had rescued from the drudgery of rural Alabama and took everywhere with her, stayed on hand to provide constant room service for the lovers. They also used a host of hotels and apartments under a variety of pseudonyms. When the government finally went looking for Hill over a small matter of several hundred-thousand dollars in unpaid taxes, they issued a wanted poster on which they described her as a "paramour and associate of gangsters and racketeers" and gave a list of twenty aliases she had used over the years.

Hill had a wardrobe a queen would have envied: a hundred pairs of shoes, a series of $5,000 designer dresses, a dozen mink stoles, a pair of persian-lamb coats. Her winter-wear was imported from England, she had $15,000 diamond rings and each year bought herself a brand-new Cadillac. Most of the money came from Epstein. But Bugsy paid too, and put a $30,000 deposit on a house at Miami Beach for her. When questioned by the Revenue, she said that she only had an income of $16,000 a year, from betting on the horses. She did bet large sums, and won huge amounts too; but it was nothing compared to the flow of money from Epstein. Chick Hill once reckoned that his sister got through around five million dollars in these years. She didn't just spend it on herself: at times she literally threw it at people, tossing sheaves of it out of the window. No one has ever satisfactorily explained why Epstein sent her so much; some say she had a share of his gambling syndicate, others that she was one of the most successful blackmailers ever. But the truth is probably that Epstein not only was smitten, but also felt responsible for her: she became his mistress when she was only seventeen. Before her death, Hill told a friend that she hated Epstein, that he never gave her any peace, and never gave up trying to buy her back.

During the Second World War, Siegel declined to fight for his country. They probably wouldn't have let him into the Army anyway. With the nation's eyes turned outwards, he was able to expand his criminal activities, encouraging bookies to subscribe to his Trans-America race-result wire service. Most bookies already subscribed to a rival service, the Continental. But the threat of physical violence generally opened their eyes to the advantages of Siegel's wire.

He bought interests in racetracks and illegal gaming clubs in California, and, across the state line, began to acquire legitimate gambling interests in Las Vegas, where he had investments in a number of small clubs. His annual income was conservatively estimated to be around $500,000, but it was never enough. His gambling and his women saw to that, and he was forever borrowing money.

Bugsy was still married to Esta, but spent most of his time with Hill, to whom he was by no means faithful. Virginia Hill was no more faithful to Bugsy: she needed, and devoured, men but she did love Bugsy Siegel. When the attention of the police became too much for him, he decided to move out of the Hollywood mansion and escape to Nevada. Virginia was keen to get away from Hollywood too, and Bugsy even intimated that despite his need to keep up pretences of married respectability he was considering divorcing his wife. The movie star

---

Naturally, Siegel wanted to be a movie star. He figured he spent all his time acting, and it seemed inevitable to him that he would one day be paid for doing so. He began turning up in the studio where George Raft was making a film with Marlene Dietrich, first watching, then going to Raft's dressing room and acting out the sequences he had witnessed. He purchased a 16mm camera, and had one of his tame hoods film his impromptu performances. He let it be known that he was interested in appearing in films and spent months trying to improve his diction and perfect his appearance. But the offers never came. He could only impersonate; he could never act.

Loretta Young offered to buy his house for $85,000, but pulled out after Bugsy refused to pay $350 to have the termites in the cellar exterminated. Bugsy, irascible as ever, took her to court, lost the case, appealed and lost again. His peculiar meanness was much in evidence when he finally moved out of the house: he forced George Raft to pay him $500 for an assortment of decaying garden furniture not worth twenty dollars, which the movie star had no need for; but one didn't refuse Bugsy. "I guess he needs the money" sighed Raft, counting out the bills.

One summer day in 1945, Bugsy Siegel took his old friend Little Moe Sedway on a trip to Las Vegas, then a poky little desert town in a sea of burning sand with a collection of run-down gambling clubs. Most of the Californians who crossed the border to gamble would head for the smarter resort of Reno. Las Vegas was for ranchers, cowpokes, poor Indians and the occasional lost tourist.

Bugsy drove Moe to a remote and bleak spot seven miles outside town, where a dilapidated motel rotted in the sun. He told him his plan: he was going to buy these thirty acres of wasteland for a few cents and build a hotel and casino costing two million dollars. It would be called "Ben Siegel's Flamingo". When Moe protested at the absurdity of the idea – what possible incentive could there be for anyone to come here? – Bugsy simply stared dreamily at the desert haze and told him that one day people would drive hundreds of miles just to see the place he planned.

Fronted by his friends, Siegel bought up the land over the next few months, and floated the Nevada Projects Corporation, raising one million dollars through a share issue, all of which were bought by close associates; Meyer Lansky took shares, as did Louis Pokross, another member of the old Bug-Meyer gang. In effect, the Flamingo was financed by the Mafia. In December 1945, building began.

Bugsy was beside himself with excitement. He engaged the popular Del Webb to build the hotel, and pulled every political string he could to obtain the necessary supplies of copper, marble and steel; wartime stringencies still applied, but while veterans down the road returned from the fighting to find that they couldn't get bricks with which to build houses, the Flamingo was made a priority building project. Truly, Bugsy Siegel was a master of graft.

In the midst of this, Bugsy forgot that he hadn't seen his family for months, and Esta finally sued for a divorce from the man who was now an utter stranger, wrapped up in his twin passions of the Flamingo and Virginia Hill. She got an unusually generous settlement: Bugsy was in an ebullient mood and signed an alimony agreement worth $1,500,000 to his ex-wife.

He was being profligate on the building, too. He flew plasterers and carpenters in from other cities, and paid them fifty dollars a day. When materials weren't forthcoming, he would obtain them at extortionate prices on the black market. Lorry drivers were turning up and delivering materials which they would return at night to steal and then sell back to him the following day. He ordered that the walls be of double thickness. When it transpired that the supporting beam of the penthouse suite he intended for his own use was only going to be 5'10" off the ground and he would have to duck humbly under it every time he entered the room, he ordered this central piece of structure to be ripped out and re-designed. His vanity cost $22,500. Bugsy decided that the layout of the kitchens was wrong: it cost $30,000 to alter. Then he complained that the boiler room was too small: another $115,000. He insisted that the ninety-two bedrooms all had their private sewage systems: the plumbing bill came to $1 million. The building was his obsession, his final play for recognition; he was going to run the most glitzy hotel and casino in the country and therefore everything must be as he desired it. He was out of control.

Throughout 1946, as the hotel took shape, his temper grew fouler and his aggressive outbursts of frustration and fury more regular. He reverted to being an irascible hood, made uglier by his imperial ambitions; the workmen who battled in the sweltering Nevada heat to finish the hotel in time for a Christmas opening were afraid of his megalomania and of the boots and guns of henchmen like Hymie Segal and Little Moe Sedway. The atmosphere was fraught.

In the summer, on impulse, Bugsy and Virginia Hill flew to Mexico and were married. Siegel gave her a ruby and diamond ring. He never mentioned the wedding to anyone else; it was five years before Hill told reporters that she had once been Bugsy's wife. Bugsy was never an emotionally articulate man, and rarely expressed any sort of tenderness. But though they might not talk about it, they both knew that theirs was the love of kindred spirits. Bugsy even wrote Hill a poem once.

The Flamingo was due to open on 26 December. Realizing that the day was fast approaching, Siegel began frantically to try and publicize the hotel. He hired press agents in Los Angeles, who inundated the newspapers with photographs of the nubile beauties that would be on display at the hotel. In Las Vegas he took full page advertisements in all the region's newspapers and hired Henry Greenspun, the editor of a monthly magazine, *Las Vegas Life*, to manage his publicity (he wanted, most particularly, to ensure that he was never again known as "Bugsy"). He assiduously courted the press, sending them cases of whisky, promises of free sex at the casino and sometimes envelopes full of cash; there was many a newspaperman who disengaged himself from a firm hand-shake with Bugsy to find himself holding a $100 bill. He drew up a list of movie stars he wanted present for the opening and ordered Billy Wilkerson, his long-time associate in Los Angeles, to make sure they turned up and chartered a fleet of aircraft to bring them to the door of the Flamingo.

But Siegel's luck was about to run out. Randolph Hearst, the newspaper magnate, let it be known that he was none too keen on either Siegel or the Flamingo. The press kept their distance, or wrote sniping articles about Siegel's shady past. The movie stars he wanted – Joan Crawford, Spencer Tracy, Greer Garson – were advised by influential figures to stay away. In despair, Siegel contemplated cancelling the opening; but Virginia Hill had just spent $3,500 on a new dress and was not going to have her big night ruined.

On 26 December the weather was appalling. A driving wind and a foul storm kept the chartered aircraft and most of the willing celebrities grounded in Los Angeles. The spectacular ornamental waterfall outside the hotel – visible for miles – wouldn't work, because a cat had had a litter of kittens in the tap, and Siegel believed it would be bad luck to flush the kittens out. When the doors opened, it was apparent that there were more staff than customers, and only two or three names of any sort – including the faithful George Raft – had made the journey by car or train. The great occasion was a disaster.

So long as the gambling side of things could hold its own, there was hope. Casinos do have runs of bad luck, but if managed with a modicum of care, they should be money-making machines: after all, the odds are invariably in favour of the house. But Siegel was on a losing streak: the casino's losses in the first week were unprecedented. Some say that the local opposition joined up to try and bust the Flamingo in its first forty-eight hours, pouring money in to break Siegel with big early winnings. But everybody – except George Raft, who went down $65,000 on the Chemin de Fer – made a small fortune. Siegel was frantic; he switched the dice, changed the cards and moved the confused dealers from table to table. Nothing changed his luck and he was even being clipped by his own staff, who were openly playing rigged games.

Siegel stalked the still unfinished hotel and casino, pumping with adrenalin, his eyes bloodshot, his temper exhausted. He began to look for fights, and tried to sock Chick Hill. He and Virginia had a vicious scrap in which she flew at him with a stiletto heel, cutting his face badly. Hill went back to Los Angeles, took a new mansion, bought new clothes and indulged herself with new lovers. She hated the desert, and was going crazy herself. One night a policeman was called to her house, to find her stalking round in her night dress, clutching a gun and announcing that she intended to kill everybody present.

Siegel's rivals in Las Vegas and Los Angeles began to spread rumours about the volcanic temper of the thug who ran the Flamingo; they said that visitors were putting their lives at risk. Finally, facing ruin, Siegel announced that he would close the Flamingo and re-open it, completely finished, in March.

He began to suspect that his backers might seriously be contemplating ridding themselves of him and might even be involved in the process of ruining him so that they could take the Flamingo over. He surrounded himself with armed hoods and lashed out wildly at anyone whom he suspected of disloyalty. He needed money so badly that he stung everyone he knew for whatever they had: George Raft was persuaded to lend him $100,000, which he never saw again.

The re-opening night in March was a downbeat, panicky affair. There were no firework displays or razzmatazz, and Siegel, his friends and their wives spent the evening running from bedroom to bedroom, frantically trying to help the workmen and chambermaids to finish preparing them. At

---

After two weeks, the Flamingo had lost $300,000. The building costs of the complex stood at four million dollars, and there were still ninety-two bedrooms to furnish at $3500 each. The mob wanted to hear some good news about their investment. Siegel was looking down the barrel of a gun.

eight p.m. there were still guests in the lobby, waiting to check into rooms that had no furniture. But, on the face of it, business looked much better. Siegel had ridden the adverse publicity, and people were making the trek across the desert to visit this fabulous, glowing palace.

But Siegel's bad luck persisted. The guests were playing in the casino, but they were still winning. The net loss for the first six months was approaching one million dollars. There was a series of other disasters too. On one hot afternoon, the occupants of the swimming pool were alarmed to see all the water disappear down a vast crack which suddenly opened up. Many mumbled about the hand of God and checked out immediately. It was just an engineering flaw, and was soon repaired, but by then the word was out: the Flamingo was cursed.

Virginia Hill was becoming more unstable. One night, after convincing herself that Siegel was sleeping with a blonde hatcheck girl, she launched herself at the woman, and put her in hospital with a dislocated vertebra and severe facial lacerations. Siegel was furious: his arbitrary explosions were adverse publicity enough. The couple argued; Hill took an overdose. She was taken to hospital in time to save her life, but it was only the first of many suicide attempts, and one day she would succeed.

Hill was exhausted. Siegel had become a raging insomniac. He now knew that his position was hopeless, that he had insufficient experience to run the Flamingo, that his vanity and bad taste had contributed to the disaster, and that he could find no more money from anywhere. But when Hill told him to sell up and move with her, he refused.

His death was inevitable. The backers wanted him out. He had long parted company with two of the mob's contacts with the project, Gus Greenbaum and Little Moe Sedway (the man he had first taken to see the windblown, desolate site). These

When the movie starlet Marie McDonald (a close friend of Siegel and Hill) came to Las Vegas they were surprised that she did not visit the Flamingo. She told them that the room clerk at her hotel, one Ray Kronsen, had flippantly said that the place was full of gangsters and murderers. Siegel was beside himself. He took Hymie Segal and Chick Hill and went round to the hotel where the clerk worked and clubbed him insensible with gun-butts.

two seem to have been remarkably well-informed about the time-table the Mafia drew up for Bugsy's last days.

Over the few days leading up to 20 June 1947 Siegel seemed to be almost constantly on the telephone. Nobody will say who he was speaking to. Sometimes the conversations were violent disagreements, sometimes he seemed to be imploring, sometimes he was rational and friendly. On 19 June Siegel called a sidekick called Fat Irish Green into his office and showed him a briefcase containing $600,000.

"I'm going to Los Angeles for a couple of days," he said. "I want you to look after this case. If anything happens to me, just sit tight and then some guys will come and take the money off your hands."

Then he called Virginia Hill's house on Linden Drive in Los Angeles. He got hold of Chick and told him that he would be over that night, accompanied by his associate, Alan Smiley. He said that he was going to have a meeting at his lawyer's the next day.

He arrived, slept, had his meeting and then went to a barber's and had a leisurely lunch. He also had a talk with an old mob friend, Mickey Cohen, and asked him if he could get hold of some guys with "equipment". Cohen dropped a couple of names, and Siegel said he'd see them the following day. To Cohen, it looked as if Siegel was even now planning to fight back. After dinner at Jack's Restaurant in Ocean Park, Siegel and Smiley returned to Linden Drive. Siegel opened the door with the solid gold key that Virginia had given him, and he and Smiley sat in the lounge, which was decorated in a curious mixture of English chintz and American camp, talking over the grim state of business.

At 10.20 p.m. on 20 June 1947, as the two men talked, Chick was upstairs, fumbling with the clothing of his girlfriend Jerri Mason. Suddenly, he heard what sounded like gunfire downstairs. When he reached the lounge, Al Smiley screamed at him to turn the lights out. He did so, and both men stood in the dark, trembling, with Jerri Mason screaming in the background. They heard a car pull away. After a while, they switched the lights back on. Chick saw that Smiley was hiding in the fireplace, and on the floor, his head nearly severed by nine shots from a .30-30 carbine, was the corpse of Benjamin "Bugsy" Siegel. His right eye was found plastered to the ceiling fifteen feet away, and his eyelids with their luxuriant lashes were glued to an adjoining door jamb.

The front-facing window of the lounge was shattered by bullets. The killer had come very close to the house, and had carefully rested his gun on the tasteful lattice-work frame that shielded the house from the road. Siegel had been a sitting target because, curiously, the curtains had been open, as if by arrangement.

Within twenty minutes of his death, Greenbaum and Moe Sedway strolled through the doors of the Flamingo and took control of the complex. Later, a group of businessmen called on Fat Irish Green, and relieved him of the cash that Bugsy had deposited with him. The Flamingo was refinanced, and given a respectable front man. In a short time, it began to make vast profits, and all along the bleak road where it had once stood as a lonely memorial to the grandiose dreams of a dead mobster sprang up a host of other, glittering gambling palaces. The modern city of Las Vegas was born.

Siegel had a handsome coffin, made of scrolled silver and bronze and lined with silk, costing $5,000. Few of his associates attended the funeral; the police and press outnumbered the mourners. Virginia Hill didn't come, nor did George Raft, nor the Countess DiFrasso. Just his family – his ex-wife, his daughters, his sister.

Virginia Hill was in Paris when Siegel was killed. She checked out of her hotel and drove to Monaco, where she sat alone in the Casino. Later that night she took an overdose of barbiturates. She survived, then returned to Paris where she took a suite in the Ritz and again tried to kill herself. She flew back to America, but the pattern of attempted suicide persisted. On each occasion she was saved only by fortunate intervention, mostly by Chick. Pursued by the Internal Revenue and eaten by depression and loneliness, she finally fled the United States and made her way, via Mexico, to Europe.

Hill went to live in the ski resort of Klosters, outside Zurich. She was increasingly unstable, and regularly assaulted her

Little Moe Sedway died of multiple ailments and was buried in the same cemetery not fifty feet from Siegel, his bitter enemy. Gus Greenbaum was not so fortunate: he fell out with his Mafia masters and in 1958 was decapitated with a butcher's knife while asleep in Las Vegas; his wife was then knifed and strangled for good measure as she lay beside him.

brother's girlfriends (throughout her life she possessed a formidable right jab). Before leaving America she had married Hans Hauser, an Austrian-born ski-instructor reputed to have the looks and body of Apollo. She even had a child, Peter, by him. But she was never happy with Hans, and soon despised him. The Revenue had already seized everything she owned in the US – her house, her cars, her mink coats. Now she tried to strike a deal with them. She would come back, try and settle her tax and serve a nominal sentence. But the deal fell apart. She lurched on: to Salzburg, then Prague and then Cuba, from where she was immediately sent back to Prague (she was unaware that Castro was now in power). Epstein stopped sending her money; she was broke, and raged against the world.

Finally, in March 1966, Hill drove to the small, beautiful mountain village of Koppl outside Salzburg and, by a waterfall, swallowed twenty-eight barbiturates and quietly died. She was forty-nine years old.

AL CAPONE: PUBLIC ENEMY NUMBER ONE

Contrary to popular belief, Al "Scarface" Capone, the most infamous of the Chicago gangsters, was unconnected to the Mafia. He was not a Sicilian, and he spent his active life quarrelling with the "Mob". Capone came from a Neapolitan family and was born in Brooklyn in 1899, the fourth son of Gabriele and Teresa Capone, who had emigrated from Naples some six years previously. Like all gangsters, he was involved in crime from an early age, running with the so-called "Five Points Gang", which was led by another Italian, John Torrio, a future partner in violence. At the age of fifteen, young Alphonse discovered that The Black Hand, a Camorra/Mafia murder squad, was extorting money from his father. He tracked down the two men responsible, shooting them dead. Torrio was impressed.

In 1919 the Volsted Act was passed, and America began its long and ultimately disastrous experiment with Prohibition. Torrio had been in Chicago for a few years already, establishing himself as a serious gangster. In Chicago, illegal drinkers were kept supplied by one of a dozen big gangs, each of which had its own clearly defined territory. Torrio controlled the South Side of the city, in conjunction with the Irish Duggan-Lake gang who supplied the Inner West Side. The rest of the West Side was run by the Genna brothers, Sicilians from Marsala, who were noted for the pleasure they derived from killing. The North Side of Chicago was the province of Dion O'Banion, a small time thief who ran a flower shop opposite the Holy Name

Cathedral. He worked in conjunction with two Poles, George "Bugs" Moran and Hymie Weiss.

At first there was little trouble between the gangs; there was enough business to go around, and the gangs' energies were devoted towards organizing themselves into efficient units. But within a year, they began to look for opportunities to muscle in on each others' profits, and the murders began. Torrio suddenly acquired rivals on the South Side, the O'Donnell gang, who started hijacking his beer trucks and smashing up his drinking dens. He had several of their drivers killed, but he realized that in the circumstances attack was the best form of defence. If he did not exert control over the whole of Chicago, it was unlikely that he would survive at all. He needed skilled, violent men who were prepared to kill without remorse and casting his mind back he remembered the young Capone, now twenty-one and a lieutenant in the Five Points Gang. Torrio lured him to Chicago with an extraordinary offer: Capone would get twenty-five per cent of all existing turnover and fifty per cent of any further business.

Within two years Capone had gained control of the middle class Chicago suburb of Cicero, which became his personal headquarters. The local police and town authorities were in his pocket, and through the classic mix of bribery and intimidation his illegal casinos, brothels and bars were left alone to flourish. He also killed in public with impunity. Nobody would testify against him and he and Torrio were raking in $100,000 a week apiece.

Both Torrio and Capone agreed that absolute control of Chicago was there for the taking but Capone, no diplomat, wanted to shoot his way to the top in an all-out gang war; Torrio was more circumspect and tried to persuade his irascible partner to bide his time. Then, in October 1924, a dispute broke out between the Gennas and the O'Banion gang. The Sicilians had stolen a cargo of the Irishman's whisky. O'Banion swore revenge, but on 4 November was himself mown down in his flower shop by three men posing as customers. The murder was almost certainly the work of Capone and Torrio, but both they and the Gennas had convenient alibis, and although the street outside the shop had been crowded, once again no one had heard or seen anything. The coroner was forced to return a verdict of "unlawful killing at the hands of a person or persons unknown".

O'Banion had a lavish funeral. His body lay in state at the

undertakers for three days. Silver angels stood at the head and feet of his corpse, bearing in their hands ten candles that burned in solid gold candlesticks. Mounted police had to maintain order as the vast procession wound its way to the cemetery; there were twenty-six trucks of floral tributes, valued at $50,000. Capone sent a bunch of red roses, with a dedication: "from Al". Both he and Torrio attended the funeral.

O'Banion's organization was taken over by Hymie Weiss, his trusted lieutenant. Weiss adored O'Banion, and wept buckets by his grave. He swore revenge and a few days later Capone's car was swept by machine-gun fire. He escaped unhurt, but Torrio was not so lucky: two weeks later he was gunned down by another of the late O'Banion's men, Bugs Moran, in front of his wife. He recovered, but soon found himself in jail on charges of operating an illegal brewery. In prison, his nerve began to crack. He had steel screens fitted to the windows of his cell and paid for three extra sheriffs to stand guard; he wanted out of Chicago. In 1925, on his release from prison, he announced he was leaving town. Chicago, he said, was "too violent". At the age of forty-eight, Torrio took retirement and Capone, then only twenty-six, inherited his criminal empire. Shortly after his ascent to power, three of the six Genna brothers – Angel, Mike and Antonio – died in gun-battles. The others decided that life in Sicily was preferable to death in America, and retired hastily to Marsala. Only Weiss and Bugs Moran now stood between Capone and absolute control of Chicago.

Weiss fought back in spectacular style. In broad daylight, no less than eight car-loads of his henchmen descended on Capone's headquarters at the Hawthorne Inn and within the space of a few seconds they pumped over a thousand bullets into the

One of Capone's first victims in Chicago was Joe Howard, a small time crook, who unwisely stole two consignments of Torrio's alcohol. The following night, as he sat enjoying the "happy hour" in his neighbourhood drinking hole, Capone walked in and shot him six times at point-blank range in front of a gallery of witnesses. The police arrested Capone, but had to release him when, after a series of personal visits from smartly-dressed men in large cars, all the witnesses became uncertain as to what, if anything, they had seen.

building. Capone escaped, but decided to bring the dispute to a swift conclusion and on 11 October 1926 Hymie Weiss was gunned down on the steps of Holy Name Cathedral. Ten days later, Capone called a meeting of the Chicago gang leaders. "We're a bunch of saps to be killing each other" he told them. They nodded their assent, and agreed to a peaceful carve-up of the whole of Cook County.

For a while there was peace, and everybody made money. Capone became fabulously wealthy. Within Cook County he controlled no less than 10,000 illegal drinking dens, or speak-easies, each of which purchased an average of six barrels of beer and two cases of liquor a week from him. The beer reputedly brought him about three and a half million dollars a week; the liquor another one point eight million. When the proceeds from his gambling and prostitution rackets were added to this, his income was estimated at six and a half million dollars a week. Though his overheads were vast, his profits still made him a multi-millionaire.

Capone thought that Chicago was no place to bring up his children. By 1928, he felt secure enough about his position to look around for a second home, somewhere away from the city. Not every state was keen on having him as a resident. He was thrown out of California, and tried Florida instead. Its citizens objected vociferously, but Capone succeeded in buying a palatial residence on Palm Island, Miami, where he quietly passed Christmas and New Year of 1929.

While he was away, Bugs Moran, the man who had shot

Capone was now a pillar of the establishment, most of which was on his payroll (it is thought that he spent some thirty million dollars annually on back-handers and bribes and blatantly bought favourable politicians, financing the re-election campaign of Mayor "Big Bill" Thompson to the tune of $260,000). A conservative man, strong on family values, he dressed immaculately, in hand-made silk shirts, and sported diamond tie-pins. He gave generously to charities, and church restoration funds. He contributed $100,000 to a fund for striking miners, and during the Depression opened a string of soup kitchens and gave more than two million dollars to help ease the plight of the poor. When an old woman was blinded in the cross-fire of an assassination attempt on him, he paid $10,000 to have her sight restored.

Al Capone winks at the camera as he arrives at the Chicago Courthouse prior to being sentenced to 11 years in prison and a £10,000 fine for tax evasion

Torrio in revenge for the murder of O'Banion, decided to settle his long-standing score with Capone. He began to muscle in on Capone's activities, regularly stealing his consignments of liquor, and threatening the other, more legitimate businesses that Capone had poured his illicit wealth into. When the source of the trouble became apparent, Capone acted swiftly. He called his right-hand man, Jake Guzik, and gave orders for the elimination of Moran. The time and place of the killing were fixed: it was to be 10.30 a.m. on 14 February 1929, St Valentine's day.

On that cold and grey Chicago morning, six of Moran's men – and one other man, an optician called Doctor Richard Schwimmer, whose presence has never been explained – were standing nonchalantly in a garage on North Clark Street, waiting for a truck-load of stolen whisky to arrive. Shortly after 10.30 a.m., a local resident, Mrs Max Landeman, heard the sound of shots coming from the adjoining garage. Looking out of the window, she saw a man leave the garage and get into a large black touring car. Another woman, Miss Josephine Morin, who lived in the flat below, saw two men come out of the garage with their hands raised above their heads. They were followed by two uniformed police officers, who had their guns drawn. She presumed she was witnessing an arrest. The four men got into a large black Cadillac and drove off.

Curiosity got the better of Mrs Landeman, and she hurried over to the garage. The doors were shut. Pushing them open, she saw seven men piled in a bloody heap on the floor. In addition to the optician, the bodies were later identified as being those of Frank and Peter Gusenberg, Moran's principal hit-men; James Clark, Moran's brother-in-law; Al Weinshank, his accountant; Adam Heyer, his business-manager; and Johnny May, a burglar. It looked as if Capone's men had entered, disguised as policemen, lined them up facing the wall and then massacred them. Frank Gusenberg was still alive when the police arrived. They tried to persuade him to talk, but he refused to say who the killers had been. He died three hours after entering hospital, without breaking the gangster's sacred code of silence.

Bugs Moran was lucky. He should have been with his men, but had been unexpectedly delayed. By the time he arrived, it was all over; he saw the police cars and ambulances and made himself scarce. He had no doubts about who had ordered the killing: only Al Capone would contemplate such a massacre. At the time of the shooting, Capone was in the office of a Miami official, arguing about his right to reside in Florida. The police picked up some other members of his gang, but they too had alibis. Jack "Machine-Gun" MacGurn, Capone's prize executioner, claimed to have been with his girlfriend at the time of the killing, and even married her so that she could not be forced to testify against him. In the end no one was ever charged in connection with the St Valentine's Day Massacre, but Moran was finished as a force.

Gang members began to whisper that there was something a little unstable about Capone. His temper had become shorter, his use of violence less selective. The killings grew indiscriminate, and men from all walks of life were gunned down, knifed and garrotted for the most petty of offences.

In the spring of 1929, Capone found himself under unusual pressure. Herbert Hoover had been elected President, and had promised the nation an onslaught against organized crime, naming Al Capone Public Enemy Number One. In addition, Capone discovered that there was a highly enticing contract out on his life. Its possible source was Moran, but it might just as easily have emanated from the families of Scalise and Anselmi, or one of the hundreds of others whose relatives had been destroyed by Capone; even his own men thought that he was becoming a liability.

Capone decided to drop out of circulation for a while, and contrived to have himself arrested for a minor firearms offence. He expected thirty quiet and safe days in jail, but was horrified to find that he had been put away for a whole year. It made

Capone came back from Florida in high spirits, only to discover that two of his trusted lieutenants, John Scalise and Albert Anselmi, had ambitions to take over the "outfit". Capone organized a communal gang meal, inviting the two to join him and other favourites in a private room at a restaurant in Hammond, Indiana. To those present, Al Capone seemed in an uncommonly good mood. He laughed and joked and kept the drink flowing. Then, towards the end of the meal, he got up and sauntered around to where Scalise and Anselmi were seated. Leaning over the backs of their chairs, he smiled sweetly at them. "I hear you boys want my job," he said. "Well come and get it!" Picking up a baseball bat that was positioned on an adjoining table, he smashed in their skulls.

little difference to his life, as he soon managed to establish good links with his Chicago operations, and continued to control events from the security of his prison cell.

Meanwhile, Hoover embarked on a series of meetings with various arms of his administration: the Prohibition Bureau, the FBI and the Treasury Department. The officials discussed how they might be able to put Capone away permanently. Since Capone had most of the police in his pocket it was impossible to find witnesses to his crimes and orthodox methods were unlikely to succeed. For a while the Justice Department launched an all-out war on his organization, smashing up his breweries and trucks, but it had little long-term effect: Capone had the resources to absorb the attacks and come back.

By far the most successful department in the fight against organized crime was the Treasury. Frank Wilson, the senior investigator of their Special Intelligence Unit, had already succeeded in putting away a number of Capone's associates, including Frank Nitti (his deputy), Jack Guzik (his accountant), and his brother Ralph; all got sentences of between eighteen months and five years.

Since Capone had no bank account in his own name, and all his assets nominally belonged to others, Wilson had little to go on. He would have to prove that Capone's lavish lifestyle indicated undeclared income and unpaid taxes.

Gangsters can't declare the source of their earnings and have a natural aversion to paying taxes. Capone claimed that he lived off $450 a month; because his earnings were therefore less than $5,000 a year, he had never filed a tax-return.

Wilson began piecing together the record of Capone's personal spending. He found that between 1926 and 1929 Capone had purchased more then $25,000 of furniture for his various homes; he had also spent $7,000 on suits and another $40,000 on telephone calls. In all, Wilson found that in that period Capone had spent some $165,000, which clearly indicated undeclared income. It would only be enough to put Capone away for three years; they needed more. Finally Wilson persuaded some of Capone's casino employees to talk, and the Treasury was able to charge Capone with failing to pay taxes on one million dollars of undeclared earnings, meriting a possible thirty years in prison.

At first Capone's attorney struck a deal with the prosecution: if his client pleaded guilty he would get no more than two years in prison. But when the Judge heard about the arrangement he was disgusted and refused to accept it.

Capone went on trial. The jurors were subject to persistent threats and attempts at bribery, which necessitated a last minute change of the entire jury. On 24 October 1931, Capone was found guilty on all counts and was sentenced to eleven years in prison and fined $50,000, the most severe sentence ever imposed for a tax offence. He was imprisoned in Cook County jail while his lawyers lodged an appeal. It failed, and in May 1932 he was shipped to Atlanta Federal Penitentiary and from there he was moved to the infamous prison on Alcatraz in San Francisco Bay.

Shortly after he began his sentence, Capone was diagnosed as suffering from syphilis. All attempts at a cure failed and by the time he was released in 1939 the disease had reached its debilitating tertiary stage: at the age of thirty-eight, Al Capone was going mad. He went to live at his home on Palm Island, Florida. Surrounded by his family, and under constant medical supervision, he survived for another seven years, a grim, haunted figure, his mind slowly consumed by syphilis. In 1947 he died following a brain haemorrhage and his body was returned to Chicago, the scene of his triumphs, where he was buried, at great cost, in a marble mausoleum in the cemetery at Mount Olive.

BONNIE AND CLYDE: DEPRESSION MOBSTERS

During the drab, poverty-stricken years of the Great Depression, the Great Plains became the hunting ground for a number of celebrated gangsters who specialized in motorized crime. Although criminals like any others, their poor backgrounds and their reputation for robbing banks rather than other struggling individuals gave them the image of latter-day Robin Hoods. As much as anything, the stories of their doomed and violent lives made good news in an otherwise dull decade.

Foremost amongst them were the young lovers Bonnie Parker and Clyde Barrow, now folk heroes and the subject of many works of fiction. In reality they were a little less scrupulous about killing than the legends suggest. Clyde Barrow, who was born on 24 March 1909 into an impoverished Texan farming family, had a particularly vicious streak, and it was claimed that from an early age he took great pleasure in torturing farm animals.

His future partner, Bonnie Parker, two years his junior, came from a devout Baptist environment. Her father died when she was four and the family moved to the gruesomely named Cement City, Texas. A pretty, petite blonde, Bonnie was much sought after and when only sixteen married a Dallas bum

Bonnie Parker

named Roy Thornton. He was soon in jail, doing life for murder, and at the age of nineteen she met the handsome, polite and pleasant Clyde, whom her mother thought a lovely boy. Her illusions were shattered when Clyde was arrested on seven counts of burglary and car theft. But her daughter was smitten and helped Clyde to escape from jail, smuggling in a gun. A few days later he was picked up again, this time for robbing a railway ticket-office at gunpoint, and sentenced to fourteen years in a grim Texas prison.

There was nothing Bonnie could do this time, so Clyde got to thinking and came up with the ingenious idea of persuading another inmate to cut off two of his toes with an axe. Thus crippled, he was deemed to have suffered enough, and released. He hobbled straight back to Bonnie. He tried going straight, but the work was dull, the pay bad and you still died at the end of it all. Crime held less prospect of such prolonged disappointment. He and Bonnie headed for West Dallas; they picked up a friend of Clyde's, one Ray Hamilton, acquired two other gang members and hit the road.

They rarely struck gold – the biggest haul was a mere $3,500 – and after a few minor heists Clyde committed his first murder, when he shot a jeweller in Hillsboro, Texas. They got away with the grand total of forty dollars. Bonnie was in custody at the time, on suspicion of auto-theft. By the time she was released, three months later, the gang had signed their death warrants by gunning down a Sheriff and his Deputy outside a Texas dance hall.

Some of their murders were the result either of a surprisingly casual attitude to killing or of sheer nerves; little else could explain the occasion on which Bonnie shot a Texas butcher three times in the stomach, or the unnecessary death of the son of a car owner whose vehicle they were stealing. The police stalked them relentlessly. In 1933, they went to hide out in Missouri, where they were joined by Clyde's hitherto respectable brother, Buck, and his neurotic wife, Blanche. Such a large group made it all the easier for the police to find them. They were duly surrounded but, by now heavily armed, they shot their way out, killing two policemen.

On the run, the two became increasingly morbid; aware that they would inevitably die, they were concerned that they would never see their parents again. A certain desperation crept into their behaviour, and the killings became even more arbitrary. They survived a nasty car crash, and escaped again

"Pretty Boy"Floyd was so christened by an affectionate whorehouse madam in Kansas City. Named Charles Arthur, he was a tall and muscular farm labourer from Oklahoma who one day tossed aside his shovel and decided on a career as a gangster. A contemporary of Bonnie and Clyde, he ploughed exactly the same furrow, robbing banks and shooting anyone who opposed him. Caught and sentenced to fifteen years for the one killing they could pin on him, Pretty Boy hopped off the train taking him to prison and went back to work. He was finally gunned down by the FBI in Ohio in 1934.

from a police assault, before they were once more cornered in Missouri. Again they managed to escape, but this time the police scored: Buck was shot in the head, and Blanche was blinded. Bonnie was still crippled from the car crash. When Clyde stopped driving to buy water and food, the police were on them. Buck was riddled with bullets and died in hospital six days later. Blanche stayed with her dead husband, and was sentenced to ten years in prison.

Bonnie and Clyde eluded the authorities for the next three months. Betrayed by a former gang member, the police staked them out and ambushed their car as they returned from shopping. On 23 May 1934 the Ford V8 sedan they were driving had nearly a hundred rounds pumped into it. They died instantly, very young and very pretty. When they were buried in Dallas, they pulled crowds from all over the country.

THE KRAYS

Charles Kray was a small, dapper man with sharp black shoes, gleaming black hair and an easy smile. A dealer in second-hand clothes and scrap precious metals, from Hoxton, East London, he came from a family of wanderers, and in the 1930s was happy to travel hundreds of miles to buy stock, knocking on doors and "pestering" people. Charles Kray was considered one of the finest "pesterers" in the business and his neighbours said that the Krays had gypsy blood and were descended from horse-dealers who had settled in this poorest part of London; a drab, depressed area, famous for its pubs and thieves. Here Charles's earnings – twenty or thirty pounds at least most weeks – were riches indeed.

At the age of twenty-four, he married Violet Lee, a seventeen-year-old blonde with blue eyes, whom he met in a dance hall in Hackney. One of three attractive sisters from Bethnal Green in the East End, Violet was a headstrong and romantic girl who had effectively eloped with Charles. When she found out a little more about him, she was content to make do. A good wife, quiet and resourceful, she tolerated his gambling and drinking and their relationship was as equable as these things came. Her own father was a celebrated street-fighter and alcoholic who ruled his family with Victorian severity, and she was grateful to escape.

They lived with Charles's parents over a shop in Stene Street, Hoxton, and Violet was soon pregnant. The doctors told her that she should expect twins. In the event, she gave birth to a single child, who was named Charles David. Three years later she was pregnant again.

On the night of 17 October 1934, Violet gave birth at home to male twins who arrived within an hour of each other; she called the first Reginald, and the second Ronald.

Violet adored her twins. Their older brother was a placid, easygoing child, but the twins were a demanding pair, and brought out their mother's protective pride. Assailed by the grinding poverty of the time, dreadful housing, disease, mal-nutrition and inevitable male drunkenness, East End working-class families were more often than not held together by the canniness and sheer persistence of their women, and Violet was to make an exacting matriarch.

Violet dressed her beloved twins in identical clothes. They were pretty babies, swathed in their white angora woolly hats and coats, and everybody clucked over them. They were unusually healthy children for those times, but at the age of three they contracted diphtheria. They were hospitalized – the first time they had been separated from their mother – and Ronald did not make a particularly good recovery. Afterwards, his mother began to worry about him and pay rather more attention to him than to his brother. Young children can be adversely affected by an early dose of diphtheria, so it was perhaps no coincidence that Ronnie was quieter and slower than Reginald; he also began to display a tendency to sulk, and as a toddler made quite violent demands on his mother's affections. The brothers vied for her attention, and watched each other closely, determined that neither should receive more love than the other.

As the pair grew up, they became a strange beast with two heads and four fists, always allied against the world, but often fighting savagely between themselves (though ten minutes later it would all be forgotten). From an early age they fought all-comers. They were surprisingly vicious, and happily took on older boys. Ronnie was the more overtly aggressive. He may have looked for opportunities to denigrate Reggie in his mother's eyes, but he knew he could count on him in a scrap.

Much to Violet's delight, the family moved back to Bethnal Green, her old neighbourhood. They took a house in Vallance Road, where they were surrounded by members of Violet's close family. The area possessed its own morality, its private code of honour, and a long tradition of villainy. For those

involved in the incessant pub fights, street brawls and stab-
bings, it was a violent world. But so long as the "decent" folk
were left alone, the police were inclined to turn a blind eye.

During the Second World War the Krays' father went into
hiding to evade the call-up; many others in the area did the
same, so much so that the street gained the name of "Deserter's
Corner". The twins became adept at lying to the police when
they came looking for their father. There were few men
around. Ronnie and Reggie spent long hours in the company
of Violet's now reformed and teetotal father, who regaled them
with the folklore of local fighters and thieves. Violet's sister,
Auntie Rose, who lived round the corner, became a favourite of
the twins. She was a tough, street-fighting woman herself, and
from the beginning she lacked Violet's sentimental illusions
about the twins. She loved them, but she knew and prized their
darker nature and spoiled them rotten. "You're a born devil,"
she said to Ronnie. "You know what those eyebrows of yours
mean, meeting in the middle like that? That you're born to
hang . . ."

Violet aspired to respectability and decency; the twins were
imbued with these virtues. This entailed proper behaviour in
public, and the local schoolteacher and vicar were hard pressed
to find fault with Reggie and Ronnie. They were polite, helpful,
punctilious and respectful to their elders. But increasingly they
had other, distinctly violent, aspirations. They formed juvenile
gangs and fought extended campaigns across the Bethnal
Green wastelands. Their elusive father introduced them to
old-time cockney villains, like Dodger Mullins, the "old guv-
nor" who taught them the code of the East End criminal.
Toughness, pride in one's fighting name, contempt for women
and their family values, a willingness to go to the limits in a
fight and an utter disregard for the law; the eleventh command-
ment in Bethnal Green was "thou shalt not grass on thy
neighbour".

Aged ten, the Kray twins began to box. Their first fight was in
a fairground ring, against each other, and they fought with
furious intensity. The bout was declared a draw, with Ronnie
taking a black eye and Reggie sporting a bleeding nose. Not
only did the fight indicate their prowess at a traditional East
End skill, but it also gave the pair an unforgettable taste of
notoriety. They were quickly snapped up by a local trainer, and
a year later were again fighting each other in the Hackney
Schoolboys Final. Reggie won on points, but the violence of the

Boxing twins vow not to fight each other

contest frightened the spectators, and Violet made them promise that they would never fight each other again.

Until the age of sixteen, when they turned professional, the
twins never lost a bout. Ronnie was tough, but Reggie was
canny, and was clearly the one to place the money on, if one
was sufficiently familiar with the pair to be able to tell them
apart. The twins received a lot of publicity, which fed their
appetite for power. At sixteen, they were dominant in the local
gang fights. Their commitment to violent force was outstanding: their opponents' serious injuries were caused not only by
fists and boots, but by coshes, bicycle chains and broken bottles,
which the twins were quick to employ. Ronnie had perfected
the technique of cutting an enemy in the face, for which
purpose he preferred to use a large sheath knife rather than
the traditional razor. The twins bought their first gun, a
revolver, and hid it under the floorboards in Vallance Road.

One of their victims, a sixteen-year-old named Harvey,
nearly died. There were witnesses, and the twins were re-
manded in custody. But, by the time the case came to trial,
the witnesses, reputedly subjected to veiled threats, were
unwilling to testify, and the twins walked free.

Already, Ronnie was getting out of hand. His father had felt
his fist, and had become wary of him. He had once had hopes
for the twins' future as professional boxers, but he now avoided
the increasingly undisciplined pair. Then Ronnie slugged a
policeman. Reggie hated the thought of his brother sitting alone
in the cells and, acting on the perverse sense of loyalty that was
to characterize their relationship, went out and hit the same
constable, successfully joining his brother down the local nick.
They got off on probation, but Ronnie's reputation as a loose
cannon effectively put paid to his professional boxing aspirations. Indeed, despite the good impression these well-man-
nered boys continued to make on naïve figures of authority, the
only people who really exerted any control over them were
their Auntie Rose and their beloved, precious and all-forgiving
mother, Violet.

In 1952, the twins were called up for National Service in the
Royal Fusiliers. Their behaviour on their first day set the tone of
their relationship with the Army. They were still being shown
around the barracks by a corporal when they announced they
didn't care for the environment and were off home. When the
corporal tried to stop them, he was hit.

Over the next two years they proceeded to make a mockery

of the machinery of army discipline. They were constantly in the guardroom, in military prisons or on the run. They were unafraid of punishment; spartan conditions were merely a trial of their manhood, and their insolent fortitude and skill of fist ensured that all attempts to re-shape them were soon abandoned.

There was something increasingly self-conscious and contrived about the way they presented themselves to the world, dressed in smart blue suits, their tight politeness and control giving way to sudden bouts of orchestrated violence. Their experience of the army sharpened this double act. When, as frequently happened, they were charged with assaulting an officer, it was customary for both to plead ignorance. The authorities found it impossible to ascertain which of these identical, stony-faced young men had actually thrown the punch. Later, towards the end of their relationship with the army, they were incarcerated in the guardroom at Howe Barracks, Canterbury, where they wreaked havoc. Ronnie amused himself by pretending to be "barmy", throwing wild tantrums; Reggie handcuffed the guards; they both burned their bedding and together roundly humiliated a succession of hardened soldiers set on subduing them.

Those with wisdom saw that the best way to treat the twins was with weary forbearance, and looked forward to the day when they could be shot of them. The only man who exerted any significant control was a long-serving, aristocratic adjutant, a languid ex-public schoolboy who had been a prisoner of the Japanese. He appeared untroubled – even bored – by their antics and thus earned their respect. They could be sentimental about a proper gentleman.

Ronnie and Reggie had by now decided that what they wanted was a piece of the "good life". Though not yet certain as to what this was, they nevertheless knew that it wasn't going to come by legitimate means but through the exercise of power in the criminal world. Ronnie was an aficionado of gangster literature and movies; he idolized the organized criminals of Chicago, like Capone, who behaved like emperors.

Military prisons enabled Ronnie and Reggie to meet a whole generation of the criminal fraternity from all over the country. They were to remain excellent networkers. Among the more local of the new friends was Dickie Morgan, a villain from a family of villains. While on the run with him they stayed at his family house in Clinton Road in the East End, a regular thieves' kitchen, where the Krays were able to mingle with a host of habitual petty criminals. While hiding from the army they also hung around the less salubrious areas of Soho, and made a useful impression on its underworld. Though they were barely nineteen, the twins appreciated that it was in the underworld of the West End, with its gambling clubs, strip joints and drinking holes, that easy money was to be made. If they were to be more than minor criminals from Bethnal Green they need a reputation out West. Out East they would give occasional, breathtaking displays of bar-room fighting. People remembered them, and began to talk about the strange atmosphere that hung around them: an impressive odour of evil.

One Christmas Eve, when the twins were on one of their spells of unauthorized leave from the Army, a policeman named Fisher (who had arrested and returned them to the army once before) came across them sipping a cup of tea in a cafe in Mile End. He invited them to accompany him to the station. They agreed and, once outside, promptly slugged him and ran off. On their capture they were tried for assaulting a policeman, and were sent to Wormwood Scrubs for a month. It made a refreshing change from military prison. Inside, they found themselves accorded a degree of respect generally reserved for important villains. They appreciated the photographs of themselves that appeared in local papers during their trial, sticking the cuttings in their personal scrap-books as evidence of their growing notoriety.

The army finally court-martialled and ignominiously dismissed the twins. Back in the East End, they began looking for a locus for their career as professional criminals, and fixed upon the Regal, a dilapidated billiard hall in Mile End. A haunt of local gangs who would come, boozed up, to fight and extort, the place was already in trouble. When Reggie and Ronnie started hanging out there, the violence inexplicably increased to such a level that when the twins offered the owners five pounds a week for the tenancy it was gratefully accepted.

The twins made an unexpected success of the place. The violence stopped abruptly, and the hall was efficiently managed and maintained. It remained open day and night, and the twins began to enjoy a heathly income from the billiard tables. They themselves were the main attraction. Their friends began to drop in regularly and hang around just to see what might happen: life was never dull. There might be a fight on the premises, as when the Maltese gang called in, looking for

protection money, and were cut to ribbons with cutlasses; or
the twins might form up a raiding party and drop in on a
neighbouring pub for a brawl. Watching them punch, kick,
slice and stab, their friends were consistently struck by the
intent and serious nature of Kray violence. Despite the twins'
small stature, they were never to come off worse in a fight. They
developed specialities. Reggie perfected a trick he called his
"cigarette punch", for which he would sucker the prospective
target by offering him a cigarette with his right hand. When the
man opened his jaw to put the cigarette in his mouth, Reggie
would catch him with a left hook. An open jaw shatters very
easily and the "cigarette punch" floored many. Ronnie preferred to cut people, though he considered the razor an
inadequate weapon, and preferred a knife or sharpened cutlass. He also fantasized about using guns, of which he had an
expanding collection. It was undoubtedly Ronnie who was the
more frightening of the pair.

At first there was little organized purpose to the twins'
violent forays. But the loose groupings of admirers and minor
criminals soon began to form into a distinct gang. Ronnie had
found new role models in Lawrence of Arabia and other

> The Regal gave them a stage on which to parade their theatrical
> personas. Ronnie was to the fore in this, playing the Chicago
> mobster, sitting impassively in a chair clad in dark, double
> breasted suit, small knotted tie and heavy jewellery, occasion-
> ally summoning a henchman for a quiet word. He ensured the
> lights were low, and demanded that the atmosphere be smoky
> and conspiratorial, as in the movies. He would hand out packets
> of cigarettes and urge people to gasp away until the room was
> choked with a fug. He had a liking for the weird and freakish, and
> would drag in a circus giant or a pair of dwarves to amuse his
> entourage.
>
> He also liked young boys. Initially, there was an air of
> philanthropy about his interest in lads culled from the streets.
> Sometimes he would justify his relationships by pointing out that
> the kids were also part of a network of informants. But, though he
> always despised effeminacy, Ronnie was homosexual. It was
> shortly common knowledge. Later he would bed lads from the
> area and then give them five pounds to take their girlfriends out
> for the night, provided they told him which experience they had
> preferred.

military heroes. He began to organize, and instil obedience
into, the evolving gang. He learned the value of intelligence
and propaganda, and began to plan raids in detail, evolving
complex tactics. One day somebody christened him "the
Colonel". The nickname stuck.

The Krays were often seen as one personality split between
two identical bodies, and in this collective psychology it was
the violent aspect of Ronnie that was in the ascendant. The
aspect of reason, and a modicum of self-restraint, represented
by Reggie, was gradually being suppressed.

For the moment, the gang – which would one day become
known throughout London as "the Firm" – served as a form of
publicity for the Krays. Their aura of control made the Regal
into a safe house and meeting place for criminals, who could
make contacts, exchange information and conceal their stolen
goods. The twins took a cut from the crimes they helped
arrange; Reggie generally negotiated. They began to pull
complicated con-tricks, and extort regular protection money
from pubs, illicit gambling dens and bookmakers.

As their activities took shape, they presented a challenge to
some of the established local gangs. Three dockers, all brothers,
who unofficially ran Mile End and Poplar, issued a challenge.
They were big men – much bigger than the Krays – and all good
amateur boxers. To the disappointment of their followers, the
Krays refused to talk about the affair. As the appointed date – a
Sunday morning – approached, many began to think that the
twins were opting for discretion rather than valour. Ronnie and
Reggie seemed wholly unconcerned. They spent the Saturday
night as usual, getting thoroughly drunk (their capacity for
alcohol was stupendous), and lounged around the Regal
quietly on the Sunday morning, sipping tea and chatting
amiably. Then, with a nod to each other, they strolled down
the road to the pub where, in an empty bar, the dockers were
waiting. By the time the manager of the pub thought the twins
must have had a good hiding and went back into the bar, it
looked like an abattoir. Two of the dockers were laid out and
Ronnie was carving some finishing touches on the third.

The twins looked forward to the day when they would
assume control of London's gangland. Nor were they content
to take it in the discreet way in which these matters were
customarily handled. None of the old criminals would start a
gang-war if it could be avoided. Not so Reggie and Ronnie.
They longed for confrontation; they were convinced of their

invulnerability, and in the face of this boundless confidence, most of their opponents simply melted away.

They allied themselves with an old villain, Jack Spot, who with another, Billy Hill, ruled the town, and constantly tried to precipitate an all-out struggle for power in the Chicago style. Armed to the teeth with guns, they prowled the streets in their car, looking for trouble. Finally, Ronnie got a chance to shoot a gun. Spot and Hill had both retired and there were new Italian gangs moving in on the West End. The twins believed they were on a hit-list of potential opponents. Ronnie took his favourite Mauser, drove to the Italians' pub and discharged three shots. Fortunately, despite his passion for guns, he was a notoriously bad shot, and missed everybody.

The "Firm" grew. By 1955 there was a buzz of money around the twins. Funded by an ever-growing protection racket, they looked like they might be on their way to wealth and now drove big American cars. Their henchmen did well too. Each could expect some forty pounds a week as their share of the proceeds from extortion, and both Reggie and Ronnie were lavish with the cash: they enhanced their charitable reputation by looking after the families of those doing a stint in prison and were always approachable for a hardship loan.

Then, on 5 November 1956, Ronald Kray was sentenced to prison for three years. He had been convicted of inflicting grievous bodily harm on a young man named Terry Martin, a member of a gang from neighbouring Watney Street. Martin's

---

The money didn't make Ronnie happy. Increasingly, he wanted to kill somebody. He fantasized about it, drawing up lists of those who merited death, and cutting the ends of his unused bullets to make them into dum-dums capable of blowing a man to pieces. When a local car-dealer got into a spot of bother with a client and asked for help, Ronnie went after him with a Luger and shot the man in the leg, just as he was apologizing to the dealer for his rash behaviour. Reggie had once again to do the tidying up. He bought time by letting himself be arrested in Ronnie's place. By the time he got round to telling the police that they had arrested Reginald, not Ronald, Kray, his brother was safely hidden away, and the victim and all witnesses were suffering from amnesia. Reggie was not best pleased with Ronnie, who retaliated by telling him that he was an amateur who'd never have the balls to kill a man.

gang had beaten up an ex-boxer named Joe Ramsey. Ramsey was important to the Krays: he had just secured them their first toe-hold in the West End as his partners in The Stragglers, a shabby drinking club. Martin was the only member of the gang the twins could get their hands on. They held him while Ramsey sliced him up with a bayonet, and then put the boot in. Martin nearly died. Reggie went home. Ronnie, still attired in blood-stained clothing and armed to the teeth, was stopped by the police, as he drove frantically around the area, looking for more trouble. Ronnie went to Wandsworth gaol, where he seemed quite happy. He was respected by both prisoners and staff, and lacked for nothing. With help from outside, he soon had the traditional prison trade in tobacco under his thumb, ate well and did no work.

With the erratic Ronnie safely under lock and key, Reggie began to prosper. He missed Ronnie, but at last it was not necessary to sacrifice business interests for the sake of theatrical violence. Reggie opened a club, The Double R (after Ronnie and himself) on the Bow Road. He had always felt that the East End lacked a decently run club with a bit of glamour. The club was respectable, and had good singers and a lively atmosphere. Its association with two men popularly believed to be violent criminals also gave it a sheen of fashionable, sexy violence. One or two playboys and pop-stars began to roll in, looking for something to stimulate their jaded palates. The legitimate world and criminal world, high life and low life, the overtly proper and the covertly perverse mingled freely at the Double R.

Charlie Kray, the twins' brother, began to work alongside Reggie. They opened another club in the East End, and then started a gambling den next to Bow Police Station. Later they formed a friendship with their former enemy, the retired gangster Billy Hill. Hill had interests in illicit gambling throughout the West End that he still needed to have minded, and gave Charlie and Reggie a stake in the lucrative business. With Parliament on the verge of legalizing gambling, the Krays realized that they could soon quit the East End and be wealthy and powerful on a grand scale, without having to resort to Ronnie's style of violence. Ronnie could be thoroughly misogynistic; free from his influence, Reggie began to enjoy the company of women. He had nights out in the West End and moved in society. He looked happy.

Ronnie was not having an enjoyable time. His good behaviour had secured his transfer to a prison on the Isle of Wight. It was easygoing, but Ronnie was lost without the familiar criminal company and respect he had been accorded in Wandsworth. He grew depressed, and then paranoid. He thought that people believed he was an informer; then he saw the outlines of a conspiracy and imagined that he was under constant surveillance by people who wanted to torture him. He retreated into himself and spent days sitting in the corner of his cell. He finally broke and, after a bout of terrifying violence, was put in a straitjacket. Then his beloved Auntie Rose died of leukaemia. Ronnie slid into madness, and shortly after Christmas 1957 was certified insane.

He was diagnosed as paranoid schizophrenic. Transferred to a Surrey mental institution, he began to make a recovery, assisted by large doses of the drug Stematol. But so long as he was certified insane, there was no prospect of his release.

Under prison regulations, anyone who was certified insane, escaped and stayed at large for longer than six weeks had to be certified again on recapture. If Ronnie could escape, and appear sane on recapture, he would be allowed to complete his original sentence.

In the summer of 1958, Reggie helped his brother to escape, and hid him in the Suffolk countryside. The twins had spent a spell there during the Blitz, and the country seemed to calm Ronnie down. He lived in a caravan deep in woodland, accompanied by a trusted bodyguard who did the cooking and cleaning. Reggie kept him well supplied with boys and alcohol and Ronnie amused himself by getting his bodyguard to play "the hunting game" in which they stalked each other with air-guns. But he was soon bored. He was jealous of Reggie's public prominence and missed London. He implored Reggie to let him make the occasional late-night foray to the Double R. Against the better advice of his brother Charlie, Reggie agreed. Soon Ronnie was dressing up as Reggie and strolling through the streets of Whitechapel.

But each time he returned to the country, Ronnie fell back into his former depression. He brooded, and began to mutter ominously about murder. He was moved from the caravan into a neighbouring farm. After the police called to make a routine check, he lapsed once more into paranoia, accusing Reggie of being an impostor: he was not his brother, but a Russian spy.

Even Reggie was frightened. The family discreetly consulted psychiatrists and doctors, but the drugs prescribed had a limited effect. Ronnie was contained by the consumption of two bottles of gin a day.

After Ronnie attempted suicide, the family realized that he had to be returned to a secure mental hospital; they must surrender him to the authorities. Reggie let the police know that if they came around to Vallance Road they could pick his brother up. Ronnie was unsuspecting, and when the police called, he went without a murmur.

With treatment, he was allowed to finish his prison sentence and was released in the spring of 1959. He immediately suffered a fit of paranoia and, convinced that the Russians were coming to get him, was sedated in a hospital. Again he recovered, but his personality was irrevocably altered. Before his breakdown he had been an unnerving presence. Now he was hysterically excitable, wholly crazed and dangerous, devoid of any vestige of conventional conscience and trapped within his own grotesque fantasies.

As a consequence of one of Ronnie's rash pledges of loyalty, Reggie found himself embroiled in a dispute over money between a shop-owner and a small-time crook. He went to prison for eighteen months. Charlie Kray melted into the background and Ronnie was free to indulge his taste for open warfare, slowly destroying the business they had built up.

Income plummeted. Then, quite coincidentally, something profitable happened. Ronnie fell out with Perac Rachman, later notorious as a landlord specializing in extortion. In order to get Ronnie off his back, Rachman showed him how the Krays

---

Ronnie liked to have the local barber come over to his house and shave him in the morning, something he had read that Chicago gangsters did. The tailor also had to call personally, and he had his shirts and suits delivered to the door. He took up riding and spent the weekends playing the country squire in a Suffolk village. He had a pet Doberman, which he adored. But he remained contemptuous of the moderate policies of Reggie and Charlie and wanted an immediate return to the old days of violence and petty extortion. He upset people, careering drunkenly around the East End, demanding protection money from clubs in which the Krays already had a stake and publicly insulting the Italian gangs with whom Reggie had carefully forged peace. He accused Reggie of having gone soft, which he blamed on his brother's taste for women.

could get their hands on Esmerelda's Barn, a Mayfair gambling club, the haunt of stars and minor royalty.

The twins now had a business advisor, Leslie Payne. A canny man, who had just been declared bankrupt and badly needed the work, "Payne the Brain" was a principal factor in the rise of the Krays. Latterly he had managed to exert some control over Ronnie. Reggie was out of prison pending appeal and, together with Payne, the twins called on the owner of Esmerelda's Barn. Acting on information Rachman had given them, Payne made the man an offer. After a glance at Reggie and Ronnie, the man decided not to refuse it. The club did well. Soon the twins were making £40,000 a year each, without having to lift a finger. But Reggie lost his appeal, and went back to prison.

Ronnie carried on playing the role of king gangster. He had money, lavish clothes, expensive cars, a flat in the West End and all the pretty boys he could manage; for a while he fell in love, and paraded his boy about as if he were a young mistress, tenderly calling him "son" and referring to himself as "your old Dad". But at heart he remained an unhappy and sick man. He despised the wealthy, confident clientele of the club. They made him feel insecure. He wanted an entourage of people he could control and began to attract a seedier variety of customer, offering hard-up nobility and habitual losers unlimited credit. Though the club's profits fell, it remained a goldmine, and its respectability was ensured for a time when they persuaded Lord Effingham – the first of a string of tame peers – to join the board of management. Charlie urged his brothers to invest their wealth quickly in clubs and betting shops, but Ronnie resisted. He knew that if the Krays became legitimate, he would cease to be of any significance.

While Ronnie now believed himself to be a reincarnation of Attila the Hun and a Samurai warrior, read *Mein Kampf* and planned to create an army that would take the world by force, Reggie kept the business going and efficiently muscled into the protection rackets of the West End. He also established fruitful contacts with foreign organizations looking for a piece of the action in London and, aided by the ingenuity of Payne, the twins were able to execute a string of lucrative frauds. They began to expand outside London, taking over clubs in Birmingham and Leicester. They cultivated a reputation for philanthropy, giving generously to charity; they were not shy of publicity, and their faces were soon appearing regularly in national newspapers. They granted interviews to eminent journalists, and Ronnie approached one to ghost his autobiography, but the offer was declined.

In 1963, they made their first important political contact: Joan Littlewood, the legendary theatre director, introduced them to the influential and corrupt Tom Driberg, then Labour MP for Barking. A future Chairman of the Labour party, who later became a respected member of the House of Lords, Driberg was one of a number of eminent pederasts whom Ronnie was to form mutually rewarding relationships with. In return for support, Ronnie provided flesh to order. His parties became famous, and he began to receive invitations to stately homes outside London.

In the summer of 1964, the *Sunday Mirror* alleged the existence of a homosexual relationship between a prominent member of the House of Lords and a "leading thug in the London underworld". It also claimed that it had pictures to

When Reggie got out of prison he was in love with Frances Shea, the sister of a man the twins had known since their youth. She was sixteen, eleven years younger than Reggie. In prison he had written to her every day. He dreamed of a perfect marriage; with his fairy-tale bride he would at last lead the good life, free of the strain of crime, and free of Ronnie. His twin knew Frances was a threat. He hated her. At first, Reggie's society contacts and wealth impressed Frances and her parents. When he first proposed to her, in the autumn of 1961, she turned him down, on the grounds that she was too young. He persisted; he was possessive but also charming and generous, and courted her assiduously over the next four years. She married him on 20 April 1965, at St James, Bethnal Green. It was the East End wedding of the year. David Bailey photographed the wedding and the church was packed with journalists and voyeurs from the world of show business. Within eight weeks Frances, at last party to the truth about Reggie's life, could take no more. She fled back to her parents. Reggie could not leave her alone. She became frightened and withdrawn. She had a breakdown and tried to kill herself a number of times. She tried to get a divorce, but then agreed to attempt a reconciliation with Reggie, who claimed he was a changed man. On 6 June 1967 they booked air-tickets for a second honeymoon. That night, Reggie dreamed she had taken her life and, as dawn broke, went around to her parents where she was staying. It was true. She apparently died a virgin.

> Ronnie met Ernest Shinwell, son of the Labour politician, who interested him in a plan to build a new township costing several million pounds in the bush outside an obscure Nigerian town. Ronnie became obsessed with the plan, certain that it would guarantee immortality, and visited the country as a VIP guest of the Nigerian government. When the grandiose design collapsed, he was bitterly upset. An old confederate of the twins had the misfortune to catch Ronnie on a night after he had received the bad news. He touched Ronnie for five pounds and made a cheerful jibe about his weight. Ronnie took him into the bathroom and cut most of his face off. It took seventy stitches to put him back together again.

prove it. Though they were not yet named, it was known that the men referred to were Lord Boothby and Ronald Kray.

The twins were in two minds about the happening. There was no such thing as bad publicity, but homosexuality was illegal, and any investigation into Boothby might lead to their activities. The police had long been looking for something that would give them a hold over the Krays. But when the police realized that a number of politicians might be involved, they backed off. The photographer who had supplied the newspaper with the pictures suddenly wanted them back; Boothby denied everything and received an apology and £40,000 from the newspaper's parent company. Even Ronnie got an apology. The editor of the *Sunday Mirror* got the sack.

The following January, a known associate of the Krays entered a West End club, demanded money for the twins and, when it was not forthcoming, smashed the place up. The police believed that they at last had something on the twins. They were arrested and charged with demanding money with menaces. It is alleged that with Boothby's help, they were able to command the services of the best criminal lawyers in London, and Boothby even had the chutzpah to raise their case sympathetically in the House of Lords. After two trials, and amid whispers that both jurors and witnesses had been subject to unseen pressure, the twins were acquitted. "To some extent I share your triumph" wrote Boothby to Ronald Kray. No doubt he had a considerable share in it. The twins walked free in a blaze of triumphant publicity. Reggie married Frances Shea almost immediately.

This perverse alliance of the Krays and respected establishment forces ensured that henceforth there was a virtual news-
blackout on their criminal activities. They seemed unchallenge-
able, and were left alone to consolidate their hold on London.
Over the next four years they re-organized protection rackets
on a scale never seen in Britain, before or since. They dealt
freely with the New York Mafia, marketing vast quantities of
stolen US bonds, looked after the Mob's interests in London,
and swindled and intimidated with absolute impunity.

In March 1966, at Ronnie's instigation, they found themselves in a rather unnecessary war with a lesser gang run by the
Richardson brothers, scrap metal merchants from South London. Their interests should never have clashed. Ronnie got hold
of a pair of Browning machine-guns, and the twins prepared
for the bloody battle the "Colonel" longed for.

On 8 March there was an unrelated shoot-out when the
Richardsons tried to steam-roller a local gang at Mr Smith's
club in Catford. It left one man dead and another two seriously
injured. The Richardsons came off worse, and there was clearly
no need for the Krays to take any further action against them:
they were finished as rivals.

But Ronnie wanted to have his say in the Richardsons'
demise. There was a lesser Richardson member called Cornell, who he knew had once called him a "fat poof". Taking his
Mauser 9mm pistol, Ronnie had himself driven to The Blind
Beggar, the Richardsons' hang-out. He and his driver walked
in; Cornell was sitting at the bar. The driver loosed off a couple
of shots to clear the bar. Then, at point-blank range, Ronnie
blew Cornell's head to pieces. It was the most satisfying
moment of his career.

It would be two years before the police could persuade
anyone to talk.

Reggie had to clear up the mess. He put his twin into hiding
in an obscure flat in Finchley, where Ronnie was engulfed by
another savage depression and bouts of waking nightmares
during which he would turn violent or attempt suicide. But
Reggie managed to contain him and still keep the business
going, though the strain was telling. There was now an air of
unnatural self-control about Reggie. Still good-looking, he had
become thin and had dark rims under his bloodshot eyes.
Ronnie was fat and swollen, his thickened face permanently
distorted with anger.

By the spring of 1967, just as Ronnie was calming down,

Reggie's wife, Frances, committed suicide. Reggie went off the rails. He drank himself insensible and veered between violent self-reproach and utter hatred for her family who, he said, had turned Frances against him. After the funeral, Reggie became more like his erratic twin. Aside from the hour he spent at Frances's grave each day, talking to her ghost, he was drunk most of the time; with encouragement from Ronnie, he started looking for people he could hurt. The first was a former friend called Frederick, who he believed might have said something derogatory about his dead wife. Fuelled by a violent row with Ronnie, Reggie turned up at Frederick's house and shot him in the leg. He shot and wounded another man at a club in Highbury, then slit open the face of an old boxer with whom he had a vague dispute. One or two of the Firm's members went missing following disagreements with the twins.

Ronnie was still determined that his brother should kill a man in cold blood. The eventual victim was Jack "The Hat" McVitie. A criminal whose nerve had long gone, McVitie was a good-natured man who derived his courage from alcohol and pills. Ronnie heard that Leslie Payne had struck a deal with the police and was grassing on the twins' activities. He offered McVitie £500 to kill Payne. Jack "The Hat" bungled the attempt. Ronnie was furious, and wanted his money back; he issued threats. Reggie briefly smoothed things over. Then McVitie got drunk, and wandered into a club waving a shotgun and saying he was looking for the twins. Word of this reached Ronnie.

On a Saturday in October 1967 Reggie and Ronnie Kray told two of their henchmen to find McVitie and bring him to a party they had arranged in a dingy flat in the East End. The owner of the flat, a blonde girl they knew well, was happy to loan them her premises for the evening. Surprisingly, McVitie, who probably had no recollection of his previous behaviour, came willingly. As he walked in through the door, Reggie shot at him. The gun jammed. McVitie tried to dive through the window, but got stuck. Ronnie pulled him back; Reggie had taken a carving knife from one of the gang. McVitie looked at him in bewilderment; Ronnie insisted; Reggie struck the point of the knife into his head below the eye. As McVitie sank to the floor, Reggie stabbed him repeatedly in the stomach and then impaled him through the throat to the floor. The twins took a holiday in Suffolk. The body was never found.

Detective Chief Inspector "Nipper" Read of Scotland Yard

had a long-standing battle with the twins. They considered him highly dangerous and had done all they could to ruin his career. His failure to get them convicted on charges of extortion two years previously had nearly done for him. He was happy to stay away from them, but on being posted to Scotland Yard in 1967 was promptly put in charge of their case. It was an unenviable task. There was very little documentation of their activities. Any possible conviction was wholly dependent on persuading victims and villains to talk and the criminal code of silence had ensured this had not happened.

But Read was convinced that if he could persuade one to talk then many would follow. Leslie Payne had heard about the offer Ronnie had made to McVitie, and was the first to agree. Once he had outlined the Krays' activities in a statement two hundred pages long, Read knew that he had the basis of a case. With exacting slowness, his team began to pick up corroborating statements from reluctant witnesses. Read hoped that once people saw the Krays were under lock and key they would be happier to come forward. In particular, the barmaid at The Blind Beggar, who had witnessed the shooting of Cornell, might at last talk.

It was 9 May 1968 before they felt they had sufficient evidence to hold the twins. It was a gamble, but they could delay no longer. At 7 a.m., the police smashed in the doors of the house where the twins were staying and dragged them out of their beds. They had been out drinking until 5 a.m.. Ronnie was with his latest boy; Reggie, with a girl from Walthamstow.

With the twins awaiting trial, the police quickly rounded up the members of the already disintegrating Firm. With no Firm, the twins had no way of reaching those who talked and the wall of silence that had protected them collapsed. Their sources of money vanished; their support melted away; they had to apply for legal aid. The barmaid from The Blind Beggar did speak as a witness for the prosecution. Reggie was charged with being an accessory to that killing, and Ronnie as an accessory to the McVitie murder. On 8 March 1969, at the end of the longest and most expensive criminal trial in Britain, Mr Justice Melford Stevenson sentenced them to life imprisonment, and recommended that this should be not less than thirty years each.

They were only thirty-four years old. Apart from attending their mother's funeral, they have remained in prison ever since. Reggie is in Parkhurst on the Isle of Wight. A "Category A" prisoner, his life is spent in solitary confinement. He now suffers from acute depression and is haunted by the past. He hopes that he will still live to re-marry and settle in the country, but there is no parole for Category A prisoners. Ronnie was originally with him in Parkhurst, but was certified insane and transferred to Broadmoor. He lives well, dresses nattily and has become rather keen on art and health food. Although sedated by drugs, he still considers himself the Colonel, and has broad fantasies about his importance. He has plenty of hopes for the future, and no regrets about the past.

JACK SPOT AND BILLY HILL: THE LONDON VILLAINS

For many years before the Kray twins brought their particular brand of American-style organized crime and violence to London, the sprawling, fog-bound city of the 1930s and 1940s was run by two legendary villains: Jack Spot and Billy Hill.

At various times close friends and bitter rivals, both claimed the title of "King of London's Underworld". Although violence was endemic in their circles, it rarely erupted onto the streets or involved the public, and so long as they remained discreet, the police – many of whom formed close relations with the villains – were content to leave the criminals to themselves.

Far better the devil you know, the argument went. Underpaid bobbies on the beat were frequently accused of "rolling" those too drunk to resist, and stealing their possessions. This is the origin of the saying: "If you want to know the time, ask a policeman". Policemen were never without a watch, often donated by an unsuspecting drunk.

Guns, although increasingly available after the First World War, were rarely used and killings were less frequent than they would become under the Krays. The old gangs rarely indulged in the spectacular gun battles that American gangsters were so fond of. Enemies and traitors were not machine-gunned from cars but visited by the "chiv-man", who would carefully slice a face up with his taped-down cut-throat razor, or chop through their collar bones with his little hatchet.

In a fight, gangs used knives, razors, pick-axe handles, hatchets and the fist and the boot. But, for generations, their favourite weapon was the beer-bottle. If you carried a gun or a knife, you could be in serious trouble if the police stopped you. But an innocuous beer-bottle was entirely legitimate. Quite apart from providing suitable sustenance before an affray, it made an excellent club. It could quickly be smashed and its broken, jagged edges thrust into the face of an opponent with devastating results. It also made an excellent missile.

The English underworld in the early part of the century provided a number of illegal but nevertheless essential services. It supplied prostitution, gambling and out of hours drinking facilities to the public. The men who ran the illegal rackets were "wide-men"; the them, the respectable, hard-working populace were "mugs", waiting to be fleeced.

During the years of acute poverty, and particularly in the 1930s, prostitution was rampant in London, as women discovered that they could make a comparatively good living on the streets. They could get through twenty or thirty clients in a shift of four hours, and as they charged from ten shillings to a pound a time, the wages of sin were quite decent. Many

In the 1920s many major criminals in London tended to be men renowned for their sheer masculine toughness rather than as businessmen-gangsters. East End villains such as Jew Jack "The Chopper King", Wassle Newman, Jimmy Spinks and Dodger Mullins (who was later to become something of a mentor to the Krays) were legendary for their displays of brute force. Newman was reputed to toughen his fists by tossing bricks in the air and punching them as they came down; but he was no master of organized crime. He simply enjoyed being a bully, and would go into pubs and take away the customers' beer, daring them to protest. Mullins was notorious for his perfunctory views on the fairer sex, and once disposed of a girlfriend he had tired of by pushing her out of a moving car. She broke her back. Spinks was a bully like Newman; when actually asked to pay for some fish and chips he was guzzling, he tossed the cat belonging to the shop's owners into the chip-fryer. One Glasgow "hard man", Jimmy "Razzle Dazzle" Dalziel, was so afraid of having his masculinity questioned that he would always dance with a member of his gang, the "Parlour Boys", rather than be seen being sentimental with a woman.

prostitutes came from abroad. Marthe Watts, a French woman, hated the English climate, but was surprised at the
leniency of the police. She was also perturbed by the sexual
tastes of the average Englishman. She once said she was
astonished at the number of men who wanted her to tie them
up and beat them. Those who controlled the prostitution
rackets also tended to come from abroad: until 1929, the
principal racketeers were a Frenchman, Casimire Micheletti,
and a Spanish dancer, Juan Antonio Castanar. When "Mad
Emile" Berthier, a known associate of Castanar, mistook a
French pimp called Charlie "The Acrobat" for Micheletti and
slashed him to death in a seedy Frith Street dive, the police
deported the rival pimps. The prostitution racket was taken
over by "Red Max" Kessel, a heavily scarred Latvian, whose
bullet ridden body turned up in a ditch in Hertfordshire.
Another infamous pimp was Eddie Manning, a Jamaican dope

The use of hard drugs such as heroin and cocaine became more
common in the 1920s. The "Bright Young Things" of the
"Roaring Twenties" were often young women determined to
live the bright life and take their chances with death. They were
known as "dopers" and lived lives which consisted principally of
drugs and parties. Countless "Bright Young Things" began to
succumb to drug overdoses. Among these were many aspiring
actresses and society hostesses. Billie Carleton, a popular
actress much sought after (not only for her acting skill), died
of cocaine poisoning after attending the victory celebrations in
November 1918. Freda Kempton, who was a hostess at a club run
by the legendary "madame" Kate Meyrick, died of an overdose of
cocaine in March 1922. The actress Brenda Dean Paul was
crippled by her addiction. These – and many other casualties
– were laid at the door of "Brilliant" Chang, an immaculately
groomed Chinese man, who owned two restaurants in the heart of
the West End. He was strongly suspected of being a substantial
gangster specializing in the opium trade, and his close liaisons
with beautiful young women caused outrage and indignation. As
late as the 1950s one national newspaper remembered him as
"an arch-fiend, who would stop at nothing to gain his mastery
over beautiful women". Chang was arrested in 1924, but only
imprisoned for fourteen months. On his release he was deported,
but in exile he was still thought to have a substantial interest in
the London drugs trade.

dealer. Being black he was viewed, in keeping with the morals of the time, with particular horror, because of the power he exerted over white women. Manning was called the "wickedest man in London". After imprisonment in 1929 he died of a cocaine habit.

In the nineteenth century, betting on racehorses became a national past-time. But it remained illegal to lay a bet anywhere other than at the racecourse. This was to remain the case until the Betting and Gaming Act of 1960. Despite the illegal status of off-course bookmakers, there were well over 15,000 of them practising in the 1920s, and it was estimated that illegal bookmaking had an annual turnover of between £350 and £450 million. The police and the bookmakers had an unofficial arrangement, whereby the police would satisfy the public desire to see an occasional prosecution by periodically rounding up a number of bookmakers. They would be compensated by their fellows for any lost earnings. In return the police could expect to be well treated, receiving regular payments, and the odd case of whisky.

Criminals are almost exclusively attracted to sources of money, and such a vast business naturally invited the attention of protection gangs. These, apart from charging a book-maker for his "pitch" at the racetrack and taking a substantial percentage of his profits from illegal off-course betting, would protect him against theft and ensure that his debtors paid up. The last was most important. Gambling debts were not enforceable by law, and losses were vast. Between 1918 and 1956, the underworld was largely dominated by the race-gangs. Jack Spot ran one of these.

The son of Polish Jews who had come to England in the 1890s, Jack Spot, who generally gave his real name as Jack Comer, was born in Whitechapel in 1912. It was an industrious, hard working and law-abiding community, and from an early age Spot, who was restless and aggressive, stood out. His brothers and sister were employed in tailoring and dressmaking but Spot hung around the local boxing clubs and gyms, where the local ne'er-do-wells would congregate.

He established a reputation as a fearless fighter and, in those days of rising anti-Semitism, he soon found himself inundated with pleas for protection from Jewish bookmakers, businessmen, promoters and shopkeepers who were threatened by the activities of fascists. When Sir Oswald Mosley attempted to march through the East End with his Blackshirts in 1936, Spot and his entourage happily decimated Mosley's bodyguard.

Billy Hill, 1956

Darby Sabini and his brothers Joe, Charles, Harry Boy and Fred came from Saffron Hill, Clerkenwell, the heart of London's Italian community. In the early 1920s they wrested control of the lucrative South of England racecourses from Billy Kimber and his Birmingham gang, with considerable assistance from the Flying Squad (then one of the first mobile police units) with which Darby Sabini had reached an "understanding". For fourteen years Sabini and his brothers maintained a discreet but all-powerful hold over the racing world. Their shootings and stab-bings went largely unreported, but the police were quick to swoop on affrays instigated by the vengeful Birmingham mob, or one of the other London race-gangs. Once Sabini was attacked at the Fratalanza Club in Great Bath Street by a rival gang, the four Cortesi brothers, who blazed away at the gangster and his family. It was their first attempted shooting, however, and they missed. The four men were quickly rounded up. But only two of them were found guilty of "attempted murder", and the judge held that this was an internecine dispute, unworthy of public concern: the men only received three years each. In the end Sabini fell from grace as a result of a lost libel case. A newspaper called him "Britain's leading gangster". Sabini sued, and then failed to turn up in court. He lost and was ordered to pay modest costs, which, being a profligate, he couldn't manage, and he had to declare himself bankrupt. The excessive publicity he received perpetually dis-credited him in the eyes of his fellow criminals.

He was increasingly drawn to the lucrative world of the racetracks and the "spielers": the small, illicit gambling clubs that were widespread throughout Soho and the West End. These were the scene of many confrontations between Jewish and Italian gangsters. Though Spot took his fair share of beatings – he was thrashed to the point of death with billiard cues by a mob from Islington – he earned a reputation for his almost foolhardy courage.

By the early 1940s Spot, backed by his ferocious race-gang, was the emerging force in the criminal underworld. Following a police clamp-down on the "spielers" in 1940, Spot and his cronies found themselves dragooned into the army. Spot hated it, objecting to the bad pay, rotten food, harsh discipline and rampant anti-Semitism. He had no compunction about belting his superiors and, after three torrid years, the marine regiment admitted failure and discharged him as mentally unstable.

Spot returned to the Blitz-devastated East End to find that his parents were dead and his family long dispersed. He became involved with the spivs, but after an altercation with a local hard man (in which he nearly succeeded in killing him with a tea-pot), he fled to Leeds, the black-market capital of the north, and a haven for deserters, gamblers and racketeers.

Here his strength, lack of fear and his alcoholic abstinence quickly gave him an advantage over the local gangsters. He looked after club-owners and bookies, and after the war moved back into London's gambling clubs. High wages, the profits of crime and the recklessness induced by realizing one was still alive created a vast boom in post-war gambling.

From a club in St Botolph's row, on the outskirts of the City, Spot also ran his extensive racetrack business. After a pitched battle with the Islington mob, which brought him control of Ascot race-course, his only serious challengers were the White gang. But the White gang had grown soft, and met their Waterloo at the Stork club in Sackville Street, where Spot and his men coshed and "chived" them into bloody submission.

Spot's gang were also involved in lorry hijacking and big "project" heists. It was thought that he was behind the abortive 1948 Heathrow airport robbery, when ten men armed with lead pipes and with nylon stockings over their heads drove up to the airport in a lorry, coshed the security guards into submission, and broke into a warehouse which was reputed to contain ten million pounds in gold ingots. Unfortunately it was a Flying Squad trap, and they were assaulted by a phalanx of psyched-up policemen. After a brutal battle, the police got eight of the men. One of the villains – Franny Daniels – escaped by clinging to the underside of a police van, eventually falling off when it stopped outside a West London police station. Daniels crawled away into the night. There was insufficient evidence to incriminate Spot.

One morning in late 1949, Jack Spot went to the gates of Wandsworth gaol to meet a released prisoner. It was Billy Hill, now middle aged. Once a major gangster, he had of late fallen on hard times.

Billy Hill was born in 1911 in Seven Dials, on the north side of Covent Garden. It was not then a fashionable area, but a rookery of the poor and criminal. His mother was a "buyer of bent gear", and his father could barely pass a policeman without hitting him, a compulsion which had brought him five

or six convictions. There were twenty-one children in the
family. Those who survived generally turned to crime. Young
Billy started his working life as a grocer's delivery boy in
Camden Town, but looked upon it largely as an opportunity
to feed a relative tasty information about prospective targets for
burglaries. He was soon doing his own, preferring "drumming" (the wholesale ransacking of a house in its owners'
absence) to "creeping" (burglary while the occupants slept).
Drumming was increasingly popular among criminals; there
were many new, quiet suburbs, whose occupants were out
during the day, and drumming tended to be more leniently
viewed by the courts than creeping.

Over the years, Hill specialized in domestic theft and smash
and grab raids. When the Second World War broke out, he
evaded military service and with his gang found that the
confusion of war-time offered new opportunities for making
easy money. He broke into post-offices and opened up safes
with a custom-built giant tin-opener; the black-out meant that
he went undisturbed, and a depleted police force lacked the
man-power to keep tabs on him. Though Hill was overtly as
proud as the next man to be British, and talked of the war-time
camaraderie, he became an important figure in the vast spiv-
ridden world of the black market, selling stolen goods and
ration cards, and keeping the well-heeled supplied with everything from petrol and nylons to fresh salmon and bacon.

The profits were huge. Hill was making £3,000 a week from
burglaries and many times that from his black-market activities. He never went on the town without a "monkey" (£500) or
a "grand" (£1,000) in his pocket. He wore forty-guinea Savile
Row suits, silk shirts and hand-made shoes.

Though not yet an ally of Spot's, Hill was also involved in the
violent demise of the White gang. Shortly afterwards he was
nicked by the police. Hill had spent nearly 15 years inside, and

Teetotal Spot often had the mickey taken for drinking only
lemonade. He didn't mind and favoured attacking his opponents
when the alcohol had rendered them incapable of retaliation. He
liked to attack the opposition in West End pub toilets. As he said
himself: "I used to knock 'em out in the lavatory, that was my
surgery. I used to follow 'em into the toilet and bomp! Leave 'em
in the piss."

objected to being imprisoned for a crime of which he claimed to
be wholly innocent. He was indignant, and on bail decided to
leave England. Pretending to be a policeman, he relieved a pair
of crooks of their haul of parachute silk, and with the proceeds
headed for South Africa. In Johannesburg he opened a gambling club. But he was soon involved in a battle with Arnold
Neville, the emperor of South African crime. Neville was found
in a pool of blood outside a night-club. He had been sliced from
head to toe with razors, and needed over a hundred stitches.
Hill was arrested, but his polite demeanour and respectable
appearance earned him a light sentence. Afraid of extradition,
he jumped bail and headed back to England. But he was sick of
running, and finally gave himself up and went to Wandsworth
gaol.

   When Spot took Hill under his wing, it was not for altruistic
reasons but because Spot's roster of trusted lieutenants had
been depleted by injury and police action. Hill was a useful
man, and Spot put him in charge of the spielers. He could be a
cold, hard man, and it was said that his eyes were like "black
glass". He was an excellent gambler, and tolerated no trouble in

Motorized crime and car theft began to boom in the 1920s. Fast
transport and the prospect of a swift getaway widened the
prospective criminal's catchment area. Two of the most famous
motor bandits were "Ruby" Sparks and his long-time lover and
side-kick the "Bobbed-Haired Bandit". Ruby earned his nickname while working as a cat-burglar: he unwittingly stole a
priceless cache of rubies from an Indian prince, but believing
they were fake, gave them all away. With the "Bobbed-Haired
Bandit" he turned to motorized smash and grab raids. The first
time he tried throwing a brick at a window it bounced back at him,
but he soon developed a successful technique, though it often
meant that he lacerated his arms. He would hold the gashes
together with bulldog clips until the "Bobbed-Haired Bandit"
sewed him up. The police admired the "Bobbed-Haired Bandit",
a Jewish girl from a respectable family who had turned to crime
after an unhappy love affair. She drove a Mercedes and sported a
black beret. After five years she and Ruby were caught, but got off
with light sentences. After Sparks escaped from a spell in prison
in 1940 they teamed up again. But they were old and tired. She
had grey in her hair and wore spectacles. After a few abortive
raids they finally retired.

the clubs he ran, though his propensity for violence elsewhere often caused Spot embarrassment. Hill fell for the charms of Gypsy Riley, a tempestuous temptress and noted good-time girl. When her ex-pimp, "Belgian Johnny", tried to put her back on the game, Hill marched into a restaurant where Johnny was eating with his Belgian friends and publicly slashed his face to shreds. Spot had to work hard to persuade the Belgian to keep his mouth shut.

Spot had married a young Irish girl named Rita, and in 1951 he planned to retire. But he could not wholly trust his chief henchmen to preserve peace in the underworld and in the end he worked out a power-sharing arrangement with Hill where the latter had control of the spielers while Spot kept a firm grasp on the race-track.

But the world of gambling was changing. The Betting and Gaming Act of 1960 would legalize many of the illicit areas which the gangsters derived their wealth from. In the run-up to it, the race-course authorities went about cleaning up the activities on the courses, licensing and policing the book-makers themselves. By the mid-1950s Spot had lost much of his authority. His less scrupulous partner was looking for opportunities to expand.

Hill had grown up when the legal system only meted out modest sentences for petty crime and theft. Such stints were regarded as an occupational hazard. The Criminal Justice Act of 1948 changed his attitude. Now he and others like him were to be regarded as "continual reoffenders", and would face longer and longer spells in jail. Hence, the rewards from petty burglary and shifting bent gear no longer justified the potential penalties. He cast around for bigger and bigger "project" crimes. In his autobiography he as good as boasted that he was responsible for the 1952 mailbag robbery, in which £287,000 in used notes – a massive sum in those days – was stolen from post office vans ambushed between Paddington Station and the sorting office in the City. The following year a lorry carrying £45,000 in gold bullion on behalf of KLM Air-ways was hijacked in Holborn. Hill never had to worry about money again.

Despite dallying with retirement, Hill still took violence seriously, and in 1953 nearly got into serious trouble when he viciously chived a young East End tearaway called Tommy Smithson, who had given offence to his beloved Gypsy. That same year Spot and Hill met two young, polite and promising

lads from the East End, Ronald and Reginald Kray. The twins
later said that they never had much time for Spot, but Hill
certainly aided their rise to prominence.

In 1954, Hill had the nerve to begin serializing his memoirs
for *The People*. The first episode blatantly explained how the
KLM bullion hijack had been executed. In the ensuing public
outcry, Hill decided to emigrate to Australia. When he got there
he was sent straight back. Spot was, as he put it, "well pissed
off" with Hill's high profile and his claims to be the emperor of
crime. They fell out, and Spot, who blamed Webb for fostering
Hill's delusions of grandeur, personally put on his favourite
knuckleduster and beat up the journalist. The subsequent court
case did nothing for his public image, and when he too tried to
serialize his memoirs, they received scant attention.

By 1955, Spot was losing what little influence he still had on
the racecourses to a bunch of Italian bookies and their strong-
men. It was at this time that the Krays saw him again at Epsom
races, at his invitation; they were happy to be noticed but
decided that they would ultimately be wrong to ally themselves with such a spent force. Hill had returned from his
abortive attempt to emigrate, and at that same Epsom race
meeting publicly allied himself with the Italians. Soon afterwards, Spot was strolling through Frith Street in Soho when he
came across Albert Dimes, a genial Italian, whom Hill had

Billy Hill found an unlikely ally in the crusading journalist Duncan
Webb, who described Hill as "a crook, a villain, a thief, a thug",
but also "a genius and a kind and tolerant man". It was Webb
who wrote a series of exposés for *The People* which brought
about the demise of the Messina brothers, who had taken over
running London's prostitution rackets. Of mixed Egyptian, Sicilian
and Maltese descent, the Messina brothers ran an efficient
operation in which their women worked strictly regulated hours
and were limited to ten minutes per customer. One prostitute
reckoned that between 1940 and 1955 she earned £150,000 for
the gang; on VE Day she got through forty-nine clients. In the
course of his investigations, Webb was constantly threatened by
the Messina thugs. Then he met Hill, got on amicably and
thereafter enjoyed the freedom of the underworld that so
fascinated him. In return Webb ensured that Hill had a favourable press and even ghosted his autobiography called, with
typical modesty, *Boss of Britain's Underworld*.

employed as a bodyguard. They began brawling outside the Bar Italia. Spot clouted Dimes on the chin. Dimes fled and tried to hide in a greengrocers shop. Spot, his temper up, seized a potato knife and stabbed Dimes with it several times before the proprietor of the shop, a formidable woman called Mrs Hyams, hit him over the head with a scoop from a set of scales. As he lay stunned, Dimes retaliated and slashed wildly at him with his knife. In the end, both men staggered off, cut to shreds. Although badly injured, they survived. But as Spot lay in hospital, the last vestiges of his criminal empire vanished.

He also ended up in court, charged with instigating the affray. Though he was acquitted, it subsequently came to light (largely as a result of work by Duncan Webb egged on by Billy Hill) that Spot's principal witness in his defence, an old and genteel clergyman called Parson Andrews, was popularly known as the "knocking Parson". Though he had a sanctimonious exterior he habitually swindled bookies and his ecclesiastical career had been devoted to whisky, gambling and women. This decrepit character had been recruited by Spot as a witness, and he and a coterie of Spot's associates and his wife Rita were eventually charged with conspiracy to pervert the course of justice. The case went badly for Spot, and this and a subsequent perjury case involving another witness ruined him.

Hill always kicked a man when he was down. One night in May, Spot and his wife Rita were strolling back to their flat in Hyde Park Mansions when they were set upon by a large group of men armed with razors, knives and coshes. Spot knew what was coming and tried to get his wife inside the door to the flats, but she refused and clung to him, screaming. Together they fell to the floor, and the men closed in on them. Rita was not cut, but Spot had seventy-eight stitches and a blood transfusion. He considered breaking the underworld code and revealing the identity of his attackers, but in the end decided not to. Although they had no respect for him, the Kray twins were looking for an opportunity to whip up a gang war in which they could assert themselves by brute force on the world of the West End, at that time still closed to them. They visited Spot in hospital, and urged him to let them start shedding blood in revenge. But such rash conflicts were anathema to Spot, and he said nothing in reply, but rolled over in his bed and faced the wall.

Rita had no qualms about talking to the law and took her husband's assailants to court. In the end, three of Hill's henchmen went to jail.

In the aftermath of the endless trials, Jack Spot was finally declared bankrupt and evicted from his Bayswater flat. Rita made a little pile of money from selling her life story and opened the Highball Club, which quickly became a popular haunt for the glitterati. But Hill didn't want Spot around in any form, and the club was constantly plagued by fires and pointless vandalism. Spot gave up and emigrated. He wanted to go to Canada, but when he was refused admission he settled for Ireland. Here he retreated into comfortable obscurity, working as a bookie's runner in Dublin and Cork. His marriage survived and his daughters went into show-business. Later, he returned to England, and lived a quiet life, making occasional appearances as a celebrity at sporting events.

Hill also assumed a lower profile, bought a villa in Marbella and delegated the handling of many of his affairs. Many of his gang drifted off to join the Richardson gang from South London, and became involved in the subsequent dispute with the Krays. Throughout the sixties Hill enjoyed a period of prosperity and respectability. He became close to the Kray twins, to whom he was invaluable as a guide to the low-life of London's West End and Soho. He was friends with journalists other than Duncan Webb and the rising media personalities of the era. He hob-nobbed with nobility, and gambled with Perac Rachman and Mandy Rice-Davies. Based for the most part in Spain, he was far removed from the unfavourable Kray-instigated scandals of the London underworld in the 1960s.

In the early 1970s he got fed up and returned to England, opening a night-club in Sunningdale. In 1976 he split up with his long-standing moll, Gypsy, and took up with a black singer, with whom, to his surprise, he fell deeply in love. It was late in the day to discover such tender feelings, and when, three years later, she committed suicide, Hill sank into depression and misanthropy and shut himself up in his flat. He was cursed to live until 1984, and died a lonely and unhappy man. Jack Spot described him as "the richest man in the graveyard".

"JUNGLE W11": RACHMAN AND MICHAEL X

"Jungle W11" was the name the London police gave to the Notting Hill area of West London in the 1950s. Now gentrified and hugely fashionable, the haunt of publishers, journalists, actors and the like, the area was once considerably run-down and seedy. The Notting Hill police station area stretched from the expensive genteel houses off Notting Hill Gate and Holland Park to the large, run-down and overcrowded properties of North Kensington and Paddington. In the poorer areas settled the West Indian immigrant population. The proximity of the area to the West End and the fact that at that time street prostitution extended from Marble Arch, all along the Bayswater Road, to Shepherds Bush, meant that the crumbling properties of Notting Hill had become coveted bases for organized operators in the field of vice. Illegal drinking clubs and rip-off joints were widespread, and the area was a bastion of the drug trade.

The immigrant West Indian community was easy prey for racketeering landlords, most notably Perac Rachman, whose name has become synonymous with rent extortion: "Rachmanism" is now in the dictionary.

Perac Rachman was born in Poland in 1920 and came to England as a penniless refugee in the wake of the Second World War; by the time he died in 1962, aged only forty-two, he was a millionaire.

When he arrived in London he started off by doing casual

work in the East End, then obtaining a job as a clerk at an estate agent's office in Shepherds Bush, a little further west than Notting Hill. The 1957 Rent Act made it possible for landlords to charge much higher rents than those hitherto paid by existing sitting tenants whose low rents were legally protected. However, Rachman had an astute mind and saw that the new Rent Act, the severe post-war shortage of housing, and the influx of immigrants desperate for accommodation offered a considerable opportunity to make money. The immigrants were a particularly vulnerable group; they had arrived in Britain to find that there was little rented accommodation available and that they were a low priority for council housing. Ignorant of the laws of the country, they would take whatever accommodation they were offered.

Rachman began to buy up large Victorian terraced properties, often on short leases, in North Kensington and Paddington. He obtained the capital principally from the Eagle Star Building Society, which in 1957 lent Rachman nearly sixty per cent of its total loans for the year, amounting to nearly £60,000; by the end of 1959 the company had lent Rachman and his associated companies – the police identified about thirty-three of which he was director and principal shareholder – over £220,000. The extent of the society's involvement was not discovered until much later, as none of Rachman's concerns was lent more than £25,000 and only details of the loans above this figure had to be disclosed in the society's annual returns.

Having purchased a property, Rachman's first move was to get rid of its existing sitting tenants. Initially he would offer them a modest pay-off to quit. If that was refused, life would become unpleasant for the tenants. Rachman would install some of his trusted henchmen in adjoining rooms, and suggest that they have a few all-night parties, turn the music up as loud as possible, let rubbish pile up in the communal areas and generally make living conditions as intolerable as possible for the existing tenants. If they still refused to go, strong-arm men would cut off the water and electrical supplies, smash up communal toilets and remove the external locks to the house, leaving it unsafe. The tenants would be left in no doubt that physical violence would follow.

Some courageous tenants did take their cases to local rent tribunals or considered legal action, but the majority tended to be poor people, for whom the complexities of civil law were a mystery. Furthermore, it was impossible to find direct evidence linking Rachman to the intimidation. Most sitting tenants quit their flats. Rachman then sent in the cowboy builders, subdivided the flats still further, made a few cosmetic repairs and re-let the accommodation at a still higher rent, either to immigrant families or to prostitutes looking for working space.

Rachman was living in a vast house in the exclusive area of Hampstead. He had a full time domestic staff, and was chauffeured around London in a Rolls-Royce, while his poverty-stricken tenants were crammed together in squalid, tiny flats, their exorbitant rents collected by men who had little time for excuses and quickly resorted to physical intimidation. A short, podgy, bespectacled and prematurely balding individual, he hardly looked like an emperor of crime and had a rather incongruous reputation as a ladies' man.

By 1959, allegations about Rachman's often violent methods were beginning to trouble the authorities, but since he avoided personal contact with tenants, it seemed impossible to mount a sustainable case against him. His financial affairs were targeted; his companies certainly owed tax, and a prosecution by the Inland Revenue would have forced him into bankruptcy. But, as his companies' shares had only a nominal face value, sometimes of a few pounds, it would have done him little damage. As much of his accommodation was let to prostitutes the police tried to get a conviction for brothel-keeping and living on the earnings of prostitutes, but could not gather sufficient evidence; Rachman was a cunning operator. The police tried again, and came sufficiently close to rattle Rachman. He sold his Notting Hill interests, and kept a low profile until his death three years later.

Rachman employed some of London's seediest types as enforcers. Among them were Raymond Nash, a Lebanese who later developed an interest in Soho's clubs and was finally barred from Britain after a conviction abroad for smuggling gold, and George Pigott, a well-known armed robber, currently serving a life sentence for his alleged involvement in the contract killing of "Italian Toni" Zomparelli, who was blown away in a Soho amusement arcade in 1974.

The most infamous of Rachman's henchmen was Michael Campbell De Freitas, a Trinidadian, who later reinvented himself as a black-power leader in the style of Malcolm X, and called himself Michael X. During the 1960s he acted as an agent for Rachman in the now prestigious areas of Colville Terrace and Powis Square in Notting Hill. He was heavily

Michael X

involved in a number of vice rackets, and for the right money arranged working accommodation for prostitutes. He was convicted for keeping a brothel, but though he had a fearsome reputation as a pimp and extortionist, he got off with a conditional discharge and a nominal fine.

Inspired by Malcolm X, he then became a Muslim, going under the name of Abdul Malik, later Michael X. He founded the "Racial Adjustment Action Society", and became the self-appointed Messiah of a black-power commune on the grimy Holloway Road in Islington, North London. De Freitas attracted a number of wealthy and influential followers, and found himself a hit with young, middle class white women, notably the ill-starred Gale Benson, daughter of the Conservative MP for Chatham. The enthusiasm of his followers did not wane when he was imprisoned for twelve months after publicly urging the shooting of any black girl seen with a white man.

His organized criminal activities continued throughout his immoderate political career. In 1969, De Freitas and four of his associates were put on trial at the Old Bailey, accused of robbery and demanding money with menaces. The proprietor of an employment agency in Soho had been subject to extortion, and when he had expressed a reluctance to pay, De Freitas had put a dog collar on his neck and forced him to crawl around the floor, begging for mercy.

De Freitas jumped bail and headed back to Trinidad, where he was followed by some of his supporters, including Gale Benson. There De Freitas formed a black-power party, and joined up with local criminals, creating a gang that was to prove a constant source of fury to the authorities. In 1972, a member of the gang, a man called Joseph Skerritt, refused to obey De Freitas's orders and carry out a raid on a local police station. De Freitas announced to his gang that he needed to improve the drainage in his garden, and ordered a number of them, including Skerritt, to dig a long trench. When this was done, De Freitas decapitated Skerritt with a cutlass and threw him into the trench. The other members of his gang became worried about their esteemed leader's erratic behaviour, and with good reason. Shortly afterwards, another of their number mysteriously drowned, and Gale Benson vanished. When De Freitas and his wife went away on a lecture tour, one of his henchmen set fire to his bungalow. While investigating the arson, a police inspector rooted around De Freitas's garden and became suspicious of some abnormally tall and horribly yellow lettuces. They began digging, and soon found the corpse of Skerritt. Two days later, Gale Benson's body was found, five foot underground. The pathologist deduced that she had been stabbed with a six-inch blade, but that it had not killed her outright. She had been buried alive.

Two of De Freitas's gang were convicted and hanged for her murder. Though De Freitas himself was indicted for the murder of Gale Benson, he was never tried for the crime. Convicted of the murder of Skerritt, he went to the gallows in 1974.

DRUG BARONS

Outside the Mafia, the international drugs trade is often controlled at its roots by a series of powerful individuals, drug barons, whose power base is the source of production within often lawless and poor countries, much of whose gross national income is connected to narcotics.

Colombia's economy has for many years depended largely on the export of cocaine; at one stage it was estimated that Colombia was exporting something like 100 tons of cocaine annually with a street value in excess of sixty billion dollars, representing forty per cent of the country's gross national product. With no alternative source of revenue in the impoverished and mountainous rural areas, government attempts to tackle the problem have met with stiff and violent local resistance; the impetus to drive out the drug producers has come largely from America, which has offered military training, equipment and financial incentives to the South American governments.

Trafficking in Colombia has long been controlled by a few powerful and wealthy dynasties. In the drug capitals of Medellin and Cali live the families of Escobar, Lehder, O'Campo and Ochoa, who have run the country with the liberal use of graft and the gun. One of the most prominent of these families is the Escobar clan. It has been claimed that Pablo Escobar, its head, a man in his early forties, is among the ten richest individuals in the world. Based in Medellin, where he runs five homes, Escobar's official status as a wanted man has done little to persuade him to keep a low profile. A public benefactor, his grandiose gifts to the poor – including building thousands of new homes – have given him the status of a hero and guaranteed that the slum-dwellers and the starving of Colombia are unlikely to surrender him to the authorities. The government does not have the funds to match the generosity of the criminals, and those politicians who refuse to be bought are murdered with impunity. In Medellin, a comparatively small regional capital city of a million people, there are nearly ten murders a day, principally drug-related, the result of quarrels between cartels, or of the enforcement of drug-law. In Colombia, it is quite customary for a cartel to kill not only an offender, but his entire family. In such surroundings of grinding poverty human life is seen as cheap.

Although Colombia is the leading exporter of cocaine, much of its output is actually grown elsewhere in South America, with Colombia forming a centre for refinement and distribution. Bolivia and its own drug baron, Roberto Suarez, are responsible for a substantial slice of the actual coca crop from which the cocaine is extracted. Suarez is unusual in that, far from being a gangster who has struggled out of the gutter, he is an educated and affluent man from a rich family. Once a cattle rancher, he discovered that his remote land holdings in the regions around Beni, Chapare and Santa Cruz could be far more profitably used for growing the stunted, wiry coca bushes.

Possessing an annual income in the region of one billion dollars, Suarez acquired a favourable public image in the accepted fashion, buying the hearts of the poor with lavish beneficence, building roads, schools and hospitals. Suarez was alleged to have had his own private army, the so-called "Fiances of Death", whose leader was reputed to be a mild-mannered German who went under the name of Klauss Altmann, better known to the world as the one-time Gestapo officer, Klaus Barbie, the "Butcher of Lyon", a resident of Bolivia since 1951.

After decades of de facto rule, the drug barons of Bolivia were disconcerted when, in 1978, the country democratically elected Silus Zuazo to the position of president. His predecessor, Hugo Banzer, had been a substantial trafficker in his own right, but Zuazo promised the Americans he would take on the cocaine kings. It was unlikely that he would have much effect, but to guarantee his failure, Suarez instigated a military coup led by disaffected officers eager for power and money. Colonel Luis Arce Gomez (a cousin of Suarez) was paid $800,000 to effect the necessary introductions, and General Luis Garcia Meza, head of the armed forces and the leader of the insurgency – the 189th coup in the short history of the Bolivian state – received a sum well in excess of one million dollars as a down payment on his future cut of the action. The coup, on 17 July 1980, was a success and Suarez became the effective ruler of Bolivia; his paid killers worked openly alongside the armed forces to suppress and exterminate civil opposition. Within two weeks of the takeover, 500 civilians had died, and several thousand more were imprisoned and subject to beatings and torture. Such authority also gave Suarez licence to break up and absorb the smaller rival cocaine cartels throughout Bolivia.

Meza's brutal and corrupt regime devastated the already tottering legitimate economy. The dictates of the International Monetary Fund were wholly ignored, inflation reached three figures and the United States suspended all aid. Perturbed by the bad reputation his nation was acquiring, and fearful of military intervention by the United States, Suarez encouraged Meza to mount a suitable weak, cosmetic and stage-managed campaign against a few minor cartels. It was enough to silence the Americans temporarily. Within the year, however, Suarez, the puppet-master of Bolivian politics, decided to bestow the crown of the bungling Meza elsewhere. In September 1981, he engineered yet another coup and replaced Meza with General Torrelio Villa, who in turn was discarded in favour of General Guido Calderon, who made the usual promises of democratic elections.

Suarez profited while Bolivia went to ruin. Finally, in the face of public unrest, Calderon was forced out of office and Zuazo returned from exile to confront the mess: a nation with no industry, massive unemployment and the highest murder rate in the world. Zuazo did good things. He deported Klaus Barbie back to Europe to face trial; he purged the army and put Gomez, Meza and a host of others to flight. But the problems of cocaine growing required dealing with at a fundamentally economic level; the poor farmers had to be financially encouraged to grow something other than coca. He turned to the Americans for help, and they created the crop substitution programme, offering forty million dollars in subsidies to farmers prepared to renounce coca in favour of legitimate crops. But no crop has such a good profit margin, and once the subsidy is

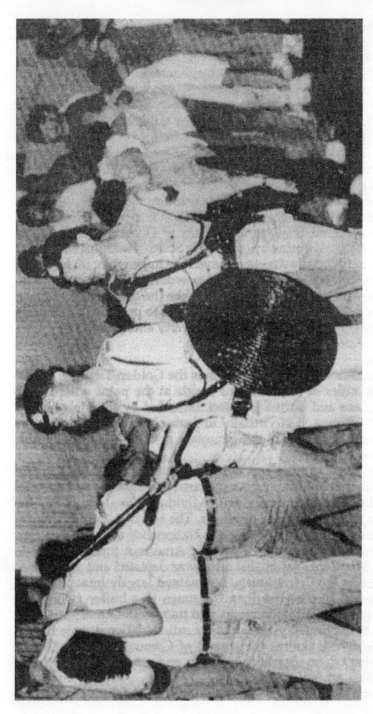

Hong Kong policemen lead away some of the 800 men suspected members of "Triads"

accepted there is little way, in the mountainous terrain of Bolivia, to ensure that the farmers actually switch crops. For the past decade the authorities have fought an increasingly bitter battle against the cocaine barons, with only a small degree of success.

For a long time, cocaine was not seen as a major problem in the same way as heroin. It was a social drug. "Cocaine" said one American "is God's way of telling you that you're too rich". That was once true; the cocaine economy depended upon the criminal manipulation of a wealthy First World, for whom cocaine was the consumer drug *par excellence*, and the poverty of the Third World, where conditions allowed unfettered production. The rich got their kicks, the poor made a living and the organizers were as wealthy as Croesus. But the over-production of cocaine by the greedy South American barons led to an excess on the streets; not even the huge white middle class of America could snort all that powder. With the street price plummeting, it was necessary to make the cocaine accessible to the huge market of the vast underclass; to put it in competition with heroin. Crack – the drug of poverty and of violent escape – was created.

The traditional source of heroin is the Golden Triangle, 80,000 square miles of mountainous jungle at the point where Thailand, Laos and Burma intersect. Bounded by the Mekong and Mae Si Rivers, it is virtually impassable except to the native inhabitants, the Shan, the mountain people. It is unpoliceable terrain.

The Shan, in turn, feel little allegiance to the three national powers that hold sway over the territory. Theirs is still a feudal society, and their lords are individuals like Khun Sa, the world's biggest opium producer. The son of a former Colonel in Chiang Kai Shek's Chinese Nationalist army, Khun Sa's power stems from the vagaries of American foreign policy in Asia. When the Nationalist army was defeated and driven into Burma by the Communists, it remained largely intact and was welcomed first by the Shan tribesmen as a buffer against the local government in Rangoon, and then by the Americans, who saw the continued presence of the exiled Nationalists in Burma as a bulwark against the spread of Communism. The Americans kept them supplied with arms and money for more than a decade.

In the late 1950s, the Burmese government, hitherto tolerant of the Nationalist presence, decided that they were now too powerful, and pushed them out towards Thailand and Laos. The Americans gradually cut off the flow of aid, although covertly the CIA continued to support them for another fifteen years. But, with their sources of revenue seriously disrupted, the Nationalists began to look for alternative income, and moved into the cultivation of opium poppies, which have for centuries been a staple cash crop of the region, a situation largely ignored by the Burmese government.

Young Khun Sa grew up to become the Nationalists' main link with the CIA, supplying them with information about Communist insurgency while exporting massive amounts of heroin to the USA. The situation was entirely hypocritical; the American administration was openly at war with Khun Sa and his compatriots while their principal intelligence organ was employing him as an agent. During the Vietnam War, as many as one in seven American soldiers took heroin, probably supplied by Khun Sa, the same man who the CIA regarded as an ally. The American soldiers disliked the coarse, brown, smoking heroin the locals used and Khun Sa obligingly turned to manufacturing heroin in the form of a fine white powder suitable for intravenous injection.

In the 1970s, Khun Sa expanded his operations, encouraging Thai farmers to increase their output of raw opium base, and began to ship heroin to Bangkok, where he had formed a link with the Triads, Chinese gangsters.

When the American servicemen went home, Khun Sa began dumping his stocks on the streets of America's cities. His profits were enormous; a kilo of raw opium base costing $3,000 at source could fetch up to three million on the streets. The operation was run with corporate efficiency and Khun Sa had his hooks in most of the authorities; the Thai police have even been known to run some of his heroin manufacturing laboratories. In 1978 he even had the nerve to propose to the American Government that they could solve the nation's heroin problems by buying 500 tons of opium base a year off him, at a cost of fifty million dollars; but the Americans decided that he had sufficient supplies to sell this to them and still flood the streets.

In 1980, the Americans put a price of $25,000 on his head and furiously urged the Thai authorities to do something about his activities. In 1982 they finally did, launching a huge, American-sponsored assault on his hilltop fortress at Ban Hin Taek, a small Thai mountain village. The attack force of 2,000 troops supported by helicopter gunships killed over 200 of Khun Sa's private army and captured ten tons of weapons, but the mastermind was gone. He and the bulk of his forces slipped across the border into Burma where he immediately went into the heroin business with Communist insurgents. Two years later, he returned to Ban Hin Taek, and there he has remained; the Thai government has now become quite desperate in its struggle against the drug traffickers – one in fifty of its own population is an addict – and customarily awards the death penalty for trafficking. But the Golden Triangle remains impossible to police and the Shan tribes are still adamantly uncooperative. A quarter of them use the drug and all of them rely on it financially. To stop the heroin, and oust Khun Sa, would require a bloody war or an aid programme of monumental proportions.

PART 2: WORLD FAMOUS ROBBERIES

"IF YOU THINK TODAY IS LAWLESS . . ."

When we complain about the rising crime rate, we speak as citizens who take the protection of the law for granted. Police patrol our streets and country lanes. Burglary and mugging may be on the increase; but at least the robbers take their freedom into their hands every time they set out to commit a crime.

If we are to understand the history of the past three thousand years we have to make an effort of imagination, and try to forget this notion of being protected by the law. In ancient Greece, the problem was not simply the brigands who haunted the roads and the pirates who infested the seas; it was the fact that the ordinary citizen became a brigand or pirate when he felt like it, and no one regarded this as abnormal. In the *Odyssey*, Ulysses describes with pride how, on the way home from Troy, his ship was driven near to the coast of Thrace; so they landed near an unprotected town, murdered all the men, and carried off the women and goods. Greece was not at war with Thrace; it was just that an unprotected town was fair game for anyone, and the war-weary Greeks felt like a little rape and plunder. This state of affairs persisted for most of the next three thousand years, and explains why so many Mediterranean towns and villages are built inland.

What is far more difficult to grasp is that "law abiding" countries like England were in exactly the same situation. Just before the time of the Black Death (as Luke Owen Pike describes in his *History of Crime in England,* 1873), "houses were set on fire day after day; men and women were captured, ransom was exacted on pain of death . . . even those who paid it might think themselves fortunate if they escaped some horrible mutilation." And this does not relate to times of war or social upheaval; according to J.F. Nicholls and John Taylor's *Bristol Past and Present* (1881) England was "prosperous in the highest degree; populous, wealthy and luxurious . . ." (p. 174). Yet the robber bands were like small armies. They would often descend on a town when a fair was taking place and everyone felt secure; they would take over the town, plunder the houses and set them on fire (for citizens who were trying to save their houses would not organize a pursuit) and then withdraw. In 1347–8, Bristol was taken over by a brigand who robbed the ships in the harbour – including some commissioned by the King – and issued his own proclamations like a conqueror. His men roamed the streets, robbing and killing as they felt inclined – the King had to send Thomas, Lord Berkeley, to restore order. When a trader was known to have jewels belonging to Queen Philippa in his house, he was besieged by a gang led by one Adam the Leper and had to hand over the jewels when his house was set on fire. The law courts were almost powerless: when a notorious robber was tried near Winchester, the gang waited outside the court and attacked everyone who came out; the case was dropped.

The Age of Gin

Around the year 1650, a Dutch professor of chemistry called Sylvius discovered that a powerful alcohol could be made by distilling corn mash – which was cheap – and a sharp and pleasant flavour could be given it with juniper berries. This drink was called "geneva" (French for juniper), and this was soon shortened to gin.

It was sold in small bottles in chemists' shops, and the Dutch soon realized that geneva was as potent as good brandy, and far cheaper. When William and Mary installed themselves on James's throne in 1688, their countrymen began to export the new drink to England. Since England was quarrelling with France, and was therefore reluctant to buy French brandy, geneva – or gin – quickly became the national drink. Because of the brandy embargo, a law was passed permitting anyone to distil his own drink, and the English soon improved on the Dutch original, distilling an even cheaper grade of corn mash, and producing a powerful spirit that would now be called

The most famous of British highwaymen, Dick Turpin, never actually made the famous ride to York on his mare Bonnie Black Bess. Neither was he the courteous and heroic outlaw depicted by legend.

Born in 1705, Turpin was a butcher who turned to sheep-stealing to stock his shop. Inevitably found out, he lived by robbery and petty theft until he joined the notorious Essex Gang in 1735. One of his two quoted utterances is to a widow who refused to divulge the whereabouts of her cash: "God damn you, you old bitch, if you won't tell us I'll set your arse on the grate." On another occasion the gang poured boiling water over a farmer – whose skull they had cracked – while they took it in turns to rape his maid.

The gang was finally betrayed in an alehouse when a reward of a hundred guineas was offered for each, but Turpin escaped by jumping out of a window. It was after this that he took up highway robbery in Epping Forest, soon becoming one of the most successful highwaymen in the country. Hiding out in a cave, he murdered a keeper who tracked him down.

Turpin retired on his ill-gotten gains and settled in Yorkshire, calling himself John Palmer. He was arrested for shooting a gamecock and sheep-stealing, but no one suspected his identity. Turpin wrote to his brother from prison in York, asking for help, but sent the letter without a stamp. His brother failed to recognize the handwriting and refused to pay the postman sixpence. But a local schoolmaster caught a glimpse of the letter, recognised the handwriting of his old pupil and claimed the £200 reward on Turpin's head. Turpin was tried and sentenced to be hanged.

In jail he became a celebrity, receiving many visitors. One of them swore he was not Turpin, whereupon Turpin told a jailer "Lay him a wager and I'll go you halves", his only other recorded utterance.

On the scaffold, he preferred to launch himself into eternity by jumping from the ladder.

moonshine. (It is also probably a safe bet that this was when someone discovered that beer could be distilled to produce whisky.) Gin shops opened all over England – one London street had six of them.

Queen Elizabeth's subjects had drunk sherry (Falstaff's "sack"), beer and wine, which were cheap – wine cost fourpence a quart. Then James I had succeeded in raising some of the money Parliament refused to grant him by taxing various commodities, including wine and sherry, so that the English working man of the seventeenth century could only afford beer. By 1688, the English working classes were alcohol-starved. The consumption of gin rose steadily, from half a million gallons around 1690 to three and a half million by 1727 and to nineteen million gallons by the middle of the century.

The result was a crime wave. Many gin shops carried the notice: "Drunk for a penny, dead drunk for twopence, clean straw for nothing." Crimes to obtain money for gin became as common as crimes to obtain money for drugs in our own society. Theft became so common that, in 1699, a particularly savage act was passed that made almost any theft punishable by hanging, provided the goods were worth more than five shillings. At the same time, anyone who helped to secure the apprehension of a thief could obtain various tax exemptions and rewards. The measures were desperate; but so was the situation. Quite suddenly, England was virtually in a state of war with criminals. The diarist Narcissus Luttrell mentions an endless series of highway robberies and similar crimes. On one Saturday in 1693, a highwayman named Whitney had been arrested after resisting for an hour, and another highwayman was arrested in St Martin's Church. A gang of seven broke into Lady Reresby's house in Gerard Street, tied her and her family up and then rifled the house. Three coaches were robbed coming from Epsom, and three rowdies had caused an affray in Holborn, broken windows and run a watchman through with a sword, leaving it in his body. The invasion of houses by robber gangs had become as common as it was before the Black Death. A few years later, the famous robber Dick Turpin – whose exploits were far less romantic than his legend – led a gang that specialized in breaking into country houses, torturing the householders to force them to disclose valuables and raping any maids.

All this makes an interesting contrast with crime in the age of Queen Elizabeth. It had been just as widespread, but far less serious. London was then full of thieves and confidence men (known as "cony catchers", a cony being a rabbit). The thieves used to meet once a week in the house of their leader, who also happened to be the brother-in-law of the hangman; there, like an aldermen's meeting, they discussed "prospects" and exchanged information. In contemporary descriptions (Robert Greene wrote several pamphlets about it), the London criminal scene in the time of Elizabeth sounds rather like Damon Runyan's New York, deplorable but fairly good-natured. A century later, this had changed. Highwaymen infested the country roads, burglars operated in the towns, and women and children appeared in the courts as frequently as men. Children were trained as pickpockets, and were also sent out to earn gin money by prostitution – the novelist Henry Fielding, who became a magistrate in 1740, wrote of the large number of children "eaten up with the foul distemper". The government's reaction was to execute almost every offender who appeared in court. In 1722, a gang of Hampshire poachers had murdered a keeper who had interrupted them; they had

Black Bess and Dick Turpin (1706–39)

blackened their faces so as to be less visible in the dark. Landowners in the Waltham area (where it took place) were so alarmed that the government was prevailed upon to pass an act – the "Waltham Black Act" – which enabled almost any poacher to be hanged. (If the act had been in existence when Shakespeare was arrested for poaching from Sir Thomas Lucy, his works would have remained unwritten.) The act included a list of more than three hundred other offences – including catching rabbits – for which a man could be hanged.

Yet these measures had no effect on the rising crime rate. They could hardly be expected to when a large proportion of the population was permanently drunk. Henry Fielding reckoned that a hundred thousand people in London alone lived mainly on gin. Another observer stood outside a gin palace for three hours one evening and counted 1,411 people going in and out. These "palaces" usually consisted of a shed, full of barrels of gin; the customers merely came to buy a pennyworth of gin, which explains the enormous number. Whole families, including, father, mother and children, then sat on the pavement and drank themselves unconscious; with gin at a penny a quart, it was not difficult. The artist William Hogarth engraved two famous pictures, "Beer Street" and "Gin Lane", to expose the evil. In Beer Street, a lot of jolly-looking men and women are drinking outside a tavern and obviously engaging in intelligent political discussion (there is a copy of the king's speech on the table). In Gin Lane, a drunken mother allows her baby to fall out of her arms into the area below, a madman impales a baby on a spit, and a man who has hanged himself can be seen through the window of a garret. Fielding remarked that the gin "disqualifies them from any honest means to acquire it, at the same time that it removes sense of fear and shame and emboldens them to commit every wicked and dangerous enterprise." The result was that pickpockets who had once relied on skill and light fingers now knocked down their victims with bludgeons in broad daylight. The novelist Horace Walpole was shot in the face by a highwayman in Hyde Park in 1752.

Punishments, both in England and on the continent, had always been barbarous; now they became sadistic. The sentence of being hanged, drawn and quartered was usually reserved for political criminals, although it might be applied to some particularly violent robber. The victim was dragged to the place of execution behind a cart; he was then half-hanged, and his bowels were torn out while he was still alive and burned in front of him.

After this the body was cut into four pieces. Female criminals were often burned alive, because it was regarded as more "decent" than allowing them to risk exposing their private parts as they swung from a rope. (In this respect our ancestors were remarkably prudish.) But it was common for women – as well as men – to be stripped to the waist before being whipped through the streets to the pillory or gallows. After the 1699 act, thieves were branded on one cheek to make their offence public knowledge – this was probably regarded as an act of clemency, since most thieves were hanged. Prisoners accused of offences that involved speech – perhaps preaching false religious doctrines – would have a hole bored through the tongue as they were held in the pillory. A confidence man named Japhet Crook was sentenced to have both ears cut off and his nose slit open, then seared with a red hot iron. The hangman, known as 'Laughing Jack' Hooper, cut off both ears from behind with a sharp knife and held them aloft for the crowd to see, then cut

Ask anyone to name a famous pirate, and the chances are that they will say: "Captain Kidd". The truth is that Kidd was never a pirate.

William Kidd was a forty-year-old sea captain with a respectable record when the British government asked him to head a "privateering" expedition in 1695. A privateer plundered the ships of nations with whom his government was at war, and England was at that time at war with France. Kidd was also supposed to hunt real pirates – the unofficial variety – in the Red Sea.

Kidd captured and plundered two Armenian ships with French passes – which he was legally entitled to do – and the owners complained in London. When he arrived in New York, Kidd found to his astonishment that he had been proclaimed a pirate. He protested that he was nothing of the sort (and hid some of his loot), but when he ventured ashore he was arrested and returned to London. In the two years before he came to trial, the passes that would have proved his right to plunder the Armenian ships disappeared, and Kidd was convicted of piracy. He was also convicted of killing a member of his crew whom he had struck with a bucket – during a mutiny, he claimed. Kidd was hanged on 23 May 1701. The best known of all pirates was actually an innocent man.

open Crook's nostrils with scissors; however, when he applied
the red hot iron to the bleeding nose, Crook leapt out of his chair
so violently that Hooper – who was a kindly man – decided not
to carry out the rest of the punishment. On the Continent,
sentences were even crueller; red hot pincers were used to tear
out the tongues of blasphemers. A madman called Damiens,
who tried – rather half heartedly – to stab Louis XV of France in
1757, was executed by being literally "quartered". He was
carried to the execution because his legs had been smashed
with sledgehammers. His chest was torn open with red hot
pincers, and lead poured into the wounds. Then his hands and
feet were tied to four dray horses, which were whipped off in
opposite directions. They were not strong enough to tear off his
arms and legs, so more horses were brought; even so, the
executioner had to partly sever the arms and legs before they
could be pulled off. Damiens remained conscious until he had
only one arm left – during the early part of the proceedings he
looked on with apparent curiosity – and his hair turned white
during the course of the execution.

The Theft of the Crown Jewels

Another villain who certainly deserved execution cheated the
hangman because the King of England – Charles II – entirely
lacked the spirit of vengefulness.

The infamous Colonel Blood was born in Sarney, County
Meath, in Ireland, in 1618, and christened Thomas. His grandfather lived in Kilnaboy Castle, and was a Member of Parliament. Blood's father was a prosperous blacksmith who owned
an ironworks. When the Civil War broke out in 1642, Blood
hurried to England to fight on the side of King Charles I. But as
it became clear that Cromwell's forces were going to win, he
changed sides and joined the Roundheads. The result was that
when Charles was defeated in 1653, Blood was made a Justice
of the Peace and granted a large estate.

His prosperity lasted only seven years; when Charles II
returned to the throne in 1660, Blood had to flee back to
Ireland. He was not entirely destitute – he had married a

Lancashire heiress, who had borne him a son. In Ireland he joined a plot with other disgruntled Cromwellians to seize Dublin Castle and take its governor, Lord Ormonde, prisoner; it failed and he had to flee again, this time to Holland. After taking part in more political plots, he became a marked man with a price on his head. A daring rescue of a fellow conspirator, who was being taken to London under an escort of eight soldiers, again made Blood one of the most wanted men in the kingdom. In spite of this, he returned to England in 1670, and, under the name of Ayloffe, practised as a doctor at Romford.

He still dreamed of revenge on Lord Ormonde, who had dispossessed him and crushed his Irish plot. On 28 May 1670, Ormonde was on his way to a banquet in the Guildhall when he was held up in his coach and dragged out by several men. Blood then told him that he was going to be hanged at Tyburn, and sent the others off to prepare the gallows. But the coachman raised the alarm, and servants ran to Ormonde's aid; Blood fired a shot at him, then ran into the shadows of Piccadilly. (It was rumoured that he escaped with the aid of the Duke of Buckingham, who would have been glad to see Ormonde hanged.)

Back in Romford, he decided on an even bolder scheme: stealing the Crown Jewels, which were kept in the Tower of London, behind a grating in a locked basement room.

The keeper, Blood learned, was a man named Talbot Edwards, who lived with his family on the floor above the jewels. So one day early in 1671, disguised as a parson, Blood went to see the Crown Jewels, and became friendly with Talbot Edwards. Next time he went he took his wife. But as they were leaving the basement of the Martin Tower, Mrs Blood had a sudden violent stomach ache, and was taken into the Edwards' apartments to rest. The grateful Parson Blood returned a few days later with four pairs of white gloves for Mrs Edwards.

Blood was soon a regular visitor. And since Talbot Edwards had a pretty daughter, he was delighted when Blood proposed a match with his own wealthy nephew, an idea that his womenfolk also received with enthusiasm.

On 9 May 1671, Parson Blood arrived at 7 am with his "nephew" and two more companions. While the good-looking young man was making the acquaintance of the ladies, Blood suggested that they might see the Crown Jewels. Edwards thought it a good way of passing the time and led the way downstairs. He unlocked the door of the room that held the jewels, led them in, and locked it behind him. At that moment, he was knocked unconscious with a mallet wielded by Blood.

The thieves wrenched away the grating that protected the jewels, and removed the crown, orb and sceptre. The crown was flattened with the mallet and stuffed into a bag, the orb stuffed down the breeches of one of the men. Edwards, who had been tied up, began to struggle at this point, and Blood ran him through with his sword. The sceptre was too big to go into the bag, and one of the accomplices – Blood's brother-in-law, Hunt – began to file it through with a mallet.

Then there was an interruption. Edwards' son had been serving in Flanders, and he now arrived unexpectedly. Blood's "nephew", looking out of the window, saw him approaching and made an excuse to go downstairs. Blood decided that it was time to leave; they dropped the sceptre and hastened away.

At this moment, Edwards regained consciousness, and began to shout "Treason! Murder!". The son, now upstairs with his mother and sisters, ran down to see what was the matter. When he found his father bleeding from a sword wound, he raised the alarm.

Blood shot a sentry who tried to stop him, then made a minor mistake that betrayed loss of nerve: instead of leaving across the nearest drawbridge, by the Bulwark Gate, he changed his mind and made for the Iron Gate, near which his horse was tied. Even so, he came close to escape – the sentries mistook other guards for the fugitives and attacked them. Fortunately, the commander of the guard recognized the mistake, and reached Blood as he was mounting his horse. Blood pointed his pistol and pulled the trigger; it misfired. Beckman wrestled with Blood and finally overcame him. By this time the three accomplices had also been arrested.

In custody, Blood refused to answer questions, repeating stubbornly: "I'll answer to none but the King himself." Blood knew that the King had a reputation for liking bold scoundrels, and reckoned on his Irish charm to save his neck.

He proved correct. Blood was taken to the Palace, where he was questioned by the King, Prince Rupert, the Duke of York, and other members of the royal family. Charles was amused by his roguery, and chuckled when Blood remarked that his escapade had not been worth it, since the Crown Jewels were certainly not worth the £100,000 they were usually valued at – £6,000 would be nearer to it. Blood then went on to invent a tale of a plot to murder the King in which he himself had taken part. They had hidden, he explained, in the reeds at Battersea when the King went to the river to bathe, but "such was the awful majesty of your unclothed form that the weapon fell out of my hand." The King may have taken this as a flattering reference to his natural endowments; at all events, he asked, "What if I should give you your life?", and Blood answered promptly, with the correct expression of deep humility, "I would endeavour to deserve it, sire!"

Blood was not only pardoned – to the disgust of Lord Ormonde – but granted Irish lands worth £500 a year. With his pockmarked face, short legs and little blue eyes, he soon became a familiar figure around central London, and made frequent appearances at court.

Talbot Edwards, who recovered, was also rewarded by the king, and achieved his own kind of celebrity as the man who had been robbed of the crown by Colonel Blood. He lived to a ripe old age, always delighted to tell the story to visitors.

Blood's downfall came eight years later, when, in 1679, he quarrelled with his former patron, the scheming Duke of Buckingham. Somehow, perhaps when drunk, Blood came to accuse Buckingham of "gross immorality". Buckingham sued him for £10,000 – which would have ruined Blood – and, to Blood's dismay, he was found guilty. But immediately after the verdict, Blood fell ill, and died on 24 August 1680, at the age of sixty-two.

Even death was quite not the end of the story. There was soon a rumour that Blood had arranged his own "death" to escape paying the fine, and that the coffin contained some other body. The coffin was dug up in the presence of the coroner; when the body had been identified at an inquest it was reburied – a disappointment to his enemies, who still hoped to see him hanged.

Farmer Porter and the Robbers

Nowadays, even in countries with a high crime rate, the countryside is at least safer than the town. In eighteenth century England, it was just as bad.

In the summer of 1751, a farmer named Porter, who lived near Pulford, in Cheshire, engaged some Irish labourers to help with the harvest. One August evening, there was a crash at the door as someone tried to force his way in; the farmer evidently kept it locked as a precaution. Five Irishmen smashed their way into the house, grabbed the farmer and his wife – who were sitting at supper – and tied them up. Porter was ordered to reveal the whereabouts of his cash box, and tried delaying tactics; at this the gang threatened to torture them both. A daughter who had been listening outside the door now rushed into the room, flung herself on her knees, and begged for her father's life; she was also tied up and threatened. She gave way, and told the gang where the valuables were kept.

The youngest daughter, a girl of thirteen, had hidden herself; now she escaped out of the rear door, tiptoed to the stable, led out a horse and rode across the fields to the village. She went to the house of her brother and told him what was happening. The brother and a friend armed themselves – probably with knives and hatchets – and hurried to the farm. A man was on watch; they managed to approach so quietly that he was taken unawares, and promptly killed him. Then they rushed into the parlour, and found the four men holding the farmer – who was naked – and trying to force him to sit on the fire to reveal where he kept his savings. One robber was promptly knocked senseless; the other three fled through the window. The rescuers organized a pursuit, and caught up with two of the robbers on Chester bridge; another man, the ringleader, was caught on a ship at Liverpool. All four men were tried and sentenced to death, but the sentence of the youngest was commuted to transportation for life. The ringleader, Stanley, managed to escape on the eve of his execution. On 25 May 1752, the other two – named M'Canelly and Morgan – were hanged, "their behaviour [being] as decent as could be expected from people of their station".

This kind of house storming was commonplace during the crime wave of the eighteenth century. The robbers organized themselves like military units. A house that was to be attacked was watched for days until the gang knew when they could burst in, and when they were likeliest to be safe from inter-ruption. Stealth and skill were unnecessary in the actual operation; it was conducted like a siege of a town. The M'Canelly and Morgan case shows that the burglars of the mid-eighteenth century had already discovered a method of torture that became common in France at the time of the Revolution, when the robbers were known as *chauffeurs* – warmers. (Professional drivers were later called chauffeurs because the earliest cars were steam driven, so that the driver was literally a stoker, or "fireman".) We have seen that the streets of London were unsafe even by day; footpads operated openly in all the parks and open spaces, while highwaymen waited in every wood and thicket along every main road.

And what were the police doing while all this was going on? The answer is that there were no police. In the countries of Europe, the army kept some kind of order – that is why French policemen were later calls *gens d'armes* or gendarmes – men at arms. But England had no standing army, for it had not been invaded since William the Conqueror. And the British were deeply suspicious of the idea of a police force, believing it would erode their freedom. So in villages, there were local watchmen, and a parish constable – who was a local tradesman who did the job in his spare time. And, as Patrick Pringle points out in his introduction to Goddard's *Memoirs of a Bow Street Runner*, this system worked well enough in the country, but tended to break down in large towns. If a citizen was robbed, he himself had to pursue the robber, setting up a "hue and cry", and if he caught him, had to prosecute him at his own expense. The government tried to make up for the lack of law and order by the barbarity of punishments, so that as many as a dozen men at a time might be hanged at Tyburn (and on several occasions, as many as twenty). The *Gentleman's Magazine* for 1750 recorded: "Executed at Tyburn, July 6, Elizabeth Banks, for stripping a child; Catherine Conway, for forging a seaman's ticket; and Margaret Harvey for robbing her master. They were all drunk." As late as 1801, a boy of thirteen was hanged for breaking into a house and stealing a spoon; two sisters, aged eight and eleven, were hanged at Lynn in 1808. In 1831, a boy of nine was hanged for setting fire to a house, and two years later, another boy of nine was hanged for pushing a stick through a cracked shop window and stealing two pennyworth of printer's colour.

When better-off people left London in the mid-eighteenth century to go to the country, they locked up their houses and took their valuables with them, for they expected the houses to be broken into and robbed. And when someone wanted to recover stolen property, they went along to some dubious characters who knew the underworld, and offered a reward. In the previous century, a retired highwaywoman named Mary Frith, or Moll Cutpurse, set up a shop in Fleet Street to sell the goods stolen by her gang of pickpockets, and her best customers were the victims themselves; she was so successful that she drove every other fence out of the business. Moll died, rich and respected, in 1659, in her mid-seventies. A century later, Jonathan Wild set himself up in the same business, and soon achieved a success far beyond that of Moll Cutpurse. He became a kind of eighteenth century Al Capone, who divided London into districts, with a gang to each; any thief or highwayman who preferred to operate alone was hunted down and hanged on evidence supplied by Wild. He owned a London house and a country mansion, as well as a ship for taking stolen goods overseas; at one point, he even had the effrontery to ask the Mayor of London for freedom of the city in consideration of his great public services. When a law was passed making it illegal to take money for restoring stolen goods to their owners, he found ways around it, and became richer than ever. Eventually, the law caught up with him, and he was hanged in 1725. And within a year or so, London was in the grip of a crime wave that made it dangerous to walk in Covent Garden in broad daylight.

Gin was not the only cause. Others attributed it to the increasing number of sailors who flooded into London as Britain's trade with the rest of the world increased. But the novelist Henry Fielding came closest to the heart of the matter in a pamphlet enquiring into "the late increase of robbers" when he blamed "the vast torrent of luxury which of late years hath poured itself into this nation". England was becoming the richest country in the world, but its wealth existed side by side with appalling poverty. Naturally, the poor tried to divert a little of the wealth into their own pockets. The same thing had happened in ancient Rome and every other civilization that achieved wealth and success . . .

London went on a crime rampage, and it was not confined to the poor. The Mohocks, a society whose members were dedicated to the ambition of "doing all possible hurt to their fellow creatures", were mostly gentlemen. They employed their ample leisure in forcing prostitutes and old women to stand on their heads in tar barrels so that they could prick their legs with their swords; or in making them jump up and down to avoid the swinging blades; in disfiguring their victims by boring out their eyes or flattening their noses; in waylaying servants and, as in the case of Lady Winchelsea's maid, beating them and slashing their faces. To work themselves up to the necessary pitch of enthusiasm for their ferocious games, they first drank so much that they were "quite beyond the possibility of attending to any notions of reason or humanity". Some of the Mohocks seem to have been members of the Bold Bucks who, apparently, had formally to deny the existence of God and eat every Sunday a dish known as Holy Ghost Pie. The ravages of the Bold Bucks were more specifically sexual than those of the Mohocks and consequently, as it was practically impossible to obtain a conviction for rape and as the age of consent was twelve, they were more openly conducted. An expectation of inviolability was, indeed, shared by many, if not most young men of this class. One evening in the 1720s, Richard Savage, who claimed to be a son of the Countess of Macclesfield, quarrelled with some people playing cards in Robinson's coffee-house, lost his temper, and ran one of them through with his sword. He was tried for murder but he was subsequently pardoned. And when a young gentleman named Plunket called at a shop to collect a wig he had ordered he did not hesitate to pick up a razor from the counter and slit the wig-maker's throat from ear to ear, because he would not reduce the price by more than one guinea. Senseless murders such as this were as common as riots . . .

Things began to change for the better in 1729 when a half-pay captain named Thomas De Veil was appointed magistrate for Westminster and Middlesex. A decade earlier, De Veil had been well on the road to ruination with his taste for wine, women and song, which ran him up enormous debts. But he had the sense to retire to a country village and live cheaply before returning to London and setting up as a kind of scrivener, drafting petitions to the government. De Veil made no secret of the fact that he accepted his post as a magistrate because it offered him the opportunity to take bribes and indulge his immense sexual appetite with young ladies who had no other means to bribe him. He had twenty-five legitimate children and an unknown number of bastards, and next door to his office he kept a private room to which he could quickly retire with any attractive woman who appeared before him and was willing to buy her freedom on the couch. But in spite of being virtually a sex maniac, De Veil was also an efficient and hard-working magistrate. Ten years after the execution of Jonathan Wild, one

of London's largest and most desperate robber gangs decided
to kill him when they heard that he was collecting evidence
against them, and well-armed groups of them waited for night
after night around Leicester Fields (the present Leicester
Square), where De Veil had his office. De Veil seems to have
got wind of the plot, and all the waiting finally preyed on the
nerves of one of the thugs, who secretly betrayed his companions to the magistrate. So one of London's most dangerous
gangs was broken up.

De Veil's greatest triumphs came after he transferred his
office to a house in Bow Street, in 1739. Already in his mid-
fifties (and therefore, in eighteenth-century terms, an old man),
De Veil began to build up a reputation as a detective. When an
eating house in Chancery Lane was burgled, he found himself
interrogating a suspect who professed total innocence of the
crime. On a "hunch", De Veil asked the man casually for a loan
of his knife, and he noted that the suspect's pocket knife had a
missing point. He sent a constable round to the eating house
with instructions to look in the lock; the missing point was
found there, and the man convicted. As with most good
detectives, De Veil's success rested upon this keen instinct
about criminal behaviour.

After the death of De Veil in 1746, his position and his house
in Bow Street were taken over by the novelist and playwright
Henry Fielding, who had made the discovery that literature
and poverty are almost synonymous. Fielding had made a
living as a political playwright, until the Prime Minister, Sir
Robert Walpole, grew tired of being satirized, and introduced a
bill that required every play to be licensed by an official called
the Lord Chamberlain – an office that aroused the fury of
generations of playwrights until it was abolished in 1968. That
put an end to Fielding's career as a dramatist, and novels like
Joseph Andrews and *Jonathan Wild* failed to make up for the loss
of income. So, with some reluctance, Fielding decided to accept
the post of Justice of the Peace. His enemies set up a chorus of
derision about the idealistic playwright who had become a
"trading justice". But Fielding had no intention of lining his
own pocket. In his few brief years of office (he was already ill in
1748, and died six years later) he became the most formidable
enemy of crime that London had ever known.

His problem was simple: for every thief and highwayman
who was sent to jail, there were a hundred more left on the
street. With no police force except part-time parish constables,

the London criminal had never known any organized opposition. Yet De Veil had shown that gangs could be destroyed by a determined magistrate. With half a dozen public-spirited friends, Fielding began to organize a group of "thief takers", all ex-parish constables who knew the villains by sight. To us, the system sounds hopelessly amateurish. Victims of robberies were urged to hurry to Fielding's house in Bow Street, whereupon the thief takers would set out in hot pursuit – which is why they soon became known as the Bow Street Runners. And since London's robbers were accustomed to immunity, and seldom bothered to leave their habitual haunts, they were captured in droves. Fielding described his satisfaction as he read the London newspapers, and saw reports of robberies diminishing day by day, until eventually they ceased altogether. He had been granted £600 by the government, and in putting a stop to London's crime wave, he used only half of it.

The next problem was the number of highwaymen and burglars who infested the roads around London. Again, it proved unexpectedly easy to solve. As soon as a few heavily armed constables patrolled the roads, the thieves became nervous, and moved elsewhere. One highwayman had become so accustomed to immunity that he returned regularly to rob the same coach just outside London. Finally, the coachman took a Bow Street Runner with him and when the robber rode up waving his pistol, the Runner fired and blew away half his jaw. The highwayman also fired, but missed; he was taken off to hospital, and thence to jail. This episode took place under the magistracy of Fielding's blind brother John, who continued to be the scourge of London's underworld for more than a quarter of a century after the novelist's death.

The Great Vidocq

At the age of 34, Eugène-François Vidocq was a short, powerfully built man with a scarred face and a jaw like a lion. Born in Arras on 24 July 1775, he had been in trouble most of his life; never serious trouble, but Vidocq had a quick temper and a powerful will, qualities that had led to a number of personal combats and jail sentences. Injustice enraged him, and his attempts to escape from jail had been determined and desperate. By 1808, when he found himself in Paris, the list of his offences was enough to ensure a lifetime in the galleys. He asked to see M. Henry, head of the criminal department of the Paris police, and made him an offer. If he could be guaranteed immunity, he would act as informer against a number of men that the police wanted far more than they wanted Vidocq.

Henry knew he had a bargain, but he felt it could be improved. He allowed Vidocq to go. And when, a few weeks later, Vidocq was denounced by criminal associates and appeared again in front of the chief of police, M. Henry drove a very hard bargain indeed. Vidocq was to become a police spy in one of Paris's toughest prisons, the Bicêtre. If Vidocq was even suspected of being a police informer, he would be found dead the next morning. But, as M. Henry knew, he had no alternative.

Vidocq's task was to obtain evidence against a burglar named Barthélemy Lacour, known to the police as Coco. He had stolen a quantity of silver from a police official. Now he was about to come up for trial, and the police had no evidence. Vidocq's task was to obtain that evidence.

It proved unexpectedly easy. Because of his reputation as an escaper, Vidocq was something of a hero to the other prisoners, and soon became a kind of unofficial lawgiver. One of the first "cases" brought before him in this capacity was, oddly enough, Coco himself, who was suspected of being a police informer. Vidocq saved Coco's life, and so became his trusted intimate. And soon Coco had confided in him that the police would never convict him, for the only witness was a street porter whom the police had failed to question. Coco did not tell Vidocq the porter's name, but he mentioned the street he lived in. Vidocq passed on this information to Henry, and the man was soon traced. Coco never knew how they obtained the evidence that convicted him . . .

For the next two years, Vidocq continued his career of betrayal. Then Henry kept his side of the bargain and allowed him to "escape" on his way to court – the other prisoners were delighted with Vidocq's latest exploit. After that, the great escaper apparently returned to his old habits, spending his days in low wine shops. But the criminals were baffled that the police seemed to know of their best laid plans in advance. No one suspected that the culprit might be the great escaper.

In due course, Vidocq's successes became so great that, in 1810, he was given his own police department; it was called the Sûreté. His priority was to establish a network of informers or "grasses" – a method most police forces now take for granted, but which was established by Vidocq. And from 1810 until he retired in 1833, he scored a remarkable series of successes.

One example will suffice to illustrate his methods. In 1821, a butcher named Fontaine stopped at a roadside inn, and fell into conversation with two respectable-looking travellers; the butcher was delighted when they said they were on their way to a fair at Corbeil, and asked if he could join them. He was carrying a large sum of money, and was worried about robbers. At a lonely spot a few miles further on, they beat him unconscious, stabbed him, and took his money, leaving him for dead. But the butcher survived, and was able to describe his assailants. At the scene of the crime, the police found a fragment of an envelope with part of an address, including "M. Raoul" and "Roche . . ." Vidocq knew a M. Raoul who kept a bar at the Barrière Rochechouart, and whose reputation was sinister.

The butcher had succeeded in delivering a powerful kick at the knee of one of the men, so Vidocq assumed he was looking for a man with a limp. His men kept the bar under surveillance, and soon observed a man with a limp who fitted the butcher's description of one of the robbers. When Vidocq saw him, he recognized a criminal named Court, whom he had arrested some time before for armed robbery. At dawn the next morning he went to Court's room. He told Court he had been accused of smuggling, and observed the expression of relief that crossed the robber's face. Court invited him to search the room, and Vidocq took possession of some weapons, then took Court to the nearest gendarme post.

Now Vidocq used the same technique on Raoul. He explained that Raoul had been denounced for holding anti-Government meetings and distributing seditious pamphlets. Raoul invited him to search the place. There was, as Vidocq expected, nothing. But Raoul had another apartment in Paris. And there, in a bureau, Vidocq found the other half of the envelope. He arrested Raoul and lodged him in prison.

Vidocq proceeded to question Court, carefully failing to mention the attack on the butcher; eventually, Court divulged that he had been concerned in the murder of a poultry dealer, who had been robbed of four louis. Now, at last, Vidocq revealed that the crime he was investigating was the attempted murder of the butcher. By now demoralized, Court also confessed to this, but accused Raoul of the stabbing. Faced with his confederate's admissions, Raoul also confessed. Both men were condemned to the guillotine. Yet it is typical of the close relationship that Vidocq was able to form with criminals that he went to enormous lengths to make their last days comfortable, and that when they knelt at the block, they regarded Vidocq as a friend.

At the age of fifty-eight, Vidocq declined to retire into civilian life, and became the first private detective in Europe. He wrote his memoirs, and became a close friend of the novelist Balzac, who immortalized Vidocq as the sinister but extraordinary criminal Vautrin; in return, Balzac helped Vidocq to write novels based on his early life.

THE WILD WEST

The First Private Eye

The American equivalent of the great Vidocq was a Scottish-born detective named Allan Pinkerton. Like Vidocq, Pinkerton retired from the official police force to become a private detective, one of the first "private eyes" in the business. (In fact, the term private eye is probably derived from the Pinkerton symbol – an open eye bearing the legend "We never sleep".) But in the second half of the nineteenth century, the Pinkerton detective agency developed an efficiency that surpassed that of Scotland Yard or the Sûreté.

Allan Pinkerton was a radical, who fled from Scotland at the age of twenty-three – in 1842 – to avoid arrest. Working as a cooper in Dundee, Kane County, Illinois, he became an ardent advocate of the abolition of slavery, and helped to smuggle runaway slaves over the border into Canada. And in 1846, chance introduced him to his true vocation: detection. Walking in the woods on an island, he found the remains of a camp fire and trails in the long grass. Many men would have minded their own business; but Pinkerton had a social conscience. The local sheriff accompanied him back to the island, and decided that the camp belonged to a gang of counterfeiters. With Pinkerton's enthusiastic help, he uncovered a cache of fake money and arrested the gang. Only one of them escaped, and

Pinkerton, flushed with triumph, offered to help run him down. He tracked the man, pretended to be a fellow crook, and succeeded in getting him arrested. The result was an overnight reputation as a detective.

On Lake Michigan, not far from Dundee, there was a new city called Chicago – although this little collection of wooden cottages and rooming-houses, with a population of 4,000, was hardly more than a town. Soon after his triumph with the counterfeiters, Pinkerton was asked to become a deputy in Kane County and Cook County, which included Chicago. Like Vidocq, he proved to be a born detective, with a phenomenal memory for faces and a sure instinct for the ways of criminals. But the Chicago police were poorly paid, and when the Post Office engaged Pinkerton as a special agent, he saw that there was more money in private work. This is why, in 1850, he founded the Pinkerton detective agency.

This new, fast-expanding America needed efficient detectives. A fast-growing economy needs to transfer large amounts of money and valuables, and in the wide empty spaces, coaches and railway trains were a great temptation to bandits. The railway came to Chicago in 1852, and the new crime of rail theft

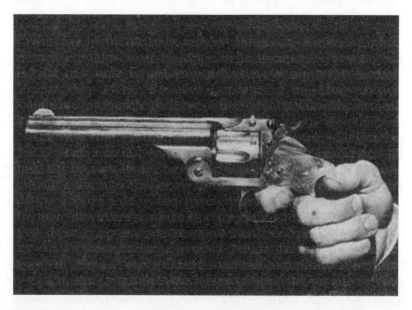

Nickel-plated Smith & Weston, used by Robert Ford to kill Jesse James

was soon costing the express companies and their customers enormous sums of money. In this vast country, Pinkerton often had to behave more like an Indian tracker than a policeman. In 1858, he was summoned to New Haven, where robbers had forced open the Adams Express car and prised open the safes with crow-bars, taking $70,000 in cash and jewellery. Near Stamford, Connecticut, Pinkerton found a bag containing $5,000, and knew he was on the right track. At Norwalk he heard of three men who had tried to hire a buggy, and tracked them down to a house where they had stayed overnight. When he learned that their host had been seen the next day on a train, carrying a heavy package that evidently made him nervous, he guessed that it contained the rest of the loot. He tracked the man to New York, but found that he had already left for Canada – but without the package. And under his questioning, the man's niece led him to the money and jewellery, hidden in the cellar. The gang was arrested, and Pinkerton completed the job by arresting the leader in Canada.

The Drysdale Bank Robbery

One early case from the Pinkerton archives is so incredible that it sounds like fiction. In 1855, a young bank teller named George Gordon was murdered late at night when working in his office; he was the nephew of the bank president. The bank vault was open, and $130,000 was missing. Gordon had been killed by a hammer blow dealt from the left. In the fireplace there were remains of burnt papers and clothing – the murderer had stayed on to burn his bloodstained coat. The only clues were two pieces of paper – a bloodstained page containing some pencilled figures – found under the body – and a partly burnt fragment of paper that had been twisted into a "spill" to light the fire. When Pinkerton unfolded this, he found that it was a note for $927.78, and that it was signed Alexander P. Drysdale, the county clerk, a man of unimpeachable reputation. The bloodstained page contained a subtraction sum – $1,252 minus $324.22 – the result being $927.78.

Pinkerton asked to see the bank balances of a number of

prominent local businessmen whom Gordon might have admitted to the bank after hours. Drysdale's account showed a
figure of $324.22. Now Pinkerton was able to reconstruct the
crime. Drysdale had come to the bank in the evening to request
a loan of $1,252. Gordon had agreed – but had subtracted from
this sum the amount already in Drysdale's account. Then he
had opened the vault. Overcome by sudden temptation, Drysdale had seized a hammer someone had left in the office and
killed his friend.

Pinkerton was certain that Drysdale was the killer, but how
to prove it? He began by finding an excuse to get Drysdale to
write something, and noted that he was left-handed, like the
killer. Next, he sent for three of his operatives from Chicago –
an older man, a woman, and a young man called Green. They
posed as visitors to the town, and began secretly investigating
Drysdale's affairs. Green, a good carpenter, found himself a job
in the local carpenter's shop, where all the old men gathered in
the evening to gossip. The older detective, who was calling

The most famous siege in criminal history began with a robbery
that went wrong.

On the freezing, windy night of 16 December 1910, a man who
lived next to a jeweller's shop in Houndsditch, East London,
heard the noise of hammering. Suspecting – correctly – that
robbers were trying to break through the wall into the jewellers,
he called the police. P.C. Piper knocked on the door of 11
Exchange Buildings and asked if the "missus" was there. A
foreigner told him she was out and he said he would call back.
Piper returned with several more policemen – all unarmed – and
knocked again. This time they were admitted, but as soon as they
were inside, shooting began. One policeman was killed outright,
two fatally injured, and four more wounded. Outside, a policeman
grabbed the gang leader, George Gardstein; another member of
the gang fired at the policeman, and hit Gardstein instead. They
hurried away, supporting Gardstein, who was bleeding to death.
Gardstein died that night at a nearby house – rented by a Russian
anarchist named Friz Svaars – at 59 Grove Street.

The doctor who had been called to attend Gardstein notified the
police, who found the body of Gardstein in the bed. Only one
member of the gang, a little hunchback named Sara Trassjonsky,
was still there, frantically burning papers. Her lover Peter Piatkow

himself Andrews, learned by chance one day that young Green bore a close resemblance to the dead George Gordon. And when Pinkerton learned of this, he formulated an incredible plan. Not far from Drysdale's home was a spot known as Rocky Creek, reputed to be haunted. "Andrews", pretending to be interested in a local plot of land, got Drysdale to take him through Rocky Creek at dusk, and as they rode among the trees, a ghostly figure walked across the path, its hair matted with blood. Drysdale shrieked; Andrews looked astonished and insisted that he could see nothing.

The woman operative had succeeded in getting herself invited into Drysdale's home as a guest of Mrs Drysdale, and she observed that her host was beginning to suffer nightmares and was prone to sleep-walking. Green, dressed as the ghost, kept up the pressure by occasionally flitting about outside the house when Drysdale was wandering around restlessly. Finally, Pinkerton appeared and arrested Drysdale, who protested his innocence. They took him to the

– who became known as Peter the Painter because he painted scenery for anarchist plays at a nearby club – had already escaped.

During the next month, a nationwide manhunt led to the arrest of eight gang members, including two women. On 2 January 1911, police received information that two more – Fritz Svaars and a man named Josef – were in the second floor room of Mrs Betsy Gershon at 100 Sidney Street. In fact, Mrs Gershon was a prisoner, and the men had taken her skirt and shoes to prevent her from going out. The police surrounded the house and evacuated the other floors. Early the next day they sent the landlady to go and ask Mrs Gershon to go and fetch a doctor, and the anarchists allowed her to go.

At dawn the police threw gravel at the window, and the anarchists opened fire. From the Tower of London the Scots Guards were sent, and the Home Secretary, Winston Churchill, arrived to watch the siege. The firing continued all morning. At one o'clock the house burst into flames, and the police refused to let firemen near it. One fireman was fatally injured as the house collapsed. The bodies of the two anarchists were found in the charred ruins, one shot in the head.

Peter the Painter was never caught, and is said to have died in America in 1914.

bank, and when the "ghost" appeared from behind the teller's counter, Drysdale fainted. When he recovered, he still continued to protest his innocence, and it began to look as if Pinkerton's bold strategy had failed. But when Drysdale was shown the two scraps of paper proving his involvement, he broke down and confessed. The stolen money was found hidden in a creek near his home.

The Reno Gang

But most of Pinkerton's early cases demanded persistence and courage rather than this kind of ingenuity. His most remarkable feat of the 1860s was undoubtedly his break-up of the Reno gang, America's first gang of organized outlaws. The five brothers – Frank, John, Simeon, Clinton, and William – were the sons of an Indiana farmer who lived at Seymour, Indiana. John left home at sixteen – in 1855 – and spent some time wandering around Mississippi, working on steamboats and learning to make a living by his wits. Back home, he propounded a scheme of amazing simplicity. The nearby small town of Rockford was prosperous and virtually unprotected. A series of arson attacks so terrified the inhabitants that they began moving elsewhere. Then the Renos bought most of Rockford at bargain prices.

During the Civil War, the Reno brothers served in the army; but most of them soon deserted. During the war, the bloodthirsty southerner William Clarke Quantrill led a band of guerrillas who were little more than robbers and murderers – it included Jesse James, "Bloody Bill" Anderson, and Cole Younger – and although most of the gang was wiped out in 1865, James and Cole Younger went on to become wandering outlaws. Meanwhile, back in Seymour, the Reno brothers formed their own outlaw gang, specializing in robbing county treasury offices. And in 1866, they invented a new crime – holding up trains. They boarded the wood-burning Ohio and Mississippi railroad coach as ordinary passengers at Seymour, then strolled down to the Adams Express car, forced the door, and held up the messenger at gunpoint. They pulled the communication cord, stopping the train, and rolled the safe off it. But they were still trying to burst it open in the woods when a posse drove them to abandon it. Nevertheless, John Reno had succeeded in seizing $10,000 in notes.

Pinkerton was asked to take on the case. The bandits had worn masks, but he had no doubt they were the Renos. A few weeks later, a new saloon was opened in Seymour – the amiable, round-faced man who ran it was really a Pinkerton operative called Dick Winscott – and the Renos soon became customers. Winscott even succeeded in persuading the brothers to allow him to take a group photograph – possibly the first time photography was used in crime detection. (Pinkerton had copies made and circulated.)

Seymour was an armed camp run by outlaws, and there was no chance of arresting the Renos on the spot. Allan Pinkerton enlisted the aid of Dick Winscott. The Renos were being sought for a bank robbery in Gallatin, Missouri, and had been identified by witnesses through their photographs. One afternoon soon after, the train stopped in Seymour, and Allan Pinkerton looked cautiously out of the window. On the platform he recognized the jovial figure of Dick Winscott, talking to John

Jesse James

Reno. Six muscular men, accompanied by a sheriff from
Cincinnati – another city that held warrants for the Renos –
strolled casually off the train, surrounded John Reno, and
hustled him aboard. Reno bellowed for help, but although
the other Reno brothers commandeered another train and
pursued the kidnappers, John Reno was handed over to the
Gallatin authorities and sentenced to twenty-five years in jail.

In February 1868, Frank Reno – now the gang leader – led a
raid on the Harrison County treasury at Magnolia, Iowa, which
netted $14,000. Using his skills as a tracker, Pinkerton found
them hiding in the home of a pillar of the Methodist church in
Council Bluffs, and arrested them in a sudden raid. But the jail
in Council Bluffs was not strong enough to hold them, and
when the sheriff arrived the next morning he found the cells
empty and a chalked inscription: "April Fool" – the date being
1 April 1868.

Local citizens were becoming enraged at the impunity the
gang seemed to enjoy. The Reno brothers were not the kind of
jolly outlaws who became folk heroes; they were bullies and
killers. In desperation, some of the bolder Seymour residents
formed a Vigilance Committee. The Renos heard the rumours,
and made bloodthirsty threats.

After a train robbery at Marshfield, Indiana, which netted the
gang $96,000, Pinkerton decided they had to be caught by
cunning. He circulated rumours that $100,000 in gold was to be
shipped via Seymour. The train's engineer pretended to agree
to co-operate with the gang and tipped off Pinkerton exactly
where the robbery would take place. And as the outlaws
stopped the train and burst open the Express car, they were
met by a volley of shots from Pinkerton's men. Most of the gang
escaped, but the next day, three of them were captured in a
thicket and arrested. But one dark night a few weeks later, the
train on which they were being sent to their trial was stopped
by men waving red lanterns; the three bandits were dragged off
the train and lynched. A few weeks later, another three bandits
who had been tracked down by Pinkerton were intercepted on
their way to jail by a mob and lynched. The Reno gang left in
Seymour began to fight back; members of the Vigilance Committee had rocks thrown through their windows; there were
night raids, beatings, and mutilations. When Simeon and
William Reno were arrested by Pinkerton detectives in India-
napolis, Vigilance Committee members received messages: "If
the Renos are lynched, you die." The Vigilance Committee

decided that if the Renos were not lynched, things would remain as bad as ever. The authorities decided to transfer the two Renos to the more secure New Albany jail. On 6 September 1868, there was a determined attempt by vigilantes to break into the Lexington jail, but the Renos had already been moved. They were joined in New Albany by their brother Frank, who had been arrested in Canada, together with a gang member named Charles Anderson. But on 11 December vigilantes surrounded the jail and burst their way in with a battering ram. The sheriff was beaten unconscious, and his keys taken. Then the Reno brothers and Anderson were dragged from their cells and lynched. As the vigilantes dispersed, prisoners watched from their cells and saw Simeon gasping for breath on the end of his rope; it took half an hour before he ceased to struggle.

The Vigilance Committee issued a notice, naming other members of the gang still in Seymour – including brother Clinton – and declaring that if they wished to remain as honest citizens, they would be welcome; otherwise they would meet the fate of the others. The gang accepted the ultimatum sullenly, and the outlaws ceased to be a power in Indiana.

Jesse James

Pinkerton was altogether less successful in his attempts to catch Jesse James. Like the Reno brothers, Jesse and his brother Frank came back from the Civil War, in which they fought for the South, wondering whether the methods of Quantrill's guerrillas could not be applied with equal success in peacetime. On 13 February 1866, ten men rode into Liberty, Missouri, and robbed the bank; on their way out of town, one of them shot down an unarmed student on his way to college, then, whooping and firing pistols, the gang rode out of town. It was the first of many pointless murders committed by the gang led by this modern "Robin Hood". In December 1869, the James gang robbed the same bank in Gallatin, Missouri, that the Reno brothers had robbed two years earlier, and James shot the manager in cold blood.

The Pinkertons began trailing the James gang at about this time, but had no success. In February 1874, a Pinkerton operative, John W. Whicher, succeeded in infiltrating the gang, but was recognized and murdered. On 6 January 1875, the Pinkertons received a tip-off that Jesse was visiting his mother, Mrs Zerelda Samuel; they surrounded the house and tossed in a "smoke bomb". It killed James's eight-year-old half-brother, and blew off his mother's arm. The incident brought much sympathy for the James brothers and indignant criticism of the brutality of Pinkerton. Jesse James was so angry that he spent four months in Chicago trying to get Pinkerton alone so he could kill him; he was unsuccessful.

On 7 August 1876, an attempt to rob the bank in Northfield,

Edward "Ned" Kelly is remembered as an outlaw in the same tradition as Robin Hood, a national hero who stole as a protest against authority. He was the son of a man transported to Tasmania from Belfast in 1841, and he himself began his criminal career early. He stole cattle and horses, and while still in his mid-teens he served a three year prison sentence.

His criminal career really took flight when in April 1878, he wounded a police officer who had come to the family home in Victoria to arrest his brother, also on a charge of rustling. As a result, the warrant was extended to cover the both of them and they took to the bush to hide out and plan. While they were away, the remaining portion of their family were arrested, tried and imprisoned for theft and resisting.

The two Kellys joined up with two other criminals, Steve Hart and Joe Byrne, and as the Kelly Gang, terrorized the local area, avoiding capture through a network of sympathizers and informants that hated the police. The gang's robbery technique often involved rounding up most of the inhabitants of a town and holding them prisoner in the local hotel while they stole anything worthwhile that they could find. The gang had no reservations about killing any policemen that got near them.

Even after the police had arrested many sympathizers under the Apprehension of Felons Act, the gang continued to evade them. The officers did not dare arrest any women, for fear of the public outcry that this would cause, yet a large proportion of the gang's "Bush telegraph" consisted of female sympathizers and

Minnesota, went disastrously wrong; the citizens all rushed outdoors with guns, and most of the bandits were either killed or wounded; James's cousin Cole Younger and his brother Bob were captured soon after and sentenced to life imprisonment. James formed a second gang, but it never met with the same success as the earlier one. On 7 August 1881, the gang committed its last train robbery, netting only $1,500. Harassment by the Pinkertons was breaking their nerve. On 3 April 1882, Jesse James was planning another robbery with two new gang members, Bob and Charlie Ford, when Bob Ford pulled out his gun and shot James in the back. He had agreed to deliver Jesse James to the state governor for reward money and amnesty. The murder of Jesse James – at the age of 34 – made

thus remained intact. As the robberies continued the police were heavily criticized in all quarters.

Meanwhile the Kelly gang were planning an ambush in which they hoped to kill many officers. A former accomplice called Sherritt was being held under police protection. As a means to attract the police, Joe Byrne shot Sherritt dead, while the rest of the gang forced two railwaymen to sabotage the track outside town. The plan was to let the train carrying the officers de-rail, and then kill them while they were still confused and wounded. As usual the gang held the local population in a hotel, but a schoolteacher succeeded in evading them and warning the police. Soon they arrived in town by different means and surrounded the hotel.

Realizing that the situation was hopeless, Dan Kelly and Steve Hart took poison and died. Joe Byrne was shot dead by the police. Ned Kelly, determined to escape the police that he hated so much, made a break for the bush and, although wounded, succeeded in making a makeshift suit of armour out of plough mouldboards. Wearing this as protection, Kelly tried to break through the police line. He was brought down by bullet wounds to his legs, but not until he had withstood twenty-five hits on the armour.

Kelly was tried in Melbourne in 1880, and was hanged on November 11. The repeated failures of the police prompted an inquiry by the Royal Commission. Kelly still remains a hero for anti-authoritarians everywhere; at his trial he was described as a quiet, self-possessed man with a fanatical hatred of the police.

him more of a folk hero than ever, and his brother Frank was acquitted several times of crimes he had obviously committed (he died of old age in 1915). Allan Pinkerton died two years after Jesse James, at the age of sixty-five but the agency continued with unabated success under sons and grandsons.

The Dalton Gang

One of the great early classics of American crime is Thomas S. Duke's *Celebrated Criminal Cases of America*, published in 1910. Duke was a captain in the San Francisco Police Force, and his style is often rough and ready; nevertheless, it has a dramatic feeling of immediacy. Here is Duke's account of the Dalton gang.

After the extermination of the James–Younger gang, the Dalton brothers stepped in and occupied the place once filled by them in the ranks of bloodthirsty criminals. In the Dalton family were six boys, named Ben, Frank, Grattan, William, Robert and Emmet.

In April, 1889, the Territory of Oklahoma was thrown open. For weeks previous to that time, thousands of people were camped along the frontier so as to be located in the most advantageous position to rush in at the appointed time and stake claims on the most valuable land, which they afterwards purchased from the Government for less than two dollars per acre.

For many months after the rush, lawlessness reigned supreme in this Territory. Bob Dalton was performing the duties of a Deputy United States Marshal at this time, but he began to associate with the outlaws and finally became a leader among them. Emmet and Grattan joined the gang, but in 1890 the Territory became "too warm" for the Daltons, so they went to California, where their brother Bill had rented a ranch in Tulare County.

At 7:50 pm, January 6, 1891, train No. 17 left Alila, Cal., for Bakersfield, but had scarcely gone one mile on its journey when Engineer Thorn and Fireman Radliff were confronted by two masked men who stood on the tender of the engine. The engineer was ordered to stop the train and the frowning muzzle of a pistol placed against his temple caused an immediate compliance with the command.

The engineer and fireman were then ordered to accompany the robbers to the express car. The express messenger, suspecting what had happened, put out the lights in his car and lay on the floor. He was ordered to open the door, but his reply was a shot from his revolver which was followed by a fusillade, during which Fireman Radliff was mortally wounded. The desperadoes then gave up the struggle and fled. A pursuit was at once begun but all trace of them was lost until 12 March. On this date Sheriff O'Neil of Paso Robles arrested William Dalton on the strength of evidence he had gathered, and upon being interrogated Dalton made some damaging admissions, which led to the arrest of his brother Grattan a few days later.

Both were taken to Visalia and charged with this crime, but William was eventually acquitted. On 7 July Grattan was convicted, after having tried to throw the entire blame on his brothers, Robert and Emmet, who were still at large. His sentence was continued until 6 October, but on Sunday night, September 26, he in some mysterious manner obtained possession of the keys to the prison kitchen and cell door, and in company with one William Smith, a convicted burglar, and W.R. Beck, a notorious character, escaped.

Services were being conducted in a church nearby, and the team belonging to George McKinley, one of the worshippers, stood awaiting him, but the three desperadoes took possession of it and made good their escape.

On December 24, Sheriff Hensly of Fresno met Grattan Dalton in the mountains, and after an exchange of several shots the bandit again escaped. He then joined Emmet and Bob in the Oklahoma reservation.

Deputy United States Marshal Ransom Payne incurred the displeasure of this gang, because he had the "audacity" to attempt to capture them. Bob and Emmet Dalton and one Charlie Bryant learned that this officer would leave Wichita, Okla. Ter., on the evening of May 9, 1891, for his home in Guthrie, so they decided to rob this train and kill the officer. They went to a little station called Wharton and ordered the stationkeeper to signal the train to stop. When the train came to a standstill, one bandit took charge of the engineer and fireman, and the remaining two went through the train inquiring for Payne. That official being alone and not knowing the number of bandits in the party, and realizing that he would probably be killed if the Daltons were in the gang and discovered him, decided to evade them and left the train and hid in the brush near the track.

Failing to locate Payne, the two desperadoes proceeded to the express car, where they obtained about $1,500. The bandits then made their escape on horses, and when the train left Payne came out of hiding and ran to the stationhouse, where he found the stationkeeper bound and gagged. The next day a posse was organized and in August, 1891, Bryant was arrested. One of the posse named Edward Short took charge of him, while the remainder continued in pursuit of the Daltons. Short boarded the train with his prisoner, and when the train stopped at a little station he left Bryant, who was handcuffed, in the charge of Wells-Fargo's agent, to whom he loaned a revolver. The agent, believing the prisoner was asleep, laid the pistol down and continued with his work. Just then Bryant jumped up, seized the weapon and attempted to escape. Short saw him leave the car and instantly drew another revolver. A duel followed with the result that both men were killed.

The Dalton gang remained in seclusion until the night of June 2, 1892, when Bob, Grattan and Emmet Dalton, assisted by three or four others, held up the Atchison, Topeka and Santa Fe train at Red Rock Station, Oklahoma. As the passenger train stopped at this station only when signalled to do so, the stationkeeper was ordered to display the necessary signal. When the train stopped the engineer was overpowered by two robbers and the remainder of the gang proceeded to the express car, where $1,800 was obtained, after which they escaped in the darkness.

In the early part of the following July, the territorial police and railroad officials learned that the Dalton gang were rendezvoused near the Missouri, Kansas and Texas Railroad in Oklahoma, and as they had profited little financially from their recent raids it was suspected that one of the trains on this road would soon be attacked. It was therefore decided to put a heavily armed posse on each train. Thus prepared, the authorities rather welcomed an attack, feeling confident that it would mean the extermination of the gang.

On the evening of July 15, 1892, the three Daltons, reinforced by five others, rode up to Adair station in Indian Territory and after robbing the agent they ordered him to signal the train to stop. Conductor George Scales and Engineer Ewing were immediately taken into custody, and the party then went to the express car which was in charge of Messenger George Williams, who reluctantly opened the safe and several thousand dollars were stolen.

The "guards," who were lounging in the smoker instead of being with the messenger, did not appear very anxious to perform their duty, although some of them ventured out and opened fire in a half-hearted way. A stray bullet struck and mortally wounded a Dr W. Goff, who was at the time in a nearby drug store. Two of the guards named Kinney and La Flore were also shot, but their wounds were superficial. During the fusillade, a wagon was driven up to the train, the bags of money were thrown in and the bandits again escaped.

The next raid attempted by these bandits occurred at their old home in Coffeyvile, Kansas, on October 5, 1892. The gang on this fatal day consisted of Bob, Grattan and Emmet Dalton, Dick Broadwell and Bill Powers. They rode into town about 9:30 am, and were recognized by a merchant named Alexander McKenna, who quickly but quietly rushed about notifying everyone he met.

The five bandits proceeded to C.M. Condon's bank and Grattan Dalton, Powers and Broadwell entered the bank, where they found President Charles Carpenter and Cashier Charles Ball.

As soon as the three men entered this bank, Bob and Emmet Dalton hastened to the First National Bank across the street, as it was planned to rob both institutions simultaneously. In each bank the bandits were informed that the time lock would not be off for several minutes and the robbers decided to wait.

In the meantime the news of the movements of the gang had spread through the town like wildfire, and the gunsmiths were loaning weapons and ammunition to all who desired them. As a result both banks were soon surrounded by determined men, all heavily armed, and the bullets began to fly through the windows of the bank.

When the vault was opened at the First National, Cashier Thomas Ayers handed out the money, amounting to over $20,000. Bob and Emmet Dalton put this in a sack and escaped out of the back entrance. They ran in the direction of Condon's Bank, but when they observed the crowd of armed men in front of that institution, they began firing, with the result that a young clerk named Lucius Baldwin was instantly killed.

In the general battle that followed, two shoemakers, named

George Cubine and Charles Brown, were killed by Bob Dalton when he saw them attempting to shoot him. Immediately after killing these men, Bob saw Cashier Ayers of the bank with his rifle raised, and Dalton shot him in the head, inflicting a serious but not fatal wound.

At this time the three robbers in Condon's Bank rushed out into the shower of bullets with about $3,000, and joining Bob and Emmet Dalton, they ran to their horses, but did not have an opportunity to mount.

John Kloehr, a stableman, and City Marshal Charles Connelly, both armed with rifles, then joined in the battle. Grat Dalton killed Connelly and almost immediately afterwards Kloehr killed Bob Dalton. Bandit Powers was the next to be killed and Grattan Dalton was then killed by Kloehr.

All of the bandits having been killed except Broadwell and Emmet Dalton, these two, realizing the great odds against them, mounted their horses and attempted to escape. They had only gone a short distance, however, when Emmet wheeled about and in the face of a heavy fire, returned to the body of his brother Bob, and as he was in the act of lifting the body with the intention of carrying it away on his horse, a load of buckshot was poured into his back and he fell unconscious.

Broadwell was fatally wounded as he attempted to escape and his body was found a short distance from town. Several horses were also killed and many citizens wounded.

Emmet Dalton finally recovered from what were diagnosed as necessarily fatal wounds, and he was sentenced to serve the remainder of his life at the State Prison at Lansing, but Governor Hock pardoned him in January, 1907.

After the tragic death of his brothers, Bill Dalton reorganized the gang and operations were resumed in Oklahoma Territory. Their rendezvous was in the extreme eastern part of the Cherokee strip, but considerable amount of their time was spent in a little village called Ingalls. As they purchased their provisions, ammunition and whisky in this village, they were shielded by those who profited from their trade.

On September 1, 1893, Bill Dalton, Bill Doolin, Arkansas Tom, George Newton and Tulca Jack were drinking at the bar in the village hotel when the place was surrounded by a posse consisting of ex-Sheriff Hixon, Deputy Marshals Thomas Houston, Lafe Hadley, Dick Speed and several other officials and civilians. The outlaws ran out of the place and at the beginning of the firing Deputy Speed was killed. Hadley killed Dalton's horse and the bandit fell and laid motionless on the ground. Hadley, believing him to be dead, approached, but as he drew near Dalton jumped up and shot the deputy in the head, killing him instantly. The bandit then mounted the murdered officer's horse, and although severely wounded, he escaped.

During the battle Deputy Houston and a clerk named Simmons were also killed, and S.W. Ransom, N.S. Murray and a twelve-year-old boy named Briggs were seriously wounded. All of the bandits escaped with the exception of Arkansas Tom, who was barricaded in the hotel and who subsequently surrendered on the condition that he would be protected from the mob. The next day it was ascertained that none of the bandits escaped without wounds.

The last raid committed by the Dalton gang occurred at the First National Bank at Longview, Texas, at 3 pm, May 23, 1894. At this time two roughly dressed men entered the bank and presented a note to President Clemmons, which read as follows:

"Home, May 23rd.

"This will introduce you to Charles Spreckelmeyers, who wants some money and is going to have it.   B. and F."

When Mr Clemmons read the note and looked up, he was covered by a rifle in the hands of one bandit while the other went behind the counter and secured $2000.00 in ten-dollar bills and nine twenty-dollar bills. City Marshal Muckley immediately learned of the raid and hurriedly gathered a posse who gave the robbers a hot battle. One of the bandits, Geo. Bennett, alias Jim Wallace, was killed as was also George Buckingham of the posse. Marshal Muckley and J.W. McQueen, a saloon-keeper, received serious wounds.

On June 7, 1894, a suspicious looking character, giving the name of Wall, came into the town of Ardmore, I.T., with two women who also acted quite mysteriously. They purchased about $200.00 worth of provisions and then called at the express office. The attention of the authorities was attracted by the peculiar actions of the trio, and while they made many conflicting statements, the information was elicited that they were living near a place called Elk. Sheriff Hart immediately organized a posse as he believed the provisions were purchased for some persons who feared to come to town, and as the Dalton gang was uppermost in his mind, he concluded that these three persons were connected with the gang. They were held prisoners and at 8 am the next morning the house where it was suspected that Dalton was hiding was surrounded.

Dalton came to one of the windows and seeing some of the posse he jumped from a window on the opposite side of the building and started to run.

Sheriff Hart called on him to halt, but as he ignored the command, one shot was fired from the sheriff's rifle and Dalton dropped dead without uttering a word.

The house was then searched and conclusive evidence was obtained, not only as to Dalton's identity, but also that he participated in the Longview bank robbery. The officials then returned to Ardmore and when the mysterious trio were informed of the death of Dalton, one of the women became hysterical and said she was Dalton's wife and that they were married at her home in Merced, California, in 1888.

The D'Autremont Brothers

In the mid-1920s, the most famous American sleuth was a man named Edward Oscar Heinrich, who became known as "the Edison of Crime Detection". Before he became Professor of Criminology at the Berkeley Campus of the University of California, Heinrich had been the city chemist in Tacoma, Washington.

The case that brought him celebrity began on 11 October 1923, when a train bound from Oregon to San Francisco was held up by bandits in the Siskiyou Mountains. The train was crawling through a tunnel when two men dropped off the roof of the engine tender and pointed guns at the engineer and fireman; they were made to stop the train and then marched up a slope at gunpoint and made to stand with raised hands. A third man placed a large package beside the mail car – which was half-way out of the tunnel – and ran. A moment later, there was a violent explosion, which blasted open the car and set it on fire. Then the engineer and fireman were ordered to pull the rest of the train out of the tunnel. This proved to be impossible. The bandits were becoming increasingly panicky, and when the brakeman ran out of the tunnel to see what was happening, one of them raised a shotgun and shot him dead. Then the engineer and fireman were deliberately executed. And the bandits, who realized that they were not going to get into the blazing mail car, disappeared. A mail clerk named Edwin Daugherty was burned to death.

Police from Ashland, Oregon, found a detonating device with batteries near the tunnel. Nearby there was a revolver, a pair of shoes, and a pair of greasy denim overalls.

Posses galloped off in all directions looking for the robbers. Meanwhile, the sheriff examining the detonator wondered whether its batteries might not have come from a nearby garage. He hurried there, and arrested the mechanic he found working in a pair of greasy overalls that looked very similar to those found near the detonator. But the mechanic maintained his innocence, and the police were unable to find the slightest shred of evidence to link him with the crime.

Edward O. Heinrich was obviously the man to approach, and the police sent him the overalls found at the scene of the crime. Within two days he told them over the telephone: "You are holding the wrong man. The grime on these overalls is not car grease. It is fir pitch. In the pocket I found particles of Douglas fir needles. The man who wore these overalls is a left-handed lumberjack. He is between twenty-one and twenty-five years of age, about five feet ten inches tall, and he weighs about 165 lb. His hair is medium light brown, his hands and feet are small, and he is a man of fastidious habits."

Later, Heinrich explained how he had made these deductions. The fir chips were in the right-hand pocket, which meant that the man stood with his right side towards the tree as he was chopping it down; a right-handed man stands with his left side to the tree. Besides, the left-handed pockets were more used than the right, and the overalls were buttoned on the left. The overall bottoms had been folded to fit into boots, and the position of the suspender buckles indicated the height and build of the wearer. A single hair adhering to a button told Heinrich that the man was white – Negro hair or Indian hair is quite different. Nail clippings that had been caught in a front pocket had been cut with a precision that indicated a man of fastidious habits. The size of the shoes had indicated a man with small feet, and it followed that his hands were also small.

Heinrich had found another clue. In the pencil pocket of the overalls he had found a scrap of folded paper that the police had missed. It was a receipt for a registered letter bearing a code number. The Post Office was able to tell the police that it had been issued in Eugene, Oregon, as a receipt for $50 sent by a man called Roy D'Autremont to Ray D'Autremont in Lakewood, New Mexico.

It was easy to locate Paul D'Autremont, the elderly father of the brothers, in Eugene. He told them that his three sons – the twins Roy and Ray, and their brother Hugh – had been missing since the day of the hold-up. And Roy was a left-handed lumberjack.

Heinrich's examination of the gun found near the detonator left no doubt that the D'Autremont brothers were the bandits. A hidden number led the police to the store in Seattle where it had been purchased by a man calling himself William Elliott. Heinrich, who was also a handwriting expert, was able to state that Elliott's handwriting was that of Roy D'Autremont.

Even the reward of $15,000 offered by the railway company failed to produce information of the brothers' whereabouts. But in March 1927, an army sergeant saw a "Wanted" poster, and thought that Hugh D'Autremont resembled a private he had known in the Philippines. Hugh D'Autremont was arrested in Manila. A month later, Roy and Ray were recognized at the steel mill in Steubenville, Ohio, where they were working. All three brothers were sentenced to life imprisonment.

VICTORIAN VILLAINIES

The Great Gold-Dust Robbery

Until the end of the eighteenth century, most robbers were clumsy amateurs – footpads, highwaymen and burglars who lived from day to day, and usually ended on the gallows before they reached their thirties. But the Industrial Revolution created new wealth, and brought a new class of criminal: the bold planner who was willing to risk ten years in jail for an ambitious coup that might make him wealthy for life. And the simplest way to go about it was to find some underpaid clerk or warehouseman, and bribe him to take part – what we now call an "inside job".

The first of the great "inside jobs" happened in London Docks in 1839.

On 25 March 1839, two boxes of gold dust addressed to Hartley and Co. arrived at St Katherine's Dock from Brazil. They had just been forwarded from Falmouth by a shipper called Carne and Co. and the contents were worth £4,600. That same morning, Hartley and Co. received a letter from Carne and Co. telling them that the gold-dust was about to arrive, and that it would be collected by a representative of the agents of the Brazilian Mining Company.

Early that afternoon, the man they were expecting arrived to collect the boxes, and produced documents that described them in detail. A clerk named Lewin Caspar, who was in charge of the boxes, was heard to mutter that he hoped the papers were genuine. But he handed over the boxes, and the man drove off in a cab. Half an hour later, his employers were thrown into panic when another man arrived from the agents, and demanded the boxes, producing another set of obviously genuine documents. It seemed that Lewin Caspar had been right, and the first man was an impostor.

For Hartley and Co. it was a serious blow – they would have to reimburse the £4,600, enough to threaten them with bankruptcy. The London police force had only been in existence for ten years, and was not noted for its efficiency. Nevertheless, two detectives named Lea and Roe were given the task of tracking down the robber.

They began by tracing the horse-drawn cab in which he had escaped. The driver said he had been paid off in Wood Street, in the City, and that the man with the two boxes had then hired another cab and driven off towards Holborn. The second cabbie was finally traced, and told them that he had driven the man to a house in New Street. But the detectives arrived too late; the man had already left and moved to lodgings in Goodman's Fields. Now several days behind him, the detectives arrived to find that he had left this lodging too, this time without leaving an address. But, to their relief, he proved to be known to his landlord in Goodman's Fields. He was a married man named Henry Moss, and he worked as a foreman to a watchmaker in Goodman's Fields. Mrs Moss's female servant had been left behind, and told the detectives that on the morning of the robbery, Moss had left home wearing his best clothes, which was unusual. He came back to his New Street lodging with two large boxes. The next morning, the servant had noticed burnt fragments of these boxes in the grate.

The detectives picked up another important piece of information. Before the robbery, Henry Moss had been seeing a great deal of a Jewish watchmaker called Ellis Caspar, who had once been his employer. And Ellis Caspar was the father of Lewin Caspar, the clerk who had handed over the boxes of gold dust. This was too much of a coincidence, and both Caspars were promptly arrested.

While they were still searching for Henry Moss, the police decided that the next step was to find out what might have happened to the gold. A check among London's bullion dealers revealed that Bull and Co. of Cheapside had recently bought a large quantity of gold bars from a man called Henry Solomon. Solomon, a gold refiner, admitted that he had sold gold bars worth £1,200 to the bullion dealer, but claimed he had made them from melting down gold snuff-boxes. The police did not believe him, and when they told him so, Mr Solomon became sullen and uncooperative. These were the days when London was full of the kind of anti-semitism reflected in Dickens' Fagin – *Oliver Twist* came out the same year – and the *New Newgate Calendar* remarks that the gold-dust robbers "were of the Jewish persuasion, and the proverbial cunning and habits of cheating of these people were exemplified throughout the enquiry". There can be no doubt Mr Solomon's civil rights were violated in the course of his interrogation. Although the evidence against him was non-existent, he appeared before the magistrates, together with the Caspars, charged with receiving the gold dust.

Meanwhile, Henry Moss, who was hiding out in Peckham, had heard of the arrest of the Caspars. It also emerged later that he suspected the Caspars of intending to cheat him. So Moss decided to give himself up and turn police informer. His story was that he had acted in complete innocence. Ellis Caspar had approached him a year ago, and told him that his son Lewin now had a job as a clerk at a shipping agents. He wanted Moss to do him a small favour – take some papers, and go and collect some boxes from Hartley and Co. Moss was assured that he was doing nothing illegal, and agreed. But on this first occasion, something had gone amiss – Caspar said that a ship had failed to arrive. He was given ten shillings, and told they might need his help on some future occasion.

The occasion came a year later, when Henry Moss was finally given the necessary papers, and told to collect two boxes from Lewin Caspar at Hartley and Co. He followed his instructions, and took the boxes back to his lodgings in a cab. When he got there, he found Ellis Caspar waiting in a state of jitters. The police were on the trail, said Mr Caspar, and Moss would have to move the next morning. After this, the boxes were opened, and proved to contain a number of tins. Then the Mosses were told to burn the boxes.

Obviously, things had gone wrong. The whole swindle depended upon Lewin Caspar remaining unsuspected. The moment the detectives learned that the robber was a friend of Lewin's father, "the game was up".

Two more accomplices were arrested: a go-between called

Emanuel Moses, and his daughter Alice Abrahams, who had sold the gold-dust to Solomons. At the trial, it emerged that there was little honour among thieves: everybody was apparently out to swindle everybody else. Henry Moss had made a determined attempt to keep all the gold for himself, but was forced to hand it over to Moses and his daughter. They sold it to Solomons, who agreed to pay £3,700, but gave an IOU for £1,800 of this, which he then refused to pay. Alice Abrahams cheated her own father of £13 which she got for the gold dust shaken out of the bottom of the empty bags; her father cheated the Caspars by claiming he only received £2,000 for the gold. The Caspars intended to cheat Henry Moss by fobbing him off with an absurdly small part of the proceeds. And Moss – indignant when he learned that he was being cheated – decided to go to the police and give evidence against his

Around mid-1911, Paris was full of anarchists who declared that the corrupt social system could only be overthrown by violence. Among these was Jules Joseph Bonnot, the son of a poor family who had educated himself, and who at one time had been a racing driver. In Paris anarchist clubs Bonnot recruited a group of fifteen idealistic young men who agreed to follow him to the death. They obtained guns by raiding a gun shop, and stole a large, fast car from a garage. On 21 December 1911, Bonnot and four followers waylaid a bank messenger with typical brutality and violence, shooting him first in the chest, then in the throat, and firing shots over the heads of the crowd as they drove off. Their haul proved to be small, consisting mostly of useless securities. (Incredibly, the bank messenger recovered.)

When they knocked down a woman as they were driving a stolen car, they drove off at top speed; a policeman who tried to intercept them was shot to death.

In March 1912 they committed another typically brutal crime. They needed a car, so they waylaid the Marquis de Rouge, who was driving out of Paris in a new sports car at six in the morning. Rouge and the chauffeur were both shot dead and dumped in a ditch; the gangsters then drove to a bank in Chantilly, and while Bonnot waited with the engine running, the others went into the bank and fired indiscriminately, killing one man and seriously wounding two more. As they rushed out with their haul, Bonnot was trying to hold an angry crowd at bay by firing over their heads.

accomplices. (By this time, Moss had admitted that he knew he was involved in a crime from the beginning.) What seems certain is that if the Caspars had not tried to cheat Moss, he would never have gone to the police, and they would have gone free for lack of evidence.

Ellis Caspar and Emanuel Moses received fourteen years each, Lewin Caspar was transported for seven years, and Alice Abrahams received only four months, on the grounds that she had been influenced by her father. Henry Moss was sentenced to a day in prison.

This complicated affair – with its tale of mutual plunder – set all London laughing. No one noticed that something highly significant had happened: that a clerk in a position of trust had planned to become a wealthy man overnight with a brilliant and cunning scheme. If it had not been for the determination of

---

While they were driving away, a bullet grazed the arm of Francois Callemin; in a rage, he began shooting at random, luckily hitting no one. This robbery brought the gang its largest haul so far.

The Bonnot gang was now being hunted by the whole French police force, and the public clamoured for their arrest. More robberies followed, and the gang lived up to its reputation for brutal and unnecessary killings. One of them, Pierre Garnier – who had shot the bank messenger – wrote the police a defiant letter enclosing his fingerprints, and declaring: "I know you will get me eventually because you have force on your side, but I shall make you pay dearly for my life."

Other anarchists were shocked by all this violence, and the police began to receive tip-offs. Inspector Jouin arrested one gang member in March 1913, and another soon after. But Jouin himself was killed when he surprised Bonnot in a hideout in Ivry; Bonnot shot his way out, wounding another policeman.

Finally, Bonnot's hiding place at Choisy-le-Roi was surrounded after a tip-off from another hostile anarchist who felt that Bonnot was giving the cause a bad name. Dubois, the man who was sheltering Bonnot, was shot dead as he fired at the police while trying to escape on a motor bike. After six hours of shooting, the police stormed the house, and found Bonnot bleeding to death; he had time to shout "Bastards" as he lapsed into a coma.

Other gang members were arrested one by one, and many – including Callemin and Garnier – ended on the guillotine.

everyone involved to swindle everyone else, he might have succeeded. The gold-dust case is the first of the robberies that are usually preceded by the epithet "great".

The Great Bullion Robbery

It has to be admitted that the great gold-dust robbery lacks the stuff of high drama. This is certainly not true of the great gold bullion robbery that took place sixteen years later.

In fact, the story begins in 1848, when a remarkable theft occurred on the British railway; when a strong-box arrived by train in Bristol, the box was found forced open, and £1,500 in gold was missing. The case was never solved. But it attracted the attention – and admiration – of a suave gentleman forger named Edgar Agar. He knew that large quantities of gold bullion were sent by train, and that, with careful planning, he might make enough money to last him the rest of his life.

Agar was introduced to an unimpressive little clerk named William Pierce, who had sandy hair and a shifty look; Pierce worked for the South-Eastern Railway as a ticket printer, and he was a man of expensive tastes who never had the money to pay for them. So when Agar disclosed his interest in the gold shipments, Pierce showed himself eager to cooperate. He set out to learn all he could about the way the gold was sent, and at what point it might be vulnerable.

What Pierce learned was not encouraging. Large quantities of gold were often sent from London to Paris. But there were *two* keys to the heavy safe, and one was kept in London and the other in Folkestone. That obviously presented enormous difficulties to the most enterprising thief. Agar decided that forgery was easier, and dropped the idea.

In 1850, the shifty little clerk was discharged on suspicion of theft, which was probably justified. Now he was more anxious than ever to take part in the scheme. Accordingly he made the acquaintance of the station master at Margate, William George Tester, and persuaded him to help. This was in 1854, six years after Agar had dreamed up the plan. With Tester's help, it should be possible, he thought, to get a duplicate of both keys.

Map showing the details of a later Bullion robbery, May 1967

Agar, just back from America, where his criminal enterprises had flourished, thought this sounded promising. He and Pierce went off to Folkestone and took rooms there, then spent a great deal of time hanging around the station, trying to learn where the second key was kept. But the railway police noticed them, and took them for pickpockets. The down-at-heel Pierce fled back to London.

Agar stayed behind a short time longer, as he had scraped an acquaintance with the clerk in charge of the keys, a man called Sharman. The problem was how to find out which of the keys fitted the bullion safe. But the railway police were watchful, and warned Sharman that they thought Agar a villain. So Sharman suddenly ceased to respond to Agar's friendly overtures.

Agar now devised a clever scheme to find out about the key. He had £200 in gold sent from London to Folkestone, to be delivered to a Mr Archer – himself. This, of course, would be sent in the gold bullion safe. Then Agar went to Folkestone to collect it. The scheme should have failed, because Sharman had been warned about Agar. But luck was on Agar's side; Sharman was away on the day he called, and the young booking clerk went to the key cupboard – watched by Agar – and removed the gold bullion key. Obstacle number one had been successfully surmounted.

So was obstacle number two. Tester, the Margate station master, was transferred to London, and soon had the opportunity to take a wax impression of the other key. Now Pierce and Agar hurried back to Folkestone, and waited for the boat train to come in. For a few minutes, the office was empty while the various clerks came out and attended to the registered luggage. Pierce slipped into the office and grabbed the key; outside, Agar pressed it into a piece of soft wax. Within a minute, the key was back on its hook, and Agar and Pierce were strolling out of the station.

A fourth – and most essential – accomplice had now been enrolled – a guard named James Burgess, who was in charge of the guard's van that contained the bullion safes. Without him, the robbery would have been impossible. Burgess agreed that he would give a signal – wiping his hankerchief across his face – when there was gold bullion on the train.

Things were still far from straightforward. Both keys were cut from the wax impressions, but it took months – it was a complicated design – and when Agar tried them out, neither would fit. They had to modify them eight times before they would open the safe. Now that success was at last in sight, Pierce and Agar moved to new lodgings, and Pierce wore a false moustache and wig and changed his name.

There was still one more problem. Unless the stolen gold was replaced by something of equal weight, the loss might be discovered at Folkestone, where the bullion was weighed before it left England. That would be too soon. So Agar and Pierce bought two hundredweights of lead grapeshot from the Shot Tower, near Waterloo, packed it into carpet bags, and staggered back with these to their lodgings.

It was now the beginning of May 1855. Every evening the men followed the same routine. They drove to London Bridge Station in a cab, with their carpet bags, each weighing half a hundredweight, and then took up their position where they could watch the bullion train. But for two weeks, Burgess failed to make the signal they were waiting for, and they drove back home. They began to worry in case railway police should notice them again. But finally, on 15 May 1855, Burgess wiped his face with his handkerchief. Agar and Pierce immediately bought tickets, and went to the luggage van, where Burgess stowed their abnormally heavy bags. But only Pierce came out of the van. He went to a first class compartment. Agar crouched in a corner of the luggage van, covered with an apron.

As soon as the train started, Agar threw off the apron. From a leather bag strapped under his arm – and concealed by his cape-overcoat – he removed his tools: wedges, pincers, sealing wax and tapers. While Burgess acted as lookout, Agar opened the first of the two safes with the keys and removed two small and very heavy wooden boxes, sealed with metal bands. Working with feverish haste – the train would soon be stopping at Reigate – he used the wedges to prise up the bands on one of the boxes, then forced it open. It contained solid gold ingots. Four of these were removed, and bags of lead shot placed in the box. Then the nails were hammered down again and the bands replaced; finally, Agar lit a taper and melted the sealing wax to replace the seals. The box was locked back in the safe, and when the train stopped at Reigate, Burgess was ready to hand over a carpet bag to a man who came to the guard's van to claim it. William Tester strolled off the station carrying the four bars of gold.

As the train left Reigate, Pierce joined Agar in the guard's van, and they forced open the second box. This proved to contain American gold coins. Again, a quantity of these were removed and replaced with lead shot. After this, the second safe was opened. This was found to contain smaller gold bars. Regretfully – because he was running out of lead shot – Agar was forced to remove only a few of these. Their total haul was worth £12,000.

In Folkestone, two passengers holding carpet bags walked out of the station, climbed into another train, and continued their journey to Dover, where they arrived before midnight. There they went into a hotel and had a meal – their train back to London left at two in the morning. While Pierce guarded the bags, Agar took a stroll along the dock and dropped the safe keys and the tools into the water.

At the station, a porter offered to take their bags; when they declined, he became suspicious, and asked to see their tickets. But Agar had thought of everything, and produced two Ostend

---

William L. Carlisle – known as the "White Bandit" – stands out as one of the most amiable robbers in American history. Between 1916 and 1919, he robbed numerous passenger train across the east and central United States. Donning a handkerchief to hide his face and waving a revolver, he would relieve passengers of their valuables in much the same way as any other petty crook, but with one important difference: he would not steal from women. At times panicked ladies would even thrust their purses and jewellery at him, but he would always courteously refuse.

On one occasion, seeing that a man had only raised a single hand when commanded he moved closer to threaten him. However, he then saw that the victim had only one arm. Carlisle immediately apologised and left the man with his belongings.

His flamboyance was amazing. He not only wrote to the police to ask how the investigation was going, he even told them which trains he was going to rob beforehand. Even with this help, it took the authorities some time to catch him, and then he promptly escaped.

He was eventually recaptured and served seventeen years before being paroled in 1936. On release he turned over a new leaf, got a job and married. For the rest of his life he devoted all his spare time to campaigning against crime. Speaking at many public rallies he stressed the need to help young offenders, not to castigate them.

tickets – the return halves. The porter thanked him – then remembered that there had been no Ostend boat that day, and asked them when they came from Ostend. ("Yesterday") said Agar breezily, holding out a tip. The porter saluted and went away.

Two hours later they were back in London. Even now they continued to take precautions. In case they had been followed, they took three cabs in succession, arriving back at their lodgings after dawn. There Tester was waiting with his carpet bag. After seven years of planning, the great bullion robbery was now successfully completed.

Meanwhile, in the Gare Maritime in Boulogne, the cross-Channel steamer lay alongside the quay, and in the Customs shed officials were checking the weight of the three iron-bound boxes against the documents that accompanied them. In fact, the boxes had been weighed at Folkestone, and one had been found to be light; but since the other was too heavy, the Folkestone Customs had decided that a simple mistake had been made. The Boulogne authorities were less casual. When it was realised that two out of three boxes were under-weight, there was deep suspicion. Customs officials re-checked the papers; there could be no possible doubt; the boxes were dozens of pounds lighter than they should be. When the boxes were finally opened, and the lead shot discovered, there was consternation. The seals were intact. But on closer examination, the officials discovered the marks of the wedges and pincers that revealed that the boxes had been opened . . .

Back in London, the gang converted around £400 in American gold sovereigns into English money, and it was divided equally.

The gold was now moved from the temporary lodgings to Agar's house in Shepherds Bush. Here he lived with a young woman called Fanny Kay, whom he had met working behind the counter in the buffet at Tonbridge station, and persuaded to move in with him. She had borne him a son. For the next week or so, Agar and Pierce worked at a furnace in the upper room, converting the gold ingots into smaller ones by running the gold into iron moulds. They sliced up some of the smaller ingots with a hammer and chisel. These smaller pieces they were able to sell at £3 an ounce, bringing in £300. Then, very slowly and cautiously, Agar began looking around for a customer for a larger part of the loot. Tester and Burgess were both given a share of the proceeds, after Agar had impressed upon them the importance of continuing in their jobs and displaying no sign of sudden affluence. A famous forger named James Townesend Saward – better known as Jim the Penman – bought £2,500-worth of the gold.

At this moment, Agar's luck turned – although he was not aware of it at the time. In spite of his new wealth, he continued in his old occupation of forging. He came across a young man named Smith, who seemed bright and willing, and employed him to do odd jobs. Smith seemed to be reliable – several lots of money were safely delivered by him – so Agar decided to employ the young man on a permanent basis. Although Smith was not told this, his job was to go to banks and cash forged cheques. In case Smith was caught, Agar made sure that he personally was untraceable; Smith did not know his real name, and he always met him at a hotel.

What Agar did not know was that Smith had spent twelve months in jail for receiving stolen goods, and had run a brothel, which had gone bankrupt. When Smith told a thief called William Humphries about his new job, Humphries advised him to be very careful, since Agar was a villain. In fact, Humphries himself had reason to dislike Agar. The latter had a roving eye, and had seduced Humphries's mistress, a girl named Emily Campbell. Fanny had found out, and after a quarrel, Agar had walked out on her and taken his new mistress to live with him elsewhere.

When Smith realised that he had been selected so that he could take all the risk, he went to the police. And the police arranged a trap. One day, Agar sent Smith to a bank in Lombard Street with a forged cheque for £700. Agar followed – in the event of Smith being caught, he wanted to make sure he was ready to disappear. The bank, apparently, handed over the £700 without suspicion; in fact, they had been tipped off by the police, and filled the bag with farthings. Smith then met his employer – whom he knew as Captain Pellatt – in Jockey's Fields (now Grays Inn) and handed over the bag. At this moment the police pounced and arrested them both. Agar was charged with forging the £700 cheque.

Agar was convinced that Humphries had "framed" him for stealing his mistress, and protested his innocence. But counterfeit notes and forged plates in his home made it clear that he was a professional crook. He was sentenced to transportation for life in Botany Bay. This was only five months after the great bullion robbery.

Now he began to feel remorse about abandoning Fanny Kay

and their son. He had £15,000 in the bank, and decided to settle
it on Fanny. But he wanted to invest it and give Fanny a
weekly income, rather than handing her the whole sum – being
unaccustomed to handling money, she would probably spend
it, whereas it could bring her an income of £2 a week for life.
Agar now made his greatest mistake so far: he decided to
entrust Pierce with the business of investing the money and
making sure that Fanny received her income: the deed was
signed in the Portland Convict Prison, where Agar was
awaiting transportation. But the slippery Pierce had no intention of investing the money; since Fanny had not been told
about it, he felt there was nothing to stop him from keeping it
for himself.

In due course, Agar wrote to Fanny, asking her to buy a silver
cup for his son, and another for Pierce's child; he also asked for
a geography book with a section on Australia. Pierce, he said,
would give her the money. Fanny – who was living with Pierce
and his wife – asked him for money, but Pierce refused. Fanny
stormed out, and went to the governor of Newgate prison,
where Agar had originally been held. She had suspected what
had been going on in the upper room with the furnace
(although she knew nothing of the robbery), and wanted to
make sure that Pierce went to jail too.

When a solicitor from the South-Eastern Railway arrived at
Portland prison, and told Agar what was happening to his
mistress and child, Agar was at first incredulous, then furious.
Encouraged by the solicitor, he went on to tell the full story of
the great bullion robbery. Pierce was arrested, and thousands
of pounds were found buried under his front step and hidden
in his pantry.

On 12 January 1857, Pierce, Tester and Burgess stood in front
of the judge at the Bailey, and were duly sentenced – Burgess
and Tester to fourteen years transportation to Botany Bay, and
Pierce – amazingly enough – to a mere two years; Pierce had
been charged as a member of the railway company, which he
was not, and a lawyer was able to obtain a shorter sentence on
this technicality. The judge said some extremely harsh words at
his sentencing, but could do nothing about it. At least the judge
succeeded in restoring Agar's money to Fanny Kay, who
thereupon became rich.

Agar served five years of his sentence and was released,
whereupon he married Fanny Kay. Unfortunately, he returned
to crime, and was transported once more to Botany Bay. Shortly

before his death, a convict who had recently arrived told him that he had become a legend in the London underworld; Agar groaned: "That means nothing at all."

Fanny herself died penniless in a workhouse. What happened to Pierce is not known, except that he was badly beaten up after he was released from jail – no doubt at Agar's request.

Tester, at least, succeeded in making good; after being released from prison in Australia, he started a highly successful grocery business, and ended a wealthy man.

The Case of Orrock's Chisel

Unlike the previous two cases, the case that follows is of a burglary that went appallingly wrong. But it has become one of the great classics of Victorian detection.

On 1 December 1882, the cobbled, gaslit streets of east London were wrapped in choking fog as a young constable set out from Dalston police station on a beat that took him down a narrow thoroughfare called Ashwin Street. As he turned the corner, he came to a sudden halt as he saw a man placing a lantern on top of the wall outside the Baptist chapel, and beginning to scramble over. PC Cole took a swift step forward, laid his hand on the man's shoulder, and asked: "What do you think you're doing?" For a moment, the man – who seemed little more than a youth – looked as if he was going to resist; then he changed his mind and agreed to "go quietly". But PC Cole and his captive had only gone as far as the pub on the corner when the man broke loose and ran. Cole ran after him and grabbed him by the left arm; as he did so, the man reached into his pocket, pulled out a revolver, and fired three shots. A woman who was walking towards them screamed and fled; as she ran, she heard another shot. Moments later, she encountered two policeman in Dalston Lane, and led them back to the scene of the shooting. PC Cole was lying on the pavement outside the Baptist chapel, his head in the gutter; a trickle of blood ran from the bullet hole behind his left ear. He died five minutes after being admitted to the local German Hospital.

Inspector Glass, who took charge of the case, ordered a search of the area where the policeman had been found; on the wall of the Baptist chapel, the burglar had left his dark lantern; behind the railings, a chisel, a jemmy, and a wooden wedge had ben left on the ground. The only other clue was a black billycock hat, which the burglar had lost in the course of the struggle. The woman who had seen him running away described him as short and slightly built; another witness gave the same description.

There was one man in the Dalston police station who believed he knew the identity of the murderer. Only minutes before Cole had arrested the burglar, Police Sergeant Cobb had been walking along Ashwin Street with another sergeant, Branwell, when they had noticed a man standing under a streetlamp. Cobb recognized him as a young cabinetmaker named Tom Orrock, and when he saw the policeman, he looked furtive and uncomfortable. Orrock had no criminal record, but he kept bad company – thugs and professional criminals – and it seemed a reasonable assumption that he would one day try his hand at crime. As they passed Orrock that night, Cobb had been tempted to arrest him for loitering. But standing under a streetlamp was no crime, and Cobb had decided against it. Now he regretted it, and was inclined to blame himself for the death of PC Cole, who was a young married man with children.

Informed of Sergeant Cobb's suspicions, Inspector Glass was inclined to be dismissive – to begin with, he disliked Cobb, regarding him as too unimaginative and too conscientious. But he ordered Tom Orrock – who was nineteen – to be brought in for an identity parade. When the witnesses who had glimpsed Cole's captive failed to identify him, Orrock was released. Soon after that, he disappeared from his usual haunts.

Months after the murder, the investigation was at a standstill. The clues seemed to lead nowhere. The hat bore no marks of identification, and the chisels and the large wooden wedge might have belonged to anybody. But the bullets looked more promising. All four had been recovered – two from the policeman's skull, one from his truncheon, another from the truncheon case. They were unusual in that they had been fired from a revolver that was little more than a toy – the kind of thing ladies sometimes carried in their handbags. The science of ballistics was unknown in 1882, but the rarity of the gun suggested that it might one day provide a valuable piece of evidence.

When studied through a magnifying glass, one of the chisels also yielded an interesting clue. A series of scratches near the handle looked like an attempt at writing, probably with a sharp nail. And when the chisel was photographed for the case file, the letters could be seen more clearly, and they resolved themselves into a capital R, followed by what looked like an o, a c, and a k. Rock. Could it be short for Orrock? Cobb began calling in every tool shop in the Hackney and Dalston area, asking if they recognized the chisels, but met with no success.

Cobb refused to give up. A year after the murder, he was talking with an acquaintance of the missing cabinetmaker named Henry Mortimer, who occasionally acted as a police informer. And Mortimer's rambling discourse suddenly arrested the sergeant's attention when he mentioned that Tom Orrock had possessed a revolver – a nickel-plated, pin-fire miniature affair, Orrock had seen it advertised in the *Exchange and Mart*, and he and Mortimer had gone to Tottenham to purchase it from the owner for the sum of half a guinea. They had also been accompanied by two men named Miles and Evans, both professional – if unsuccessful – criminals. On the way home, the four men had stopped on Tottenham Marshes and used a tree for target practice. At Cobb's request, Mortimer accompanied him to Tottenham and showed him the tree. The following day, Cobb returned alone, and dug some bullets out of the tree with his penknife. One of them was relatively undamaged, and was obviously of the same calibre as the bullets that had been fired at PC Cole.

Now Cobb was sure he had his man, and that view was confirmed when Mortimer admitted that Orrock had virtually confessed to killing PC Cole. When Mortimer had expressed disbelief, Orrock had replied: "If they can prove it against me, I'm willing to take the consequences." This is precisely what Cobb now set out to do.

The first step was to lay the new evidence before his immediate superior. Inspector Glass was still inclined to be indifferent, but he agreed to ask for help from New Scotland Yard in trying to trace the shop that had sold the chisel. And, it was the Scotland Yard team that finally located a woman named Preston, a widow who carried on her husband's tool-sharpening business. She recognized the chisel because she always made a practice of scratching the name of the owner near the handle; she remembered the young man who brought in the chisel for grinding had given the name Orrock, which she had shortened to "Rock".

Now at last, they had the kind of evidence that might impress a jury. All that remained was to locate Tom Orrock. Scotland Yard was asked to circulate his description to every police station in the country. This would normally have brought prompt results, for in those days before the population explosion, most police stations were aware of any strangers who had moved into their district. So when another year failed to bring news of the wanted man, Glass was inclined to assume either that he was dead or that he had gone abroad. Cobb refused to believe it. And one day he had an inspiration. One place where a man could "lie low" with reasonable chance of escaping recognition was prison. Once again, Cobb began painstaking enquiries – enquiries that entitle him to be ranked with Canler and Macé as a distinguished practitioner of the needle-in-the-haystack method. And he soon learned that a man answering Orrock's description had been serving a term for burglary in Coldbath Fields for the past two years. Coldbath Fields, in Farringdon Road, was one of London's newer prisons, and had a reputation for severity. The name under which the prisoner was serving his sentence was not Tom Orrock, and when he was summoned to the governor's office, the man denied that he was called Orrock or had ever been in Dalston. Sergeant Cobb attended an identity parade, and had to admit reluctantly that he was unable to recognize Orrock among the seven uniformed convicts who now faced him. But as the men filed out again, they passed under a light, and Cobb suddenly recognized the profile of the man he had last seen standing under a gaslamp in Dalston more that two years earlier. He stepped forward and laid his hand on the shoulder of Thomas Henry Orrock.

Now it was a question of building up the web of circumstantial evidence. Orrock's sister, Mrs Bere, was questioned, and admitted that on the night of the murder her brother had returned home with a torn trouser leg, and without his hat, claiming that he had been involved in a street brawl. Orrock's two friends Miles and Evans were questioned separately. They admitted that they had spent the day of the murder drinking with Tom Orrock in various pubs, and that soon after 10 o'clock in the evening, the three had been in the Railway Tavern in Ashwin Street when Orrock boasted that he intended to embark on a criminal career by "cracking a crib" – stealing the silver plate of the Baptist church, which he attended regularly, and taking it to his brother-in-law to be melted down. Orrock had then left the pub. Not long after, Miles and Evans heard the sound of revolver shots, but claimed they had taken them for fog signals. All the same, they had left the pub and been among the crowd that gathered around the wounded policeman. Three weeks later, when a reward of £200 had been offered for information leading to the capture of the murderer, Orrock went to Evans and begged him not to inform on him; Evans swore that he would not "ruck" on a comrade even for a thousand pounds.

But all this was merely hearsay evidence. The vital link between Tom Orrock and the murder of PC Cole was the revolver. This had disappeared – one witness said that Orrock admitted throwing it into the River Lea. But the police were able to track down the man who had sold Orrock the revolver – his name was McLellan – and he unhesitatingly identified bullets and cartridge cases as being the calibre of those he had sold to a young man in the last week of November 1882, one week before the murder. McLellan's description of the purchaser fitted Thomas Henry Orrock.

A few decades later, all this corroborative evidence would have been unnecessary. Examination of the bullets under a comparison microscope would have proved that the bullet found in the tree at Tottenham was identical with the bullet that killed PC Cole.

But in the year 1884, no one had yet thought of studying the pattern of rifle marks on the side of a bullet; it would be another five years before Edmond Locard's mentor, Professor Alexandre Lacassagne, would provide the evidence to convict a murderer by studying bullet grooves under a microscope. Nevertheless, when Tom Orrock came to trial in September 1884, it was the bullet evidence that carried most weight with the jury. The bullet found in the tree at Tottenham was "precisely similar to the one found in the brain of the dead constable", said the prosecution. "If the prisoner purchased the revolver, where was it? A man did not throw away a revolver that cost him 10 shillings without good cause." The jury was convinced. On Saturday 20 September 1884, Thomas Orrock was convicted of the murder of PC Cole and sentenced to be hanged. The jury added a special recommendation to Sergeant Cobb for his persistence in tracking down the killer. But the chronicler relates that, in after years, Inspector Glass liked to claim credit for capturing Orrock, and "has often remarked that the man who in reality put the police in possession of their information to this day is ignorant that he disclosed to them this knowledge" – from which it would appear that Glass continued to resent the success of his subordinate and to deny him any of the credit.

THE AGE OF DETECTION

Fingerprints

The greatest single advance in crime-fighting was the discovery of fingerprints. As long ago as the 1820s, it had been noticed that no two fingerprints are ever alike. But what good was that when there was no method of classifying them? This had to wait until the 1890s, when Sir Francis Galton and Edward Henry finally worked out a way of classifying them according to "loops" "arches" and "whorls". But it was not until 1902 that Henry set up a fingerprint system at Scotland Yard. It proved its value on Derby Day, 1902, when the police were able to prove that twenty-nine arrested men were pickpockets with previous convictions. Later the same year, a burglar named Henry Jackson was caught when he left his fingerprints on some fresh paint in a house in Denmark Hill.

The first major crime solved by fingerprints in England was committed by two brothers named Alfred and Edward Stratton; early in the morning of 27 March 1905, they broke into a shop in Deptford, East London, hoping to find a large sum of money. They knocked out the shopkeeper and his wife with a jemmy, hitting them so violently that both died. But Alfred Stratton left behind a fingerprint on the cash box – in which there had only been a few pounds – and both brothers were hanged.

The Great Bertillon

In France, fingerprinting took longer to establish itself; this was largely because the French had already invented their own method of criminal identification, called "Bertillonage", after its inventor, Alphonse Bertillon.

Bertillon's story would be ideal for Hollywood. He compared photographs of criminals to see if there was some way of classifying noses and faces. Then he thought it might be a good idea to take measurements of criminals when they were arrested – height, reach, circumference of head, height sitting down, length of left hand, left foot, left leg – Bertillon chose the left-hand side because it was unlikely to be affected by work. He was subject to constipation, stomach upsets, headaches and nosebleeds; but he had a certain stubbornness that made him ignore the knowing smiles of colleagues. A doctor named Adolphe Quetelet had asserted that the chances of two people being exactly the same height are four to one. If that was so, and the same thing applied to the other statistics, then you needed only two or three measurements of each criminal to raise the odds to a hundred to one. When the prefect of police ignored Bertillon's letter about this method, Bertillon bought himself a set of filing cards, and started to work on his own, staying in the office until late at night. Macé revealed a lack of insight when he read Bertillon's report, and said it was too theoretical. The prefect, Andrieux, told Bertillon to stop making a nuisance of himself. And three years went by before Bertillon could persuade a new prefect Jean Camecasse to give him an interview. Camecasse was as sceptical as his predecessor, but he was impressed by the clerk's persistence. He told Bertillon that they would introduce his method experimentally for three months. This was obviously absurd; it would take more than three months to build up a file, and a method like Bertillon's depended on accumulation. He knew his only chance lay in working on and praying for luck. His card index swelled at the rate of a few hundred a month. But with more than twenty thousand criminals in Paris alone, the chances of identifying one of them was low. Towards the end of the third month, Bertillon had towards two thousand cards. Theoretically, his chance of identification was one in ten – fairly high. But it must be remembered that a large number of his criminals were sent to jail, often for years, so most of his file was lying fallow, so to speak.

On 20 February 1883, luck was with him. His system led him to identify a petty criminal who had been measured three months earlier. It was a very small triumph, but it was enough to make Camecasse decide to allow the experiment to continue. This was not far-sightedness. The post of prefect was a political appointment; Camecasse was hoping for fame. Unfortunately, a new prefect had been appointed by the time Bertillon became a celebrity; but history allows Camecasse the credit. As the file swelled, identification became more frequent. Before long, it averaged one a day.

Bertillon's system was soon being used by most of the major police forces of the world. And when fingerprinting arrived, Bertillon immediately incorporated this into his system, making sure that the file on every criminal included his fingerprints. Unfortunately, Bertillon refused to face up to the truth: that fingerprinting had completely superseded his own methods.

On 22 July 1934, John Dillinger, a farm boy turned bank robber, went to the Biograph cinema in Chicago with his girlfriend Polly Hamilton and her friend Anna Sage to see Clark Gable in *Manhattan Melodrama*. Anna Sage, who was under threat of deportation, had decided to try and curry favour with the authorities by betraying the gangster, and was wearing a bright red dress. As they left the cinema, FBI agents surrounded him, and as Dillinger sprinted away, three agents fired, killing him.

But did he really die? The autopsy notes reveal that the corpse's eyes were brown; Dillinger's were blue. The dead man suffered from a heart condition; Dillinger did not. Neither did the corpse possess various marks and scars that Dillinger was known to have on his body.

Crime writer Jay Robert Nash has argued that the dead man was a small-time hoodlum called Jimmy Lawrence, and that J. Edgar Hoover was too embarrassed to acknowledge the mistake. Lawrence, he believes, was "set up" by the "lady in red" so Dillinger could escape. A fellow gang member, Blackie Audett, claims that Dillinger married and escaped to Oregon. The rest of Dillinger's gang was wiped out not long after their leader's "death".

He refused to take the obvious step and classify fingerprints so they could be identified immediately. If a French policeman wished to identify a burglar who had left his fingerprint at the scene of a crime, he had to go through every single file until he found it. It was the sheer cumbersomeness of this method that led to Bertillon's downfall.

The Theft of the Mona Lisa

On 21 August 1911, someone stole Leonardo's *Mona Lisa* from the Louvre. It should, of course, have been a total impossibility, with so many guards; but it happened on a Monday, when the Louvre was closed to the public. The painting, which is on a panel, was housed in a case with a glass cover. This case was found, empty, on the service stairs.

Bertillon was immediately summoned, and careful examination revealed fingerprints. A fingerprint is made by sweat – that is to say, the skin's secretions which include fatty substances; this comes from sweat pores along the papillary ridges, and also from contact of the fingertips with parts of the body where there are sebaceous glands, such as the face. Latent or invisible prints on smooth surfaces can be made visible by dusting the surface with fine powder, such as talc, aluminium, or lead powder. (On white surfaces, such as china, a black powder is used.) And when Bertillon dusted the glass with powder, he realized with delight that the thief had left behind a good set of fingerprints. And now if the thief happened to have a criminal record, it should be a matter of the utmost simplicity to identify him . . .

And if the theft had taken place in London or Berlin or Madrid, it would have been. But Bertillon's fingerprints were still unclassified. And since 1902, when he had solved the Scheffer case, he had accumulated more than 100,000 additional cards. So, in fact, it was an impossible task. Bertillon and his assistants searched for weeks and months – Bertillon was such an obsessive that he probably went through every card individually. But after a few hundred prints, the eyes grow tired, and the attention flags. Bertillon must have ended day after day in a state of exhausted defeat. Nothing could have brought home to him more clearly that his system was a waste of time, and that he should have adopted Henry's fingerprint classification, as improved by Inspector Collins.

Two years later, the thief was arrested in Florence. The police had been tipped off by an art dealer named Alfredo Geri, who had been offered the painting in a letter signed "Leonard". Leonard proved to be an Italian house painter named Vicenzo Perrugia, and he was carrying the *Mona Lisa* with him. His story of the theft caused astonishment, and some amusement at the expense of the Louvre authorities. The crime had not been planned. Perrugia had been a friend of a painter working in the Louvre, and the guards were familiar with him; they let him past without question. Finding himself quite alone in the Salon Carré with the famous painting, the temptation had been too much. He had simply lifted the case off the wall, walked down the service staircase, and extracted the painting, leaving his fingerprints on the glass. Then he had hidden the painting – which is small – beneath his smock and walked out unchallenged. For the next two years the *Mona Lisa* lay hidden under his bed.

John Dillinger 1934

But for Bertillon, the final bitterness must have been that he had Perrugia's card in his file, for Perrugia was a petty thief who had been arrested several times.

Significantly, in this same year 1913, Bertillon was found to be suffering from pernicious anaemia; he died in February 1914, and France immediately accepted the same fingerprint classification as the rest of the world.

The Great Pearl Robbery

In fact, fingerprint evidence played no part in the most famous robbery of 1913, which was a kind of throw-back to the "great" robberies of the Victorian age.

The story begins on 16 July 1913, in the office of a diamond merchant called Max Mayer, in Hatton Garden. Mr Mayer was anxious to go away on holiday, but first he wanted to replace in his safe his most precious possession: a pearl necklace worth £130,000, which he had built up over many years. The necklace had been in Paris, in the hands of a dealer named Henri Salomons, who had been showing it to a wealthy customer. Unfortunately, the deal had fallen through, and the necklace had been returned back to Mr Mayer by registered post. This was not the first time that the famous necklace – whose existence was known to the whole of the jewellery trade – had been back and forth across the Channel, and so far, it had been perfectly safe.

But when Mr Mayer opened the sealed package on that July morning just before the First World War, he was shocked to find that it contained only several lumps of sugar. Scotland Yard was notified immediately, and a telegram despatched to M. Salomons in Paris. He immediately rushed to London, and confirmed that he and his wife had packed the pearls themselves, and sent them from the local post office in the Rue de Provence. Salomons was above suspicion. So it was obvious that the necklace had been stolen in transit. The sugar lumps were French, which suggested that the substitution had taken place in France, probably on the mail train. Clearly, the theft had been carefully planned, for the package had been re-sealed with identical string, and with sealing-wax that bore Mr Mayer's seal, MM.

The Paris police were also informed, and immediately began tracing the passage of the necklace from the post office to the Cross-Channel ferry. They ended by admitting their bafflement. There was simply no point at which the registered package could have been opened.

Fortunately for Mr Mayer, the necklace was insured. Nevertheless, it was his most precious possession, and he longed – against all the odds – for its return. Mr Mayer therefore offered a £10,000 reward for its recovery.

To the delight of Scotland Yard, this worked. They received a letter from an Antwerp jewel dealer named Samuel Brandstater, who said he and his cousin Meyer Quadratstein – another diamond merchant – had been offered the necklace. In due course, Brandstater and Quatratstein arrived at Scotland Yard. Brandstater then explained that he had been contacted by a relative from London, a diamond broker named Leiser Gutwirth, who had offered him the pearl necklace – admitting it was stolen – for one and a half million francs. Brandstater had offered 300,000 francs, which Gutwirth had indignantly rejected. So Brandstater told him he would try and raise more money, and Gutwirth had returned to London.

So now Scotland Yard knew the name of at least one of the thieves. And now that Brandstater had betrayed his relative, they could rely on his help to recover the necklace and earn the reward. But the whole transaction obviously required care. If the thieves suspected they were betrayed, they would scatter, and Mr Mayer would never see the return of his necklace.

Now began the long and nerve-racking business that Chief Inspector Ward of Scotland Yard – who was in charge of the case – called "playing the fish". First the informer Brandstater met Gutwirth at Charing Cross station, and raised his offer to half a millon francs. Gutwirth replied angrily: "Go back to Paris. The necklace cannot be bought at less than a million francs." Brandstater said he would try and raise more money, and agreed to meet Gutwirth again.

And so it went on – meetings at Gutwirth's home, at Lyons tea-shops, and various hotels. Usually, two policemen were sitting a few tables away, carefully observing everything. One by one, the other members of the gang revealed themselves. They were all "diamond merchants" who were also known to the police as high-powered crooks: Simon Silverman, Joseph

Grizzard and James Lockett. The police (and insurance company) enlisted the aid of a Paris diamond merchant named Max Spanier, who agreed to meet the thieves and make them an offer. At one meeting in a Strand tea-shop, Grizzard asked Lockett: "Have you got a match?", and Lockett tossed him a match box. Grizzard opened this and revealed three beautiful pearls lying in cotton wool. This was merely to prove that they really had the pearl necklace.

To convince the crooks that he was serious, Spanier bought two of the pearls for 50,000 francs each, and promised to buy the rest in a few days' time. Spanier, Brandstater and his cousin Quadratstein knew they were taking their lives in their hands every time they met the crooks in some hotel room, and the police provided them with loaded revolvers.

Unfortunately, the members of the Scotland Yard team were not all equally skilful at the art of shadowing. One day, the crooks spotted four obvious plain-clothes policemen watching the hotel. They lost no time in fleeing to the Continent, and for a while it looked as if the clumsiness of the police had destroyed months of patient work. But after a few weeks, the crooks were lulled once more into a sense of security, and when Spanier told

Captured booze during the Prohibition – 1921

them that he had a wealthy Indian prince who was interested in the necklace, they allowed themselves to be lured back to London. This time, Scotland Yard pounced immediately. It was at the British Museum tube station, and Gutwirth, Silverman, Lockett and Grizzard were all present when the police quietly took their arms and told them they were under arrest.

But now once again there was dismay at Scotland Yard. The thieves were not carrying the pearls. And although the police had enough evidence to convict them – the two pearls sold to Spanier – the case would certainly be counted a failure if the rest of the necklace was not recovered.

Then, totally unexpectedly, the necklace turned up – lying in the gutter in St Paul's Road, Highbury. A piano-maker named Horne picked up a match box wrapped in paper, and found that it contained some white beads. He took them to the local police station, where the police agreed they were probably valueless. When he got home, Horne found that one of the beads had fallen into his pocket, and in the local pub, offered it to anyone who wanted to buy it for the price of a pint – one penny. No one did. And later, Horne lost it. In fact the missing pearl was the largest in the necklace, and was worth thousands of pounds. It was never recovered.

The Highbury police finally realized that the box of "beads" might be the missing pearls that everyone was talking about, and asked someone from Scotland Yard to come and look at them. And so Mr Mayer finally received back most of his necklace, minus its largest pearl.

Now the story slowly emerged. The gang, led by Silverman, often ate in a Hatton Garden restaurant known as the "Diamond Club", where diamond brokers met and talked shop. It was there that they planned the coup – almost certainly overhearing Mr Mayer telling someone that his necklace was on its way back from Paris. But how could they get their hands on it? The answer was simple and obvious. When the necklace was on its way back, in a registered parcel bearing French stamps, the postman merely had to be bribed to take it to Silverman's office, where it would be opened and re-sealed. A craftsman had even made a replica of Mayer's MM seal for a shilling. Sugar would be substituted for the pearls – French sugar, to give the impression that the substitution had taken place in France – and the postman would then deliver it to Mr Mayer's office, and collect his receipt.

The gang refused to admit that there had been a postman

involved, but Gutwirth had told the informer Brandstater that £400 had been set aside as "expenses", to pay two postmen £200 each. No postman was ever charged as an accomplice.

The gang was let off surprisingly lightly. Lockett and Grizzard received seven years each, Silverman (who planned it) a mere five years, and Gutwirth only eighteen months, because he had no police record.

The final puzzle remains: how did the pearls end up in a London gutter? The answer, almost certainly, is that the gang had given them into the care of some accomplice, who heard that the thieves had been arrested, and suspected that he was next on the list. When the piano-maker Horne picked up the packet, he saw a man and a woman just climbing on to a nearby bus, and called to them to ask if they had dropped it; they did not reply. No one has ever learned whether the pearls were dropped in the gutter by accident or design, and Mr Mayer certainly did not care one way or the other.

The First Cat-Burglar

Fingerprinting had the effect of making burglars more careful. The old-fashioned Bill Sikes, with his checked cap and jemmy, was soon an endangered species, and a new and more sophisticated type of burglar appeared on the scene. The first to draw the attention of Scotland Yard is described by ex-Superintendent Robert Fabian, in his book *Fabian of the Yard*.

> Robert Augustus Delaney will be remembered at Scotland Yard as the man who started a new fashion in crime that was to become known as "cat-burglary". Delaney trod the crags and precipices of Park Lane's roofs with nonchalant skill. Wearing faultless evening clothes, he could apparently climb the sheer side of a house. I think he imagined himself a kind of acrobatic Raffles.
>
> He certainly made the great criminals of the past – like Charles Peace, who carried a collapsible ladder disguised as a bundle of firewood – look clumsy. In

his pocket was a slender steel tool like a putty-knife for slipping window catches – it could also open jewel-boxes. Around his trimly tailored waist coiled four yards of black silk rope. Two men died trying to imitate Delaney: "Irish Mac" impaled himself on spiked railings, and "The Doctor" – who should have known better – fell forty feet from a portico in St James's. He had £8,000 of jewels in his pocket and crawled grimly for two miles before dying.

In 1924, when the rich and noble residents of Park Lane were trooping splendidly in to dinner, Delaney would crouch beneath their windows, unwinding his gossamer rope. The tinkle of polished cutlery . . . or was it the clink of a dulled steel hook catching in the balcony drain gutter . . . and Gussie Delaney robbed their bedrooms like a wraith and departed before coffee wafted fragrantly into the victim's drawing-room and cigar smoke hazed the wine.

The thefts were reported to us in Vine Street, where I was a probationer detective fresh from training school. We questioned indignant flunkeys, far haughtier than their masters, but they knew nothing, and next week another robbery from a Park Lane bedroom – and so on at weekly intervals.

It was not really my case, nor was my probationer pal, Tommy Symes (now Chief Inspector), assigned to it. One night we sat stirring police-canteen coffee, waiting to go out on a routine club raid, but the Park Lane mystery burglaries intrigued us more.

"One each week for the past five weeks," I said. "A total of £30,000. He should be ready to retire soon. And none of us will have caught a whiff of him!"

Tommy leaned forward. "Keep it to yourself," he murmured. "I've been putting in some spare-time work on those burglaries – I've been making a sort of map . . ."

I had to laugh. "So have I, Tommy!" We compared efforts, and found that both of us had the same idea – a map of the Park Lane district, indicating those houses where residents were known to be outstandingly wealthy and where the dining-room could be kept under observation.

"And it looks as if he's working in some sort of sequence, too," I said quickly. "See – top end of Park Lane, then the bottom end, then St James's. Fourth burglary top of Park Lane again, fifth burglary at the bottom end . . ."

"And the next one around here!" Tommy's broad thumb covered Arlington Street at the Ritz Hotel corner. "It might be tonight," he added.

We left the canteen and went into the CID main room. The duty inspector called: "Oh, you two – that club job – it's off for tonight. We shan't be needing you."

We looked at each other. It was a crisp, starlit October evening, just gone dark. "Care for a bit of fresh air, Tommy?" I asked casually. He grinned. "Green Park it is!"

Concealed in the shadow and shrubbery of Green Park, we knew we could keep watch on the backs of all those tempting mansions by the Ritz corner. Three hours later we were chilled, cramped, disap-

---

For a brief period in the 1920s, the gang led by brothers Matt and George Kimes and Ray Terrill was one of the most successful in America. The members were all farm boys, many of whom had decided that bootlegging was more profitable than ploughing.

Terrill persuaded the Kimes brothers that bank robbery would be even more profitable than bootlegging, and so it proved. A raid at the Farmer's National Bank in Beggs, Oklahoma, netted $20,000. They were captured when their car hit a tree but Terrill and Matt Kimes escaped and robbed the same bank again, this time taking $18,000.

In Pampa, Texas, in 1927, the gang learned that the huge old iron bank safe was almost uncrackable, so they rolled it outside – while customers were held up by other gang members – loaded it on to a truck and drove away with it. It proved to contain $35,000.

Matt Kimes was caught soon after this and sentenced to life. Terrill teamed up with Herman Barker, eldest of Ma Barker's sons, but in September 1927, after a shoot-out during which they escaped, Barker was found dead in a ditch. (Ma Barker always claimed he had been "executed" by the police.) Terrill was captured soon after and spent most of his life behind bars.

pointed. Nothing had happened.

The next night was cloudy. Once again Tommy took the Green Park bandstand, while I waited in the garden behind Wimborne House. Faintly we heard the austere chimes of dinner gongs from the big mansions. One by one, bedroom lights winked out from costly chandeliers. I fumbled for a peppermint and stared into the shadows until my eyes felt aglow like a stoat's . . . A dark figure was creeping along the nearest garden boundary. Quick, agile as a cat, it vaulted the high railing and disappeared.

We next saw the shadowy intruder flit across one of the white balconies. How did he get up there? Tommy, flattened against the wall beneath the balcony, turned as I crept near him.

"Did you see that?" His voice was hoarse with suppressed excitement. "Like a blooming cat!"

"I'll wait for him here," I whispered. "You give the alarm inside."

The lights began to flash on in each of the spacious upstairs rooms as Tommy Symes raced through the bedrooms and corridors, with alarmed householders behind him. I heard excited voices – then the re-peated thud of sturdy shoulders at an equally sturdy thick mahogany door. The thief had jammed it with a wooden wedge, ready for such an emergency. He reappeared on the balcony, made no attempt to descend into the garden, but ran light-footed along the balcony, leapt a nine-foot gap to the next, and alighted soundlessly. He threw something up on to the gutter of the neighbouring roof and in six seconds was across the slanted tiles, away . . . For hours we scoured the district, but our quarry had vanished among the chimneys. All I had seen was the glint of a diamond stud in what was obviously a dress-shirt front.

The Inspector was scathing. "You really must forgive me for intruding upon your beautiful part-nership," he said. "But I would like to know about all this before it happened, so we could have one or two more men on the scene – " Upon me he cast a withering glance. "You say you saw him – but you can't describe him – except he climbed like a cat – he didn't have fur by any chance?''

Afterwards I said solemnly: ''Tommy, we've got to catch that blighter – that cat-burglar – and rub butter on his paws!'' That was not all I said.

We went to the scene of the previous night's burglary. Jewels valued £2,000 were missing, which didn't make us feel better. By daylight that leap from one balcony to its neighbour seemed no less remarkable. We measured it, Tommy throwing the end of a tape-measure across the space to me. And as I leaned to catch it I noticed something . . .

It was a footprint on the balcony ledge – so small and so exquisitely pointed in the toe that it might have been made by a woman's dancing shoe. We got a ladder and in the soft mould of the drainage gutter on the roof found another imprint of the wedge-shaped shoe, the smooth tiles showing clearly the porous tread of crêpe soles. ''Rubber-soled evening pumps!'' said Tommy. ''He'd need to get those made specially!''

I spent the day visiting those exclusive shoe emporiums of Jermyn Street, York Street (as it was then), Dover Street and Shepherd's Market, where craftsmen took pride in hand-made shoes to suit clients' whims. In Albemarle Street I was lucky.

''Most remarkable,'' said the proprietor earnestly, ''that any gentleman should require crêpe rubber soles, however thin, on patent-leather evening shoes. I remember strongly advising the gentleman against it – but he was insistent.'' The order-book showed name and address as: ''R. Radd, 52, Half Moon Street. Five guineas – paid.''

A good address. I went to Half Moon Street, but the numbers stopped at 42, and there had never been a 52. A stranger to the district would have been unlikely to know that. It seemed worth investigating the bars and lounges around Half Moon Street. Those were the days of evening clothes for gentlemen in London's West End, so my laundry bill became staggering . . . and the days passed.

More than a week afterwards I walked into the Range Bar. My dress shoes clacked like sabots on the polished parquet corridor. A man passed me. He wore good evening clothes, a diamond sparkled in his laundered shirt-bosom, and as he walked it occurred to me that his feet were making no noise at all! I glanced quickly – and saw tiny pointed toes . . . Outside he hesitated at the taxi-rank, then decided to walk. I jumped into the cab at the tail of the rank.

"I'm a police officer. Follow that man. Don't put your flag down. I'll lie on the floor."

We rolled after the man with the pointed shoes – round the corner from Half Moon Street, up another side street, then: "He's gone into No. 43, Gov'nor," said the taxi-driver.

"Right," I said. "Don't stop. Keep going to New Scotland Yard."

I took the lift to the Criminal Record Office, but there they knew nothing about the address. I searched some picked photo files. There was no record on the man. Still . . . back at Vine Street I made a report.

For two days we trailed our man without success. Then he strolled down to Hatton Garden, met a man in a café, and went with him in a taxi to Southgate, where they entered a comfortable-looking private house. After about twenty minutes the man with the pointed shoes came out alone. I left a colleague to make inquiries at the house and followed him back to No. 43.

In a brown van a concealed spark morse receiver buzzed and stuttered: "Inquiries at house in Southgate – occupier known – admits receiving jewellery – has just paid £800 – jewellery answers description of part proceeds from Park Lane thefts."

That did it. We called at No. 43, and a middle-aged woman answered the polished bell and regarded us haughtily. She was dressed pompously in rustling black, and a black taffeta ribbon at her throat held a cameo brooch.

"Have you a man living here . . .?" I described my suspect. The woman considered me as though she suspected some fault with the drains.

"That may well be Mr Delaney, who has the upstairs flat. Is he expecting you?"

I brushed past her. "We'll just find out!" I called

cheerfully from the stairway.

She gasped, "I think you're very rude!"

So did Mr Augustus Delaney, as his engraved name-plate described him, who looked up coolly as we entered without knocking. "What the blazes do you want?" His accent was slightly Canadian.

"Quite all right," I said, soothingly. "We're just looking for some money and jewellery. You don't mind, do you?" He stood up, suddenly pale, and then his mouth twitched into a wistful smile. "I suppose – it's too much to hope that you gentlemen are burglars?" The £800 was hidden under the mattress. Stolen jewels were concealed in the dressing-table, behind the drawer backs.

On his first conviction he received three years' penal servitude at the Old Bailey for those six Park Lane burglaries. That was in 1924. Would you like to know what this daring, well-educated and quick-witted young man did with the rest of his life and with that superb acrobat's body that fate had given him? By the time he died in Parkhurst Prison on 14 December 1948, he had spent twenty years in various gaols. In his brief intervals of freedom his pointed, immaculate shoes had scarcely time to become worn down at the heels!

The Count of Gramercy Park

Gerald Chapman, the "man prisons couldn't hold", the crook who wore tailor-made suits and spoke with a near-impeccable English accent, was regarded by the American public as a modern Robin Hood, and accordingly lionized. One writer speculates that his parents were comfortably off and that he had a good education. It was all untrue. Chapman was born in Brooklyn in 1890, of Irish parents, and had the usual criminal apprenticeship of petty theft and reformatories. When he was fourteen a judge prophesied he would end in the electric chair. In fact, he was hanged.

It was when he was eighteen, and was transferred from Sing Sing to Auburn, N.Y., that Chapman met a man he came to admire passionately, George "Dutch" Anderson, a graduate of Heidelberg and Uppsala Universities, who spoke several languages. (His real name was Ivan Dahl von Teller, and he was a Dane.) Anderson was a swindler and a "gentleman crook", and he advised Chapman to give up armed robbery and use his brains. Chapman began to educate himself with books and acquired an English accent.

Released from prison, he went back to robbery, and this time was so successful – for a time – that he was able to buy himself expensive clothes, rent a fashionable apartment, and dine in good restaurants. He decided that being a gentleman suited him. But in 1911 he received ten years for armed robbery, and was sent back to Sing Sing. There he became friendly with a man named Charles Loerber, who was in for armed robbery, and who was totally lacking in any kind of finesse.

In 1919, Chapman, Anderson and Loerber were all paroled. Chapman joined Anderson on a tour of the Midwest, and was soon convinced of the soundness of Anderson's methods when they managed to acquire a fortune of $100,000 through confidence trickery. Chapman rented an apartment in New York's exclusive Gramercy Park. Here he called himself G. Vincent Colwell, and acquired a pretty English "wife" called Betty, who was as much a born lady as he was a born gentleman.

It was Charles Loerber who persuaded Chapman to return to armed robbery. He had been observing the mail trucks on Wall Street, and noted that they had minimum security, and that their wire-mesh sides gave a good view of the amount of mail they were carrying.

On the cold, foggy night of 14 October 1921, Chapman, Anderson and Loerber, driving a stolen black touring car, followed one of these post office vans along Wall Street, which becomes deserted after the offices close. Suddenly Loerber accelerated and pulled alongside the mail van as it halted at a red light. Within seconds, Chapman was on the running board, holding a gun to the driver's ribs. This was the dangerous part, when someone might have seen him and given the alarm; fortunately, no one did, and he pulled open the door and sank into the passenger seat. The driver, Frank Havernack, obeyed his instructions to pull over into a quiet side street – Leonard Street. The stolen car pulled up behind them, and Anderson demanded the keys to the van. Then, while Chapman sat with his gun in the driver's ribs, Anderson and Loerber located five sacks of registered mail and tossed it into the car. They drove off leaving Havernack tied up, with a mail bag over his head.

In a hideout across the river – a farm belonging to an uncle of Loerber's – they opened the sacks, and counted out the money and bonds. It amounted to $2,643,720 – the biggest haul so far in American criminal history. More than three hundred thousand of this was in cash, and more than twice that amount in traveller's cheques.

While the police were searching frantically for leads, and Federal agents kept a watch on all the ports, G. Vincent Colwell was back at 12 Gramercy Park, throwing parties to which his wealthy neighbours were invited. He even organized the theft of an expensive pearl necklace from one of his guests. Then the driver identified Chapman and Anderson from "mugshots", and their pictures appeared in "wanted" posters in every post office. But still no one thought of looking in Gramercy Park. Chapman, impeccably dressed, with a neat moustache, often stood in front of the wanted poster, and reflected how little this rough-looking character looked like Vincent Colwell.

Prohibition had arrived. Chapman and Anderson invested some of their money in the bootleg business, and prospered. And in another robbery at an American Express office in Niagara Falls, the gang added a further $70,000 to their capital.

Loerber was their undoing. He was picked up while trying to "fence" some of the securities, and gave away his associates in exchange for a lighter sentence. On 3 July 1922, Chapman and Anderson were arrested. But while Chapman sat alone with a detective in the Federal Building on Broadway, he pretended to have some kind of attack, slumping in his chair and gasping for water. As the detective rushed out of the room, Chapman rushed out of the window, ran along a narrow cornice – his hands shackled – and climbed in at another window. But he was soon located and re-arrested. The escape attempt made the headlines, and Chapman was delighted to see himself described as a modern Robin Hood.

In the Atlanta penitentiary, faced with a twenty-five-year sentence, Chapman swore he would escape. The governor assured him he wouldn't. But with immense patience, Chapman stole small pieces of cord from the workshops and braided them into a rope, which he buried in a flower bed. From stolen cutlery he made a file and a crude hook. Then he began to complain of stomach pains. After several days he was admitted to hospital for observation. There he was placed in a room with a "trusty" named John Grey. He soon persuaded Grey to join him in an escape attempt. They filed through the bars, severed an electric cable – plunging the prison into darkness – then used a rope of bed sheets to get to the ground. Five minutes later, both men were over the wall.

Two days later, Chapman was tracked by bloodhounds as he lay in a field; as he tried to run away, he was shot twice, then handcuffed.

In a civilian hospital in Athens, Betty came to visit him. She succeeded in smuggling in a gun, and Chapman used it to force an intern to give him his white coat. Then, after binding and gagging the intern, he walked out of the hospital and climbed into the waiting car driven by a fellow-crook, Charlie Wolfe. Betty joined him a few minutes later and they drove away – and vanished.

In fact, they made their way to a hideout in Muncie, Indiana, where Chapman recovered from his wounds in the home of Dr Harry Spickerman – a man he had met in Atlanta. Then he persuaded a farmer named Ben Hance to take him in as a boarder. There, in January 1924, he was joined by Dutch Anderson, who made an equally remarkable escape from Atlanta. Anderson had managed to get himself assigned to the tubercular unit, and was housed in a tent in the prison grounds – the notion being that plenty of fresh air would cure tuberculosis. He and a number of other prisoners had tunnelled their way sixty feet under the prison yard and wall.

Chapman now stole himself an expensive car from a show-room in Stanton, and changed the numberplates. Then he and Anderson drove east, committing burglaries and robberies as they went along. Their aim was to set up in the counterfeiting business, but in New Britain, Connecticut, they decided that the department store of Davidson and Leventhal looked as if it would be easy to burgle, and that early on Sunday morning would be a good time, when the safe would be full of Saturday's takings. They were accompanied by a new confederate, Walter Shean, the spoiled son of a businessman in Springfield, Mass., who enjoyed hanging around with two famous robbers.

In the early hours of 12 October 1924, Chapman blew one of the store's safes with nitro-glycerine; to his disgust, it contained ledgers and an envelope with a few dollars. And while he was working on the other safes, the police arrived, alerted by a local livery-stableman, who had become suspicious of the well-dressed men entering a large store at dawn on a Sunday. As two armed policemen blocked the doorway of the room in which he was hiding, Chapman fired, then made his escape, followed by flying bullets. The shot policeman, James Skelly, died on the operating table two hours after Chapman and Anderson had escaped.

When the police arrived in force a few minutes after the shooting, they found Walter Shean dozing in the car, and the incriminating envelope containing a few dollars on the back seat. In the warehouse of Shean's advertising agency in Springfield, police found a large quantity of stolen goods, including fur coats, oriental rugs and jewellery. There were also firearms. It took a large removal van to transfer all the loot to police headquarters.

It was while going through this loot for the hundredth time that Detective Ed Hickey noticed a loose label on a carpet bag, and steamed it off to reveal another underneath; this carried the name of Dr Harry Spickerman of Muncie, Indiana. Spickerman was the doctor who had cured Chapman's bullet wounds. Hickey and his team moved into the Braun Hotel, opposite the surgery of Dr Spickerman, and waited patiently for two months. And in the lobby of the Braun Hotel, on 17 January 1925, one of Hickey's men noticed a well-dressed man with an English accent buying a newspaper. He immediately recognized Chapman. The following morning, shortly after leaving Dr Spickerman's house, Chapman was arrested. He put up a fierce struggle and succeeded in firing one shot before he was overpowered.

When the gun was turned over to the forensic lab, it proved to be the same weapon that had killed officer Skelly. Chapman was extradited to Connecticut to stand trial for the murder. His defence was that he was in Holyoke, Mass., at the time of the shooting, but Walter Shean testified against him. So did his former landlord Ben Hance, on whose premises more incriminating evidence was found. On 4 April 1925, Chapman was sentenced to death. In spite of appeals, he was hanged a year later, on 6 April 1926.

By then, Dutch Anderson was already dead. On 15 August 1925, Anderson and a gunman named Charlie Wolfe sought out Ben Hance and his wife Mary, the farmer who had sheltered Chapman and Anderson; they shot them both in their car. Mary died immediately; her husband died later in hospital – but not before he had named his killers. Charlie Wolfe was quickly arrested, and was sentenced to life for the murders. Anderson moved on through northern Michigan, leaving behind a trail of counterfeit bills. On 31 October 1925, he passed a counterfeit twenty-dollar bill in a cafe in Muskegon, Michigan. The manager called a policeman, who caught up with Anderson a few streets away, and Anderson agreed to accompany him for questioning. Suddenly, Anderson darted away into the crowd; the policeman, Charles Hammond, followed him. In a deserted street, Anderson hid under a loading platform behind an empty factory, and as Hammond approached, shot him down. As Anderson ran out from under the platform and took to his heels, Hammond fired after him and brought him down. Both the policeman and the counterfeiter died.

The Inside Job of All Time: The Rondout Heist

Late on the night of 12 June 1924, mail train No. 57 of the Chicago and Pacific Railroad was just passing through the small town of Rondout, Illinois; thirty-two miles northwest of Chicago. The eleven-coach train was ten minutes behind schedule and the driver had pushed the speed up to sixty-five miles-an-hour to try to make up time. So intent were he and the fireman on keeping the boiler at full steam, they completely failed to notice two intruders entering the engine compartment. The fireman looked up from his shovelling to see the muzzle of a rifle levelled at his head and at the same moment the driver felt a pistol in his back.

"Do as I say and you won't get hurt," they were told. "Put on the brakes then flash your headlight three times." As they coasted to a stop the gunman looked back down the train and shouted: "Now back the train three car-lengths." The driver co-operated, positioning the third mail coach over a level-crossing. Four armed men then jumped from two cars parked on the road and ran to the train, firing into the air like archetypal Mexican bandits.

Showing no interest in the other coaches, the robbers made straight for the one straddling the crossing. They dealt with the mail clerks inside by throwing a tear-gas grenade through the upper window. Then, as the agonized clerks stumbled out the door, two robbers in gas masks stepped forward to ransack the coach.

It was at this moment that the men on watch saw a dark figure approaching along the path that skirted the train tracks. "Who the hell is that?" one demanded.

"I don't know," replied another.

Then someone shouted: "Let him have it." The bandits opened fire and the figure staggered and fell to the ground. The robbers ran to the slumped figure and carried it to one of the cars. From their swearing it was evident that they had accidentally shot one of their own people.

Undeterred, the thieves looted the mail coach then sped into the night. They took with them $50,000 in jewellery, $450,000 in newly issued currency and $1,500,000 in readily negotiable bonds; a neat two million dollars in all.

The police started with little to go upon. The train crew were so frightened they reported seeing twenty bandits in all – far too many to fit into the two getaway vehicles. As such their testimony would stand for little at any trial. This, and the lack of any physical evidence, left the police with only two leads.

The first was the wounded man – if he was still alive – he would be difficult to conceal. The police informers were told to keep their eyes open for any underworld medical activity.

The second was the apparent efficiency of the actual robbery. The thieves had known which of the eleven coaches held the richest plunder and in which mail bags to search most thoroughly. This suggested an inside job.

Fortunately, the Chicago police had an expert in such matters on their staff. He was Inspector William Fahy, on secondment from the investigative branch of the US Post Office. He had been sent to put a stop to the growing influence of organized crime in the dealings of the Chicago Post Office – a role similar to the one in which the gangbusting Eliot Ness was to later bring down Al Capone.

At thirty-six, Fahy had an excellent record. Known as the "Lone Wolf" by colleagues for his habit of working alone, he had caught numerous "inside job" robbers, including "Big Tim" Murphy.

Murphy – both a labour racketeer and popular State Senator – had been involved in several major robberies from the Post Office, but had covered his tracks with great care. However, despite much pressure to drop the case, Fahy eventually secured a conviction and lengthy sentence for the mobster. At the time of the Rondout robbery, Fahy was one of the most highly thought of officers in the city. There was no question of anyone else handling the Post Office side of the investigation.

The case soon took a turn for the better. An informant reported that someone who had "soaked up a lot of lead", was secretly being treated at an address in the North Washtenaw sector of the city. The police arrived and found a badly shot up man attended by a friend. In the pocket of the second man they found $1,500 in brand new bills, just like the ones taken at the train heist. A stake-out at the house over the next twenty-four hours netted two more visitors, one being a well-known bootlegger named James Murray.

Inspector Fahy interrogated the suspects personally and it was not long before one broke. Willis Newton identified the wounded man and his nurse as his brothers Willie and Joe. They, Murray and two men called Holliday and Glasscock – from the infamous St Louis gang "Egan's Rats" – had been in on the robbery. Unfortunately, he did not know the identity of the Post Office informer. Only the "Boss", James Murray, had any contact with this person, Newton said.

The engine driver and fireman easily identified Willis and Joe Newton as being two of the robbers. Then, soon afterwards, the police picked up Holliday and Glasscock as well as a fourth Newton brother called Jessie, who Willis had left out of the confession.

Jessie confessed as well and led the police to his stash of the cash. Investigation of the other gang members' haunts also turned up much of the stolen money. However, the investigation into the criminal informant got nowhere. Then the case took a very surprising turn.

One day, a woman calling herself Nan Ryan walked into the office of Police Captain William Schoemaker. She told him that she was the wife of Jerry Ryan, a man William Fahy had recently arrested for robbery. Convinced of her husband's innocence she had set out to find evidence that Fahy was corrupt. Pretending that she had hated her husband she had started to date the officer – he was apparently totally unconcerned that she might be trying to destroy him.

Eventually her self-sacrifice had paid off. Fahy, when drunk, had complained that she always wore the same dress. She replied that she had no money to buy another and Fahy had said; "You just be patient for a couple more days. I'm going to get $14,000 tomorrow."

Incredulous though they were, the Chicago police had to take the accusation seriously. They had Fahy secretly followed and it was soon realized that he was spending far more than he earned. To settle the matter a fake telegram concerning the undercover surveillance of the bailed James Murray was planted on a detective's desk. As soon as he saw it, Fahy sneaked out and rang Murray to warn him. Fahy had not been informed that the bootlegger's telephone was bugged.

The detective was arrested and charged with aiding and abetting the Rondout train robbers. At the subsequent trial, he and Murray – both insisting on their innocence – were sentenced to twenty-five years each. The other robbers were sentenced to between twenty-five years and a year-and-a-day, depending on their co-operation in recovering the stolen loot. Jerry Ryan, husband of the unofficial undercover agent Nan Ryan, was quietly released without trial.

Of the valuables taken from mail train No. 57, all were eventually accounted for but $14,000 – the sum William Fahy had told Nan he was due to receive.

THE AGE OF GANGSTERS

Prohibition, which began in 1919, brought the era of gangsterism to the United States. But at least it also brought prosperity to men like Dutch Schultz, Dion O'Banion and Al Capone, and made bank robbery unnecessary. The repeal of Prohibition in 1933 meant that America was full of out-of-work gangsters. Worse still, the great slump of 1929 brought widespread poverty and misery to the wealthiest nation in the world. The inevitable result was a steep increase in crime. And since banks were the places that held the money, bank robbery became the profession of some of the most ruthless of Al Capone's successors – John Dillinger, Pretty Boy Floyd, Clyde Barrow and Bonnie Parker, Alvin "Creepy" Karpis and the Ma Barker gang. Some of their stories have been told earlier in this book. But it is worth mentioning that much of their success depended on an absurd law that did not permit police officers to pursue bandits over a state line (ie bank robbery was not a "Federal offence".)

The largest bank theft so far was made at the Lincoln National Bank in Lincoln, Nebraska, in September 1930, which broke bank-robbery records with a haul of more than two million dollars in cash and securities – it actually forced the bank to close down. The man who planned this coup was a remarkable character called Harvey Bailey, who had been a respectable farmer until he returned from the First World War, and became a bootlegger. Trouble caught up with him when he lent his car to four bank robbers and they got caught; he was indicted, and skipped his bail. It was this mischance that turned him into a full-time bank robber – although periodically he tried to retire and live quietly with his family. The Lincoln National Bank robbery was the high point of Bailey's career. After that he became – to his regret – involved with the Barker gang and a bumbling gangster called Machine Gun Kelly, whose ambitious wife Kathryn was determined that her husband should be America's foremost law-breaker.

Bailey made two daring prison escapes. But his downfall came when he was on the run with a wounded leg, and took refuge in the Shannon Ranch, in Paradise, Texas, just after Machine Gun Kelly had kidnapped a wealthy oilman, Charles Urschel. Urschel was released on the payment of a ransom of $200,000 – Machine Gun Kelly overruled suggestions that they should kill him anyway. When de-briefed by police, Urschel was able to help them with a series of brilliant deductions and observations he had made while blindfolded in captivity – in particular, the precise time that a commercial plane flew over the ranch every day. This enabled the police to pinpoint Paradise, Texas. Bailey was captured there, with a $500 bill that one of the fleeing gangsters had given him. It proved to be from the ransom money, and Bailey was sentenced to life in Alcatraz for a crime he had no part in.

When Kelly was finally captured in a hideout in Memphis, Tennessee, newspapers reported that he yelled "Don't shoot, G-men", so coining the popular abbreviation for government agents.

The Rubel Ice Company Robbery

One of the boldest robberies of the 1930s took place on the morning of 24 August 1934 in Brooklyn, New York. Just after noon, an armoured car from the United States Trucking Company arrived to collect cash from the Rubel Ice Company on Bay and Nineteenth Street. Before leaving the vehicle the guards scanned the area; everything looked normal, and one guard entered the building while the other waited outside. At this moment, a kerbside pedlar threw a sack off his cart revealing two machine guns. Other men who had looked like innocent loiterers ran up with drawn guns. In a few minutes, bags of money were transferred from the armoured car to two cars belonging to the robbers. By the time the guard emerged from the Ice Company, the cars were speeding away. The New York police were on the scene within minutes, looking for the two cars, but the gang was already unloading the money at a pier less than a mile away into two waiting boats. The gang took their haul to a New Jersey hideout, and found that they had netted just under half a million dollars. The robbers then split up, taking an oath not to speak of their part in the hold-up.

Two years later, the police began to learn the names of men they believed had taken part in the robbery: John Manning, a top criminal, Joseph Kress, who had stolen the cars, two ex-bootleggers called John Hughes and Thomas Quinn, John and Francis Oley, kidnapper Percy Geary and forger Stewart Wallace. Most of these men were later imprisoned for other crimes, but remained loyal to their oath of denying all knowledge of the crime. John Manning, who was almost certainly the planner, was shot and killed in a gang feud on 6 July 1936.

The Invisible Bank Robbers

For sheer skill and planning, the case of the "invisible bank robbers" remains one of the most memorable in America's criminal history.

These thieves were not gangsters, but cracksmen of unusual ability, high-skilled professionals who burned their way into bank safes with an oxy-acetylene torch. But the real mystery was their apparent ability to walk through solid doors. In the majority of cases, the police were unable to discover how the men had broken into the bank. Moreover, the thieves were able to walk the streets with heavy oxygen tanks, apparently without attracting attention. These abilities led one reporter who worked on the case, Edward Radin, to christen the robbers "the phantoms".

Albert Spaggiari had been a hired gun for a right-wing terrorist organisation and had served in the paratroopers in French Indochina. By 1976, however, he was running a photographic supply shop in Nice, ostensibly a settled man. Yet he was planning one of the biggest and most daring bank robberies ever.

The Société Générale Bank in Nice had an ancient vault, built in the 1900s, and Spaggiari knew that this made it a relatively easy target. He surveyed the bank for hours, looking for a way to get to the vault without having to go through the modern building above ground. One day he saw his chance: a team of city cleaners were leaving the sewer from a manhole in a direct line with the vault. If he could tunnel through the underground masonry into the bank while the vault was locked, he could loot the safe deposit boxes and bullion almost at his leisure.

He recruited accomplices of equally dubious backgrounds, including Gaby Anglade, who in 1962 had tried to assassinate Charles De Gaulle, and Jean Kay, a conman who once cheated a rich industrialist out of 8,000,000 francs.

The tunnel was started in an underground parking facility opposite the bank, and took two months to complete. The diggers worked by the light of a fluorescent strip light attached to half a mile of cable, and Spaggiari catered the excavations, regularly bringing large amounts of food and wine down into the tunnel for his partners.

The tunnel complete, the robbery was carried off on 20 July 1976, France's Independence holiday. The gang moved sixty million francs in cash, bonds and jewellery from the vault, leaving the vault's doors welded shut to delay discovery of the crime. Supposedly the gang found some pornographic photographs belonging to a blackmailer in one of the deposit boxes, and pinned them up all around the vault. They also left a message that read: "Without weapons, without hate and without violence."

By October the police had found some of the stolen bonds being sold by a garage owner in Nice. Following this lead, they arrested Spaggiari at Nice Côte d'Azur airport, where he had just returned from a holiday in New York, Hong Kong and Bangkok.

He remained in custody for only four months. Expecting a fifteen to twenty year jail sentence, he broke free of the court security and dived through a loosely secured window onto the street below. As his defence lawyer shouted: "No! not that!" he was picked up by a waiting motorcyclist and driven to freedom.

The first robbery took place on the night of 19 October 1944, at the Long Island City Savings and Loan Association. But the thieves had either been interrupted, or forced to abandon the job because of defects in their equipment. A hole had been burned neatly through the door of the safe, but the contents remained untouched. And the door of the building was locked, exactly as it had been when the manager had left the previous evening. There were no fingerprints – the police did not expect any, since all burglars wore gloves as a matter of course.

In the days of the D'Autremont brothers, safe-breakers had used explosives – usually nitro-glycerine – or "can-openers", huge jemmies that can rip off a safe door. In 1944, oxy-acetylene was the most sophisticated method.

Twelve days later, the "phantoms" broke into a safe in Brooklyn and removed sugar coupons and rationing stamps; again, there was no sign of forced entry. An almost identical robbery took place in Queens thirteen days later. Twelve days after that, the thieves got away with $11,000 in cash and $5,000 in war stamps; this time they had entered by a rear window. A robbery at another Brooklyn Savings and Loan Association in January was less successful – the thieves got away with blank war bonds. But again, the detectives could find no obvious means of entry.

The police interviewed every bank burglar in New York and eliminated most of them from their enquiries; the rest were kept under surveillance. This seemed to deter the "phantoms"; there were no more robberies for two months, and the next one occurred in Newark, New Jersey; the thieves drove off with the safe containing $7,000, and it was found the next day, with the neat burn-hole that had become the trademark of the raiders. But in March 1945, after the retirement of Captain Richard A. Fennelly, the man who headed the "Safe and Loft" Squad – specializing in safe-crackers – the "phantoms" moved back to New York and committed a series of robberies. Fennelly's assistant, Lieutenant Maguire – now promoted to chief of the squad – decided to keep a watch on all savings and loan associations. It required a vast number of officers, but it seemed to be the only way to approach the baffling case.

One day, two policemen sitting in a car in downtown Manhattan noticed two men standing outside a bank. Neither of the men was a known safe-breaker, but the policemen nevertheless felt they looked familiar. Then one of them remembered: they had seen them a week before near a savings and loan association. One was big and muscular, the other small and slim. Now the policemen watched them enter the building, pick up an advertising booklet, then stand by the door, apparently deep in conversation, while they glanced around the room. After this they strolled across to a restaurant opposite. Within a few minutes, two additional police cars had been summoned. When the men emerged from the restaurant and entered a grey Dodge sedan, a plain-clothed detective strolled past and noted its number.

A check with the Bureau of Identification revealed that it was registered in the name of Stanley Patrek, of Clay Street, Brooklyn. A check with the Motor Vehicle Bureau uncovered Patrek's driving licence, complete with a physical description. The Bureau of Criminal Identification was then able to tell Maguire that Patrek, who had been born in 1915, had a record as a hold-up man. He had been paroled in the previous year. His description indicated that he was the shorter of the two men.

Patrek and his companion were shadowed to a garage in Astoria, and later to their separate addresses. The following day, a plain-clothed detective in an unmarked car saw the heavily-built suspect come out of his apartment building, looking as if he was on a shopping errand. The detective slipped into the building and waited on the stairs. When the man returned, he observed which apartment he entered. A name on the door identified him as Joseph Stepka. He, it seemed, had a criminal record as a burglar as well as a stick-up man.

Now the two men were carefully shadowed; it was the constant aim of the police to make sure they had no suspicion they were under surveillance. If they were suspicious, both had sufficient money from robberies to lie low indefinitely. Both men seemed to be happily married, and spent much time at home playing with their children. But they also spent a good part of most days patrolling the streets and surveying loan association offices. One night, the detectives observed them having dinner with two attractive blondes, and deduced that they were deceiving their wives – the women proved to be a dance-hall hostess and a cigarette girl.

On 28 May 1945, a night of torrential downpour, the men left home late at night and returned to their Astoria garage. Three police cars proceeded to trail them as they drove off in the Dodge sedan. But near the Triboro Bridge, the suspects began

Chicago cops with armored car

to weave in and out of side streets, and the police lost them. The following morning, Maguire learned that the "phantoms" had struck again at the Whitestone Savings and Loan Association, and got away with a safe containing $9,000. Again, there was no sign of forced entry, and the door was locked normally when the manager came to open the bank.

The following day, detectives trailed the two men from bank to bank as they made small deposits totalling $9,000. And when Maguire checked with the banks, he discovered that similar deposits had always been made in the past on days following the "phantom" robberies.

On the night of 1 June 1945, Patrek and Stepka again left home late in the evening and drove to the Astoria garage, lifting a bulky suitcase into the trunk. Once again they were shadowed as they followed a circuitous route to their destination, which proved to be Yonkers. The police lost them again, but eventually found the grey sedan parked not far from the Yonkers Savings and Loan Association on Broadway. For the next three hours they waited in darkness. Then the two men returned, both carrying heavy objects. The police ordered them to halt, and both men turned to run. Shots fired in the air made them change their minds. Stepka proved to be carrying the oxy-acetylene equipment, while Patrek held a briefcase containing more than $15,000.

The two men surrendered philosophically, and admitted that they had no idea they had been under surveillance for months. The Astoria garage proved to contain elaborate and expensive safe-breaking equipment – the most elaborate the police had ever seen.

But although they had been caught red-handed, there was no conclusive proof that Patrek and Stepka were the "phantoms" who had committed the previous robberies; understandably, they preferred to leave this problem to the police. The Astoria garage was studied carefully, and the detective in charge noticed some metal filings on the floor. These were turned over to the Technical Research Laboratory. The safe from the Whitestone Savings and Loan Association, which had subsequently been found abandoned, was also handed over. Under the microscope, the floor sweepings were found to consist of asbestos as well as metal filings, a strong indication that they came from a safe – most safes at that time were fire-proofed with asbestos inside the door, and often in the rear wall. Then samples of the filings and asbestos were compared with samples from the safe by means of the spectroscope. In emission spectroscopy, the sample is placed between two carbon electrodes, and a spark struck between them; the light from the burning sample is then split into a spectrum, whose emission lines are as distinctive as a fingerprint. The spectroscope revealed beyond all doubt that the filings and asbestos came from the Whitestone safe.

The chief mystery remained: how had the phantoms succeeded in walking in and out of locked doors? They refused to say; but a small box in their garage workshop finally revealed the secret. The box contained a well-known make of lock, together with an extra cylinder – the part the key slips into – and a tiny screwdriver. If the lock could be approached from the inside – the side that became accessible when the door was open – the screwdriver could be used to loosen a screw in the cylinder. Once this screw had been loosened, the cylinder could be worked out of the lock by pushing in a key, and twisting it back and forth. Eventually, it could be slipped out of the lock, and another cylinder – to which the thieves had the key – substituted. When the robbery was over, the original cylinder was replaced, the screw tightened, and there was no sign of the substitution.

Another lock in the box, partly sawed away, revealed how the thieves had stumbled upon this interesting secret. One of them had obviously made a scientific study of every make of lock until he found one with this flaw. When the watching detectives had observed Patrek and Stepka engaged in earnest conversation as they stood in the doorway of the bank, they had assumed that the men were simply observing the layout of the place; in fact, Patrek was unobtrusively inserting the screwdriver, using the big man's body as cover, and loosening the screw. Here was a case in which the thieves applied to crime the same scientific techniques that forensic experts were applying to their solution. It was a relief for the New York police when both men received long prison sentences for grand larceny.

The Brinks Bank Robbery

Not be be confused with Brinks-Mat, which we shall discuss in a moment, the Brinks bank robbery achieved another record, with a haul of nearly $3 million.

On 17 January, 1950, in the early evening Thomas Lloyd and his fellow employees were checking the day's consignment of cash and cheques. They worked for Brinks Incorporated, the American money-moving firm, in the Boston branch. They worked in the locked wire cage that surrounded the vault, among over three million dollars worth of different forms of money. As they counted and checked, Lloyd was distracted by faint sounds of movement on the other side of the wire. Looking up, he saw seven masked men wearing similar uniforms to his own. Each held a pistol; they were covering all the Brinks staff.

One of the men shouted: "Open up this door. This is a stick-up! Don't give us no trouble."

They had entered the room so quietly that they had given Lloyd and his co-workers no time to reach for the loaded shotguns that rested in a rack by the safe. Thus the Brinks men had no choice but to cooperate.

Lloyd opened the mesh door and, at the gang's command,

lay on the ground with the others. Their hands were bound with cord and their mouths sealed closed with adhesive tape. Over the next twenty minutes the robbers worked hard, stuffing sacks with the money that lay around and also blowing open the vault door with a 20 mm anti-tank weapon. At the end of this time, around seven p.m., they left quietly and almost nonchalantly.

It took half an hour for Lloyd to wriggle free of his bonds and activate the alarm. The signal went direct to the police, and they were on the premises by eight. The gang had taken a staggering amount: $1,218,211.29 in cash and $1,557,183.83 in money orders and cheques. Among the haul were bundles of cheques intended for war veterans and half a million belonging to the Federal Bank Reserve. This meant that the robbery was accounted a Federal crime, and soon the bank was filled with FBI agents.

The ease with which the criminals had slipped into the central vault of the holding bank seemed to indicate help from an employee. The locks were intact; somehow the intruders had got hold of duplicate keys for most of the building. Checks on the branches employees revealed nothing, and the police and FBI turned to other methods. They pulled in hundreds of people and questioned them all.

The answer to the puzzling question of how the gang had got in without inside help was actually rather simple. About two years before the robbery, two men, Joseph "Specs" O'Keefe and Stanlet "Gus" Gusciora had been asked by a friend, Anthony Pino, to scout out the Brinks building, with a view to seeing if it was possible to rob it. When O'Keefe and Gusciora checked the bank late one night, they were astounded to find that the outer lock could be turned with only an ice pick, and that the inner doors opened when a strip of celluloid was slid through between the frame and the handle. Using these two simple burglary techniques, the prowlers were able to get right into the vault. There, the alarm was evidently switched on, and the safe door bolted. Hanging on a nail close by was a clipboard with the total amount of money in the vault scribbled on it. The two men let themselves out silently and reported back to Pino.

The main problem, then, was that at the time of day that they could easily use burglary techniques to gain entry, the alarm was always activated. In order to rob the bank, they would have to catch the employees before they left, and this would require a respectable and quiet means of entering the vault. The solution was simple – one night, O'Keefe and Gusciora stole all the locks from the Brinks Incorporated doors and had a fast and discreet locksmith create keys for them. They then sneaked back and replaced the locks well before the morning shift arrived.

Equipped with keys, Pino and associates gathered a group of accomplices and began planning the rest of the crime. They acquired uniforms that resembled the Brinks standard outfit, so that people on the street would not think twice about seeing them loading fat Brinks sacks into their getaway vehicle. Pino ordered that they get some rope, but that it must be stolen so that the police could not trace it. In the event those told to acquire the rope were too lazy to steal it and instead mail ordered it from Sears and Roebuck.

All signs pointed to 17 January being a very busy day for Brinks and consequently a very lucrative day upon which to rob it. Seven men including O'Keefe and Gusciora were detailed to enter the building and commit the robbery while two men, among them Pino, attended the getaway car in the street. One man was to keep watch from a roof top; the final, eleventh man was to dispose of all the evidence that they brought away from the crime, including the truck.

As we have seen, all went very smoothly, and late that evening the gang met to divide up the profits. They gathered at the house of one of the robbers' parents, a couple that spoke no English and were apparently unaware that their son's business activities took place on the wrong side of the law. In a back room the gang divided the usable money from the unusable, which was to be burnt. $98,000 was new, sealed and sequentially numbered, and thus useless without a massive money-laundering operation. Nearly all the cheques and money orders were "trouble money" too, being far too risky to attempt to cash. In all about $1,100,000 was salvageable, making each share worth $100,000. Each of the eleven wandered off into the night rich.

They did not have long to enjoy it however. Within two days all of the eleven had been questioned by the police in their massive sifting operation. Two gang members were given safe-keeping of all the shares, during this difficult time. After they had all been released due to the lack of any evidence against them, $35,000 was found to have disappeared. The keepers maintained that the money had gone while they were being questioned, and thus that they knew nothing about it. Grudgingly the gang accepted this and took back their depleted shares. Soon however the police were back, centring their attention upon O'Keefe. After first removing $5,000 for spending money, O'Keefe handed his money to another gang member, Adolph Maffie, to keep while he and Gusciora temporarily left town.

They set out westward, into Pennsylvania, and it was not long before they began to practise their trade again. They broke into a hardware store and stole five handguns. They then used these to hold up a clothes shop and steal six suits. The fact that there was already FBI and police interest in the pair, coupled with the fact that they were careless, soon led to their apprehension. O'Keefe was given three years, while Gusciora received five to twenty years in prison.

Meanwhile the Boston police had found pieces of the getaway truck in local scrap yards. The gang had intended to bury the sections, but the frozen ground that January had frustrated their efforts. On the strength of evidence gained from examination of the truck parts and also on close observation of some of the gang, the FBI produced a list of eight suspects, including O'Keefe, Gusciora and Pino. As the Statute of Limitations on robbery as a Federal crime means that no criminal can be tried more then three years after the event, the FBI were forced to subpoena the eight men to appear before a Grand Jury in late 1952. They had little chance of success because they lacked solid evidence, and sure enough the prosecution failed early in 1953.

The gang seemed to have escaped punishment; the only chance that the police had was to acquire more evidence and try them under Massachusetts state law. In Massachusetts, the Statute of Limitations occurs only after six years. There seemed little chance however that new evidence would surface after such a long interval, and by the time of O'Keefe's release from jail in 1954, the case was all but closed.

O'Keefe returned expecting to receive his $93,000 dollars from Maffie. Maffie had, unsurprisingly, spent the lot. O'Keefe showed great restraint and did not do anything to Maffie, saying that he could not kill him because he might "get lucky again and pay me back". Instead, O'Keefe tried to extort money from Pino. He kidnapped Pino's brother-in-law and demanded $25,000 from his old boss "for starters". Pino gave him $2,500, and O'Keefe, oddly obliging, gave Pino's brother-in-law back.

His all-but-failed extortion was a mistake in more than one way; soon afterwards his Oldsmobile was sprayed with sub-machine gun bullets and O'Keefe only escaped injury by flinging himself to the floor. A second attempt on his life left him with gunshot wounds in his chest and wrist. It must have almost been a relief when he was jailed for twenty-seven months on an old offence.

The FBI had heard of O'Keefe's problems, and agents visited him in prison, off-handedly telling stories about the new cars and houses that his old compatriots had been purchasing with their new-found wealth. Within three visits O'Keefe was ready to name his fellow Brinks robbers and testify against them. He was put under twenty-four-hour armed guard, and the re-mainder of the gang were arrested. O'Keefe's old accomplice Gusciora did not survive to stand trial. While being held in Boston he experienced fits of unconsciousness and vomiting. Within weeks he had died of a brain tumour.

With the testimony of one of the robbers, the rest of the gang were doomed; each received a life sentence. O'Keefe's counsel plead for leniency on the grouds of the help that he had given to the authorities:

"Where would we be – the Commonwealth of Massachusetts or the FBI – if it weren't for Specky?"

O'Keefe was released in 1960. The vast majority of the haul was never recovered.

Hermann Goering, the head of Hitler's Luftwaffe, deserves to be included a book on robbers, since he was one of the most successful art thieves of all time. A member of the German "junker" class and a highly educated man, he was passionately fond of art; so whenever German troops marched into some city with a famous art gallery or museum, Goering had its art treasures sent back to Berlin, many for his own private collec-tion. In late twentieth century currency the value of the plunder would run to billions; even in the 1940s it reached millions.

In 1945 Goering took refuge in Bavaria and tried to take control from Hitler, who denounced him as a traitor. Captured by the allies, Goering was sentenced to death as a war criminal at Nuremberg; he committed suicide by poison before he could be executed.

Emile the Nut

Across the Atlantic, gangsters in Paris and Marseilles were studying the exploits of their American counterparts with admiration. One of these was perhaps France's most notorious and dangerous gangster since the far-off days of the Bonnot gang: Emile Buisson.

Buisson's heredity seems to have been extremely bad. His father was a drunkard, a builder of bakers' ovens, addicted to absinthe. Only four of his nine children survived, and one of them was a weak-minded deaf-mute girl. The two criminals of the family, Jean-Baptiste and Émile, were its only two healthy members; a third brother died of tuberculosis at the age of twenty. The mother, worn out by overwork, starvation, and continual brutal beatings from her husband, was taken to an asylum. The father took to exhibiting his deaf-mute daughter in cafés for money; he was sent to jail for carnal knowledge of minors – including his daughter – and died in an asylum.

Émile was born at Paray-le-Monial, in the Sâone-et-Loire department of southern France, on 19 August 1902. His elder brother fought in the war, deserted, and was sent to a penal battalion in Algeria. Released in 1921, he promptly became a pimp in Paris.

Émile served his first term in jail at the age of sixteen, and then twenty months' imprisonment for theft. He was due for military service, and so sent out to a penal battalion in North Africa. The brutality of these battalions was unspeakable. However, Émile managed to distinguish himself in the fighting, and got the Croix de Guerre. Back in France, he took up a life of petty crime and served many short terms in jail.

In 1932, he helped to rescue his brother from jail. The plan was bold. Jean-Baptiste got himself transferred to Strasbourg model prison at Ensisheim by confessing to a crime in Strasbourg and getting three years added to his eight-year sentence. He there broke his leg by smashing it with a table leg. He was transferred into the hospital, and the same night jumped from a first-floor window, breaking it again. However, with the help of Émile he made a clean getaway.

Émile Buisson committed his first big robbery on 27 December 1937, and got himself the nickname "Mimile le Dingue" – Crazy Mimile. He was driving a "traction avant" Citröen – front-wheel drive (known generally simply as "tractions"), and he and a gangster named Charles Desgrandschamps (known as "Bigfooted Charlie") robbed two bank messengers outside the Banque de France in Troyes. Émile fired at one messenger, wounding him in the thigh, and then, to the surprise of Bigfooted Charlie, began to fire at random down the street and into the bank.

He was arrested a month later. French justice was slow, and in 1940, at the time of the invasion, he was still awaiting trial in Troyes Prison. He escaped. In early 1941, he robbed the Credit Lyonnais bank in Rue Notre Dame des Victoires, Paris, killing two bank messengers in cold blood.

Shortly after this he was caught by the Gestapo carrying arms and sent to a military prison; he was then sentenced for the Troyes hold-up in 1937. He escaped by simulating lunacy until he was transferred to the asylum. In 1947, with four associates, he robbed a café in the Rue Lesueur (site of Petiot's crimes) and later executed one of his associates who kept back a brooch. This gave him such a terrible reputation in the underworld that he was not betrayed by professional informers in the usual way, and stayed at liberty a great deal longer than he might otherwise have done.

Over the next few years he took part in many hold-ups, always using sten-guns and Citröen "tractions". After the war, Paris had become a great deal more dangerous than Chicago in the Prohibition era, and gang killings were commonplace. Finally, the police were armed with sub-machine guns, but after accidentally shooting up an old gentleman who was drunk and a bus full of passengers, they were forced by public opinion to be a little more cautious. Finally, a special bandit squad was formed, adequately financed, and run by Charles Chenevier of the Sûreté, who had arrested Buisson in 1937. There was one unsuccessful attempt to arrest Buisson, when a whole convoy of heavily armed police cars rushed out of Paris towards a hotel at Arpajon; but their spectacular exit from Paris excited attention, and someone phoned Buisson, who escaped. However, he was finally arrested in 1955; and tried for the murder of the gangster whom he had "executed". He was guillotined in 1956.

His brother, Jean-Baptiste, nicknamed "Fatalitas" because of his fatalism, shot a restaurant proprietor, Jean Cardéur, when the latter cast aspersions on his dead brother's memory. Maître Carboni, who defended him, turned to the jury as they filed out and said pathetically: "Do not let me have two heads from the same family on my conscience for the rest of my life." (He had defended Émile.) The appeal was successful; Jean-Baptiste was found guilty with a recommendation to mercy, and sentenced to a life sentence of hard labour in Melun Prison.

Jacques Mesrine: "Public Enemy Number One".

At the time of Buisson's execution, a young Frenchman named Jacques Mesrine was already contemplating a career of crime that was to make him for a while the most famous criminal in Europe. Like so many of his larcenous predecessors, Mesrine liked to think of crime as a way of achieving the fame he deserved, and he revelled in his reputation as a modern Robin Hood.

Mesrine was born in Clichy, Paris, in 1937. In 1940, his mother moved her family to Château-Merle, near Poitiers, where she had been brought up, while her husband was in the army. Mesrine was an attractive child, and his biographer Carey Schofield reports that he was usually able to get what he wanted from adults by smiling at them. But he was also solitary. Once, when asked to go and play with other children, he replied; "No, I always have a nicer time on my own."

After the war, the Mesrines returned to Clichy. Mesrine later claimed that he never had enough affection from his father, who worked hard in a textile designing business. He was a poor student at school, but made a strong impression on his schoolmates with his charm, his prowess at fighting, and his love of argument. His constant absenteeism led to his expulsion from two schools. He began joining other teenagers stealing cars for joyrides. At the age of eighteen, he married a beautiful black girl from Martinique, and they moved into a small flat. But he soon found marriage boring and when his wife had a baby, decided that his mother could bring it up.

At nineteen, Mesrine was conscripted into the army, and asked to be sent to Algeria, where the French were trying to put down a Muslim revolt. There was much brutality on both sides.

Mesrine thoroughly enjoyed being in action, and received the
Military Cross for valour. While in the army, he was divorced
from his wife.

His return to civilian life was an anticlimax. He soon
committed his first burglary. With two other men, he broke
into the flat of a wealthy financier. When a drill broke off in the
lock of the safe, he went out to a hardware shop, broke in and
got more drills. They escaped with twenty-five million francs.

When de Gaulle came to power in 1958, he began seeking a
political solution to the Algerian problem. Mesrine, like many
Frenchmen, regarded this as a betrayal. The right-wing General
Salan set up a secret organization, the Organisation Armée Secrète.
Mesrine became involved, and it reinforced Mesrine's attitude to
law and order – the typical criminal attitude that it is a question of
individual choice and that men who can think for themselves
should make up their own minds whether to obey the law.

In the spring of 1962, Mesrine was arrested when on his way
to rob a bank, and sentenced to three years in prison. He was
released on parole a year later. For a while he decided to "go
straight". He married a second time, had a young daughter,
and now with his father's help, began to study to become an
architect. There is evidence that he was a good architect. But
when, in late 1964, he was made redundant, he went back to
crime. His cool nerve served him remarkably well. Once, in the
course of holding up a jewellery shop, the police arrived.
Mesrine ran into the back yard, unlatched the gate to make
it look as if he had run through, then hid in a dustbin until the
coast was clear. On another occasion, he escaped from a flat he
was burgling through a lavatory window, and escaped across
the roof-tops, walking out of a building further down the street,
and asking the police what all the commotion was about.

In 1967 another attempt to "go straight" as an innkeeper –
financed by his father – again proved to be a failure as he found
respectability too unexciting. He went off with a woman,
Jeanne Schneider, and together they carried out a daring
robbery at a hotel in Switzerland. In 1968, as one of the most
wanted robbers in France, he decided to move to Canada.

He and Schneider went to work for a Montreal millionaire,
Georges Deslauriers, as chauffeur and housekeeper, but the
gardener took a dislike to Jeanne, and Deslauriers dismissed
them. Mesrine's response was to kidnap Deslauriers, and hold
him for a $200,000 ransom. Deslauriers managed to escape
before the ransom was paid, and Mesrine and Schneider moved

to a small town, Percé, where they made the acquaintance of a
wealthy widow called Evelyne le Bouthillier. After an evening
spent with the pair, Mme le Bouthillier was found strangled.
Mesrine always claimed that he knew nothing about the
murder.

They slipped over the border into the United States, but were
arrested by a border patrol and taken back to Canada. There
they were charged with the murder of Mme le Bouthillier.
Mesrine was furious at being accused of the murder of an old
woman. He claimed that he *had* committed several murders,
and tortured people who had insulted him, but that he would
have been incapable of this particular crime. Held in the Percé
prison pending trial, Mesrine succeeded in escaping by attacking a guard and stealing his keys. He also released Jeanne. They
were recaptured only two miles away. Mesrine was given ten
years for the kidnapping of Georges Deslauriers; Schneider was
given five. But they were acquitted of the murder of Evelyne le
Bouthillier.

A year later, Mesrine led a number of other prisoners in a
spectacular escape from the "escape-proof" prison of St Vincent
de Paul at Laval. He became a celebrity in Canada and it gave
him the idea of a still more daring exploit. After robbing a bank in
Montreal, he and another escaped convict drove back to the
St Vincent de Paul prison with the intention of freeing the
remaining prisoners in the top security wing. But when a police
car approached them on the way to the prison, Mesrine opened
fire. With bullets whistling past them, they escaped back to
Montreal. A week later, Mesrine and two accomplices were in
the forests near Montreal where they were stopped by two forest
rangers. One of the rangers recognized Mesrine, and made the
mistake of showing it. Both were shot down, and their bodies
dumped in a nearby ditch and covered with branches.

There were more bank robberies – on one occasion, Mesrine
robbed the same bank twice because a cashier had scowled at
him as he walked out after the first robbery. Then Mesrine met
a beautiful nineteen-year-old, Jocelyne Deraiche, who became
his mistress. With two accomplices, they crossed the border
again into the United States, continuing south to Venezuela
where they were able to live comfortably on the profits of their
bank robberies, aided by ex-OAS men living there. When a
police official told them that Interpol was on their trail, Mesrine
and Deraiche flew to Madrid.

All the publicity he had received in Canada had given

Mesrine a taste for fame. He decided to become the best known criminal in the world. In the remaining seven years of his life, he achieved that ambition.

Back in France, in 1973 Mesrine committed a dozen armed robberies, netting millions of francs. He gathered around him a gang he could trust. As the hunt for him intensified, he made preparations for the future by examining the courthouse at Compiègne. The precaution proved useful. When police finally caught up with him on 8 March, Mesrine staged a spectacular escape from the Palais de Justice in Compiègne, getting hold of a gun that an accomplice had left in a lavatory, then holding up the court, and escaping with the judge as a human shield. He was shot in the arm in the course of his escape, but had the bullet removed when he was safe in a hideout.

Once again at his old occupation of robbing banks and factories, he carefully nurtured the image of the gentleman crook, the modern Robin Hood. When a female bank clerk accidentally pushed the alarm button, Mesrine commented courteously, "Don't worry, I like to work to music", and went on collecting the money. When he heard his father was dying of cancer in hospital, he made a daring visit to see him dressed as a doctor in a white coat with a stethoscope round his neck. Not long after this, a bank robbery went wrong, and the accomplice waiting in the getaway car was arrested. As a result, the police tracked down Mesrine to his flat in the rue Vergniaud and placed him under arrest.

La Santé prison proved to be escape-proof, and Mesrine passed the time by writing a book, *L'Instinct de Mort* (*The Killer Instinct*), which was smuggled out and appeared in February 1977. In it Mesrine admitted that a previous claim to have killed thirty-nine people was a lie, but it contained detailed descriptions of other murders – for none of which a body had been found. After three and a half years, the prosecution finally opened in May 1977. Mesrine astounded the court by telling his audience that it was easy enough to buy the keys that could open any pair of handcuffs, then extracted a matchbox from the knot of his tie and within seconds had removed his handcuffs. The gesture brought him the kind of publicity that he had now come to crave. He was nevertheless sentenced to twenty years.

A year later Mesrine staged another of his spectacular escapes. An accomplice named Francois Besse squirted soapy water into the eyes of a guard, and Mesrine, who was in the interview room with his lawyer, grabbed some guns from a ventilation shaft. Two warders were made to undress, and the convicts dressed in their uniforms. They let another prisoner, Carman Rives, out of his cell, and then all three rushed across the prison yard. Mesrine and Besse escaped over the wall with a ladder, but Rives was shot.

The police commissioner, Serge Devos, was placed in charge of the squad whose business was to recapture Mesrine. Mesrine moved to Deauville, a seaside resort in Normandy. He was unable to resist the temptation of walking into the local police station, announcing that he was a police inspector from the Gaming Squad, and asking to see the duty inspector. They were told he was not there. As they walked out, one of the policemen said, "That's Mesrine", and the other told him that was impossible. Mesrine then robbed a casino in Deauville, and in the desperate chase that followed, was almost caught. After this, he invaded the home of a bank employee who had given evidence against him at his trial, and forced him to go to the bank and hand over nearly half a million francs.

A Paris department store was the scene of another one of Mesrine's typically quixotic gestures in the summer of 1978. He saw the floor-walker seizing a shoplifter – a boy of fifteen. Mesrine announced himself as a police inspector with special responsibility for juvenile affairs, flashing a fake identity card, then grabbed the boy by the scruff of the neck and led him out of the store. There he let him go. In August, he gave an interview to a journalist from *Paris Match*, which caused a sensation. Then Mesrine came to London where he spent several weeks undisturbed by police. There he planned another astonishing crime – to kidnap the judge who had sentenced him to twenty years in prison. On 10 November 1978 Mesrine and an accomplice returned to France, went to the judge's flat and held up his wife, daughter and son-in-law. But the accomplice was inexperienced, and the daughter succeeded in getting word to the judge's son when he came to the door. Mesrine saw the arrival of the police, ran down the stairs, and as he came face to face with several policemen, pointed behind him. "Quick, Mesrine's up there." And they went rushing past. A young policeman who recognized Mesrine outside was handcuffed to a drainpipe.

In hiding, Mesrine wrote an open letter to the French police denouncing conditions in French prisons and claiming that this had "evoked a fanatical passion for human rights". During his last year there was an obvious deterioration in Mesrine's character. "Mesrine believed in his lies more than anyone else did," said his biographer. "Any suggestion, even from his closest friends, that perhaps he was exaggerating a little, could send him into an uncontrollable fury. He had always been subject to fits of rage, and these were becoming more and more frequent . . . He would smash everything that was in his way, and it is extraordinary that he never killed anyone while in a rage." Mesrine explained to journalists – whom he still allowed to interview him – that he now "identified ideologically with the extreme left".

When the police finally located his hideout, in a flat in the rue Belliard, they decided to take no chances. Mesrine had sworn never to be taken alive. On 2 November 1979 Mesrine came out of the building with his girlfriend, Sylvie Jean-Jacquot, and walked towards his BMW, parked nearby. At a road junction, a blue lorry signalled that he wanted to cut across him and turn right. Mesrine waved him on. The lorry stopped in front of the car, and another lorry drew up behind. Four policemen climbed out, and within seconds, twenty-one bullets had shattered the windscreen. Mesrine was killed immediately. Sylvie Jean-Jacquot was shot in the arm, and her dog was also hit. The police flung their arms around one another and danced for joy.

The Great Train Robbery

If Mesrine was the most famous bank robber since World War Two, the most famous single "heist" was undoubtedly the Great Train Robbery. In fact, the *New York Herald Tribune* of 21 January 1964, described it in a headline as "History's Greatest Bank Robbery", followed by the unfathomable comment: "There'll Always Be An England."

On the night of 7–8 August 1963 the mail train travelled southwards as usual, making scheduled stops to load letters and packages into its twelve coaches. Packed into the second coach from the engine on this particular night were 128 large bags filled with paper money, mainly five and one pound notes. The cash had been spent over the August bank holiday that had just passed, and was returning to the head offices of several banks in London. The driver of the train, Jack Mills, and his fireman David Whitby, had taken over the running of the train at Crewe at about midnight. By 2 am they were past Leighton Buzzard in Bedfordshire and were only about half an hour from Euston. Unexpectedly however a signal showed amber rather than green, a sign that the driver should slow down in anticipation of a red signal soon. Sure enough the next signal at Sears Crossing showed red, and Mills brought the train to a halt.

In order to find out what had caused the stoppage, Whitby jumped off the train and made his way to a trackside telephone that was connected to the nearest signal box. The line was dead, the wires having been deliberately severed. Whitby shouted to the driver that the phone had been sabotaged, and ran back towards the engine. As he reached the second coach however a figure stepped from the rear. Thinking that this must be one of the postal workers on the train, Whitby asked, "What's up, mate?" Without replying the figure beckoned him over to the embankment. Suddenly the figure shoved Whitby down the slope where he was overpowered by two waiting accomplices.

"If you shout, I'll kill you," threatened one, holding a cosh

The Great Train Robbery – August 30th 1963 – Mrs Frances Reynolds, Bruce Richard Reynolds, Mrs Barbara Daly and John Thomas Daly are helping with enquiries

over Whitby's head. Panicked, he replied, "All right mate, I'm on your side."

Whitby was taken back to the engine where he found Mills on his knees and bleeding copiously from a head wound. The cab was full of men in boiler suits and balaclavas. The robber who was evidently the train expert was having difficulty operating the engine – it was a new design. Finally Mills, still bleeding, was forced to drive the engine and its first two carriages down the track for about half a mile, to Bridego Bridge where the track goes over a road.

The gang smashed the windows of the second coach with an axe, and overpowered the postal workers inside. All but eight of the bags were unloaded and thrown to a lorry waiting below. Mills and Whitby were handcuffed together and left in the smashed coach; the lorry sped away with over two million pounds.

The police were called from the nearby village of Linslade by two of the postal workers after they judged that the gang were no longer watching the coach. Scotland Yard arrived and began the process of interviewing everyone in the district about new-comers or strange activities.

Within five days, the police had found the gang's abandoned base, Leatherslade Farm, about twenty miles from the robbery location. Neighbours had seen many cars coming and going until up to three days after the crime. They also reported that the windows had been habitually covered while the occupants were at home, and that they had claimed to be decorating the farmhouse. A Mrs Brooke was found, who had actually handed the keys over to the gang so that they could examine it with view to a sale.

The farm was bursting with evidence; almost every surface carried fingerprints. The gang had left a collection of personal objects lying around, including a can of paint, a monopoly set and two Land Rovers with identical number plates.

While the police were cataloguing the bewildering array of clues from the farm, two of the robbers were being captured in Bournemouth. The owner of a lock-up garage on Tweedale Road had become suspicious when the two men had wanted to pay for three months rental in advance with a huge sheaf of notes. While they were moving their van into the garage the owner called the police saying that she thought that she was in the company of two of the Great Train Robbers. Two plain clothes officers arrived and began questioning the owners of the van. Suddenly one of them dashed off down the road.

While the officers were tackling this one, the other also tried to make his escape. Both were recaptured with relative ease and taken into custody. The two men's names were Gerald Boale and Roger Cordrey, and their van proved to be stuffed with money, £141,000 in used notes.

At this point the rest of the gang evidently panicked. Two walkers in Redlands Wood, near Dorking in Surrey, found two holdalls by the side of the path. They were filled with bank notes. Police sniffer dogs also turned up a suitcase around the same location; altogether the bags contained £101,000.

Arrests based upon the evidence from the farm followed quickly, six more men identified by their associates and their carelessly distributed fingerprints. Also the lawyer that organized the sale of the farm to the gang, John Wheater, was charged with conspiracy and the harbouring of Leonard Field, one of the arrested men.

Lastly the police raided the flat of Bruce Reynolds, a man believed to be the organising force behind the crime. The police did not find Reynolds at home, but they did find Roy "The Weasel" James, a man also wanted in connection with the robbery. The police were forced to chase James across the length of St John's Wood before they could capture him. In all, thirteen men had been apprehended.

The trial opened on 20 January 1964, in Aylesbury assize court. The Crown had over two hundred witnesses and a network of circumstantial evidence that seemed incontrovertible. Among the witnesses called to the stand was Jack Mills, the driver of the train. The savage beating that he had received had permanently disabled him; his speech was halting and he had difficulty walking. British Railways had paid him £25 compensation. His evidence was however inconclusive, as he could not identify any of the accused.

Nearly all the defendants had left some fingerprints in Leatherslade Farm and this evidence alone was near damning. Only John Daly successfully overturned the evidence of his prints: his lawyer argued that although they were present on the Monopoly set, the Crown could not prove that they had got there while the set was in the house. He was discharged.

On 26 March 1964, eight of the defendants were found guilty of conspiracy and armed robbery. Three further were found guilty of conspiracy only. The final defendant was Ronald Arthur Biggs, who had succeeded in having his trial held separately from the other men.

The sentencing followed and it was shocking in its severity. Roger Cordrey, who had helped the police extensively, was sentenced to twenty years. All those convicted of armed robbery received thirty years, except Boale, who was given twenty-four years. Brian Field and Leonard Field, convicted only of conspiracy, also received twenty-four years. John Wheater, the gang's lawyer, was treated leniently because of his conduct in the Second World War, and was sentenced to only three years. Appeals were lodged, and in four cases these eventually resulted in reduced sentences.

The press was disgusted with the length of the terms handed down. The *Guardian* described them as "out of all proportion with everything except the value of the property involved". The *Daily Herald* calculated that the prisoners would have been punished less for a combination of manslaughter, blackmail, and breaking a baby's arm.

Three of the gang were wanted at the time of the trial and later tracked down. Bruce Reynolds, James Edward White and Ronald "Buster" Edwards received between fifteen and twenty-five years each upon their eventual capture. Ronald Biggs was sentenced to thirty years in prison, but he succeeded in escaping with Charles Wilson, another of the armed robbers. Wilson was recaptured, but Biggs left the country. He narrowly avoided arrest in Australia, and eventually settled in Rio, where he leads a relatively rich and high-profile life, running his own nightclub and even appearing as himself in Malcolm Maclaren's film *The Great Rock 'n' Roll Swindle*.

The Brinks-Mat Bullion Robbery

In November 1983, robbers in England created another world record.

At 6:40 am on Saturday 26 November 1983, the men of the day security shift had just entered the Brinks-Mat high security warehouse in Houndslow, West London, and were preparing the day's orders. The nondescript factory unit was a stop-off point for valuable shipments travelling to and from nearby

Heathrow airport and contained one of the country's largest vaults. As such, its security systems were state of the art and an undetected entry would have seemed next to impossible.

Nevertheless, as four of the six security guards stood chatting in the locker room a bizarre figure stepped through the entrance. He was wearing a black suit and tie with a trilby on his head. He was also wearing a yellow balaclava and brandishing a 9 mm Browning automatic pistol.

"Get on the floor or you're fucking dead", he roared. Three of the guards complied immediately, but the fourth, Peter Bentley, just stared. The intruder crossed the room and struck him over the head with the weapon, hurling him to the floor with a badly gashed scalp. More armed, balaclavaed men ran into the room and proceeded to bind the guards' arms and legs with tape and to cover their heads with black cloth bags tied at the neck with drawstrings.

The two other guards, Tony Black and Michael Scouse, were in the radio room at the time and were similarly surprised and bound. At this point the man who appeared to be leading the intruders ordered that a radio be tuned to the police waveband to pre-warn them of any alert. The security guards noted that he had a clipped, well-spoken voice with no discernible accent – unlike the others who sounded cockney.

Whoever the raiders were, they knew the Brinks-Mat security systems intimately. The only way to open the vault and safes was with two different keys and two different sets of combinations. These were held by the senior security guards, Robin Riseley and Mick Scouse; the robbers demanded these "keymen" specifically *by name*. Also, on the way to the vault the raiders used *their own key* to open an intervening door.

Outside the vault, Scouse and Riseley were subjected to a fresh incentive to cooperate. Their trousers were cut open and petrol was poured on their bellies and genitals. Scouse was then told: "You better do as I say, or I'll put a match to the petrol and a bullet through your head."

The keymen were given no opportunity to "accidentally" set-off the alarms as they proceeded to access the vault and its safes. The robbers gave specific orders as to which systems had to be deactivated and in what order. This, and other facts, later convinced the police that the criminals had been working with inside information.

Entering the vault they were forced to clamber around a large number of shoebox-sized, grey cardboard boxes to gain access to the three safes. Here the raiders' plan broke down. Riseley had become so frightened he was unable to remember his half of the codes for the safes and no amount of blows or threats could make him remember the numbers.

In frustration the robbers demanded what was in the little boxes. Scouse, realizing that they might kill Riseley if there was nothing to distract them from the safes, replied that the boxes contained gold ingots. Some of the boxes were torn open and the fact was confirmed. In their haste the thieves had almost missed three tonnes of purest gold bullion with an approximate market value of twenty-six million pounds.

Soon afterwards, the other guards – lying in blindfolded darkness – heard the familiar squeak of the loading trolley, the sound of the entry bay doors opening and a vehicle entering. Then they heard one of the robbers shout, "We're going to need another van." Evidently they had come prepared, because another vehicle roared in moments later.

The two keymen were brought back as this went on and one of the robbers sympathetically asked Scouse, "Are you all right, Mick?" Riseley, on the other hand, who the raiders had though was being "a hero", was dismissed with a derisive, "It's a good job it's Christmas."

The vault was emptied and the robbers jumped into the vans. Just as the guards started to relax a little, one of the raiders re-appeared in the doorway. "Merry Christmas!" he shouted, then ran to the departing vehicles.

The six man gang got clean away with £26 million in gold plus £160,000 of platinum, £113,000 worth of rough diamonds and £250,000 in untraceable traveller's cheques. It was the most profitable robbery in British history.

The police had little firm evidence to go upon. The security guards all agreed that the gang was made up of white males between thirty and forty years old, but so were most of the London armed robber fraternity. However, during the hour-long raid some of the thieves had lifted the lower half of their balaclavas to speak more clearly. The guards thought that they might be able to identify the "Bully" and the "Boss", if they saw them again. These were the man who had clubbed Bentley to the ground and the well-spoken leader.

The insurance company that had to shoulder the burden of the robbery issued a £2 million reward for the identities of the thieves, but nobody came forward. The police were left with only one solid line of enquiry, the fact that somebody on the inside of the Brinks-Mat organization seemed to have fed the robbers security secrets.

Although many people had access to this information, there was the fact that the robbers had passed under several security cameras to gain access to the building to consider. This suggested that the two men in the radio room – which also housed the monitors – had not been doing their duty. Interrogation showed that Mick Scouse had been engrossed in organizing the day's shipments, leaving Tony Black to watch the screens alone.

An investigation of Black's background revealed an interesting fact. Although he had a clean criminal record, he was the brother-in-law of Brian Robinson: one of the top ten suspected armed robbers in the country. Robinson's nickname in the criminal underworld was "The Colonel", due to his excellent organizing abilities and military-style, accentless voice.

After intensive interrogation Black broke down and admitted he had been the informant. He had been meeting regularly with his brother-in-law to hand over information, photos of the warehouse security systems and even a copy of the entrance key. Black, thereafter, cooperated fully with the investigation, but in one matter he could not help the police: he had no idea where the bullion was hidden.

The police quickly arrested Robinson and several other suspects. The security guards, at identity parades, singled Robinson out as the "Boss" and a second man, Michael McAvoy, as the "Bully". On 29 October 1984, these two and a third suspect, Tony White, were sent for trial at the Old Bailey under heavy security.

At the trial, Tony Black – who had already been given seven years for his part in the robbery – testified for the prosecution wearing a bullet-proof vest. It was rumoured that the man the press had dubbed "The Gold Mole" had a million pound contract on his head; perhaps the very money he had been promised as his share of the criminal proceeds.

He told the court that neither he or the robbers had any idea that the vault would contain so much loot when they agreed the date of the raid; it had been a matter of pure luck.

Eventually, on 3 December, the trial came to a close. Robinson and McAvoy were both found guilty, but White was acquitted. Outside the court he told reporters: "The evidence against us was the same. We should all have been acquitted." As the judge passed down twenty-five year sentences on

Robinson and McAvoy they both smiled: they had expected life imprisonment.

As the months passed the press interest in what had happened to the king's ransom taken in the raid decreased. It was rumoured that both the gold and the unprosecuted thieves were now safely abroad in countries with no extradition treaty with Britain. The police, of course, continued to investigate with vigour. Such a vast sum of gold was bound to leave some trace of its passing.

Most armed robberies can only hope to net a few thousands of pounds. The safes in the Brinks-Mat vault had held several hundred thousand pounds in used notes on the day of the robbery, and this in itself would have been an excellent haul. Millions of pounds worth of bullion, on the other hand, was quite another matter. The London underworld would not have had the resources to launder such a huge load, so the police began an extensive, national investigation to find those who were handling the gold.

Fourteen months after the robbery, on a freezing evening in January 1985, an incident took place at the Kent country home of wealthy property dealer and businessman Kenneth Noye, which reawakened public interest.

The police had been keeping Noye under surveillance for just over two weeks. They had reason to believe that he was an important link in the Brinks-Mat "gold chain", a group of seemingly legitimate businessmen who were re-casting and selling the gold for the absent robbers. The police team included men from the elite C11 squad – espionage-level experts in covert surveillance – whose job it was to hide as close to Noye's grounds as possible.

On that evening the two C11 officers were Detective Constables John Fordham and Neil Murphy. At 6:15 pm the order was give for them to close in on the house, entering the grounds, to reconnoitre. It has not since been made clear if this was just a standard check of the area or the preliminary to the serving of a search warrant on the Noye property. Either way, the two men were surprised by Noye's young Rottweiler guard dogs and DC Murphy retreated back to the fence. This was standard procedure in such a case and he did not bother to look to see if his partner was following. For some reason though, Fordham continued into the property, despite the barking dogs.

Kenneth Noye heard the dogs and went to investigate. Since darkness had already fallen he first went to his car to get a torch. He also picked-up a kitchen knife, which he later told the police he had been using to scrape clean a battery terminal. He said that as he walked to where his dogs were barking a terrifying figure loomed out of the shadows.

It is true that Fordham would have looked a fearsome sight that evening. He was wearing several thick layers of clothes under a combat style jacket and must have looked huge. He was also wearing a dark coloured balaclava through which only his eyes and mouth could be seen.

Noye stabbed him ten times in the heart region of the chest. He was still conscious when other officers arrived, but was pronounced dead on arrival at Queen Mary's Hospital in Sidcup.

At the subsequent murder trial the prosecution tried to prove that Noye, and another man called Brian Reader, had gone out with the deliberate intention of killing D.C. Fordham. As evidence they produced eleven re-moulded 1 kilo bars of gold found at Noye's house and pointed out to the jury that Reader, who had been visiting the house at the time, was a fugitive from justice – he had been on the run in Spain for some years, trying to avoid a burglary charge at home. To stop Fordham discovering these facts they had, said the Crown, cold blood-edly killed the officer.

Noye replied in the witness stand that he had been unaware of Reader's criminal status. He freely admitted that he was involved in the illegal smuggling of gold bullion, but he was not, he insisted, a murderer. Fordham, he said, had reared up at him in the darkness and struck him across the face. In a panic, and thinking he was about to be killed, he had stabbed wildly at the figure, but it just kept coming towards him. Later he realized that Fordham had been collapsing from the wounds.

Medical evidence showed that Noye had indeed suffered some battering to the face, but could not ascertain if this had happened before or during the knifing. A defence forensics expert also testified that after the killing, Fordham's balaclava had been clumsily tampered with, by persons unknown, to make it look less frightening. This was, presumably, to under-mine Noye's claim to striking out of fear.

In the absence of any immediate witnesses to the killing and the lack of any conclusive physical evidence, the jury found both defendants not guilty. However, Noye had admitted to gold smuggling and thus had little chance of avoiding jail.

He, Reader and a third man, called Garth Chappell, were

later found guilty of conspiracy to handle stolen bullion and evasion of VAT payments. Noye was sentenced to a total of fourteen years imprisonment and was fined £500,000. Reader and Chappell were jailed for nine and ten years respectively.

Since that time the police have failed to retrieve any of the Brinks-Mat bullion or catch any of the other robbers. For a short time a deal was struck with the imprisoned McAvoy and Robinson that if they returned the gold they would greatly increase their chance of early probation; but, in the end, this came to nothing.

The prisoners trusted their associates to keep their shares until they were released, but when they asked for their portions early, they were refused. The authorities offered them a similar deal for the names of the other criminals, but up to now they have maintained the underworld code of loyalty and kept silent.

It is believed that most, if not all the bullion has now been converted into legitimate property and cash and with interest it must now be worth many times the original value of the haul. Much is rumoured to have been invested in London's Dockland refurbishment project.

The identities of the four remaining thieves and many of their associates are now said to be known by the police. They are believed to be living in Spain's Costa del Sol. At the time of writing, August 1993, Britain has no extradition treaty with Spain.

The Knightsbridge Safe Deposit Robbery

Nothing seemed less likely than that someone would break the record established – albeit accidentally – in the Brinks-Mat robbery. But within three years, the gang who robbed the Knightsbridge Safe Deposit had almost doubled it. This may also be regarded as *the* "inside job" of all time, since the man who planned it was the manager and part-owner.

Security Deposits of Brompton Road, Kensington, catered for the kind of customer who found banks a bore. The business provided lockable safe deposit boxes in a secure building and also a discreet lack of curiosity as to their customers' affairs. The owners, Zahid Adamjee and Parvez Latif, had spent £825,000 acquiring the business in 1986, believing that the economic boom of the time would lead to huge demand for high security storage. Things had not gone well however, and in their first year they lost £400,000 and rented out only a quarter of their capacity. Latif stood to lose most, as his background was far less wealthy than that of his partner. He had a £100,000 overdraft, and little prospect of paying it off.

Around this time, Latif became friendly with a client of the firm, a man named Valerio Viccei. Viccei was a conspicuously wealthy young man, with a taste for Ferraris and rich living. He was also wanted in his native Italy, for bank robbery, and was also suspected of involvement with ultra-right wing terrorism. He remained financially afloat in London in much the same way as he had in Italy, robbing banks when he was short of cash. Unsurprisingly, he himself used Latif's business rather than entrust his money to a bank.

The two men socialized, often going to restaurants together. At some stage the fact that Viccei's main skill was the answer to Latif's main problem occurred to them both, and they set about planning the robbery of *Security Deposits*.

Latif increased the value of the business's insurance to £1 million, while Viccei gathered four accomplices and contacted a fence, Israel Pinkas, to help him dispose of any expensive items that the crime might turn up. At around 3 pm, on Sunday 12 July 1987, Viccei rang *Security Deposits* posing as a prospective customer, and asked to be shown around.

That Sunday the business was being run by Latif with only two security guards. One of these took Viccei's call and told his employer that a customer was coming to look at the arrangements. Around 3:15 pm, Viccei arrived with one of his team, and was shown into the secure area by Latif, who all the time was playing the attentive manager eager to acquire a new account. Viccei pulled out a pistol, and in a performance that the police later described as "worthy of an Oscar" Latif "panicked" and allowed the thieves to do what they liked.

Viccei smashed the locks of each box with a sledgehammer, while his accomplice followed with a crowbar and a sack, wrenching open the wrecked doors and grabbing the contents. In the rush, Viccei cut his hand badly, but carried on his work in a very professional manner. At around 5 pm the gang left the building, about £40 million richer.

For the moment however Viccei and the others were not sure of how much they had taken. £2,500 was given out to each of the accomplices as spending money, and the gang split.

It is not known exactly how much was stolen that day. Estimates are low as £20 million and as high as £60 million. Rumours suggested that the gang also got away with some of the laundered money from the Brinks-Mat Bullion robbery two years earlier. The police were, naturally, desperate to apprehend the gang.

The ease with which the crime was achieved seemed to indicate inside help, but for the moment the police did not suspect Latif. He continued his performance, returning to work every morning and trying to deal with the flood of outraged customers.

Some things about the business puzzled the investigating officers. For example there was no video-taped surveillance of the robbery. Latif pointed out, not unreasonably, that many of his customers objected strenuously to being filmed, and that the lack of this security feature was a positive selling point of his service. The absence of any alarm that connected directly to the police was more difficult to explain; Latif's answer to this query was that his staff dialled 999 if there was any problem. For the time being the police were stumped.

Forensic examination of the smashed lockers soon provided a hugely significant clue. There was a fingerprint in blood on one of the doors. The print was so clear and prominent that at first the police imagined that it might be a kind of arrogant challenge from the robbers. Although their attempts to identify the print at first were unsuccessful, searching the records of foreign criminals thought to be in the UK soon produced the name "Valerio Viccei".

Police next set up surveillance on a group of people thought to be Viccei's friends. Among them was Israel Pinkas, who had been very busy since the robbery. Officers observed that some of the group, including Pinkas, frequented White's Hotel on the Bayswater Road. Pinkas seemed often to be looking out for a black Ferrari that regularly parked in the Hotel's drive. The police checked the car's details in their computer, but it showed that the owner was not Viccei.

Observation finally paid off however, and one day the officers recognized Viccei leaving the hotel and climbing into the black Ferrari. Viccei *had* bought the car only a few weeks before, for £87,000 cash. The registration documents had not yet been processed. As the Ferrari pulled into a virtually stationary queue of traffic, an officer tried to reach in through the open window and take the ignition key. Viccei dragged the police-man about twenty yards down the road before another officer succeeded in getting on the car's bonnet and smashing the windscreen with his truncheon. Viccei was under arrest.

Having trapped the man that they believed to be the kingpin of the gang, the police set about following the trails of evidence to his accomplices. While searching Viccei's flat, they came upon an interesting piece of paper: a phone bill from Viccei's room in an Israeli hotel. Among the calls to Pinkas and to other people that the police already suspected was a call logged to Parvez Latif, the owner of the robbed business and supposed victim of the crime. This was damning evidence, and he too was soon arrested, along with Israel Pinkas, Latif's girlfriend and all but two of the rest of the gang.

The trial took place at the Old Bailey, and there was little doubt as to the outcome. Viccei received twenty-two years, Latif eighteen. One of the gang testified against his fellows, and was given only five years. Sixteen months later another gang member, Eric Rubin, was caught and sentenced to twelve years.

The capture of Viccei, and the consequent arrests of the others, could have been avoided entirely were it not for the black Ferrari. Viccei had planned to travel to Colombia and to lie low there. He would not go, however, without his new car. The Colombian embassy were making bureaucratic difficulties, and it seemed that the license to import the car would not be granted for many days. Viccei determined to wait, and in doing so doomed himself and his accomplices to long prison sentences.

The Whitchelo Case

The 1980s witnessed the advent of a new type of crime: consumer terrorism, in which large companies were black-mailed by criminals who threaten to tamper with their pro-ducts and so cause a slump in their sales. One of the most memorable practitioners of this new dimension in extortion was an ex-police sergeant called Rodney Whitchelo, who was inspired to try consumer terrorism after hearing a lecture about it at the Detective Training School in Ripley, Derbyshire, in the summer of 1986.

Soon after hearing the lecture, Whitchelo – still in the force – opened three building society accounts in the names of John and Sandra Norman. The cash-cards and statements were sent to a mailing address in Hammersmith, so no one ever saw the face of the account holder.

During the course of the next two years Whitchelo was transferred from the Regional Crime Squad to the CID in Hackney; but he took care to keep up with his old mates.

In August 1988, the Managing Director of Pedigree Petfoods in Leicestershire received a tin of his own firm's pet food, together with a letter which demanded £100,000 to prevent its products from being contaminated. The tin of pet food had been injected with poison. If they did not pay, said the letter-writer, dozens of similarly contaminated tins would appear on supermarket shelves. It instructed the company to insert an advertisement in the personal columns of the *Daily Telegraph*.

Pedigree contacted the police, who told them to obey the instructions. So a happy birthday message to "Sandra" was inserted in the *Telegraph*. They added a telephone number suggested by the police.

In a second letter, the blackmailer explained how the "ransom" was to be handed over. It was to be paid into three building society accounts that were in the names of John and Sandra Norman. Here Whitchelo revealed something like criminal genius. Most consumer terrorists, like most kidnappers, were caught during the hand-over of cash. But he could go and draw out money from thousands of cash machines all over the country.

Here the police scored their first minor triumph. Detective Inspector Ian Leacey, who was in charge of the case, authorized some of the money to be paid into only one of the Normans' three accounts – the Halifax. This at least limited the number of machines he could use to nine hundred.

The blackmailer soon began to withdraw cash, at the rate of £300 per day (the maximum). Withdrawals were as far apart as Wales and Scotland. And there was no obvious way to catch the blackmailer except by placing a constant watch on all nine hundred cash machines.

In spite of his success, the blackmailer was furious that the police had restricted him to the Halifax account. He telephoned four supermarkets, warning them that their pet food had been tampered with. Three of the calls turned out to be hoaxes; but the fourth – to a supermarket in Basildon – was not; several tins with minute holes proved to contain injections of salicylic acid. Then he wrote to Pedigree Petfoods again, warning them that in future he would contaminate their tins with razor blades. But Leacey kept his nerve, and declined to authorize payment of ransom money into the other accounts.

In March 1989, Heinz Babyfoods became the target of the blackmailer; they were told that if they failed to pay £100,000 a year for five years, their products would be contaminated with caustic soda.

Now the operation to trap the gang (as the police assumed it to be) was transferred to Scotland Yard, and placed in the hands of Chief Superintendent Pat Fleming. And Fleming decided that he had only one option: to organize a huge operation to watch all nine hundred machines. It would be impossible to mount the watch all the time – the cost would have been prohibitive. But since withdrawals were being made virtually every day, it should be enough to watch all machines on the same day.

The immense operation was a failure. For what Fleming had failed to take into account was that he might be dealing with a blackmailer with "inside" knowledge. Whitchelo had, in fact, resigned from the force in 1988 on health grounds – asthma – but he kept in touch with his old colleagues, who spoke freely in front of him. So whenever detectives – three thousand of them – were engaged in watching cash machines, Whitchelo stayed home. As soon as the operation ceased, he started withdrawals again.

Fleming installed video-cameras at some of the cashpoints. One day, a withdrawal was made at one of these. The tape was rushed to London, and eagerly wound to the right time. The watchers groaned as they saw that the blackmailer was wearing a crash helmet with a tinted visor; he had outsmarted them again.

The blackmailer again tried to force his victims to put money into other accounts. He had so far netted over £14,000, but he wanted bigger sums. Heinz became aware that he was putting on the pressure when a baby in Cowley, Oxford, began to bleed from the mouth as his mother fed him pear yoghurt; the forensic lab found it to be full of tiny fragments of razor blade. A lady in Rayleigh, Essex, was luckier: she had poured

Heinz beef dinner onto a plate for her puppy when she saw a piece of paper that said: "Poisoned with NaOH" in the bottom of the jar. (NaOH is the chemical formula for caustic soda.)

Fleming now tried telling the Halifax to make their machine swallow the card of John and Sandra Norman next time it was presented; they were hoping to get a fingerprint from it. In fact, the card had been handled with gloves; but Whitchelo's response was to threaten to put cyanide in the food. In doing so, he forced Fleming to "go public"; at a press conference on 27 April 1989, he called a press conference and told the reporters about the blackmail. The result, of course, was a slump in the sale of Heinz babyfoods. Oddly enough, it also led to two thousand copycat offences.

Now his account had been closed, Whitchelo's cash supply had been cut off. But when Heinz offered a reward of £100,000 for information about the blackmailer, he saw his chance. He contacted Heinz – using a stencil – and claimed to be someone close to the blackmailers, who would cooperate with the police if the reward money was paid into two building society accounts held in the name of Ian and Nina Fox. Police attempts to trace who opened these accounts were as unsuccessfull as in the case of John and Sandra Norman, which convinced them that this was no informant, but the original blackmailer. Fleming authorised Heinz to pay the reward into the building societies the blackmailer had named.

Fleming was now beginning to suspect that the blackmailer was *too* lucky – that is, that there was some kind of leak. His response was to set up a new and secret operation, code-named Agincourt, and to allow the rest of the force to believe that the cooperation was being run down. Fleming's hunch was confirmed when the blackmailer grew lazy, and began limiting himself to cash machines in and around London. It looked as if he was a Londoner. In which case, he could be caught with a much more limited operation. Fleming's secret group consisted of only enough men to watch fifteen cashpoint machines. The operation was set for 20 and 21 October. Fifteen Woolwich Society cashpoints were staked out, since the blackmailer seemed to favour the Woolwich.

At this point, "Agincourt" was struck by what – at the time – seemed appalling bad luck. A workman with a drill sliced through a cable servicing the Woolwich computer, putting many machines out of action. But since the men were now in position, Fleming decided they might as well press ahead.

Whitchelo had decided on one of his favourite tactics: to go out just before midnight and withdraw £300. Then he could wait until a few minutes after midnight, and withdraw another £300 – the limit being £300 on any specific date.

He chose the machine in Uxbridge, Middlesex. As it happened, this was not covered by a surveillance team. But it was also one of the machines put out of action by the severed cable. Whitchelo drove on to Enfield.

At half past midnight, the surveillance team – of two – at Enfield saw a Peugeot pull up and a man in a crash helmet climb out. They watched him withdraw £300, then stepped up to him as he climbed back into his car. Detective Constable Mark Kiarton asked what the crash helmet was for; the man said that it was raining. Meanwhile, the other constable had found the cashcard in the name of Ian and Nina Fox. "We are placing you under arrest." As he spoke, Rodney Whitchelo slumped in a faint.

Whitchelo pleaded not guilty, but the typewriter on which he had typed the "ransom" demands was found in his bachelor flat in Hornchurch, Essex. So was a tape he had made with a journalist friend with whom he intended to collaborate on a book. Its subject: how to commit the perfect crime.

On 17 December 1990, at the Old Bailey, Whitchelo was found guilty of blackmail and contaminating food products, and sentenced to seventeen years in prison.

PART 3: SWINDLES AND HOAXES

SPORTING SWINDLES

Ben Johnson: Cheats Never Prosper?

On 30 December 1961, a legend was born in Falmouth, Jamaica. By 1977, only a year after emigrating to Canada, he had caught the eye of one of Canada's top athletics coaches. His talent was so prodigious, his determination to win so fierce, that it was predicted, even at this early age, that he would soon conquer the athletics world. His name is, of course, Ben Johnson. His coach, Charlie Francis. Together they were determined to win the ultimate prize: the Olympic 100 metres gold medal.

Francis pushed the athlete to his physical peak and beyond and, by 1980, Johnson had made such progress that he had qualified for the Olympic games in Moscow. Canada, however, in response to the Soviet Union's ill fated invasion of Afghanistan, boycotted the games and Johnson stayed at home. It was probably better that way, as he was still not fully prepared. The Pan American games had pitted him against Carl Lewis for the first time; Lewis finished first, with Johnson trailing behind in sixth position.

That defeat ensured that Johnson returned to the training ground with renewed motivation. He had seen the standard that he needed to achieve and believed himself capable of attaining it. And indeed the years 1980 to 1984 were years of constant, if undramatic, improvement. In 1981 he became the Canadian champion. In 1982, he finished second to Alan Wells in the Commonwealth games. By 1983 he had reached the semi-finals of the World Championships and the Olympic year saw him grab the bronze medal in Los Angeles.

Improvement indeed, but Lewis still finished the races before him and that hurt. Fired by the desire to beat the American, Johnson threw himself into training with a maniacal fervour. And soon his inner belief was justified. Only a year after the Olympics, Johnson defeated Lewis for the first time. Soon after, he won the World Cup and stated categorically that his talent and his talent alone would make him the fastest human on earth. It was a bold statement, but one that over the next three years was to come true. First, he easily won the 1986 Commonwealth games and throughout that year posed a serious threat to the world record. Then, at the start of 1987, he stunned Lewis and his fellow competitors by setting a new indoor world record for the 60 metres. Lewis, crowned prince of the sprints for so long, looked more and more unsettled as the year passed. By the start of the World Championships, Johnson was tipped to win and win he did, in a breathtaking world record time of 9.83 seconds.

But the Canadian was not content with a World Championship gold and the world record. What use was being the fastest man on earth, unless he had won the ultimate prize: the Olympic gold medal. The year 1988 was to be his crowning glory. Lewis might be smarting from defeat, he might return quicker than ever before, but he would not regain his crown. On that, Johnson was decided.

Nonetheless, it was not to be a walkover. Lewis did return

The Olympian ideal is one of the utmost integrity, courage and dedication. But Spridon Belokas had other ideas. The year was 1896, the race was the marathon and anabolic steroids had not been invented, yet alone used to improve an athlete's performance. So what did Spridon do? Hired a horse and carriage, of course. As soon as he was free from the crowds, he slipped into the carriage and rode in luxury. Even with this help, however, he could only finish third and was soon detected and stripped of his bronze medal.

quicker and brimming with aggression. All year long, the two athletes traded year-best times, and it began to look as if the winner of the Olympic games would be whoever kept his head for longest. But then, only a few weeks before the Games, Johnson's form dipped so dramatically that doubts were cast on his ability to win the gold medal, or indeed any medal. It was a critical time for the athlete: he needed to draw upon all his strength of character and inner belief to overcome this setback. That he succeeded at all is a great credit to him, but his response was truly herculean: Johnson scorched to a time of 9.79 seconds a new world record and, more importantly, the Olympic gold medal. His dreams had been realized and his place in the record books was secure. Ben Johnson would forever be known as the greatest sprinter the world had ever seen.

How many accounts similar to the above do you think were produced on the eve of 25 September 1988? Hundreds for certain, probably thousands. For there is no doubt that the Johnson/Lewis duel had captured the imagination of the entire world. The manner of Johson's victory left people dumbfounded. The fact that he had been able to slow down before the finish was amazing. He could have gone faster, if he had needed to. He had competed at the top level, run in the fastest race of all time, yet he could have gone faster. What did the future hold in store, people wondered.

Not, as it happened, the string of world records and imperious victories which, on the eve of 25 September, had seemed more likely than possible; Johnson's glory was to be shortlived. On 27 September, an IOC spokesperson, Michelle Verdier, stepped forward and made an announcement that shocked the sporting world: Ben Johnson's urine sample, taken after the final as was routine, had been found to contain traces of a banned anabolic steroid. Johnson was, therefore, to be stripped of his Olympic title.

The world looked on in bewilderment. The man that only two days before had been hailed as the embodiment of honourable struggle was now exposed as a sham. The remarkable surge in his fortunes after the Los Angeles Olympics had not, after all, been achieved by his inner strength and conviction that he was the best. His repeated statements that his talent and his talent alone would make him the best were seen to be filthy lies: soundbytes for the media. He had betrayed the trust placed in him and was now to reap the reward: by the end of that fateful September day, he had been banned from international athletics by both the International Amateur Athletics Federation and the Canadian Government. Stripped of the Olympic gold medal and both the world records he had set in the last year, Johnson had been effectively wiped from the record books.

It had been a woeful day. Juan Antonio Samaranch, head of the Olympic Federation, gave a fitting summary. "This" he intoned "has been a blow for the Olympic games and the Olympic movement." Johnson had, briefly, represented all that was good in the human spirit. Now he was exposed as just another gambler, greedy for the big prize.

Larry Heiderbrecht, Johnson's business manager, tried an appeal. "Ben" he stated "is obviously sick at the news and will appeal. He is shattered." Almost as an afterthought, he added: "Ben does not take drugs." It was a lame attempt: trying to pin the blame on a mysterious third party, rather than expressing the athlete's innocence. He would have done better to have withdrawn in silence.

The question was not "Had he cheated?", but "Why?" And it was an issue reflected upon at length. The panegyrics were torn up and in their place came article upon article analysing his motives. Theories abounded, but why he cheated seems uncomfortably clear. Any Olympic title guarantees an athlete fame, but an Olympic gold in the 100 metres is a passport to fame and fortune. No doubt his manager, Mr Heiderbrecht, had informed him that he stood to gain five million pounds in endorsements alone, with his Olympic victory. Johnson was simple, but not that simple.

The reason for his detection, however, was and still is much less apparent. Doubt had been raised long before the Olympics about Johnson's expanding physique, especially during the 1987 World Championships, yet nothing had been proven.

> **Ben Johnson may have changed the shape of his body illegally, but Stella Walsh of Poland went one better. Stella was the 1932 Olympic 100 metres champion. Nothing much wrong there, it appears, and indeed for nearly fifty years the name of Stella Walsh remained pure and unblemished. But in 1980, Stella was visiting a bank in Cleveland when she became the tragic victim of a bank robber's bullet. At the autopsy, the truth came out. Stella was no more a woman than Linford Christie!**

So why was it that he had been caught a year later? Again, countless articles debated this topic and countless theories were proposed. The most likely reason is that he simply mis-timed his course of treatment. His form began to drop off before the Olympics, and on 17 and 21 August both Carl Lewis and Calvin Smith had beaten him. Most probably, this panicked him into taking a booster injection close to the Games themselves and it was this intake that was picked up by the Olympic testers. Johnson, it would seem, was caught, not because he had been dishonest, but because he had failed to follow the instructions properly.

If we accept this hypothesis, then a very ugly fact is staring straight at us: cheats do prosper, and only the reckless are caught. Can this be true?

Close examination of the facts suggests that it is. Since Johnson's capture, the International Amateur Athletics Federation have taken the problem of drugs in sport much more seriously and have instituted more rigorous testing procedures. Nowhere has this had more effect than in women's athletics. Superstars such as Katrin Krabbe, the 1991 100 and 200 metre world champion, and Tatyana Dorovskikh, also a 1991 world champion (in the 3,000 metres) have been banned. But more importantly, there has been an incredible fall in performance. Petra Felke, for instance, threw the javelin 80 metres in 1988 to set a stunning world record. By 1992, the leading throw of the year was 10 metres behind that mark. And it is the same throughout all the events. Florence Griffith Joyner's records of 10.49 seconds in the 100 metres and 21.34 seconds in the 200 metres, also set in 1988, look impregnable. The shot and the discus events have seen distances thrown drop by 10%, and the 400, 1,500, 3,000 and 10,000 metres are all run in much slower

---

Does the name Boris Onischenko ring a bell? Well, it should. For this ingenious pentathlete is one of the most famous cheats in Olympic history. Rather worried by his lack of form in the fencing discipline, he decided to take the chance out of the contest. Thus, he fixed up his sword electronically, in order to obtain a hit at the touch of a button. Outraged opponents protested their innocence, but could never prove him a cheat, until he was caught in the act of rigging his equipment. It certainly took the drudgery out of his training!

times now than they were in 1988. What conclusion can one reach, except that cheats did prosper.

What, then, does this make Johnson? A fool for cheating, or a fool for being caught? It is tempting to describe him as athletics's biggest fraud, but how can this be true, if there are dozens, perhaps hundreds, of athletes who have committed the same crime, but have not been caught. Ben Johnson is simply the most visible example of exactly how far humans will go to be the best. Is it not, in fact, we, the audience, who are being somewhat hypocritical in demanding ultimate fairness in sport? "All's fair in love and war" is a well trodden cliché, but why should sport be any different? Cheating in sport did not begin and end in 1988, it has been with us for all time. Johnson was not the first Olympian to be disqualified – to be accurate he was the forty-third – and he certainly won't be the last. But, for a short time, he was an ideal to look up to, an inspiration to be drawn upon. He was the centre of that wonderfully uplifting delusion we are all under, that sport is somehow different from, and superior to, the world we live in. His crime was to shatter that illusion.

Marseille: Architects of Their Own Downfall?

Which athlete came a gallant sixth in the 1992 Olympic 400 metres final?

Which football team finished seventh behind Leeds United in the 1991–1992 Football League season?

Very difficult questions to answer. But that is how sport works. It is gloriously black or white. There are no fudged issues or demoralizing compromises. There are winners who are revered as gods or losers whose name no one remembers. This state of affairs applies equally to individual or team sports. It may not be fair, but it is compelling.

Given that winning is so important, it is none too surprising to find that not only individuals but also entire teams are prepared to alter the odds in their favour. What athletes achieve through the abuse of drugs, football teams achieve through bribery. But the end result is the same: to win by cheating.

Nowhere in football is this creed better examplified than in France. Over the last twenty years, hundreds of scandals have been exposed. May 1971 saw Saint-Etienne furiously accuse Marseille of having tried to bribe their French internationals, Georges Carnus and Bernard Bosquier, after Marseille had narrowly pipped them to the French title. By December 1977, Paris Saint-Germain had become so desperate to tempt players of high quality to the club that they actually sold match tickets on the black market, in order to increase their bargaining power. The same club was then caught, in 1982, operating a slush fund that made undeclared payments to nine of their stars, one of whom was France's present football manager, Michel Platini. The club chairman, Monsieur Rocher, was thrown in gaol.

As if these crimes were not enough, Bordeaux president Claude Bez admitted to having prostitutes on the club's pay-roll, in order that they might "take care of" match officials after European matches, and the same man was later found guilty of driving the club to debts of thirty million pounds and conse-quently imprisoned for fraud. After that, one might be forgiven for thinking that the worst was over, but that would be a misguided assumption. Marseille returned to the front pages in 1991 when allegations were made, by more than one source, that the club had tried to fix matches against Caen, Brest, Saint-Etienne and Bordeaux (who were themselves later relegated for financial irregularities). The allegations did not stick, but they were good enough to suspend the club owner Bernard Tapie for a year and to induce the Marseille players to strike.

A lively list of wrongdoing, which did nothing to improve France's club record in Europe. By the end of the 1992 season, not one European trophy had ever been won by a French side, for all their misdeeds and machiavellian intrigues. 1993 was to be different, they hoped. But the 1993 affair was to outstrip all France's previous scandals.

Here is some background: Marseille Football Club is more, much more than a football club. Set in the south of France, it stands head and shoulders above its rivals. It has more super-stars, more money and more supporters. It has won the French football league every year since 1989 (not even the mighty Liverpool can lay claim to that record) and is led by France's

> Brian Glanville is a journalist with a mission, which involves
> studying the Italians and their antics in the football arena. He has
> uncovered innumerable swindles. None could have been so
> bizarre, however, as Roma's attempt to curry favour with the
> referee before their European Cup semi-final second leg against
> Dundee United.
>   They sent a bribe of £50,000 to the referee, who not only did
> not receive it until after the match, but did not realize what it was
> and handed it back.

most outrageous entrepreneur, Bernard Tapie. The theme of his
ownership has been success, more success and even more
success. For Tapie had never done anything other than succeed, whether as head of a company, or as a minister in the
French government. He did not buy a football team for love, he
bought it for success, which in Tapie's terms meant the
European Cup.

As he had bought Marseille in 1986, it is apparent that he had
to wait longer than usual for the reward he craved. Perhaps the
club and its officials felt his impatience and decided to tip the
odds slightly in their favour. Perhaps they had been bribing
their way to success for all that time. Who knows? What is
certain is that they decided to make it easier for the team to win
the league – by means of an odd bribe here, a fixed match there
– so that all their concentration could be focused upon the true
goal: the European Cup.

However, although Tapie's desire to carry off Europe's
greatest prize was undoubtedly the driving force in this
affair, the business was conducted by a cast of thousands
who would not have been out of place in a Cecil B. de Mille
movie. The most important of these seem to have been the
general manager, Jean Pierre Bernes, and the Marseille midfielder, Jean Jacques Eydelie.

And now for the scandal itself. In short, Marseille stand
accused of buying a 1–0 league victory against Valenciennes on
20 May 1993, a victory which, to all intents and purposes,
clinched their fifth consecutive league title. The knowledge that
they would not have to try too hard to win the title – states the
prosecution – allowed them to focus with total dedication on
the imminent European Cup final in Munich.

At first sight, these allegations appear ridiculous. Valenciennes were having a wretched season and did not pose a realistic threat to Marseille. However, the allegations came not from unsubstantiated sources, but from one of the players who accepted the bribes. Christophe Robert, the Valenciennes forward, admitted taking a bribe from Marseille midfielder, Jean Jacques Eydelie, after he had been approached first of all by the Marseille general manager, Jean Pierre Bernes. He then added that team mates Jacques Glassman, a defender, and Jorge Burruchaga, a midfielder, were also approached.

On taking this confession, police immediately raided the house of Robert's aunt and dug up her garden; not because they had lost their minds, but because that was where Robert had hidden his bribe of 250,000 francs (nearly £35,000). The central characters in the case were then rounded up and taken in for interrogation on 6 July and the media event of the year had begun.

That a bribe had been offered was confirmed by the Valenciennes midfielder, Burruchaga, and, eventually (but only after his wife had confessed for him), by Eydelie. However, it was not to be all plain sailing for the prosecution, as the charges of active corruption were successfully refuted by Jean Pierre Bernes – he was released from custody at the end of July – and Jacques Glassman, the Valenciennes defender, who denied all knowledge of the plot. And there, at the time of writing, it stands. No doubt the truth will come out, albeit slowly, and the relevant legal action will be taken.

But putting aside the legal case, Marseille have already begun to suffer from the allegations. No thanks to the French football authorities, who allowed Marseille to start the new football season on 24 July as if nothing had happened, but to the swift movement of UEFA, who have banned Marseille from

---

Match fixing swindles do not occur only amongst the glory addicted football clubs. International football is affected too. But the prize at stake was not the World Cup; in one instance the prize at stake was the President's Cup held in South Korea. During this competition, the mighty Australian team alleged that they were approached by players from Romania, anxious to avoid defeat by an apparently weaker opposition (a fate the honourable English team suffer regularly). The Australians of course refused the bribe – it was only £3,000 – and lost anyway.

playing in the very competition that the club had so earnestly desired to win: the European Cup.

How ironic that, having worked so hard (whether by fair means or foul) to obtain its goal, the club has now lost the chance of repeating that success. Perhaps Marseille have been architects of both their glory and their humiliation.

But what of the French people's reaction to this affair? Bribery certainly appears to have taken place, and it did, in however small a way, help Marseille to win the league. Surely there was an upsurge of anger and disgust against this fraud? Well . . . yes and no. From those outside the confines of Marseille came warm approval of the investigation and sincere calls for the corruption in the French game to be rooted out. Noel le Graet, the French league president, even exclaimed that he would "deal with this gangrene". Yet from those who live in and around Marseille, the crisis seemed no more than a Parisian plot against Marseille, the city, Marseille, the football club, and Tapie, the club's owner. Instead of marching on Marseille's ground and demanding that justice prevail, the locals took to the streets in a noisy and defiant demonstration of solidarity. Proving the point that as long as you give people what they want they will willingly overlook the methods used, the supporters simply refuted the allegations by pointing to Marseille's success over the last few years. Why would such a successful club want to use bribery, they asked, neatly side-stepping the issue of how the club became successful in the first place.

Marseille was accused of using the most dishonest methods to gain victory, but in place of vitriol and denouncement, the

---

"Who's the bastard in the black?" A charming ditty heard on many an English football terrace. Referees are usually considered incompetent when they make yet another outrageous mistake, but in fact they are as susceptible to bribes as the players. In Portugal, the President of Penafiel and a FIFA referee were implicated in a bribery scandal and two years later, in 1993, the head of Portugal's referees' association reckoned that there could be many hundreds of his officials taking bribes every week. A Russian referee, Alexei Spirin, is the latest to be caught. He has been struck off the UEFA list for taking a bribe from Torino in their match with Norrkoping of Sweden.

club received plaudits and support. Indeed had it not been for the press exposure, one wonders whether the affair would have even surfaced. As Eric de Montgolfier, the public prosecutor dealing with the case, admitted, the press is his guarantee that the case will not be prevented from running its whole course.

Unfortunately, this is not an attitude peculiar to Marseille alone, nor even to France. Wherever one looks in the football world, one will find football teams ready to bribe their way to success and supporters ready to defend that success, however it was gained. There is none of the shame and disillusionment which was so apparent when Ben Johnson was found guilty of using performance-enhancing drugs. There is only a desperate need for victory.

A need that clubs are only too anxious to cater for. In Italy, for instance, Luciano Gaucci, the club president of Perugia, regularly offered horses to referees, in return for their services. In Cyprus, all four clubs on the brink of relegation paid their opponents for victory in the final match of the season, which led the newspapers to publish blank spaces where the reports would have been. And in Poland, so many teams were involved in bribery and match fixing that when Legia Warsaw were stripped of their title, it was not second place LKS Lodz who were made champions – as they had already been removed from the competition – but third placed Lech Poznan.

Where does all this intrigue and wheeler dealing leave football? Is playing the game for better or worse an outdated concept? If the swindles and frauds committed by the clubs are done with the backing of the supporters then are they really swindles and frauds? After all, a swindler needs someone to swindle and you can't commit fraud unless someone is there to be deceived. What used to be considered criminal now simply adds to the drama on the pitch. If anything, the scandals have made football more popular than before. They may not be morally upright, but they are magnetic.

Ben Johnson winning the Gold in the 100 metres, Seoul, Sept 26 1988.

The Chicago White Sox and the 1919 World Series

To talk about baseball and fair play in the same breath would be naïve. From its very conception, corruption was endemic, with gamblers openly boasting that they could control ball games with as much ease as they controlled horse races. Incidents where spectators, who had been paid to ensure fielding errors, stoned the players waiting for a high ball, were commonplace in baseball's early days and the American public soon seemed to have lost the ability to be shocked by the many various fixing and bribery scares. Until, that is, the infamous 1919 World Series.

Coming as it did so soon after the end of the First World War, this World Series was to be a happy celebration and confirmation of what it was to be American. The Chicago White Sox, the most powerful force in baseball, were expected to outclass and outperform the Cincinnati Reds, who by their own admission were simply making up the numbers. It was said that the Chicago fans were queuing up to see not whether their team would win, but how it would win. That they saw nothing of the sort was down to the biggest scandal baseball has ever seen: the Chicago White Sox had decided to throw the series.

The war had taken its toll on the entertainment business, of which baseball was the most important component. Accordingly, when play resumed in 1919, belts had to be tightened. Players in every team were forced to accept not only lower wages, but also a longer season. The Chicago team was worst affected, however, run as it was by the meanest owner in the land, Charles Albert Comiskey. As the season progressed and their superiority became more and more apparent, discontent rose, leading to angry threats of strike action by July of that year. The strike was averted, but the bitterness prevailed. All the players grumbled, but one man did more than that; he decided to take the situation into his own hands.

His name was Chick Gandil and he was especially embittered by the low wages, as he had grown used to the limelight and wanted the lifestyle to go with it. For some time he had wondered if his feelings were shared by any of the other players and in the July crisis he saw that they were. One

man in particular had voiced his frustration with anger: Eddie
Cicotte, the pitcher. Here was a man approaching the end of his
career, a career which had been outstandingly distinguished,
and yet he was paid less than many of the rookies at other
clubs. Gandil knew that if he could only devise a good enough
scam and persuade Cicotte to join him, then the others would
follow, such was the respect and admiration they felt for him.

For the remainder of the season, Gandil pondered on what
that scam might be, but as soon as the White Sox had stormed
into the World Series as red hot favourites, he knew that the
ideal opportunity had arisen. Three weeks before the World
Series was due to begin he asked the renowned gambler,
bookmaker and baseball expert, Joseph "Sport" Sullivan, to
visit him at his hotel, the Buckminster. On his arrival, Gandil
offered the simplest of propositions: If Sullivan could raise
$80,000 in cash, in advance, then Gandil would guarantee to
raise a sufficient number of players to throw the series. It was
too good an offer to refuse. Sullivan, despite not having access
to such a large sum, readily agreed. They shook hands on the
deal and both men went their separate ways: Gandil to raise the
players, Sullivan to raise the backers.

Gandil's task was to prove the simpler. He already had a
good idea as to who would be willing to join him and on 21
September 1919 he invited them to dinner. They were: Eddie
Cicotte, pitcher; "Swede" Risberg, shortstop; Fred McMullin,
utility infielder; Claude "Lefty" Williams, pitcher; George
"Buck" Weaver, third hitter; "Shoeless" Joe Jackson, fourth
hitter; and Oscar "Happy" Felsch, fifth hitter. Seven men who
could make or break the Chicago team. Gandil did not beat
about the bush. He told them of Sullivan and his $80,000
payment. All that was needed was to throw the series. The
deal was not immediately applauded, but by the end of the
night all had agreed to its terms.

Sullivan, in contrast, knew of only one person who would be
able to provide the necessary funds and that man was out of his
league. His name was Arthur Rothstein and he ran the biggest
gambling operation in America. Sullivan needed time to work
out how he might tempt Rothstein into this scam, and for the
meantime, he laid low.

These arrangements might seem somewhat carefree. But
none of the players involved thought that they were taking
any risk in arranging to throw the series, for they knew that
they would not be caught. This was baseball, and games were

In 1985 the Volga club of Gorky were disbanded by the Soviet Sports Committee, not for bribing other teams, not even for bribing the officials, but for bribing themselves. So desperate were the young players to gain a place in the team that they began to bribe their coach. This course of action had been suggested to them by the old hands, who implied it was an old tradition. That was not surprising, for when the club was investigated, these very same old hands were found to be taking a cut of the manager's bribe!

fixed all the time; it was part of their job. So it was not beyond belief that other gamblers – most notably, "Sleepy" Bill Burns – soon came to hear of their preparations. "Sleepy" Bill had been so named because of his somnolent personality and performances in the major league. Having retired in 1917, after one of the least distinguished careers in baseball, he had entered the oil business and, over the course of one year, had managed to earn a small fortune. On hearing of Gandil's plan to throw the series, Burns saw a second get rich quick opportunity. Accordingly, he offered to provide the money as well; he heard that Sullivan was supplying $80,000, so he proposed a sum of $100,000.

Gandil was overjoyed. His main worry had been getting the money; now here he was, two weeks before the Series began, with two men vying to pay him. It all seemed too good to be true; and it was. For, just as Sullivan did not have the money, neither did Burns, and he, too, knew of no other potential backer than Arnold Rothstein. The whole undertaking was likely to collapse unless one of the two gamblers, neither of whom were on intimate terms with Rothstein, could persuade him to underwrite it.

Burns, belying his nickname, was the first to strike. On 23 September he and his associate, Billy Maharg, approached Rothstein at the Jamaica race track and tried to enlist his support. Rothstein would not even meet them. Instead he sent his sidekick, the ex featherweight champion of the world, Abe Attell, to hear what they had to say. Impressed, Attell met Rothstein for dinner at the Reubens Restaurant and plugged the plan as hard as he could. In his opinion the plan could not fail. Rothstein, however, was not so sure. He did not know anything about either Burns or his partner, Maharg, and he was worried at the sheer number of people who were either directly involved, or seemed to know of the preparations. His answer, despite Attell's urgings, was: no. On hearing of Rothstein's decision Burns tried one last direct approach. When that failed, he threw in the towel. Gandil's plan was beginning to falter.

Sullivan, however, was still in the running and was prepared to chance his luck. He called the master gambler at home on 26 September and, to his surprise, Rothstein agreed to meet him the next day. What's more, the meeting was a success. Rothstein had had time to consider the scheme and, despite his reservations, he agreed to send another sidekick, Nat Evans, along with Sullivan to meet the players.

It was on 29 September, just two days before the Series was to start, that Evans, travelling as Mr Brown, and Sullivan arrived at the Warner Hotel. They were only just in time, for the players had lost hope of receiving anything more concrete than promises and at first their mood was black. For a time it grew even blacker, because Evans stated that he would pay after and not before the series was thrown, but eventually a deal was struck. $40,000 would be paid to the players in advance, while the other half would be placed in the safe at the Hotel Congress in Chicago, to be handed over after the games had been lost. Gandil's plan was saved and it had been saved by Sullivan. Burns, it appeared, would just have to kick his heels and think of what could have been.

Except that he had no intention of doing anything of the sort. For Burns thought that it was he who had succeeded in gaining Rothstein's support. On the day before Evans and Sullivan met the players, Burns had received a phone call from Abe Attell. During the course of this conversation, he learnt that Rothstein had reconsidered his position and would now go through with the whole scheme. He did not wish to be disturbed by any of the arrangements, however, so all contact should be with Mr Attell himself. This was music to Burns's ear, and, once again dreaming of dollar signs, he contacted the players to tell them of his success.

So with less than three days to go before the Series was due to start, the players seemed to be in the best of all positions. After having waited on tenterhooks for more than a week, they had suddenly been made a firm offer by Sullivan, followed immediately by Burns's. Again, too good to be true. For two reasons. First, the phone call from Attell was a con. The little man had been mesmerized by the riches to be obtained from

The maximum wage for footballers, which had existed for many years in England, had recently been abolished, when Tony Kay, Peter Swan and David Layne of Sheffield Wednesday – all three young men with outstanding future prospects – and a plethora of journeymen from the lower divisions decided that their wages still needed supplementing. Accordingly, they agreed to fix the results of the matches in which they played. Initially successful, they grew careless and were soon detected and thrown in prison, where they spent the rest of their footballing careers.

this scheme and on Rothstein's refusal had decided to go ahead with the plan regardless. His delay in ringing Burns was simply good, old fashioned fear. Rothstein did not like being double-crossed and would, more likely than not, have him killed. It goes without saying that he had no money at all. Second, Sullivan, on receiving the $40,000 advance, kept $30,000 for his own use, giving Gandil only $10,000, some $70,000 less than had been agreed on their first meeting only two weeks before.

Gandil was outraged, but he had gone too far to stop and begrudgingly accepted the $10,000, all of which he gave to Cicotte to keep him sweet. He knew that if Cicotte dropped out, the whole scheme would disintegrate. What's more, he reasoned, $10,000 was $10,000 more than Burns had come up with. Consequently, he fed the other players excuses and made ready to ensure that the series would be lost.

The real winners in this conspiracy, however, were never going to be the players. Acting out of an understandable sense of frustration, they had seized the only opportunity they had, but it led them into a world in which they were too naïve to compete. The gamblers quite simply used them. Rothstein might have guaranteed the players $80,000, but in behind the scenes bets, he placed over three times that amount on a Cincinnati win. He stood to win a fortune and he did not care one iota about the players who would help him win it. The same could be said about Sullivan, Burns, Attell and countless others who were all determined to make a killing out of the worst kept secret in baseball.

In theory, it was still possible for the players to change their minds, and that might have been the most sensible course of action, but the promise of riches proved too great a lure. Despite their reservations, they decided to throw the first game, and see what happened. Thus on 1 October 1919 the Cincinnati Reds came away with an unbelievable 9-1 victory.

Yet still their money did not materialize. Sullivan had begun to avoid the players and Attell, Burns's only source of cash, was decidedly unforthcoming. He had made a small fortune betting on a Cincinnati win, but was not prepared to give the players their just rewards. This threatened the whole scam.

Upset and anxious, the players were beginning to turn and although they threw the second game as well, this seemed likely to be the end of the swindle. Not even the $10,000 from Burns, which he had managed to extricate with great difficulty from Attell, was good enough now. They knew that the gamblers were taking them for a ride and their pride had been hurt. The Reds were nowhere near as good as the Chicago White Sox but they were 2-0 up in the series and receiving the plaudits of all America.

Besides, while travelling back to Chicago after the second game, they had to endure the taunts of Ring Lardner, the most popular and influential sportswriter of the day. He had even made up a ditty to the tune of *I'm forever blowing bubbles*, which went as follows:

> *I'm forever blowing ball games,*
> *Pretty ball games in the air.*
> *I come from Chi,*
> *I hardly try,*
> *Just go to bat and fade and die;*
> *Fortune's coming my way,*
> *That's why I don't care.*
> *I'm forever blowing ball games,*
> *And the gamblers treat us fair . . .*

Humiliated and angry, the players had had enough of intrigue and double dealing. They were baseball players and in the third game of the series, they would show themselves and America exactly what they could do.

Sullivan watched in horror as the third game was won by Chicago. Rothstein still believed the scheme to be on and had betted accordingly. Sullivan realized that he would be the proud owner of a pair of concrete shoes if the master gambler found out that the players were not in possession of the $40,000 he had sent. The only thing he could do to prevent this happening was to get the scheme working again. Hours of desperate pleas for money later, he had raised $20,000 and was standing in front of Gandil. He was greeted by a frosty smile. Gandil knew that Sullivan had doublecrossed him and was not happy. The players, he said, had decided to win the series. But on seeing the money, his resolve snapped. The fix was back on. Taking nothing for himself, he gave $5,000 each to "Swede" Risberg, "Happy" Felsch, "Lefty" Williams and "Shoeless" Joe Jackson.

So the White Sox suffered their third and fourth defeats of the nine game series. To all intents and purposes the swindle was now proceeding well. The players, one way or another, had received their $40,000 and the gamblers had backed Cincinnati successfully.

But Sullivan, in his desperation to restart the scheme, had promised a further payment of $20,000 if the Sox lost both the ensuing games. He had, of course, no intention of paying and was conspicuously absent when the players duly threw those games. Also, as the winners' and losers' prize money was calculated from the takings from the first five games, the players learnt how much they were to earn from the series after this fourth defeat. It came as quite a shock for them to realize that they could have earned more for winning the series than for throwing it. Once again their frustration and anger at being exploited, combined with their desperate desire to win, led them to abandon the fix.

Chicago's renaissance was staggering. The team that had been badly thrashed in four of the first five games, and that had been completely written off, bounced back with amazing force. A close victory in the sixth game was followed by a crushing triumph in the seventh. The series was wide open once again, and with the deficit reduced to only one game, with two games to play, the White Sox were the iron cast favourites once again.

Except with Arthur Rothstein. He had bet $270,000 on a

In September 1991, the Algerian distance runner Abbes Tehami cruised to victory in the Brussels Marathon. The manner of his victory – at the finish he had looked remarkably fresh – seemed to signal his arrival on the world stage. After a performance as convincing as this, what more was the man capable of? Moments later, however, opinions had changed, when it was discovered that his coach had run the first ten miles of the race for him!

Cincinnati win and he was not prepared to countenance a White Sox last minute victory. He phoned Sullivan and angrily demanded satisfaction. He made it quite clear that were Chicago to win, Sullivan would die. The terrifying nature of the world into which the naïve, ill educated baseball players had stumbled had finally revealed itself. There was more than their pride at stake.

Sullivan acted with speed and aggression. He pinpointed "Lefty" Williams as the weak link as it was well known that he was devoted to his wife. The night before game number eight was due to be played, he cornered Williams and gave him a simple threat. Throw the game, and throw it in the first innings, and your wife will be safe. Refuse and she might not be. The pitcher needed no more persuading and the fate of the series was decided. The next day Williams, none too subtly, threw the game, as requested, in the first innings and Cincinnati ran out winners of the series by five games to three.

And so the scheme, which had stumbled and faltered throughout, had been carried through. Gamblers everywhere rejoiced: Sullivan himself won $50,000; Rothstein's winnings were easily ten times as great.

But the players were never rewarded: although Sullivan did give Gandil the $40,000 which had been sitting in the Hotel Congress's safe all along, only Gandil and Risberg took advantage of this. The others had long since grown sick of the intrigue, and they all had been playing to win in that last game; all that is, except Williams. So, on losing that final game, they simply packed their bags and left, poorer in spirit and pocket than they would have been had they played to win. All they wished to do was to forget about the whole conspiracy and concentrate on winning the World Series in 1920.

But it was not that easy: many people were crying fraud.

Hundreds of Hungarian footballers thought that they had master-minded a pools coup. Needless to say, none of them became millionaires, as they were soon discovered and suspended. Many of the players, but mainly those from the lower division, were later sent to jail.

And in Czechoslavakia, Zbrojovka Brno tried to bribe their way to promotion. Unfortunately this only succeeded in securing their president a fifteen-month prison sentence.

Chicago's owner, Charles Comiskey, was forced to act. Despite having no intention of unearthing any unsavoury truths, which he knew would cut the revenue he could expect from his club, he offered $20,000 reward for any information regarding a possible swindle. In addition, he identified the players most likely to have been involved – it was, after all, quite obvious who they were – and withheld their losers' cheques until the matter was resolved. Luck had dealt the players another poor hand.

Nonetheless, it still did not occur to the players or Comiskey that any serious consequences might arise from this affair. It had been a bad business, certainly, but there was always next year. Indeed, by November 1919 the furore had died down, the players had their cheques and Comiskey's PR exercise seemed to have convinced everyone that the series had been fairly lost.

Unfortunately for them, two men were to ruin this nifty cover up. The first was a journalist, Hugh Fullerton, who published the first of a series of condemnatory articles about baseball on 15 December of that year. The headline in the New York *World* ran: "IS BIG LEAGUE BASEBALL BEING RUN FOR GAMBLERS, WITH BALL PLAYERS IN THE DEAL?"

This article and the articles that followed were not in themselves dangerous to either Comiskey or the players. However, they served two important purposes: they kept the topic of "fixing" in the news, and they gave Bancroft Johnson, a bitter opponent of Comisky's and President of the American League, the opportunity he desired to ruin Comiskey. This was the second man, and he was dangerous.

By 7 September 1920, the constant publicity had caused a Grand Jury to be convened to investigate the 1919 World Series. Baseball did not enjoy having its affairs meddled with and normally nothing irregular would have been uncovered. But Ban Johnson wanted Comiskey ruined more than anything else in the world, more, indeed, than keeping baseball's facade intact. He had already made investigations of his own and knew much of the detail of the previous year's fraud. As soon as he heard about the Grand Jury he visited the presiding Judge, a Judge Macdonald, and told him all.

As a result subpoenas were sent to Comiskey and the players, and by 22 October the Grand Jury had named the eight ball players, together with Attell, Burns and Sullivan, as conspirators in a plot to throw the series. This was dreadful news both for the players, who were suspended from playing

pending trial, and for Comiskey, whose team – and consequently whose bank balance – suffered. Johnson's ploy had
worked: he had ruined Comiskey by destroying his club.

Comiskey, however, could survive, but the ball players were
broken men. Despite subsequent acquittal on criminal charges,
they were banned from playing baseball ever again. A bad
situation had grown worse. A scam which they had been
uneasy with all the way through had enriched others and
shattered them.

As Oscar "Happy" Felsch stated: "The joke seems to be on
us."

German artist Lothar Malskat served a prison sentence for his 'Old
Masters'

FAKERS AND FORGERS

Hans Van Meegeren: the Artistic Rebel

Dr Abraham Bredius was foremost in his field. His dominion? The art world. His profession? Art expert. At times his opinions held a weight which seemed almost divine. His was often the final decision as to what was real or fake. Many a fortune, many a career relied on his ability to perceive the truth.

Take, for example, the experience of one Theo van Wijngaarden, himself a painter of some promise and a capable restorer. He had uncovered what was, in all probability, a seventeenth-century painting by Frans Hals. His attempts to clean the painting were, however, rather clumsy and he softened the paint. Theo realized that this would create problems in obtaining a sale, as some paints took nearly fifty years to harden fully and it was standard practice for a buyer to test the hardness of the painting's surface, before making a commitment. He knew that he had no choice but to admit his mistake and hope that it would not unduly deter potential buyers. Indeed, he soon gained his reward, subject, of course, to verification by the expert, Dr Bredius. Bredius took little time in declaring the picture a fake and Theo's fate was sealed – he would not now be able to sell the painting as an original.

Bredius's position, then, was a privileged one, but not one that was without peril. If he could be deceived, tempted into accepting the untrue, then the foundations upon which the art world relied would be without substance and open to ridicule.

Step forward Hans van Meegeren. Here was a man full of talent, a man with the potential for greatness. During an architectural course at Delft, with no formal painting training, he had won the college's five yearly gold medal with a watercolour painted in his spare time. On receipt of this award, he abruptly tossed aside his architectural studies, and enrolled at the Hague Academy of Art, simply to take the final exams. Such talent was quickly recognized. He breezed through the exams and was offered a professorship at the Academy itself. Typically, he refused and set off to pursue his own career.

This talent allowed him, initially, to obtain a healthy living. Before he was thirty he had held two exhibitions of his work, which had both sold out. There were commissions from advertising companies and he could always turn his hand to portraits or poster drawing. Yet somehow, as the years progressed, his talent was never fulfilled.

And then there was his lifestyle. He had married early, at the age of twenty-two, to Anna de Voogt, but his was an ego in constant need of attention. He was a hard man to live with and they separated five years later, finally divorcing in 1923. Years of heavy drinking and conspicuous sexual encounters followed and, notwithstanding his second marriage in 1929, he proved too great a handful for the restrained and highly proper burghers of the Hague. In 1932 he moved to Roquebrun in

In the 1950s appeared a fascinating biography, which sold many thousands of copies, of a certain Lobsang Rampa. In it, Lobsang claimed to be a Tibetan Lama, duly recounting his days training to be a monk, under the auspices of the guru Lama Mingyar. He told of the operation which made him clairvoyant (a hole was drilled in his head) and of his experiences of levitation and astral travel, not to mention his friendship with the Dalai Lama. So it was with some disappointment that the public learnt that Lobsang Rampa was not, in fact, Lobsang Rampa, but one Cyril Henry Hoskins, the son of a plumber, from Plympton, in Devon.

the South of France and despite continuing his highly successful portrait business, he began to fade from the art scene.

But it was his attitude more than his lifestyle, riotous as it
may have been, that accounted for his unfulfilled promise in the
orthodox world. Van Meegeren had little respect for the
accepted tenets of the art world and he had even less for
those, such as Dr Bredius, who enjoyed the most acclaim.
His opposition was wide ranging – he had run an anti-estab-
lishment magazine shortly after leaving college – but in
particular he disagreed with the standard notion that one
can prove a painting's worth. To van Meegeren a painting
was as good as a buyer believed it to be. For this reason, he had
had no qualms in faking his gold medal painting and selling it
for a handsome amount to a foreigner soon to leave the
country.

One incident, in particular, served to cement this jaundiced
view. The same Theo van Wijngaarden who had suffered at the
hands of Dr Bredius was also a friend of van Meegeren. On
being told by Bredius that his Hals was a fake, van Wijngaarden determined to show how flimsy the guidelines were that
determined a painting's true worth. After a year of industrious
zeal, he returned to Bredius, this time with a Rembrandt.
Bredius knew the history of the work's former ownership
and, believing its provenance to be sound, confirmed the
painting with hardly a glance. At this Theo laughed out loud
and began slowly to destroy the painting, stating with glee that
he had painted it himself. His point made and with Bredius
looking foolish, he went no further. Van Meegeren, however,
was entranced.

But perhaps he would never have embarked with such
diligence on his future deception, had it not been for his
childhood. During his childhood his natural ability to paint
had been constantly overlooked. And not simply overlooked,
but actively discouraged: his father religiously tore up all his
son's drawings. It was during these years that van Meegeren
had invented another world which was at odds with his
surroundings. He had grown up silently rebelling and now
he was to take his revenge. His objective was simple: to fake a
masterpiece so perfectly that it had to be taken as genuine.

In Dr Bredius, van Meegeren spotted the victim for his fraud.
The art historian was now an old man and for all his successes,
he earnestly desired the fulfilment of one wish: that of finding a
series of religious paintings by Vermeer. In 1901, Bredius had

identified "Christ with Martha and Mary" as being the early work of Vermeer. And when "The Procuress" followed a few years later, a great debate had arisen over Vermeer's Early Christian Period, with Bredius in the vanguard of those who believed that the artist had painted a series of Biblical scenes. Van Meegeren was decided. If the great art historian himself believed this to be so, so it should be.

Van Meegeren studied the principles of forgery with a diligence he had not shown in his own work. He did not simply attempt to become fully the master of Vermeer's technique, although in the years following his arrival in Roquebrun he had produced many paintings in the style of Terboch, Hals and Vermeer, but he focused with as much concentration on the faking of the canvas and the paints. His was to be no mere moral victory, as his friend van Wijngaarden's had been. He wanted to ensure that the painting would withstand any of the tests the experts were likely to use, for he intended to be richly paid for his work.

First of all, he needed to use authentic colours. In the twentieth century, for example, white was made from a stable zinc compound, which was unknown three hundred years before. Therefore, he had painstakingly to make all colours from natural ingredients: white from white lead, ultramarine from lapis lazuli and black from carbon.

Next, he tackled the problem which had so undone van Wijngaarden: that of the hardness of the paint. He may have been patient, but he could not afford to wait fifty years watching the paint dry. So, he turned scientist. Having found the components, phenol and formaldehyde, that gave bakelite its hardness, he introduced a small measure of oil of lilac into the paint substance before dyeing it. Luckily, the formaldehyde disappeared when dry, so his artificial hardness was, to the tests of the time, foolproof.

A French court found itself in difficulties in 1991: its job was to decide when a fake was a fake. A simple enough task, but not when the fakes have issued from the very same mould as the original. For that is apparently what Diego Giacometti, the younger brother of the famous sculptor, Alberto Giacometti, had been using. The case was hard to prove either way, because no one could distinguish the fakes from the originals.

Finally, he confronted by far the most complex obstruction to the success of his project; he needed to find a way to age the painting on the canvas. One of the easiest ways of checking a painting's age is to look for the tiny cracks which appear as a result of the paint drying and the environment in which it has been stored. A new painting, even with specially hardened paint, would not have these cracks. Van Meegeren hit on a tortuous but brilliant solution. Having found an authentic canvas, he removed all traces of the original painting, applied a layer of paint to the blank canvas and baked it. This process was repeated several times, until cracks began to appear in the paint. He would then paint on this artificially aged surface and bake the finished work at a high temperature, at which point the cracks would reappear.

His techniques perfected, van Meegeren felt ready to paint a true Vermeer: "The Disciples at Emmaus". The nature of this gamble cannot be underestimated. This painting was very different to the extant Vermeers. Absent were the reassuring domestic scenes and his commonplace themes. Van Meegeren, to succeed, had to hope that the experts, Bredius foremost, would greet this picture as proof of Vermeer's Early Christian Period. He had good reason to believe he would succeed. After all, this was the work that Bredius so earnestly wished to be found; but would he be fooled?

He was. It was 1937, Bredius was eighty-three years old and his expertise was confirmed. He had been right all along. He not only accepted the work, he championed it and, by the end of the year, a consortium representing the Boyman's Foundation had paid the staggering amount of 550,000 florins for it. Van Meegeren, on receiving his two-third's share of the price was rich and victorious. His point had been made.

His thirst for money, however, had not been assuaged. He continued to fake Vermeers, producing "The Last Supper" twice, "The Head of Christ", "Isaac Blessing Jacob", "Christ and the Adulteress", and "The Foot Washing". The little known Vermeer had been an inspired choice. Once the belief in his Early Christian Period had been nurtured, then it was an easy task for someone as talented and cynical as van Meegeren to churn out more of the same. He became inordinately wealthy, owning, by the time of his confession, over fifty houses, a handful of night clubs and hotels, as well as many genuine works of art.

But if he was such a master of his art, why do we know of him? What made him confess?

Ironically, he was a victim of his own success. His living and succeeding in the Europe of the 1930s and early 1940s, brought him to the attention of the Nazis. Herr Goering took a fancy to "The Adulteress" and bought it for 1.6 million florins. Unsurprisingly, when the war was over everyone believed van Meegeren, the art dealer, to have been a Nazi conspirator. How else could selling national treasures to the enemy be construed? In order to avoid prison, he had to confess to fraud: not such an easy task, as no one believed him at first. After all, he had taken great pains to eradicate any signs which might give him away. Indeed, it was only by openly painting a copy of "Jesus Teaching in the Temple" that he proved his case.

The truth finally out, his duping of Goering gave him celebrity status in Holland – as indeed Tom Keating would enjoy in England after his disclosures – and although he had spent nearly twenty years of his life exploiting and ridiculing the society in which he lived, he only received a sentence of one year's imprisonment. By then, however, he was a frail man and despite being only in his late fifties, he died within two months of his trial. His was a great talent and no matter how one judges his achievements, there is no doubting that he was the arch art faker of all time.

Tom Keating: the Laughing Rogue

Tom Keating was briefly the most famous artist in England. During the late seventies a newspaper could hardly be opened, the television scarcely turned on, without his beaming presence announcing itself. He was a man in his element. Like van Meegeren before him, he had dedicated his life to producing art fakes. Like him, he also had little faith or trust in the power brokers of the art world; and he had small difficulty in justifying his chosen profession to himself.

Yet van Meegeren lived his life by an alternative set of rules. A high profile career within the establishment could easily have been his, but he deliberately turned his back on this world and set about ridiculing and exploiting it with great intensity and even malice. Keating, on the other hand, was a much more straightforward personality. He did not begin faking because of a terrible grudge with society. He did it because he could. It paid him better than anything else open to him and it amused him.

The two men had similarities: both Keating and van Meegeren had shown natural talent for their subject. Van Meegeren's gold medal can be compared with Keating's scholarship to the renowned Goldsmith's College in New Cross. Both had started their careers, with a great deal of promise, as painters in their own right. And both had realized that the lot of a painter was not a happy one. In the Dutchman's case, many of the critics proved so corrupt that they asked him to pay for good reviews of his work. As for Keating, he could never reconcile himself to the fact that a painting which he could sell for, say, five pounds would sell for upwards of £500 the next day, when it was placed in a chic Mayfair art gallery.

But here the similarity ends.

Tom Keating was born, in 1917, into a large and poverty stricken household in the London suburb of Forest Hill. His father, a painter and decorator by trade, and his uncles, brothers and cousins were all artisans and it was not unexpected that Tom felt at ease when painting. His early promise was shown when, aged seven, he won a painting competition, using a paintbox he had received for swimming a length underwater in his local swimming pool.

However, the Depression left the family almost destitute, hardly able to feed itself, let alone encourage one small boy in his hobby. At age fourteen, Tom was forced to leave school and fend for himself. His interest in art was still apparent and in between the odd jobs that presented themselves, mainly in his father's trade, he studied signwriting and commercial art at Croydon and then Camberwell School of Art. Still, had it not been for the advent of the Second World War, this pattern of dead-end jobs might have been set for life.

He was sent to work in the Far East as a stoker for the Royal

---

What do Mickey Mouse, Ronald McDonald and Count Dracula have in common? They are all claiming unemployment benefit. These are some of the more blatantly false names used by the dole cheats, who are currently defrauding the British welfare system of some £34 million a year.

Navy and while there he suffered badly in a torpedo attack on his vessel. As a consequence, he was invalided out of the navy and never quite recovered his health. His having served in the forces enabled him to apply for and receive a serviceman's grant, sending him to Goldsmith's College for two years, in order to study art. This was the break he had needed: for once in his life he had the chance of pursuing a career which might provide both financial and intellectual nourishment.

Unfortunately, although his technical skills were well developed, he did not possess an imaginative flair. He lacked the ability to do anything other than imitate. The professors at Goldsmiths recognized this: no professorships were on offer and, unlike van Meegeren, he failed the course. To add to this misfortune, Tom was once again beaten by his own lack of funds. Undeterred by his failure at college, he had started out as an independent painter, and very soon offers to exhibit his work were forthcoming. But to display a paintings, one needs frames and Tom could not afford this luxury.

So, he found his true calling almost by default. He was in constant need of a regular wage; the only choice open to him was to train as a picture restorer. Having taken that step, he entered a world wholly separate from that which had been his up until now. His presence was welcomed in some of the most luxurious and commanding stately homes in England. He was a regular visitor to the castles and mansions of Scotland. His work was commented upon by some of the "cream of society". Tom was in his element: his confidence grew and with it he forged a new cheeky, chirpy persona, which was far removed from the quiet, downbeaten character he had been before the war. He was determined to make the most of his new found good fortune and for several years remained a eager pupil, learning the skills he was later to put to use in his fakes. In particular, he saw how pictures were altered to appeal to the tastes of the buyers and how easily this could be done. The fact that these changes meant that a hitherto worthless painting could be sold for thousands on the open market was not lost on him.

The exact reason why he began to fake works of art will never be known. Tom himself gave more than one explanation, some more plausible than others. At one point he claimed that he had acted as he did because he could no longer tolerate the exploitation of artists by the art dealers. Why, he demanded, with some justification, should the dealers grab all the profits, when the artist, whose work it is, is left penniless? At other times, in a more flippant mood, he stated that he was divinely inspired by such great painters as Rembrandt and Goya. Indeed, one picture even painted itself!

In 1964, he set up in business with his girlfriend Jane Kelly, superficially as a picture restorer. His output was prodigious and, in one weekend alone, he painted sixteen pictures. And it is this output of Keating's which so marks him out from van Meegeren, who had spent five years researching and painting his first fake. Keating was no bespoke tailor: his was off the peg art. "Buy five, get one free" might have been an appropriate catchphrase. His experience had taught him that as long as he was giving the market what it desired, no one would check the origins of the goods.

Keating's gaze fell on a little known, but up-and-coming artist, Samuel Palmer. This artist's period of painting was from the late 1820s to the late 1830s, but the best thing about him, as far as Keating was concerned was both that he had continued to paint until well into the 1870s and that very little was known of him. His links with William Blake, popular again after a long rejection, guaranteed public interest and, with nearly fifty years of undiscovered painting at his disposal, Keating had an almost totally free hand.

The problem he faced, however, was not one of production, but of distribution. He might be able to paint sixteen pictures in one weekend, but how on earth was he to sell them for a decent price? He could, and did, produce forgeries of virtually every artist popular in the last two centuries, which he could sell, but none made any real money. This taxed him for some time, until in 1970 Jane and he were ready.

In December 1992, believers in the poor Santiago suburb of La Cisterna saw a miracle occur in front of their very own eyes. Indeed, all of Chile was captivated as the Nunez family recounted how they had found their six inch porcelain statue of the Virgin weeping tears of blood.

Predictably enough, disappointment soon followed. Although initial tests seemed to confirm the miracle, the blood was eventually found to be that of Mr Nunez himself. Denials were issued by the family, but the spell had been broken and the miracle of the weeping Virgin was no longer headline news.

Jane's grandfather's father-in-law had been a contemporary of Palmer and, on being posted to the East, had bought several paintings directly from the artist himself. These had been carefully handed down and on Jane's grandfather's death – he had lived, conveniently enough, all his life in Ceylon – they had been left to her. Jane approached the Leger Galleries, who, true to form, smelt a huge profit and eagerly snapped up the first Palmer for £9,400, while expressing interest in any further Palmers she might have. Consquently, during 1970 and 1971, Jane brought three more Palmers to the Leger and each time they were taken without argument, despite protestations from some quarters that they were not quite what they seemed.

Now he was playing for higher stakes, Keating aroused more suspicion and when in 1974 he offered four more Palmers as a job lot for £60,000, the doubting Thomases had increased. It proved impossible for Keating to sell them. However, this did not stem his output: more forgeries were thrust out into the marketplace and some sold, but again, not for the prices that van Meegeren's work had obtained. And now the hunt was on. His paintings were tested and proved to be modern and in 1976 the Times arts correspondent, Geraldine Norman, named him as the originator of the fakes.

Unlike van Meegeren, who would have been destroyed had his deception been discovered by the experts, Keating revelled in the exposure. Always on the lookout for a quick buck, he spotted his chance and contacted Norman to confess all. Their joint book appeared in 1977, only days before his arrest, which had seemed likely the moment he had been uncovered.

If he had believed that his fame was to peak at the time of his arrest, he was misguided. The longer the trial lasted, the greater his star burned. And it is easy to see why. Keating presented a flamboyant, almost showmanlike front and the facts were far from commonplace. When asked how many forgeries he had committed during his lifetime, his own estimates varied between two and two and a half thousand! And he had to admit he hardly knew to whom he had sold these works of art. All told, he believed that he had painted in the style of over one hundred artists, ranging from Monet to Degas, Rembrandt to Goya. He had been nothing if not a hard worker.

The scale of his deception might have enhanced his reputation, but it did nothing for the art world as a whole. To the British public and even to some MPs Keating had simply exploited the superficial, greedy little clique that controlled art in this country. The corrupt, money grabbing ethos had been exposed for all to see. Nevertheless, Keating had still transgressed the rule of law and had to expect due punishment, along with his former girlfriend Jane (Kelly) Maurice. The trial was beginning to draw to a close when he suffered a motorcyle accident, and the ill-health which had plagued him since the war returned with a vengeance. Realizing the futility of sentencing a dying man, the court allowed him to walk free, early in 1979. Jane was given a slightly tougher, but still lenient, suspended sentence.

What does a former art faker do, after he has been exposed? Van Meegeren died soon after his disclosure; Keating simply set up his own business, producing art fakes to order! And such was the demand for his skills and his ability to communicate the true nature of art, that he was even given the opportunity of recording a series on how to paint Impressionist masterpieces. He died, in September 1984, soon after making this series, at the height of his fame: a fame which he enjoyed and never expected.

The final twist in the tale occurred when his hoard of paintings were auctioned immediately after his death. As no doubt he would have expected, his demise had breathed new life into the prices the pictures could obtain. Initial estimates of a couple of hundred pounds, at most, for each picture were blown to pieces, as hungry buyers, in some cases the very same people who had been lambasted at the time of his trial, rubbed shoulders with members of the public, in order to gain possession of a celebrated Keating. In all, the 204 paintings sold for a total of £250,000, almost five times the price they would have sold for just a month before.

In 1704 the *Historical and Geographical Description of Formosa* was published to great acclaim. In it the author, George Psalmanazar, told of a people who lived to be one hundred years old by drinking snake's blood and eating raw meat, who dealt with murderers by hanging them head downwards and shooting them to death with arrows, and – as if this were not enough – who each year sacrificed 18,000 young boys in order to appease the gods. All pure bunkum of course, but undeniably riveting.

Gerd Heidemann show the books which Stern Magazine claims are Adolf Hitler's personal diaries.

Clifford Irving: The Howard Hughes Biography

In June 1971 an author was sentenced to prison after having signed a contract worth nearly $1,000,000 with a major publishing house. His crime? He had claimed to have written the official biography of one of America's richest and most powerful men, Howard Hughes; but in fact he had made the whole story up.

Clifford Irving is to the book world what van Meegeren and Keating were to the art world. They were all disappointed in their careers, they all knew a great deal about forgery and deception, and they were all, to a man, determined to trip up and ridicule the experts in their field. Besides, they all had an eye for financial reward. But there is one large difference which makes Irving's fraud so daring and so compelling. While van Meegeren and Keating concentrated on reproducing the works of those long dead, Irving set out to fake a biography of a living man!

No ordinary man at that. After all, who has not heard the name Howard Hughes? Even in the 1990s, his position as the richest man in the world long gone, his name still has a mesmeric effect. An aura of mystery surrounds him: at his peak, he was one of the most powerful men alive, yet so little is known about him. And that is the reason for Irving's choice of subject. In the 1970s, Hughes was the richest man in the world, with interests in oil fields, airlines and who knows how many

> The fall of the Communist bloc opened up a wealth of opportunities not only for keen eyed businessmen, but for hoaxers as well. In mid 1992, the front pages of German newspapers were screaming about the latest find: an archive film showing the body of Adolf Hitler lying in the yard of the Berlin Chancellery. The old theories that he had either shot or poisoned himself, rather than be captured, were already beginning to be discarded by the time that Spiegel TV announced that the body was in fact that of a German soldier, whose only resemblance to the Führer was his moustache!

other businesses. There was constant interest, which had been recently spurred to new heights by the publication of a letter written by Hughes himself to two survivors of the merciless reorganization of TWA (the airline he owned) at the end of the 1960s. But Hughes had withdrawn completely from public life and no interviewer had been able to tempt even the smallest soundbite from him for over thirteen years. Aware of the immense publicity and sales there would be for any biographies that might be published about him, Hughes had even set up a company whose sole concern was to destroy at birth these potential time bombs.

In short, Irving took a gigantic gamble that he would be able to bamboozle Hughes's own forces for just long enough to give the world what it wanted and for himself to gain the reward he wanted. He was risking his liberty for the big prize. Irving felt that he had next to nothing to lose. Aged forty, he had been plying his trade as a writer for some years, but had not received the acclaim he had hoped for. His living was reasonably secure, but he found it frustrating and he was always on the look out for an idea that would elevate him above the rank and file. His instinct shouted that the Howard Hughes biography was that idea and that once he had embarked on the project he should be as reckless as possible. After all, the more unbelievable it is, he reasoned, the more they believe it. To a certain extent, he was right. His bravado took him tantalizingly close to his objective, but in the end it was his undoing.

Irving's idea came like this . . . He was sitting in his Ibiza home in late 1970 working on his latest project for McGraw Hill, a major American publisher, when he was struck by a brilliant thought. He had a publisher, he had a subject, all he needed was for his publisher and subject to agree to his writing the book. As it was certain that McGraw Hill would jump at the chance of publishing a biography of Howard Hughes, all that

Some fakes are just too good to be disbelieved. In 1917, H. L. Mencken wrote what he thought was a humorous piece on the history of the bath tub. He believed that the readers of the New York *Evening Mail* were discerning enough to be able to spot his hoax, especially after reading his section on bath tub taxes. But not a bit of it. All who read it were totally convinced, even after Mencken had admitted his deception!

was missing was Hughes's agreement. Had there not been a letter, handwritten by Hughes himself, published in the press recently?

Could this not be used to good effect? Of course it could. Thereupon, he contacted his friend and fellow writer, Richard Suskind, to discuss how to put the plan into action. Several days later, after careful analysis of Hughes's writing, Irving was in possession of three letters which stated the great man's tepid approval of an Irving biography. The reason given for this amazing volte-face by Hughes were rather weak – he had once met Irving's father and had remembered a small act of gallantry on Irving's behalf towards him – and perhaps the fraud might have been suspected much earlier had not everyone at McGraw Hill been completely carried away by a wave of euphoria on receipt of these letters. One would think that the mere existence of the Hughes owned company dedicated solely to stamping out these biographies would have thrown a dampener on the proceedings, but not at all. Iriving was instructed to proceed full steam ahead. Part one of his fraud had been completed without a hitch.

Nevertheless, Irving was now left with a book to write and no way of obtaining any accurate information. Even allowing for the fact that not much was known about Hughes by the general public, it was foolish to hope that he could produce a biography of complete fiction and not be caught out immediately by those who had known the man himself, however slightly. The project looked doomed, but at this point Irving received the most amazing piece of good fortune. An acquaintance of his, Stanley Mayer, approached him to rewrite, of all things, a biography of Hughes written by a former bodyguard, Noah Dietrich. Without lifting a finger, Irving had at his disposal exactly what he wanted. Here were details of the most personal nature, tales from Hughes's early days as an aviator, as an engineer. It even recounted the time he had spent in Hollywood. Undoubtedly, this was a gift from the gods. Irving kept the script long enough to photocopy it and then politely declined Mayer's offer. All was, miraculously, going to plan.

However, a contract still had not been signed. McGraw Hill, keen as they were, needed to believe that Irving was in contact with Hughes and starting his research. Irving, therefore, set up a research base in New York, with McGraw Hill money of course, and made a pretence of meeting Hughes for a couple of short, preparatory discussions, during which they talked about how Irving was to learn the facts of Hughes's life. It had been decided, Irving told the eager executives at McGraw Hill, to base the book on a series of taped interviews. Mr Hughes, shy of publicity and secretive by nature, would choose the locations, at which only Irving was to be present. This was swallowed hook, line and sinker and in March he signed a contract worth $750,000.

During the months from March to December 1971, Irving was probably at home, sipping champagne, rejoicing in his good luck. To the world at large, however, he attended a series of over 100 interviews with Howard Hughes in many weird and wonderful locations and at bizarre times of day. One meeting apparently took place at five o'clock in the morning in a car park in Palm Springs. The extraordinary, he reasoned, was not only more likely to be believed than the mundane, but also less likely to be checked. He was not quite correct in that assumption, as his travel arrangements were in fact analyzed and it was found that it was physically impossible for him to have been in all the places he described at the times he gave. But that was all still to come and for the moment everything was going smoothly. Irving finished the manuscript and handed it to his eager publisher.

McGraw Hill badly wanted this book to be genuine and they had not been as painstaking in their research about Irving's activities as they might have been. Yet it would be wrong to suggest that they rushed straight into this project without a thought. They had commissioned several graphologists to examine the first three letters presented to them and although

> Where there is money, there is deception. And no one was more developed in the art of deception than William Harkins, the master cheque forger. Indeed the New York *Times* said of his career that it was "so fantastic as to seem the creation of some errant imagination". His method was straightforward but effective. Harkins would visit a company "on business", steal a supply of its blank cheques, in addition to several cancelled cheques, and then leave. Later, having studied the signature on the cancelled cheques, he would simply walk into a bank and cash the stolen blank cheques by forging the relevant signature. What could be easier?

the experts did not all agree, not one of them suggested that the letters were faked. In addition, the publisher demanded that Irving take a lie detector test. He passed. Perhaps a second rate manuscript would have alerted the firm to the fraud that was being perpetrated, but the manuscript was better than they could have hoped. Indeed, it was so good that *Life* magazine, which had already agreed to serialize the biography, decided, on reading it, that they would also run a serialization of Irving's life. Besides, the ever lengthening queue of film directors, TV and publishing magnates forming at McGraw Hill's door strongly disinclined them to reject the book. Not even Hughes' personal denial could dent their confidence.

Amazingly, Irving had fulfilled his objective. His book had been accepted, he had already received $100,000. There seemed nothing more to do than sit back and let the money pile up. Unfortunately, Irving had been just a little too reckless in his activities. First a reporter from *Life* checked, as we have seen, on the travel details of Irving and Hughes. Then a Swiss bank announced that the Mr Howard Hughes who had opened an account several months before was a woman (who turned out to be Irving's wife!). Finally, another freelance writer, Jim Phelan, who had also seen Dietrich's attempted biography, recognized where Irving had obtained his information and immediately contacted McGraw Hill. The countdown to exposure had started in earnest and only a man with superhuman resolve could have resisted. Irving, however, was not such a man and, indeed, had confessed his guilt even before his publishers had met Mr Phelan. Although, to be fair to Irving, he had been caught out by a piece of bad luck as great as his earlier slice of good luck.

A journalist called MacCulloch had been suspicious of this biography for some time, as had many people, and had set out several months earlier to prove the book a fake. His investigations led him to think that Irving's source was not Hughes, but a man named Meier. Believing the only way to discover the truth was to speak to Irving face to face, he visited him. But as the author was now under tight security, the journalist was not allowed to see him and was forced to leave a verbal message, which Irving would receive in due course. In it, he simply stated that he knew all about Meier and that he would expose Irving as a fraud. As it happens, he was about as wide of the mark as he could be. He was not talking about Stanley Mayer and the Noah Dietrich biography, but about another person entirely. However, Irving in his state of nervous tension did not wait to find out the fact: he heard the name Mayer and believed himself discovered. When the journalist called back later, Irving was waiting for him with his confession.

Soon after, Irving and his accomplice, Richard Suskind, were arrested amid a flurry of publicity. For some months, he became the subject of everyone's conversation and, if nothing else, he added some light relief to America's everyday life. In June 1971, he was sentenced to two and half years imprisonment, while Suskind received just a couple of months for his part. It is a sad ending to the tale, but one that almost had to be.

William Henry Ireland: the Second Shakespeare

A famous English playwright told a tale of the murder of a goodly king by a depraved tyrant, of the love of that tyrant's daughter for the rightful heir, and of the treacherous battles which ensued before order was restored. Who could it be, but Shakespeare? That is, of course, what William Henry Ireland wanted people to think when he put pen to paper in the late eighteenth century. Or, more accurately, that is what he wanted his father to think. For this fraud was not set in motion for any monetary gain. There was no bitterness towards the literary critics, or society in general. The only point William wished to

---

A male nurse, Edwin Bayron, of Bukidnon Provincial Hospital in the Philippines, claimed that he was having a baby and what's more he fooled everyone. So much so, that Antonio Periquet, the country's health minister, offered to meet all Edwin's expenses for the delivery, and doctors at the hospital told reporters that they could feel the foetus kicking. So great was the interest in his biological abnormality that Edwin was on the verge of becoming a truly wealthy man, until a court demanded a full medical examination and the truth came out.

prove was that he was a worthy son and heir to his father Samuel, who, in his capacity as an antiquarian bookseller, cared deeply about Shakespeare and not a jot about his son.

The reason we know about this fake and others perpetrated by Ireland is mostly to do with the intense reverence with which the eighteenth century regarded the Bard and the zeal with which it greeted any Shakespearean memento, however small. His will had been joyously discovered in 1747; a mulberry tree planted by the bard himself was dissected and distributed to an excited crowd ten years later. And there were numerous Shakespearean festivals each year, the most conspicuous of which were held in Stratford and in Drury Lane, London. Naturally, the uncovering of a complete new play was bound to have far reaching repercussions.

The climate for fraud, then, was perfect; but was Ireland up to the task? After all, his father, when he was not disowning him, reckoned him a dullard with no talent whatsoever, a waste of time. Throughout William's childhood, his father not only refused to believe the boy was his, but used the possible disclosure of his true father as a threat to keep the boy in his place. Regardless of whether or not his view of William's abilities was correct, it is hard to believe that a true literary talent could flourish in such an oppressive atmosphere. Yet, fortunately for William, he was educated for the most part in post-revolutionary France, a society in which there was much intellectual debate and where his desire to be a writer was hatched.

It was in 1793, while on a buying trip with his father – who had begrudgingly let him come along – that William saw his chance to pursue both his ambitions: to gain the respect of his father and to become a writer. One night, Ireland senior pontificated at length on Shakespeare's virtues, letting slip what a great achievement it would be to unearth even a fragment of the Bard's handiwork. The point was not lost on William. It was he who should make the discovery.

A year later, William produced a title deed to a property near

It is an exceptionally hard task even for experts to tell fakes from the real thing. Nonetheless, Ernst Bloch believed that he had the answer, pleasingly simple and straightforward: 'A forgery can be distinguished from an original, because it looks more genuine."

the Old Globe Theatre. Its importance lay in the fact that the contract was between an actor, John Heminge, and William Shakespeare. As fakes go, it was pretty poor: William simply wrote Heminge's signature with his left hand! Nevertheless, it was pronounced genuine by various experts and it paved the way for a series of Shakespeare finds over the next couple of months. They came from the same source, a conveniently publicity shy Mr H. who had asked William to sort through his papers. Again, hardly a well thought out excuse. Had anyone checked, William's fraud would have been over almost before it began. But, as with many frauds, fortune favoured the brave. Samuel Ireland, overjoyed by this good fortune, championed the finds and they were soon the talk of the town.

The new memorabilia covered a variety of topics and were much more substantial than the initial discovery. Some illuminated the personal side of the playwright, revealing his correspondence with the Earl of Southampton, his love poetry written for Anne Hathaway, and even a letter from Elizabeth the First. The main bulk, however, was from his professional life. Uncovered were two theatre contracts, the original manuscripts of *Hamlet* and *King Lear*, and his "Profession of Faith" (which moved Boswell to tears). And to cap these all, there was a previously unknown play, the *Vortigern*.

Interest in every household in the country had been aroused. When Samuel Ireland put them on show, thousands flocked to gaze upon the treasures. Many experts, including Boswell and the poet laureate, Henry Pye, stated that the articles were genuine and even the Royal Family warmed to them. In an atmosphere of euphoria such as this, the fact that many great literary critics, particularly Edmond Malone, did not give them credit as genuine seems not to have mattered. William had inadvertently given the public what they wanted and they were going to believe in it, come what may.

Two men, Kemble, the actor/manager of the Drury Lane Theatre, and Sheridan, the theatre's owner, understood this well and snapped *Vortigern* up for production sometime during 1795. They believed it to be a fake, and not a particularly good one at that, but it would be good box office stuff. The theatre, they reasoned, would be full whatever verdict was finally delivered. And if they had staged the play in that year, there is every reason to believe that it would have had a long and successful run. However, as was to happen with Clifford Irving two centuries later, Ireland's luck began to turn. In December

1795, an authentic signature of John Heminge was brought to light. Unsurprisingly, it was completely different to Ireland's left handed attempt. Not in itself damning evidence, because the signature could just as easily have been fraudulent as real. But it sowed the seeds of doubt, which were given further sustenance by Edmond Malone's impending work *Inquiry into the validity of the Papers attributed to Shakespeare*. In it, he was known to have compiled a whole section devoted to *Vortigern* and its inconsistencies.

By January 1796, Ireland's former supporters were changing their allegiance. Both the *Oracle* and the *Monthly Mirror* condemned the finds and, more importantly, the crowds that had thronged outside the showroom were dwindling. Production of *Vortigern* had been delayed until March or April of that year and there was much debate as to why Ireland had, so far, only shown the transcript in modern copy form. Kemble and Sheridan, sensing the change in tides, began to ask for their money back and said that they would only proceed if the original manuscript was produced. It appeared that Ireland's fraud had stumbled and fallen. He could not produce the original manuscript, he could not prove Heminge's signature a fake, nor could he answer the one query which Malone, in advance of his book, had raised.

This last point seemed to be the final nail in the coffin. Malone had analyzed the letters carefully, especially that which purported to be from Elizabeth the First. Why, he

---

I have recently been the victim of a swindle. Not a serious one, admittedly, but a swindle nonetheless. Attempting to travel by London Underground from Oxford Circus to Victoria, I slotted a one pound coin in the automatic ticket machine and waited for my ticket. The pound was rejected. I tried again only to be met with another rejection. And when a final try yielded my third rebuttal, I walked angrily to an official and complained that the ticket machine had broken down. He patiently heard me out and then asked to examine the coin, which on closer inspection proved to be counterfeit: its coating had worn thin and the surface was pitted. As he graciously explained, saving my blushes, there had been a flood of fake pounds recently. Indeed official figures show that in July 1993 alone London Underground received more than 20,000 of these coins!

asked, does the Queen state that she is expecting the Earl of Leicester at the Globe Theatre, when, at the time of the letter's writing, the Earl of Leicester had been dead for six years?

Yet, just when all appeared lost, there came succour from the Royal Family. The Duke of Clarence (whose mistress was Dorothea Jordan, the female lead in the *Vortigern*) exclaimed that the findings were most definitely sprung from Shakespeare's hand and that the Drury Lane Theatre had better proceed as quickly as possible with the staging of the new play. The old manuscript would be produced in due course, but for the moment the modern transcript should be used. At the time, this must have seemed like divine intervention, although, given the eventual fate of the play, it might have been better for Ireland if the Duke had stayed aloof.

The date fixed for the opening night, 2 April, would be, it was hoped, some weeks before the publication of Malone's book, thus giving the play time to gain the support it would need to survive. In practice, this did not happen as Malone's book came out on 31 March. The spotlight was thrown onto the play, and although Samuel Ireland (who would remain convinced of the findings' authenticity, even after William had confessed) was unconcerned and simply added a footnote urging the public to be judge, this time it was really the beginning of the end. Despite a last minute show of support for *Vortigern* from some twenty literary dignitaries, the play was torn apart by the actors and audience alike. It survived as a serious work for the first act, but after that, with Kemble leading the way, the actors hammed their lines up and egged the audience on to greater and greater shows of ridicule. It was the first and last night of *Vortigern's* stage performance. The public had given their judgement, reserving their worst humiliation for the Duke of Clarence by pelting him with oranges, as he rather drunkenly tried to defend the play.

In the days that followed, Malone's book provided more and more examples of inconsistencies and errors, such as spelling mistakes, anachronisms, impossible dates and meetings. The fraud was well and truly exposed. The fraudster, however, was not.

If William Ireland had had the same motives as Irving or Keating or van Meegeren, then he could have considered himself a success. But his forgeries had not been executed for any other reason than to gain the respect of a man, who still, after twenty-one years, did not recognize him as his son and did not credit him with any talent. It was frustrating and hurtful, and, not surprisingly, William could not keep his secret hidden any longer. He wanted to show his father just how ingenious he had been and he wanted to receive some recognition for that ingenuity. Consequently, in May 1796, he announced to Samuel Ireland that he alone could vouch for the findings, that he alone knew the identity of Mr H. To his bitter regret, he got no reaction from his father. Finally, unable to bear this silence anymore, William revealed that he himself was the author. Sadly, even this failed to win his father over, as the very papers William had forged had become Samuel's life. All that the son obtained was a brief argument rejecting both Malone's criticisms and William himself. They never talked to one another again.

Unlike Irving, Keating and van Meegeren, Ireland was not sentenced to prison. However, his demise is somehow more distressing. All three of the other fraudsters became folk-heroes in their own right. They were all recognized as masters of their art, albeit an unusual one. Ireland saw none of this but it was he who really desired it. In addition, his prolific writing skills – he had already written "Shakespeare"'s *Henry II* and had been in the process of starting his *William the Conqueror* when the *Vortigern* dived so disastrously that April night – were never given an outlet. He was, truly, a tragic figure.

FINANCIAL FRAUDSTERS

BCCI: The Bank Which Broke All the Rules

Agha Hasan Abedi was a poet and a mystic, but he set up a bank. It was not just any bank, however, but the Bank of Credit and Commerce International, or, as it is more famously known, BCCI. It was characterized by the high ideals of Abedi himself, who stated that it was to be a caring bank that would nurture developing countries to financial health.

Established in 1972, it was initially based in Abu Dhabi, where Abedi, although Pakistani by birth, was a close friend of the ruler. Its appeal was great and its growth was huge. By the start of the eighties, it had become the seventh largest private banking group in the world, with its major markets being the third world countries in the Middle East, Asia, China, Africa and South America. By 1988, just sixteen years after its founding, it claimed to have assets worth $20 billion, spread throughout its 400 branches which themselves were dispersed across over seventy countries worldwide. Large branches of the bank were to be found even in the United States, Britain and Europe.

On the face of it, this was a triumphant venture: a venture, for once, that benefited the poor Third World countries rather than

Michael Milken, employee of the bank Drexel Burnham Lambert

their rich First World colleagues. But even at its peak it was surrounded by more intense secrecy than other financial institutions, and it had gained a reputation of being the Saudi-Arabians' private bank. Furthermore, the fact that it had moved from its original base in Abu Dhabi to Luxembourg, with control now lying in a holding company registered in the Cayman Islands, raised suspicions that all was not quite as it seemed on the surface.

Vociferous critics rose to attack the bank, and its proposed expansion into England and Wales, where it wanted to build a further 200 branches, was thwarted in 1988. Unlike Robert Maxwell, the doubts about the bank's dealings did not remain doubts, but very quickly developed into concrete accusations.

The Americans were the first to act and in the autumn of 1988 the American Customs indicted the bank for money laundering and accused it of working for the cocaine cartels of Colombia. A total of forty suspects were rounded up and British Customs searched the bank's London headquarters. The pretence that BCCI was a modern day Robin Hood, taking from the rich to help the poor, seemed to have been exposed for what it was: a complete and utter sham.

According to the American indictment, the bank turned drug money into certificates of deposit in its American branches. Phoney loans were then arranged by bank officials for other branches abroad, thus enabling the drug traffickers to withdraw funds completely legally. It was a difficult case to prove for the effects would be monumental if the bank was shown to be corrupt, but after two years and enquiries carried out in Washington, Miami and Tampa, Robert Morganthau, one of the United States' toughest and most respected state prosecu-

---

Here's an example of initiative and quick thinking which Mrs Thatcher would be proud of. After all, did she not state that she wanted England to be a nation of home owners? Well, that's what Mark Acklom, aged 16, thought, anyway. Eager to fulfil his part in the bargain, he deceived the Leeds, one of England's largest building societies, into granting him a £440,000 mortgage on a property in Dulwich, only minutes' walk away from the Thatcher residence. Apparently all that was necessary for this fraud to succeed was a fake curriculum vitae and some spurious business addresses.

tors, succeeded. By 1990, the bank had pleaded guilty to laundering $32 million of drug money and was duly fined $15 million, with several executives receiving jail sentences.

One would believe that BCCI's cover had been completely blown: since they had pleaded guilty to corrupt activities in the US, it would be logical to assume that their activities were equally spurious in the other countries in which they operated. But the Bank of England and the English government were blind to the scandal which was so obviously brewing beneath their noses. Despite being fully informed of events in the United States and receiving a report in March 1990 – one of ten reports on the bank's dealings prepared by auditors since 1988 – that revealed that BCCI was in serious trouble, with huge holes in their accounts indicating a massive abuse of the bank's funds, the Bank of England did nothing.

Even when it was told that there were a large number of highly irregular and ill documented loans of considerable size being processed, even when it learnt of the lax international controls, and even when the report openly suggested that the depositors' funds were being plundered by a small number of Arab sheiks and bank officials for their personal use, still the Bank of England stalled.

Furthermore the Bank of England was actually asked – as early as 1989 – by the state prosecutor, Robert Morganthau, for documents relating to the bank's affairs, which should have alerted it that something major was underfoot. But whatever the officials' reasonings, Morganthau was given no documents and very little assistance until 17 May 1991, two years after his first request.

Instead of acting to curtail the corruption which was endemic in the bank's structure, the Bank of England simply demanded a change in management and a new injection of capital. This was hardly tough talking: Agha Hasan Abedi had been suffering from heart trouble for some time and was likely to step down at any moment. The BCCI duly complied with the Bank

> Two great conmen depended on the unusual gullibility of their victims for their swindles: Arthur Furgurson and Victor Lustig. Between them, they peddled a couple of national museums in New York, let the "White House", and sold the Eiffel Tower, not once, but twice!

of England's conditions and in 1990 Sheik Zayed bin Sultan al-Nahyan, the ruler of Abu Dhabi and Abedi's close personal friend, took over, injecting, in the process, the sum of $1.8 billion. The American action was effectively ignored and the bank was allowed to continue trading in the United Kingdom, with what we know now were disastrous consequences for the small investor.

BCCI might have been living a charmed life, so far, in the United Kingdom, but its days were numbered. Other countries were joining the United States and in early 1991 the Panamanian authorities began suing the bank for deposits which had been placed in the London branches and which were linked to the recently deposed dictator, Manuel Noriega. And even in the United Kingdom, the start of 1991 saw the Bank of England launch an inquiry after a senior employee stated that he had evidence of a major fraud. By 5 July 1991 matters had come to a head and Eddie George, the deputy governor of the Bank of England, finally closed the bank down. What has become known as the world's biggest ever banking scandal had been exposed completely.

As soon as the scandal broke, the media pounced on the Bank of England, demanding the reasons behind their inactivity, for it was very quickly revealed that the Bank of England's senior executives had known that BCCI was in desperate straits for at least sixteen months prior to the collapse. The Bank asserted that it had not acted beforehand because it had not possessed enough evidence of fraud or gross mismanagement.

Given the amount of evidence which it did have, it is hard to understand what more the Bank was waiting for. But as questionable and as heated a topic of debate as the Bank of

One of the most common ways the police spot thieves is by checking up on their lifestyle. If, for no apparent reason, someone starts throwing parties and frequenting the best restaurants in town, then their suspicions are raised. So when at the end of 1991 a man in Egypt began to enjoy the highlife, he had some explaining to do. Found wanting, he was duly accused of theft and was facing a hefty prison sentence, before he saved his skin by explaining the cause of his sudden good fortune was not the theft for which he stood accused, but his kidney, which he had sold on the black market for £20,000.

England's slowness was it was quickly overshadowed by the enormity of the fraud which had been perpetrated. There was much more wrongdoing besides the money laundering service the bank provided for its more shady customers.

Far and away the most shocking revelation was the uncovering of an unofficial bank within a bank. Reference had been made to this in the March 1990 report, which highlighted an amount nearing $800 million that had been lent to a small group of rich Arabs, who had not been required to sign any loan agreements and whose capacity to pay back the loans had not been appraised. Yet, although it was clear that the correct procedures were not being followed, no one at the time believed that a deliberate policy to defraud the bank's investors of their money had been uncovered. The loans showed irregularities, that was all.

How wrong this proved to be. Ten days after the bank was closed, all the countries in which it had operated were showing frauds on such a scale that they defied belief, and many of these frauds displayed the same structure: that of the bank within the bank. It quickly came to light that the deposits, which had come from mainly Asian small businessmen, were being systematically siphoned off and dispersed around the world, ending up in rich financiers' pockets. Many loans, it was discovered, were made to clients who were never asked, or indeed expected, to repay them. A favoured clique of the owner's friends were the main beneficiaries of this corrupt system.

One of these was Ghaith Pharaon, a Saudi Arabian who had been educated at Harvard. He was often used as a front man for Abedi and was well rewarded for his services. The auditors, Price Waterhouse, reckoned that his loans were $100 million in excess of limits and that they exceeded 10% of the bank's capital base. Bearing in mind that the bank claimed assets of $20 billion in 1988, those loans can be seen to be inordinately huge. Another was Sheikh Kamal Adham, the former head of Saudi Arabia's intelligence service, who had "borrowed", by the end of 1989, the somewhat smaller but still startlingly large amount of $313 million. And there were several others who received

---

There was one conman who was so confident in his abilities and so sure of his targets' gullibility that he adopted the name of Mr D. S. Windle. And no one ever suspected a thing!

healthy handouts, such as dignitaries like Sheikh Mohammed bin Rashid al Maktoum, M. M. Hammoud and the Ibrahim family.

At least these were real people. One loan totalling more than $150 million by the end of 1989 was paid to an A. R. Khalil. No signed loan agreements, no correspondence between the bank and the customer and no net worth statements were found. Added to this lack of information, it transpired that nobody at BCCI had actually contacted Khalil since 1987. This was such an irregular way even for BCCI to handle their business that A. R. Khalil's existence was brought into doubt, adding insult to the injury already suffered by the small investors.

Indeed, as if the injuries incurred by the investors had not been brutal enough – many lost all their savings and were ruined overnight – Abedi had gone one step further. For he had been revered throughout the Muslim world, and for this reason many people had placed their faith in him and his bank. That he should betray those very people who had shown him such loyalty was the ultimate affront in an episode which had contained so many terrible surprises.

BCCI had quite brazenly broken all the rules. It is amazing that it succeeded in doing so for so long. From its very inception it had aroused the suspicions of the financial community world-wide, and yet it was still allowed to continue operating. When the rewards are so large and seemingly so easily obtained, how long will BCCI remain the world's largest banking scandal?

Michael Milken: the Fall of a National Hero

Michael Milken was a serious earner. At his peak he was the highest paid employee the world has ever seen. In 1986, his employer, the bank Drexel Burnham Lambert, paid him the astronomical sum of $296 million. But his earnings did not stop there: in 1987 he had a pay rise, which led to him being paid the monumental sum of $550 million.

To put these staggering sums in to context: Milken's salary was more than 170 times the £1.9 million that Britain's highest paid man, William Brown, a Lloyd's insurance broker, received in 1987. Not even Michael Jackson, the highest paid pop star in history, could challenge these sort of earnings; in 1988 he earned a mere $35 million. Indeed to find anyone to run Milken close in this earnings contest, we have to go back in time to the era of American gangsters, and, specifically, to Al Capone. For Capone was estimated to have earnt $62 million in 1927, which translates to a total of roughly £350 million in 1988, still some $200 million adrift.

No one person, then, has ever come close to taking home as much money as Milken. There are only a small number of British companies who can make $550 million a year. Indeed, there are entire countries throughout the world whose Gross National Product falls far short of Milken's salary!

Aside from being nauseatingly wealthy, Michael Milken was also an incredibly popular guy. Admittedly, there were a number of people – mainly from the government services – who were rooting for his downfall, but these were easily outnumbered by those who regarded him as a national hero. Days after his indictment by a grand jury on racketeering charges there appeared a full page advertisement in the New York *Times*. It ran: "His vision has enabled many of our businesses, our employees and our communities to enjoy tremendous growth and opportunity." And above the signatures of those endorsing that statement the stark headline stood out: "MIKE MILKEN WE BELIEVE IN YOU."

Ivar Kreuger was friends with many heads of state and was so wealthy that he personally loaned money to several governments. And yet his death, in March 1932, revealed debts of more than £50 million (a huge amount in those days) and helped to prolong the already harsh depression of the 1930s.

Here's another fishy tale. In 1992, a sturgeon the size of a small lorry was pulled, or should that be winched, from the Yangtze River. Its sheer scale provoked great excitement and interest, until, that is, an official from the Sturgeon Artificial Reproduction Institute confessed that the whole story was a fraud.

This is hardly the kind of support one would have expected for a man soon to stand trial for charges so serious that he faced a theoretical 520 years in prison and fines of more than $3.7 billion. And it raises the question of exactly what it was that Milken had done to deserve such earnest attention from the US Government and such unbending loyalty from his supporters.

The answer is that he broke new ground within Wall Street by establishing, in the early eighties, a completely new market, which grew so rapidly that it was worth $300 billion by the end of 1988. This market dealt in "junk bonds", so called because they raised money for new businesses that the big banks, unwilling to take risks on unknown quantities, had shunned. Hardly an imprisonable offence, one might think. And, indeed, not even the US Government begrudged Milken his success, while this new junk bond market was seen to be free from fault. The opinions of Government and supporters only diverged when doubts began to arise as to how Milken operated within this market.

To his supporters, his manner of operating was either beyond reproach or did not matter, and they applauded his genius and foresight in establishing such a vibrant and success-ful market. They constantly pointed to the fact that this market not only enabled the financial community to make a healthy living, but also gave businesses which had just been founded or had inferior credit ratings a better chance of survival than they would have had under the old system.

The Government, on the other hand, saw matters slightly differently. To it, Milken, who was unquestionably a financial genius, was also a criminal. It believed that he had transgressed the law in several areas and charged him with violating the laws forbidding securities and mail fraud, showing false statements to the government, being involved in insider deal-ing and racketeering. In addition, the prosecutors claimed that he had cheated clients and stockholders, manipulated the marketplace and tricked a corporation into being taken over.

With such a divergence in views, this case is clear cut. Perhaps without the intervention of one key witness, Ivan Boesky, it would never have been proved either way.

Boesky was hardly a knight in shining armour: in 1987, he had pleaded guilty to insider trading and had been duly convicted for three years. It was a lenient sentence, for the simple reason that he had agreed to supply the Government with information on other insider traders; one such being

Michael Milken. Boesky's information – he claimed that Milken had directed an enormous conspiracy, centred on the junk bond market, and that Milken had given him instructions about when to buy and sell stock – had a powerful effect. For in conjunction with all the information that Rudolph Giuliani, the Mafia busting US attorney for Manhattan, had acquired in the course of his three year investigation into securities fraud, it led to Milken's indictment on ninety-eight assorted criminal charges.

This indictment, however, signalled only the start of the battle. For it still remained for the Government to prove its case, which was no easy thing to do against a man like Milken. Despite being accused by a grand jury of racketeering, along with his brother, Lowell Milken, and a former colleague, Bruce Newberg, Milken was prepared to fight.

On 29 March 1989, the Government finally pounced. In the largest criminal action ever taken against a Wall Street figure, the prosecution sought an unprecedented amount, asking for $1.8 billion in forfeitures against Milken and his two accomplices. Despite facing a theoretical prison sentence of over 500 years and fines which would bankrupt most countries, Milken remained unbowed. What's more, he was backed by a wall of supporters who hailed him as a misunderstood genius. One day after his indictment, hundreds of businessmen named him as the saviour of Los Angeles, the city to which Milken had moved the junk bond department of Drexel Burnham Lambert. Without him, they declared, the city would have been much poorer, in terms of both employment and entrepreneurial spirit. These individual statements of good faith were then followed by the now legendary New York Times advertisement, in

---

It's not just the financial giants who are tempted to participate in the odd bit of fraud. Christopher Wright, for example, at the age of eighteen, started the Garston Amhurst Investment Group, with the intention of making big money fast. Ten years later he was in court, after having swindled more than 400 people out of £4 million.

And Terry Peffer and Roland Cartwright persuaded the footballers Gary Lineker and Glen Hoddle to appear in advertisements for non-existent timeshare homes.

which almost one hundred American bankers and businessmen joined together to create an impression of unswerving and
universal support from within the financial community.

It is easy to understand why Milken was the object of such
loyalty, for he had made many people besides himself rich.
Within his own department there were eighty-one corporate
deal makers who enjoyed seven figure salaries, and Drexel
Burnham Lambert itself owed nearly all its success to Milken.
By 1988, Drexel ranked top in the junk bond market, carrying
out one in every four deals, but more importantly this junk
bond business earned over 90% of Drexel's profits (which in
1987 were $522.5 million). Furthermore, Milken had been
involved in raising finance for two of California's largest
housebuilders, not to mention his dealings for Safeway and
Wickes, the DIY company. Unsurprisingly, he had made
powerful allies during these and the many other deals over
which he had presided.

Armed with support such as this and an iron determination
to fend off the prosecution, Milken began to fight back. His
attitude can be summed up in the words of his spokesperson,
Elizabeth Maas, who stated: "He has maintained all along that
he will defend himself against any charges and that remains his
position."

Accordingly, he put up a bond of $1 billion to prevent the
freezing of much of his and his brother's fortune and made
certain that his daily activities continued as before, in an
attempt to prove the injustice of the Government's case; being
helped in this by Drexel's refusal to dismiss him and their
frequent positive statements about him.

However, this was a fight which the Government did not
expect to lose. And only two weeks after Milken's indictment, it
gained the upper hand, when Drexel agreed a $650 million
settlement with the Government. In a short statement given by
the bank, it promised new practices, policies and procedures
which would ultimately benefit the firm. While in no way
implicating Milken in any misdealings which might have
occurred, this settlement effectively isolated Milken, ensuring
that he would have to fight all alone against the whole
machinery of the US Government.

To his credit, Milken remained outwardly steady and by
hiring two of the very best defence lawyers in the business,
Arthur Linman, Senate Counsel in the Iran Contra hearings,
and Vincent Fuller, the man who had won an acquittal for

President Reagan's potential assassin, John Hinckley, he ensured that his trial was eagerly awaited by the American media.

And for a couple of months after Drexel's settlement, Milken managed to soldier gamely on, helped once again by Drexel's refusal to fire him. However, the screws were being slowly tightened by the Government, and it was only a matter of time before Drexel, who had been severely damaged by this whole affair, and Milken, the cause of that damage, parted company. In June 1989, Milken announced that he had resigned as the head of the high yield junk bond division, and that he was forming his own financial consulting firm, "International Capital Access".

The writing was now well and truly on the wall. And although his departure from Drexel, the firm which he had joined as a graduate in 1964, was an honourable one, it was not enough to save him. In the months following his indictment he had become increasingly isolated and on 12 September 1989 he formally entered a plea of guilty on six charges relating to insider trading. His battle with the Government forces had ended in failure and just over one year later, after a long and complex investigation and trial, Milken was sentenced to ten years in prison.

Nonetheless, it would be unwise to assume that America has seen the last of Michael Milken. For whatever the rights and wrongs of the case, Milken, although convicted, was never crushed. Unlike Abedi, the founder of BCCI, who was suffering from heart complaints when the bank began to flounder, Milken is a relatively young man, even now only approaching his late forties. This is the man who prompted the billionaire Donald Trump, a man not renowned for his abstemious nature, to pronounce that, in his opinion, a man earning half a billion

---

There is also the self-styled minicab lord, Daniel Hughes. Having bought the title of Lord of the Manor of Newnham for £30,000, he used it to enjoy a lavish and luxurious lifestyle. Unfortunately for him, he was discovered and jailed for five years.

And Maigrage Goomany, a BT operator, who charged friends, relatives and business associates in return for half price international calls, thus making an extra £30,000 a year. Unsurprisingly, a computer exchange system was installed soon after.

dollars a year should be able to be happy on less. Is it likely that he will be able to settle for less, or will his drive and ambition once again propel him to the very zenith of the financial world?

Nauru is an island made rich by guano – seabird excrement. Ravaged by the extraction of the high grade phosphate found in the guano, the islanders decided to safeguard their future and set up a trust fund, to the tune of $60 million, with the London office of the old and respected Australian law firm, Allen, Allen and Hemsley. Unfortunately for them, when they tried to reclaim this trust fund, they found they had been swindled . . . Luckily, however, with the help of Detective Inspector Drain, a member of the City of London Fraud Squad, they have already recovered all but $12 million and are hopeful of obtaining the remainder in the near future.

IMPISH IMPOSTORS

The Tichborne Claimant: True or False?

How can a twenty-one stone man sporting a shock of red hair begin to prove that he is, in fact, an eleven stone man with brown hair? It sounds like a task from "Mission Impossible", but this is what the Tichborne Claimant tried, with a staggering amount of success, to do. It was not just his size that was incompatible with his claim. When he was tested on any number of small points, such as the name of his relatives, the school he went to, the country in which he had spent his early childhood, he was found wanting. And yet he so very nearly pulled it off.

What makes this such an amazing swindle is the gullibility of everyone involved: the man was quite obviously an impostor. Or so it seems in the cold light of day, when there is a chance to review dispassionately the facts. So what exactly are the facts?

First, a little about the man whom this impostor claimed to be. Sir Roger Tichborne was a man of great wealth, heir to several country estates and a baronetcy, if he so desired. Born in 1829, he had spent most of his childhood in France, on account of his half French mother, Henriette, who wanted nothing to do with his father or the traditional English schooling. A family funeral finally ended his French sojourn at the age of sixteen, when his father smuggled the boy back to England while Henriette's gaze was averted. He completed his education at a strict Catholic establishment, Stonyhurst School, and eventually passed into the army. The years that followed were unremarkable, but when he was twenty-four he started to date, and wished to marry, his cousin Kate. The marriage would have been an excellent financial proposition, but the two families were not entirely happy about the situation and enforced a delay, during which Sir Roger was posted to South America. Unfortunately, his journey back proved fatal, as the ship upon which he was travelling sank leaving no known survivors. Sir Roger, a man noted for his slender good looks, had met an untimely end, or had he?

There is no doubt that everyone, except his mother, believed him dead and for good reason too. The ship had been lost with all hands on deck and no survivors had been found. Nonetheless, Henriette refused to abandon hope and she set about placing advertisements all over the world, asking for information about her son and offering a handsome reward. A year passed and no one came forward. After three more years still there had not been one solid piece of evidence presented to Henriette. Amazingly, her conviction that Roger was still alive grew. If so, he was keeping a low profile, and another six years

---

Horace Cole and Adrian Stephen, both Cambridge undergraduates, were the architects of many an outrageous hoax. Indeed, one of their earlier plans was to obtain the uniform of a couple of German army officers, travel to Alsace and once there, march a squadron of German troops over the border. Thankfully, they did not attempt this potentially perilous escapade, but focused their attentions nearer home. Their next attempt was safer, but much more bizarre. Learning of the visit of the Sultan of Zanzibar to England, they sent a telegram to the Mayor of Cambridge, telling him to expect an official visit by the Sultan's uncle. Not noted for painstaking preparations, they did no more than assume the flimsiest of disguises and turn up at the Town Hall, where, incredibly enough, they were taken for real and given a tour of the Cambridge Colleges. Their deceit was only discovered at the end of the day, when the Town Clerk tried to put them on a train to London, at which point the two men ran away to their college rooms.

passed before the impossible happened. A solicitor claiming to represent Sir Roger Tichborne had stepped forward. It was May 1865, some ten years after his ship had sunk, but, if he were to be believed, Henriette's long wait was over.

Matters were not quite as simple as they could have been, however. The solicitor, on further questioning, revealed that his client was living in Wagga Wagga, Australia, under the name of Castro. He had little money and as he could only prove his claim in person, Henriette would have to pay for his travelling expenses. Perhaps this first request might have caused some suspicion, but if it did, we do not know of it. Henriette seems so overjoyed by the fact that she might be regaining a son, that she not only agreed to pay for his travel, she also sent the family servant, Bogle, to Australia, in order to accompany him back to Paris.

What Castro was expecting to happen when he finally arrived in Paris and met Henriette is impossible to say, but it is probably that his hopes, however great, were as nothing as to what actually happened. He was greeted by his "mother" in a Paris hotel room, conveniently darkened by the inhospitable weather outside. Despite the fact that he bore no resemblance whatsoever to Tichborne, and he was a mere twice the weight "he" had been before his disappearance, Henriette fell into his arms, and welcomed him as her long lost son. As such, he was installed in the family house in England with his wife and children (whose existence he had inadvertently forgotten to mention until he reached Paris) and a small – to Henriette, perhaps, but almost certainly not to Castro himself – allowance of £1000 per year.

Indeed, there were some reasons why Castro's claim might have seemed genuine. The family solicitor, a Mr Hopkins, for instance, as well an antiquary named Mr Baigent, were both convinced immediately of his authenticity. He also received support from many of the local villagers, neighbours and officers of the 6th Dragoon Guards, his old regiment. Furthermore, he could recall incidents which had happened at Stonyhurst, intimate conversations with his tailor, the shops he was accustomed to buy his clothes from as a youth, and all his childhood aches and pains.

There was at least a slim chance that he was the man he claimed to be. Castro, for one, was confident, and in 1867 he filed a lawsuit for his rightful inheritance, which had, in his absence, passed on to "his" two year old nephew. In addition, he began to spend way in advance of his allowance, presumably on the basis that he would pay off his debts when his identity was confirmed (alternatively, a cynic might suggest that he realized he was living on borrowed time and was going to make the most of his good fortune while he could). Henriette apparently continued in her steadfast belief that she had been delivered her son a second time. And the rest of the family, respectful of their mother's wishes, kept a discreet silence.

Yet there were inconsistencies in Castro's behaviour and knowledge that were hard, even for Henriette, to understand. He had not, at first, recognized anyone in the family but Henriette, not even his sisters. He spoke no French, which must have seemed somewhat odd in someone who had lived in France for the first sixteen years of his life and who had left that country fluent in her tongue. He now called Henriette "mamma", rather than the more formal "mother" of his early years. Besides these, there were the less glaring, but still worrying errors in identifying his country estates and the places that his regiment had served. But if these faults are too great to stand close inspection, there is still the problem of his scanty but intimate knowledge of Tichborne's life. Where could he have gained enough information to bluff his way through his initial questioning?

As the likelihood of Wagga Wagga being a hotbed of Tichborne gossip is minimal, the first opportunity presented Castro has to be Bogle, the family servant. There is no doubt that much of the talk during the trip from Australia to Paris centred on Tich-

"SPIRIT VOICES SPOKE EVEN WHEN MEDIUM'S MOUTH WAS FILLED WITH DYED WATER". So proclaimed the front page of a daily newspaper, sometime in the mid 1950s. The medium in question was William Roy, and he certainly had people fooled. He had become famous for holding seances where he would "summon" direct messages from the dead and tell clients details about themselves which they had never made public. He was a complete fraud, of course, communicating by means of an earpiece with no one more mysterious than his assistant in another room. However, for a short time he ruled supreme, and his greatest coup was when he convinced the Canadian Prime Minister, Mackenzie King, that he had actually spoken with Queen Victoria and Gladstone.

borne and the family. Castro might even have promised Bogle a share of his takings if the servant were to furnish him with sufficient information to convince the family. All other accounts deny this possibility, preferring to describe Bogle as the family's faithful old servant; but surely even the most faithful of employees can be tempted by the lure of a handsome nest egg for an uncertain future? However, once Henriette recognized him, Castro was allowed free range of all Roger's personal diaries and correspondence, which must have proved a goldmine of information about the private side of the man.

Nevertheless, while Henriette was alive, no one was allowed to investigate the man fully and he had time to uncover and adapt to his role. The fact that he could have been Sir Roger was all that mattered. But when Henriette died, in 1868, the situation changed dramatically. The family went on the attack and shouted fraud. They said that Castro was none other than Arthur Orton, a butcher's son from Wapping, born in 1834. As the youngest of twelve children he learnt to fend for himself and by the age of seventeen was already fiercesomely overweight, earning himself the nickname "Bullock Orton". Constantly in need of money he plied any number of trades from butcher to merchant sailor, until he emigrated, in 1852, to Australia under a false name. While there, his immense size and strength enabled him to become an expert slaughterman, an occupation in which he continued until 1865 and the beginning of this latest episode. The reason behind his claim was, the family stated, debt. He was married with a child on the way and he had been living beyond his means. On hearing of the reward for information about Tichborne, he approached the solicitor and told him that he had property back home; that he was, in fact, Sir Roger Tichborne and his pipe proved this. He had handed the solicitor a pipe with RCT scratched into it and the rest, as they say, is history.

This spelt disaster for Castro. The onus was on him to prove beyond doubt that he was who he claimed to be. All the defense needed to do was to give a reasonable alternative to his claim, and they would win. 102 days later, the inevitable happened. It was decided that whoever Castro was, he was not Sir Roger Tichborne. Castro had put up a surprisingly good defence, but his ignorance on the subject of the Tichborne dogs and their nicknames, his atrocious handwriting and even more atrocious spelling, proved too much for the jury to believe.

Matters were to get a lot worse for Castro, however. The Lord

Chief Justice Bovill decided to take the case further and opened a second trial; this time for perjury. In the first trial Castro had nothing to lose and all to gain: he would either be accepted as Sir Roger Tichborne or he would simply remain as Castro. In this second trial, he had everything to lose and nothing to gain: he would either be found to have lied and receive a heavy prison sentence, or he would simply remain as Castro. But he was not a man to surrender before the final die had been cast. If he were to go down, he was determined to go down fighting.

As a consequence, this second trial, which began in 1869, became the longest running criminal case in legal history, lasting a total of 188 days. And it was a case which mesmerized the British public, millions of whom believed him. On a number of occasions the prosecuting counsel were booed by the enormous crowds which gathered outside the court room and eventually they started appearing at the court under police protection. The same topics were discussed as in the previous case, but in much greater depth. Castro alone called 300 witnesses, all, it has to be said, fervent in their support of him. Many of the prosecution witnesses were from Australia and Chile (where he had spent some time as a merchant sailor)

Invigorated by their success as the Sultan of Zanzibar's relatives, Horace Cole and Adrian Stephen fulfilled their desire for a military mockery. Rather than lead a German invasion of France, this time they determined to fool the might of the British Navy. And so, on 10 February 1910, they sent a telegram to Vice Admiral Sir William May, commander in chief of the Home Fleet, warning him that HMS Dreadnought, which had recently docked at Weymouth, would be the proud recipient of a visit by no less than the Emperor of Abyssinia. As before, preparations were kept to a minimum, with the hoaxers simply blacking their faces on the train down to Weymouth. It did not matter, since the Navy was truly fooled. On arrival, the two men and their entourage (they had persuaded some of their friends to join in the hoax as well) were met by taxis which ferried them to the quayside. And once on board they were truly treated like royalty. A national anthem (not that of Abysinnia however, as no one knew it) was played, they were offered luncheon, given a tour of the ship and finally honoured with a salvo of guns. The tour finally ended without mishap and no one would have been any the wiser had not Cole, anxious for publicity, leaked the story to the Daily Mirror.

and all had to have their transport to England paid for. It was a ludicrous situation, as it didn't look likely that Castro could ever be proved beyond doubt to be Orton, as long as he maintained his innocence and had supporters. This ridiculous state of affairs is underlined by the fact that the prosecutor's summing up lasted twenty days and Castro's opening and closing remarks took an amazing forty-four days. How could any truth come out of this rambling and garbled trial? Nonetheless Castro, after having shown complete ignorance about his days in France and countless other areas, was declared to be Arthur Orton and to be guilty on all charges. He even had the honour of placing a new crime, "False Personation", in the statute book. A fourteen year prison sentence was meted out.

But Castro continued to profess his innocence from within his Dartmoor prison cell and so impressed a visiting QC, a Dr Kenealy, that the latter promised to plead Castro's case. Kenealy argued that the jury had been misled by Castro's weight, which at the trial was an incredible twenty-four stone. Since his incarceration, he had slimmed down considerably and his bone structure could be seen to resemble Sir Roger's. Secondly, Castro's hair was brown, not red. Thirdly, he possessed, as did Sir Roger, a retractable penis. All pretty spurious evidence, but in a case where nothing had ever been proved for certain, it was good enough to revive public opinion. On the back of which, Kenealy set up a scandal mag named *The Englishman*, which purported to plead Castro's case by threatening to reveal the indiscretions of the high and mighty. Promptly dismissed from the bench, he founded the Magna Carta Association and began to travel the length and breadth of the country proclaiming Castro's innocence. With such great success, it seems, that when he stood as MP for Stoke in 1875, some five years after Castro's trial, he was elected in a landslide. Unfortunately for the man in prison, Kenealy's crusading did him no good at all. When his trial had been discussed in the Houses of Commons and Kenealy had suggested sending it to the Royal Commission for review, the House had overwhelmingly refused (by 433 votes to 1). There was nothing for Castro to do except serve his sentence.

On his release in 1884 he sold his confession to a newspaper. But on receiving payment for the confession he immediately retracted his statement and continued to claim that he was Sir Roger Tichborne right up to his death.

Martin Guerre: Here Today, Gone Tomorrow

Jodie Foster, Richard Gere and Gerard Depardieu are all connected with the following story of deception, intrigue and betrayal, even though it happened in France in the sixteenth century. In 1982, Gerard Depardieu took the leading role in *Le retour de Martin Guerre*, which was followed ten years later by Jodie Foster and Martin Gere's blockbuster *Sommersby*. Some of the details may have changed in the telling (*Sommersby* was set in Civil War America, rather than France) but the essence of the story has remained intact, and has lost none of its power to intrigue.

It is the tale of a woman who faces a painful moral dilemma. Her husband, who had left without explanation many years previously, suddenly returns, and with his return comes a happiness greater than she has felt before. Not much of a problem on the surface, but there is one small inconvenience: the returned husband is an impostor and she knows it. What should she do? Renounce the man who has made her happy, thus sending him to almost certain death, or risk her own life and live a lie?

This is not a cut and dried example of deception for financial gain, as was the Tichborne saga. There was not, in any real sense, a victim. After all, the husband had left his wife to fend

> In 1906 Wilhelm Voigt, a cobbler by trade, became a national hero overnight. Tired of mending shoes as he had done for so many years, he obtained the uniform of a captain in the German infantry and began to parade through the streets of the capital. Bumping into a squad of ten soldiers led by a rather pathetic corporal, Voigt took charge. First of all he marched them up and down the street. Then he commandeered a bus, drove to Kopenick, a suburb of Berlin, marched into the Town Hall and arrested the Burgomaster and Town Treasurer. His appetite whetted, he ordered theTown Council to give him 4,000 marks and promptly placed them under arrest as well. His get away was secured by packing everyone into the bus and ordering it to drive into Berlin without him.

for herself and she willingly accepted the impostor. No force was necessary, no blackmail occurred. All was well, except for the impostor's identity, but, unfortunately, that proved to be the straw that broke the camel's back.

The story begins in 1538, when a young couple, Martin Guerre and Bertrande de Rols, were married in Artigat in the Ariege. Bertrande was just fourteen years old. Eight years passed and no children were born, most probably because the couple lived separate lives, but the superstitious people of the sixteenth century, held that they had been cursed and a "wise woman" was hired to break the spell. Which she did immediately. Nonetheless, although Bertrande enjoyed Martin's sisters' company, the baby did nothing to bring bride and groom closer. Martin was constantly restless, his main skills being fencing and boxing, which in Artigat could not be used to any good effect. Indeed, he did little to good effect, since he was too well placed to become a shepherd and too lowly to enter one of the professions (none of which he would have relished anyway). So it was not too startling when, in 1548, after a raging quarrel with his father, he disappeared from his home town to seek his fortune further afield.

Regardless of her feelings for Martin, his departure was a great blow to Bertrande. Not financially, since Martin's family was fond of her and would not hear of anything except that she continue living with them, but emotionally. The law forbade remarriage unless her husband were dead, and it was not the done thing for a married woman to come into contact, however platonic, with a man not her husband. So Bertrande knew that, although still a young woman, she would never find love.

But life had to go on and it would be a mistake to imply that her existence was totally miserable. She was comfortable, secure and well looked after, especially when Martin's uncle, Pierre, married her widowed mother and they all moved into her childhood home. Eight years passed and Bertrande still remained faithful to her absent husband. She might have desired love, but she would do only what was right. That is, until her husband returned. From that point on, her life was thrown into chaos.

He did not reappear with any pomp or ceremony, preferring instead simply to walk into town, as if he had been on an outing to market rather than having vanished without trace eight years before. His arrival, however, did not catch Bernadette completely unawares: news of Martin Guerre swept through the village like the mistral. Whether she was as delighted by this unforeseen development as his sisters and the rest of the village were we will never know, but she did not hurry to greet him, allowing his sisters to run on ahead and bring him in. And when they did finally meet, it was an awkward, uncertain welcome she gave him. Doubts raced through her mind: he seemed smaller than she remembered and was more open and effusive than he had been in the past. Yet, he had been recognized instantly by the villagers and he in turn had greeted them warmly. He had to be her husband. Who else could he be? Still undecided, she invited him in. Once inside her doubts crumbled. As soon as he was alone with her, he asked about the long white stockings that he had liked so much. Had she kept them? Would she wear them for him once again? This was such an impossibly intimate detail that he could be no one else but Martin.

Their marriage was reborn. The commotion caused by Martin's reappearance soon died down and village life returned to normal. If there were any doubters they did not raise their heads and Martin with Bertrande and their son Sanxi moved back to their old house in Artigat. Bertrande was happier than ever she had been before. If this were the real Martin, she reasoned, then he had changed for the better. He was more attentive, more loving and more industrious. There was none of the irritated restlessness that had so characterized his early years. Moreover, he was proving quite an astute businessman. By buying, leasing and selling land he had increased the Guerres' wealth considerably and looked set to expand it further in the future. In short, he was too good to be true.

When Bertrande discovered the truth about her husband is hard to say, but it was more likely to have been sooner rather

April Fool's Day has provided many entertaining hoaxes throughout the years, but these two must be amongst the best. On 1 April 1957, the normally serious minded current affairs programme, Panorama, fooled almost the whole nation by devoting an entire programme to the spaghetti trees of Italy. Twenty-two years later, London's Capital Radio had many people convinced that the 5th and 12th of April had been cancelled, in order to bring Britain back into line with the rest of the world.

than later. The real Martin had had a scar above one eyebrow, a detail which in the heat of a first meeting is easily overlooked, but cannot remain hidden for long. What can be said with certainty is that on unearthing his fraud she determined to ignore it. Contrary to her expectations, she had found love. And it was a fruitful love at that. Two babies followed in quick succession, one dying soon after birth, but the other, Bernarde, bursting with health.

Unfortunately, as with so many frauds and swindles, the luck had to run out. Martin saw another strip of land which was ripe for sale. This time, however, he had chosen a piece of ancestral land in the Basque country, which held special memories for his uncle Pierre. Pierre argued strongly against the sale and although the two men had, up until that point, been on the best of terms, they sank into a bitter argument, which could only be resolved by a court battle. As Martin was the rightful owner of the land, it should have been a simple case, but by then Pierre had become so incensed that he cast doubt on Martin's genuineness. The size of his feet, his height, his scar (or lack of it) were mentioned, and despite winning the case, the man claiming to be Martin had ceased to be thought of as Martin by many of the villagers. He was in a vulnerable position and had it not been for Bertrande's steadfast support, he would probably have been driven from the village there and then.

As it was, the storm wasted little time in breaking. A local landlord had long harboured the idea that Martin had destroyed one of his barns and in 1559 he took him to court for this offence. During the trial, doubt was again raised as to Martin's authenticity and, for the first time, he was accused of being a marriage breaker. Thrown into jail for arson, he must have known that worse was to come. Pierre had made no secret that he was determined to prove him an impostor. He was, it was said, scouring the district for information. Furthermore, the village was alight with rumour and counter rumour. He knew he would have to prove his case in court.

In the meantime, while Martin was languishing in prison, matters were proceeding apace. Pierre had found two men who maintained that they knew Martin in a previous existence. Bertrande was informed that, on his release, Martin was to be arrested immediately and taken to trial. There was little she could do but acquiesce and hope that her husband's story held. And there was good reason to believe that it would. After all, they had lived together as man and wife for three years: he could not fail to have learnt many details of "their" former life. What's more, as soon as misgivings had been raised by Pierre and the villagers, Martin had carefully memorized all the most intimate acts and conversations the two had had in the years leading up to the abrupt departure.

But Bertrande, under pressure from Pierre, denounced the accused as an impostor, and although she refused to deny him under oath, the case was lost. The impostor was found guilty and Pierre's pride had been restored. For he had only undertaken this prosecution out of anger, demanding no more than a fine and an apology, as he was genuinely fond of the new man. Unfortunately, there was also the King's attorney to take into account, a man who had taken a prominent part in the prosecution and who now decreed that instead of a fine, the accused was to be beheaded. Both "Martin" and Bertrande were now facing the ultimate sanction.

The couple immediately appealed to the Parliament at Toulouse and, in April 1560, a new trial was begun. A trial in which "Martin" shone, demonstrating such wit and knowledge that the judges were convinced. Especially as Pierre had begun to make wild accusations and violent threats, which were obviously without substance. The verdict was undoubtedly going to be favourable to Bertrande and her husband, until the impossible happened. The real Martin Guerre, with an astounding sense of drama and timing, walked into the courtroom.

Twelve years after his abrupt departure, he was back, and this time there was no doubting he was the real man. Bertrande was crushed. She had welcomed a stranger into her home, hoping (and most probably believing) that her true husband, the husband she loved less, would never return. What should she do? In an abrupt change of allegiance, she disowned the impostor, declaring him a trickster and a fraud. She broke

---

Who is the impostor of all time? A tricky question. But the name Stanley Weyman must surely be considered. For Stanley loved pretending to be who he was not and over the years appeared as a Romanian consul-general, a bogus lawyer, a doctor, a lieutenant-commander in the US Navy, a journalist, a UN official and an owner of a chain of motels. Not bad going for one man.

down and begged the real Martin for forgiveness. Had she not, after all, declared him an impostor as soon as she had discovered her mistake? The fake Martin's fate had been sealed. He was found guilty a second time and sentenced to death.

Shortly before his execution, the impostor confessed all: he was Arnaud de Tilh, from the village of Sajas, which lay in the north west of the region, not far from Artigat itself. Like Martin, he had grown restless in his youth and had left to be a mercenary. While fighting as a foot soldier for Henry II in Picardy, he had been mistaken for Martin Guerre on a number of occasions. His curiosity raised, he had started to study the man, his wife and his property. When he discovered that Martin had been drafted into the army of Philip II of Spain and was unlikely to return, he took his chance. The fault was entirely his and he begged Martin to treat Bertrande kindly, as she had acted with honour and integrity.

With these last words, he revealed a heroic and touching love for the woman who had remained deliberately blind to his deception, until she finally betrayed him in his moment of need. What started out as a mere fraud had blossomed into love.

Major Martin: the Man Who Didn't Exist

On 3 May 1943, disaster struck the Allied war effort. The Spanish had just found a high ranking soldier in the sea off their coast. Padlocked to his body was a briefcase holding documents of the utmost importance to the success of the impending Allied invasion of Europe. The British naval attaché in Madrid anxiously relayed this information to Naval Intelligence in London and awaited orders. He did not have long to wait. His intructions were to retrieve both the body and the papers as soon as discretion would allow. Unfortunately for the British, they were overheard. By the end of the transmission, the Spanish had forced open the briefcase, removed the contents and sent them on their way to Berlin.

It is impossible to understate the significance of the docu-

ments Major Martin had been in possession of. Berlin had been
aware, for some time, of plans by the Allies to invade Europe
from the North African coast. But they had been unable to
discover by which route this invasion would come. There were
any number of entry points possible, but three sites presented
themselves as most likely: Sicily, Greece or the area around
Sardinia and Corsica. Unable to defend all three, they were
desperate for information which would indicate the direction
whence the storm would come. Major Martin had all that they
desired. His briefcase contained word to General Alexander in
Tunisia that the attack would come via Greece and would use a
feigned move, via Sicily, as cover. The Allies' double bluff had
been exposed: the Germans could now plan their defence of
Europe with confidence.

Thus on 14 May 1943 Admiral Donitz, having checked the
documents' validity and accuracy, went to see Hitler himself.
The attack, he said, would most definitely come via Greece. As
a result, it would be necessary to run down defences on Sicily to
a minimum. The Allied attack would be met with maximum
force and would result in humiliating defeat.

But . . . Major Martin had never existed. He was a figment of
British Naval Intelligence's imagination. It had been recognized
that the outcome of the war would be heavily influenced by the
invasion of Europe and any measures which might give the
Allies the edge in this phase of battle had to be used. The top
brass also understood the enormous efforts the Germans would
be making to second guess their modus operandi, but instead
of viewing this as solely an awkward and potentially dangerous obstruction, they decided to use the German Intelligence
Service to their own advantage. They came up with Major
Martin.

If it could be arranged for false plans to fall into the enemy's
hands seemingly by accident, then, the Allies contended, they

---

It is a well known fact that "children of amputees are noticeably
short of limbs". At least that is what the Soviet Government held
to be true, until its quite transparent falsehood led this "fact" to
be quietly consigned to the rubbish bin. Among other untruths
championed by governments are: "green apples give you in-
digestion" and "milk turns sour during a thunderstorm". Interesting . . .

would be able indirectly to dictate the Germans movements. It was a risky plan, and one that could not work in isolation. It would be necessary to make the Germans, by many and various means, believe that the attack would be in Sicily, before allowing Martin's information about Greece to be caught. The whole operation was to be strictly top secret – not even General Alexander knew what was going on – and was to be called, rather menacingly, "Operation Mincemeat".

Their course of action decided, Lieutenant Ewen Montagu, the leader of the operation, set out to find a suitable candidate: not just any corpse would do. He had to have the right type of frame for a marine, be the right age and recently deceased. That done, the task of building a real identity for Major Martin began in earnest. Letters from his girlfriend, bills from his tailor and a couple of theatre tickets were planted on him. There was even a letter from his bank advising him that he had recently become overdrawn. And in his briefcase, beside the fraudulent battle plans, was a letter of introduction from Mountbatten to Eisenhower and the commander in chief of the Mediterranean, recommending him as an expert in the use of landing craft. The impostor was ready and for the moment packed in ice, until the time was deemed correct to deliver him to the Germans.

There still remained the problem of allowing him to fall into enemy hands without provoking suspicion. After all, he was rather too good to be true. He could not be found behind the German lines, as there would be no reasonable excuse for his being there. He could not be left in Allied territory with the slim hope that German spies would locate him before their own troops did. The only method which guaranteed any kind of success was to drop him in the sea and hope that he would wash conveniently into the Germans' grateful arms. This meant that a third party, favourable to the Germans, had to discover the body and relay the findings to Berlin. Hence the sea outside the Spanish coast was chosen for the drop, for not only were the Spanish favourable to the Germans, despite their official neutrality, but they were known to harbour many German spies, who worked out of the Spanish ports and Huelva in particular.

Preparations ready, the date for commencement was set, and on 19 April 1942 Major Martin, still tightly packed in his icy bed, was loaded on board the *Seraph*, a British submarine. She sailed undetected to her destination and ten days later William

Martin was defrosted, furnished with an inflated life jacket and left to float towards Spain. A nervous four days ensued in which no news was heard, but on 3 May, the British naval attaché learnt of his capture by some Spanish fishermen. All that was left to do, now, was to tempt the Spanish and in turn the Germans into believing that the discovery was a vital blow to the Allies. Hence the great concern expressed by both the naval attaché in Madrid and his superiors in London. The bait was taken, and when the Allies landed in Sicily on 10 July 1943 they were met with little resistance. An incredible gamble had paid off.

Several decades later, it seems incredible that an entire army could have been taken in by this impostor. Surely the Germans should have been suspicious that the very information that they needed turned up, neatly giftwrapped, at just the right time? Surely they should have acted with more caution? But the very success of this fraud, played, as it was, for the highest stakes, underlines why there will always be impostors and fraudsters. Just as with Tom Keating or Clifford Irving and their targets, Major Martin gave the Germans what they wanted. He simply allowed the Germans' immense desire for information to overcome their caution. Had more pressure been applied to make them believe this double bluff, they would, no doubt, have smelt a rat. But as it was, he proved too tempting to ignore.

The hoaxer's primary object is not always to make money. Some just like exposing the posturings of self-important men to ridicule. One such hoaxer was Humphrey Berkeley, who, as a Cambridge undergraduate, invented the character of H. Rochester Sneath, Head of Selhurst School. With the utmost cheek and the aid of writing paper printed with Selhurst's imaginary address, Berkeley, alias Sneath, proceeded to enter into correspondence with the heads of some of the most prestigious public schools in England, such as Eton, Harrow, Marlborough and Rugby. Such correspondence covered topics as sensitive as homosexuality among the boys, and as practical as arranging an art tour to South Africa; but not once was he quizzed about the origins and whereabouts of his fictitious school. However, he was eventually discovered and the authorities, revealing no sense of humour whatsoever, sent him down from university for two years.

LADY LIARS

Dr James Barry: the Female Physician

Not all swindlers, hoaxers and fraudsters are men. It is true that there are fewer recorded cases of women being involved in such chicanery, but perhaps this proves not that women are less likely to engage in these activities, but that they are more successful in achieving their aims. Dr James Barry, for instance, lived her whole life pretending to be a man and yet she was never detected at least officially.

Her fraud differs from the majority of those described in this book, however. She did not set out to take money from innocent hands, nor to ridicule those in authority. Her crime, if crime it can be called, was the wish to enter the profession of medicine. She merely wanted to be a doctor. And in the nineteenth century the essential prerequisite was to be a man; so she became a man.

She was born sometime around the turn of the nineteenth century – the details of her earlier life are understandably shadowy – and came with her father to England when still a young child of six, maybe seven, years of age. Her family were Irish, and she may have been a niece of the artist James Barry, but what is certain is that she grew up accustomed to wealth and privilege. Her daily life exposed her to challenging and exciting possibilities, which she wanted to explore. And so she left London, and womanhood, for Edinburgh, its university and life as a man.

Already her nerve must be applauded: she was only ten or eleven years old on enrolment and had left her family for an alien city. The fact that she also had to pretend to be a boy must only have added to her problems. But she was not quite alone. Her family contacts included some of the most high ranking aristocracy in the land and it seems likely that one of these, Lord Buchan, became her mentor during her studies. Whether he knew that his ward was a girl, rather than a bright young boy, is more uncertain, but if he did, he did not give her away. Thankfully, for James, as she was now known, was an outstanding student. So good, in fact, that she graduated with flying colours at the age of twelve – a child prodigy, if ever there were one – and was immediately engaged by a London hospital, where she worked as assistant to some of the top surgeons of the day. A truly great talent had been allowed to flourish and it was soon detected by the army.

In 1816 she was posted to South Africa, soon becoming the personal doctor of Lord Charles Somerset, Governor of the Cape. This was a high ranking post to obtain so early on in one's career – she was no more than seventeen – and it may be true that once again she did not succeed without the help of her mentor, Lord Buchan or of some other powerful family, such as the Beauforts. But still it is quite clear that she was more than capable of performing her duties efficiently.

These duties did not take up all her time: she also urged the building of a leper colony, changed official attitudes towards lunatics by registering them as sick people, rather than criminals, and promoted the idea of healthy diets by urging all she met to eat more fruit and vegetables. These achievements coupled with a colourful, flamboyant character soon got her promoted to Medical Inspector of the province.

It would be untrue to claim that no doubts were ever raised about her sex, for she was ever the subject of the colony's gossip mongers. They noted her slight build and effeminate stature and were constantly calling into the question the exact nature of her relationship with the Governor, Lord Charles Somerset. As the years passed – she was six years his personal doctor – he must have realized the truth, if he did not know in the beginning, and it was probably the tenderness and affection with which he viewed her that enabled her to play the role of a man so well. For it was obvious that he would protect her, whatever the circumstances.

She pursued her work with a religious zeal and was ready to do whatever was necessary to reform a lazy and corrupt service. To great uproar she replaced the unqualified and incompetent apothecaries who had been allowed to continue in their work only because they were well liked. In 1825, she refused to certify a drunken prisoner as insane, and her letter complaining of the mishandling of the affair led to the Governor's secretary putting her in prison, until the Governor himself pardoned her. Unfortunately, this challenging spirit led to her professional undoing. Her ideas might have been good, but she had a way of upsetting her colleagues that made progress difficult. Hence, the medical board stripped her of her unique powers as Inspector later on in 1825 and when she resisted, they demoted her.

To her credit, she remained unbowed. Ever confident in her own abilities, she surged back to national prominence when she saved both a mother and her baby by using the Caesarian technique: a technique which she had only read about some months beforehand. To this day the Munnik family name the first boy in each generation James Barry.

But perhaps she overplayed her role and became more of a "man" than other men. Her career was marked by constant confrontation – whether she was dealing with the care of patients or the administration of various hospital services – and eventually petered out because of it. When the army's most

---

Stella Newborough (1773–1843) was a strange woman. Born to a peasant family in Modigliana, Tuscany, she married twice, first to an English lord and then to a Russian baron, thereby obtaining a position on the periphery of Europe's aristocracy. But Stella had further ambitions: she claimed that her father had swapped her on birth with Louis-Philippe of Orleans, who was soon to be King of France. Not surprisingly, he was somewhat reluctant to give up this esteemed position – especially as she had no proof whatsoever – and Stella's hopes were never realized. Nonetheless, she continued her campaign until her very deathbed, calling Louis-Philippe "the involuntary usurper of rights which henceforth he cannot keep without guilt".

powerful medical post fell vacant, she, despite her sparkling talent, was not even shortlisted. How ironic that becoming a man had both enabled her to enjoy the demanding and rigorous lifestyle which she so desired, and yet ultimately led to her exclusion from the highest echelon.

Her days ended in enforced quiet, with her final posting, as Inspector General of Hospitals in Canada, cut short because of illness. After nearly fifty years in active service she spent the remaining decade of her life visiting friends and travelling, never once throwing off her disguise. Only on her death in 1865, when her body was being laid out, did it become clear that James Barry was a woman.

Sophie Lloyd: This Boy's Magic!

The twentieth century: a time of opportunities, an age where talent is free to flourish, an era of unparalleled advancement in every sphere. Equal rights for all, men and women alike. There are women accountants, lawyers, doctors. The most famous Prime Minister in England since the war? Not Harold Wilson or Ted Heath but Margaret Thatcher . . .

So what possible reason would any woman have for denying her sex in recent times? The age old reason, unfortunately. Prospects for women may have changed for the better this century, but equality is still a long way away.

> James Graham was a genius of fraud. For he spent much of his life making a handsome living out of promoting "the bed which makes you fertile". He claimed it brought "immediate conception to any gentleman and his lady desirous of progeny" and all for only £50 a night (which in the late eighteenth century was a very princely sum). How he was able to make anybody believe his claim is remarkable, but as the bed was something of a masterpiece in itself – twelve feet wide by nine feet long, supported by forty pillars of coloured glass, with a huge mirror overhead – there was never a shortage of people willing to give it a try.

And this is proved by the story of Sophie Lloyd, as recently as 1989.

Her aim should have been easily obtained. After all, she only wanted to enter the Magic Circle and, as everyone knows, if you've got the talent, you're in. As long, of course, as you are male. This puzzled Sophie. It seemed strange that a group of entertainers, not normally the most reactionary of people, should be so narrow minded. In fact, it did more than puzzle her, it annoyed her intensely. And so, in league with her agent, Jenny Winstanley, Sophie set out to gain entrance. Her aim was less long term than James Barry's; she did intend to work as Sophie Lloyd as well. Yet her preparations were much more elaborate. Sophie could not depend on such heavyweights as Lord Buchan or the Governor of South Africa to give her support. Her deception had to be complete and convincing not just to the naked eye, but to the unforgiving gaze of the camera.

First of all, she had to invent a character which was likely to convince. Being small and fragile herself, the logical choice was to play a slight, non athletic, teenage boy. So she would not have to talk too much, this boy was to have a quiet introverted personality, whose true talent could only be shown on the stage. So far, it was plausible. There are many teenage boys who hate sports and even more whose conversation verges on the monosyllabic.

Next, Sophie studied how men carry themselves, what they do with their hands, how they talk and interact with each other. It was crucial for the success of her plans that she move and speak like a man, especially as she would be under intense scrutiny while on stage. Although the moments after her performance, when she was invited to sit in the bar to discuss the finer points of the act, were eventually to prove the more demanding.

Having decided how her character would act and move, Sophie still had to make herself look like a convincing sixteen-year-old boy. So, whenever she was to perform, she had to undergo a rigorous makeup session in the hours beforehand. This entailed donning a wig and glasses, a set of body plumpers, which gave her face a much fuller aspect, and a rigid body harness to flatten her torso. Indeed, the only parts of her body that could not benefit from the careful use of props were her hands. All she could do was to keep them out of sight for as long as possible, which did not pose a problem at all, on

Mme Marthe Hanau, France's 'Woman wizard of finance'

stage. After all, the audience would be concentrating on the trick in hand, not on the hands themselves. But in the bar afterwards, she had to keep her hands in her pockets for such lengths of time that it must have seemed slightly unusual even for a teenage boy.

Preparations complete, Sophie gave her character a name, Raymond, and after inventing a whole family history, replete with school tales and family arguments, she was ready to begin her assault on the Magic Circle. It was no overnight success. Raymond's act had to be forged in the open. The basics had been learnt beforehand, but the only way to find an act good enough to be allowed into the Magic Circle, was to test the tricks in front of the public. Consequently, Raymond toured the London circuit for over a year, steadily building up both his act and support from the audience.

By the end of this period, reports of his work, although never fraught with excitement, seemed to suggest that a shot at entering the Magic Circle would be worthwhile. Ironically, these reports were more fulsome in their praise of the boy himself, than of his magic. Sophie had almost succeeded in her aim. The last hurdle was the examination, which was to be held in front of an audience of 200 and, more importantly, an official from the Magic Circle. Her makeup session that night lasted two hours – a testament to her determination – but she need not have worried: the show was a great success and Raymond was admitted into the Magic Circle.

Once again, the fraudster had been victorious, proving to herself at least the ludicrous reasoning of the powers that be. But for Sophie Lloyd and her agent Jenny, there was a vicious twist in the tale. For the Magic Circle had been under siege, for some time, on the subject of its all male membership and soon

> The urge to reinvent oneself burns in many people. Mary Willcocks, however, went one step further. She actually did reinvent herself: as Princess Caraboo from Javasu. Her deception was soon uncovered, but as there seemed to be nothing underhand about her actions, she was left in peace, or at least, she would have been, had she not been such a great attraction. Thousands flocked to see her and hear her tell of the ceremonies and festivals which she had presided over, and the fact that she was making it all up seemed not to bother anyone.

after Raymond's entry into that esteemed body it was agreed that women would be allowed to join: the only proviso being that, like the men, they would have to prove themselves good enough. Sophie thought that she would be the first woman member. It would mean admitting her deception, it was true, but everyone was bound to see the funny side of it. Who wouldn't?

Unfortunately the Magic Circle's members had only bowed to pressure to change the rules. They had no intention of letting any women actually join. It was simply a PR ploy. So, when Sophie Lloyd knocked on the door demanding to be allowed in, they laughed in her face. Until that is, she said that she was already a member: that soon wiped the smile off their faces, and there was no humour left whatsoever by the time she had finished her tale of Raymond, the magician. Instead of honorably accepting that they had been duped, and admitting that she was quite obviously skilled in the magic arts, they slammed the door in her face. Angrily they revoked Raymond's licence and denied Sophie entrance. Ironically, when one considers that deception is, after all, the Magic Circle's stock in trade.

Thérèse Humbert: the Impecunious Millionaire

Thérèse Humbert probably wins the prize for "con woman of all time". For her tale of dissimulation and deceit is worthy of any grand stage: she became one of the richest, most powerful people in nineteenth-century France by sealing up a safe and declaring that it contained a fortune which she was soon to inherit. Hardly a foolproof plan, but it worked. Creditors virtually queued at her door to give her money.

It was not even an original idea. Her father, Monsieur Aurignac, was fond of telling a tale or two, himself. And he wasn't choosy about whom he told them to. In particular, he enjoyed regaling his listeners with the fact that his name was not really Aurignac, but d'Aurignac, and his home was not the small cottage he lived in now but a mighty château in the

Auvergne. Unfortunately, he had quarrelled most terribly with his parents and they had cast him out. But after his death, his children would inherit the castle, title and fortune of d'Aurignac. Unbelieving listeners were shown, as proof, a brass-studded chest, in which – he stated – lay all the documents necessary for his children to claim their fortune. On inspection after his death, the chest proved to contained nothing more than a brick.

It is not completely clear whether Thérèse had believed her father and was so mortified by his deception that she took up telling wild tales in the hope of one day regaining her fortune, or whether she simply wished to carry on the family tradition. However, there were other, more forceful, reasons as to why Thérèse began to lie for a living.

On the death of her father in 1874, the family – Thérèse was the eldest of four children – was forced to move to Toulouse to support itself. Her mother opened a small linen shop while Thérèse, not particularly enchanting in looks, started work as a washerwoman. To a child raised on dreams of the highest expectations, this was a crushing blow. For she knew that if she continued as a washerwoman she would end her days unmarried and poor. Furthermore, there were her brothers, Emile and Romain, and her sister, Marie, to support. She had to do something for all their sakes. She could not capture a rich husband with her looks, but there are other ways and Thérèse knew it. Her strength was her intelligence: she was sharp and persuasive. All she had to do was find the right man.

Working as a laundry maid in the house of Gustave Humbert, a prosperous lawyer and at that time Mayor of Toulouse, she found her ideal man: Gustave's son, Frédéric. Not only was he weak and insecure, he desperately needed to talk to someone. He was a sensitive, creative person, who wished to spend his days in the gentler pursuits, but his strict father had insisted that he train to become a lawyer. He wanted Frédéric to follow in his footsteps. It was terrible for Frédéric. Thérèse would murmur in sympathy, stroke his furrowed brow and say that she would help. For, she said, a kind old lady, Mademoiselle de Mariotte, had bequeathed to her a chateau, a large estate and riches beyond imagination. As soon as she turned twenty-one it would be hers and she would give it all to her dear Frédéric.

Her father had used that line a thousand times during his life, and never got anywhere. But Thérèse had chosen her target wisely. Frédéric was enchanted. For the first time in his life

there was someone who cared about his feelings, and she was
even prepared to give away all her money to help him. He
proposed marriage. And when his father objected, on the
grounds that she was tricking him and would never have
two centimes to rub together, the couple eloped, married in
secret and moved to Paris.

Although Thérèse could have been forgiven for counting her
blessings and living out her life in comfort and some luxury,
she had no intention of being so cautious. Once in Paris, the
couple's lifestyle grew and grew in extravagance. They dined in
the best restaurants, took the best seats in the theatre, and
acquired property at an astounding rate. It was a lifestyle far
beyond their means and which very soon brought them into
trouble with their creditors. Matters were turning very nasty –
it had long since become apparent, even to Frédéric, that there
was no Mademoiselle or chateau – when Gustave Humbert,
now the Minister of Justice who could not afford any scandals,
stepped in and paid their debts. Thérèse and Frédéric were
saved. The sight of hard cash had calmed the nerves of the
creditors and Thérèse noted that they seemed even more eager
to lend the Humberts money than before. It was a situation
which had to be exploited.
A few months later, a windfall occurred. Thérèse had, it
transpired, been left millions of dollars by a rich American,
named Crawford. The reason for this good fortune? Thérèse
had, as a young woman, been travelling on the Ceinture
Railway in Paris when she fell to chatting to Mr Crawford,
who was in France on holiday. She had been remarking on the
sights to see, when he started to complain that he was not
feeling very well. Thérèse, had kind heartedly taken him to her
house and nursed him back to health: the illness having been
worse than it at first appeared. So grateful had Mr Crawford
been that he had duly included her in his will, unbeknown to
her. Or, to be accurate, he had included Thérèse's sister Marie in
his will: a girl he had never laid eyes upon.
Suspicions might have been raised at this point, especially
bearing in mind the fictitious Mademoiselle de Mariotte and
her chateau.
Besides, Thérèse would not be getting any money immediately, for there were certain conditions which had to be
fulfilled. First of all, the legacy was tripartite. Marie was to
receive a third of the estate, as were two cousins of Mr

Crawford. Secondly, no part of the legacy was to be touched until Marie's twenty-first birthday. And last, but certainly not least, the will would not be valid unless one of the nephews married Marie.

However, Thérèse knew her audience. She might not be in full possession of the money quite yet, she stated, but she had been left all the necessary deeds and securities. All was needed was some patience. Marie would soon be twenty-one and neither of the Crawford nephews could fail to want such a charming girl for a wife.

Thérèse knew that she had to ensure that her story was believed by all. It was time to play her trump card. She and Frédéric had recently moved to a splendid house in the Avenue de la Grande Armée. In a blaze of publicity, she installed a fireproof safe in the bedroom of the mansion, hired a provincial magistrate to act as a notary and placed the documents and securities in the safe. The magistrate testified that the procedure had been above board and then Thérèse sealed the safe with hot wax. It would not be opened until Marie's twenty-first birthday. The inheritance was secure.

It was a brilliant move. All doubt vanished about the truth of her claim and Thérèse was able to borrow as much as she liked on the strength of it. She and Frédéric went on a spending spree that made their previous extravagance look shabby. They bought three country mansions and a steam yacht, countless hats and clothes and thousands of other things besides. In total,

---

In 1917, two girls, Frances Wright and Elsie Griffiths, cut some pictures of fairies out of a magazine, borrowed a camera and photographed Elsie surrounded by the fairies. It was just a little bit of fun and they soon forgot about the photographs. But one way or another, news leaked out that real fairies had been captured on camera. All of a sudden the Cottingley Fairies were famous.

Both Frances and Elsie must have believed that the truth would soon be discovered, but it amused them to remain quiet and see what happened. And how they must have chuckled as expert after expert queued up to verify the little creatures. Indeed, such was the fervour with which they were acclaimed that many people still believed that they were real, until the two women finally broke their silence in 1976.

they borrowed 50 million francs, on the strength of an empty safe. Monsieur Aurignac would have smiled.

Indeed, there was nothing of any worth inside the safe: the deeds and securities which Thérèse had placed in it had been forged by her brothers using fake letterheads.

Thérèse's deception grew: she borrowed using a promise of riches, and soon had the riches which enabled her to borrow even more. The initial 50 million francs which the legacy brought her helped her borrow almost twice as much again. In addition, if any creditor expressed reservations about the repayment of her loan, the conditions of the will, which initially could have brought her downfall, were now made to work for her. Various legal technicalities arose to slow down the inheritance process and explain the delay; the Crawford cousins could quibble about who was to marry Marie, and Marie herself might declare that she had no wish to marry either of the Americans. Thérèse Humbert was in crook's paradise. But she was not content with borrowing only from rich greedy Parisian bankers: she was out to obtain money from wherever she could. So she established an insurance company, the Rente Viagère.

Aimed very much at peasants and small businessmen and other people who were unable to save large amounts of money for their final days, it succeeded not simply because it offered large returns from small investments, but because it was seen to honour its settlements quickly and without fuss. Unfortunately for the investors, Rente Viagère was a sham. All deposits and payments received were left unsecured and any settlement which had to be paid was taken directly from these incoming payments. During its existence it took more than 40 million francs, most of which went into Thérèse's private bank account.

Unbeknown to Thérèse, however, the tide had turned. There was one weakness in her story: the Crawfords. Why no one had

---

Marthe Hanau was a woman after Thérèse Humbert's heart. Having built up a successful business empire, she ensured its success by creating a whole network of small journals which manipulated share prices and investments to her benefit. Fraud aside, she was a gutsy woman: when she was finally put in jail, she went on hunger strike for three weeks, escaped and then returned to prison in a taxi!

checked to see whether this family existed in the first place is a mystery, but it was done eventually. Monsieur Delatte, a banker from Lyons, travelled to America, discovered the truth and wrote to a friend detailing his findings. At first the friend did nothing, but when Monsieur Delatte was murdered, he confronted Thérèse and threatened to reveal the truth. Thérèse, using the full force of her powers, managed to persuade him to remain quiet, but she could not stop other people from following their suspicions. In particular, she could not stop Jules Bizat, an official at the Bank of France, because he did not confront her directly.

Intrigued by the workings of Rente Viagère, he started to make some enquiries and found out that while the company claimed to invest in gilt-edged securities, closer investigation proved otherwise. He nearly stayed silent, as he stood to lose personally from any damaging revelations: nearly every banker in France had lent money to Madame Humbert. But instead he made a visit to no less a person than Waldeck-Rousseau, the Prime Minister. The countdown to disaster had started for Madame Humbert.

It is a sign of how peculiarly powerful she now was that Waldeck-Rousseau did not act overtly against Thérèse. He preferred to undermine her position by leaking news of her financial misconduct to *Le Matin*. Normally, this would not have bothered Thérèse, but fate was starting to conspire against her. Before she could issue a denial, her lawyer, Monsieur De Buit, seemingly as convinced as anyone of Thérèse's innocence, decided to act. The safe would be opened, he declared. The truth will out.

How Thérèse must have cursed her luck. Her powers of persuasion had been so great that they led to her downfall. And that downfall was now assured, since there was nothing she could do to stop the opening of the safe: the date had been fixed and all of France was on tenterhooks. Thérèse started planning her escape. On 8 May, two days before the safe was due to be opened, her house mysteriously burnt down and the Humberts fled. Perhaps she thought the fire would wipe out the evidence, but she had overlooked one tiny detail: the safe really was fireproof! It remained intact, and on 10 May its contents were withdrawn, revealing a handful of worthless papers.

Seven months later, the authorities apprehended Frédéric, Thérèse, her brothers and sister. They were all accused of complicity in the frauds, although it was Thérèse whose name was repeated the most often. During the early part of 1903, the pressures rose, and in March, Marie was excused trial on the grounds that she had lost her mind and would not be able to answer with any kind of coherence. By that time Thérèse had already handled one court case – an Armenian had accused her of libel – and her actions had won her much support from the public. She was a feisty woman, and it seemed that she would go down fighting. That did not prove to be the case, however. The second trial, which opened on 8 August 1903, revealed a broken figure, who offered no resistance to the prosecution case. Two weeks later she was sentenced to five years in prison for her crimes, a sentence which was decidedly lighter than could have been expected, but which still seemed to fill her with dread. Frédéric, Émile, Romain and Marie were also found guilty on varying charges.

Thus came to an end one of the most incredible swindles of all time. For twenty years, Thérèse had enjoyed a life that only royalty can expect. But her years after prison were passed in neither luxury nor excitement, and she died an old, forgotten woman.

Anna Anderson: a Fairytale Princess?

The case of Anna Anderson is difficult to categorize, for it is impossible to discover the truth about her.

While in a lunatic asylum in Germany, she claimed to be Princess Anastasia, the youngest child of the last Tsar of Russia. Sixty years later, this claim still has to be disproved.

Was she just an impostor looking for a quick gain? If so, she was a complete failure: sixty years of wrangling brought her no financial reward. Was she insane? Or was she simply telling the truth?

All three suggestions have worth. She did stand to gain a fortune, had her claim been recognized. She clearly suffered several nervous breakdowns, and spent long periods in mental institutions. She did tell a plausible story, which in many points was verified. But to state definitively which is the true answer seems to be impossible.

The story of the last royal family of Russia is shadowed by much doubt and confusion: this arose from the bloody chaos of the Russian Revolution, in the days and months just after the initial overthrow of power. That the Tsar and his family were taken prisoner cannot be denied: to the Bolsheviks now in power, they were an embarrassment and a future threat. But, after that, events are not clear. The Bolsheviks were not a military operation and needed time to organize efficient chains of command. In the meantime, it was very much a free for all. Bands of men roamed the country, nominally under the same leader, but really without control, free to do whatever they pleased. In these conditions, anything could have happened to the Imperial Family.

The most widely held belief was that the Tsar Nicholas, his wife Alexandra, and their five children, along with several members of the Imperial Household, were shot and bayoneted on the night of 16 July 1918 in Ekaterinberg. This is also the official version, which arose from an investigation by the Bolsheviks, who were only too keen to ensure that the Royal Family were put to rest (it was in the Bolsheviks' interest to confirm that all possible pretenders to the throne had been destroyed). But judging from the official statements put out by the Soviet Government in the years following the revolution, it is hardly startling that there are many other opinions about the events of 1918. These range from the ludicrous to the plausible and generally include the conviction that one or more of the

A conman took an advert in a daily newspaper recently, in order to plug a special bankruptcy sale of sex aids. The prices were so low that people responded in their thousands. But they were to be disappointed: for all they received was a letter of apology, explaining that stocks had run out. The con, however, was not that their cheques had not been returned, but it relied on the sensibilities of the customers for its success. For the cheques that were returned were drawn from an account bearing the name of "The National Sex Aids Company". The conman obviously believed that there would be a sufficient number of people who would be too embarrassed to cash a cheque drawn from such an account. And how right he was!

Royal Family escaped death through betrayal and double-crossings in the captors' camp. The most plausible of these variant accounts suggests that several members of the family escaped capture by the Bolsheviks and were evacuated westward to the town of Perm, whence they fled later.

So, when a young woman in a lunatic asylum in Germany began to claim royal blood, it would have been wise to listen to her story, especially since it bore the stamp of truth. Her account was that she had been rescued by a young man – whom she was later to marry and have a child by – and had travelled with him to Romania, where, in the general unrest of Bucharest, he had died. Deserted and desperate, she then had made her way to Germany, in an attempt to seek refuge with the man's relatives. In 1920, failing to find any trace of his kin, she had attempted suicide, but the Berlin police had saved her and transported her to the Dalldorf Asylum. This woman was, of course, Anna Anderson. And although there were weaknesses in her narrative and it was puzzling she had only told her story after another inmate had mistaken her for a Russian Royal, her case was undoubtedly stronger and more convincing than any other.

Her real quest for recognition did not start until 1928, a point which many commentators have used to prove her a fake. However, she had been deeply distressed by events at the end of the last decade – whether or not she had survived the execution of the Romanovs – and had suffered bouts of severe mental illness in the following years. Throughout this time, she had consistently held to her claim, but had not been in a fit state to prove it. But by 1928 she was healthy and ready to begin her assault. In October of that year she made a much publicized journey to America, reasserting her demand for recognition. Such was the media interest in her that the officially remaining members of the Romanov family were forced to issue a public denial, in which they described Anna as the "fairytale princess".

Undaunted, Anna formed her own company, Grandanor, which was registered in 1929 with the sole purpose of proving her assertion. During the ensuing years she gained notable supporters, such as Crown Princess Cecilie of Germany, Prince Frederick of Saxe-Altenburg, and Sigismund of Prussia, the nephew of Tsar Nicholas. Even the Tsar's sister, Olga, and the wife of the family's Russian teacher accepted her in the beginning, and their change of heart came about only after huge pressure had been applied by the official Romanovs (who, it could be thought, were simply eager to keep the last Tsar's fortune to themselves).

These supporters did not rally to Anna's case for no reason. She did look remarkably like the Anastasia they had known in pre-Revolution times and she did know intimate details that would have been extremely hard for anyone but Anastasia to know. For instance, on one occasion an army captain was recalling Anastasia's visits to his hospital in pre-Revolution times and mentioned a particularly impolite patient. "Ah, the man with the pockets", Anna exclaimed. At first, the captain was puzzled. But then he remembered that that had been their private nickname for the patient. No one else had known. Also, she knew about a secret peace-making trip to St Petersburg that her German uncle had made during the middle of the First World War. For obvious reasons, this trip had been kept top secret and only close family members knew anything of it.

Yet, her narrative did have weaknesses, and there was one imposing reason for disbelieving her story: she never spoke Russian. Various reasons were put forward for this – that she had blocked out all knowledge of the language on account of the terrible suffering she had endured; that she had become more used to speaking in other tongues, after such a long absence from her native land – but they failed to convince. People could not believe that a Russian Princess was unable to speak Russian.

In 1933, her fate seemed sealed, regardless of the arguments still raging. For the German government issued certificates of inheritance to the Tsar's official remaining relatives. This was not in itself important, as the bulk of the Romanov's fortune lay elsewhere, but the certificates stated that Anastasia had died. Who would believe Anna now? Five years later, she tried to regain the initiative by taking legal action against the Duchess of Mecklenburg, who represented all certificate holders, but although the case was never lost and ran for over thirty years, Anna gained nothing from it. The final verdict, given in 1970, was one of no result.

A sensible conclusion. But the newest scientific techniques might still be able to come up with the truth . . .

In September 1992, a leading Russian forensic scientist, Dr Pavel Ivanov, arrived in Britain with the fragments of humerus and femur bones taken from the burial pit in Ekaterinberg, which had been discovered only a short time before. The bone fragments were submitted for tests to a group of scientists at

Anna Anderson (left) Anastasia (right)

Aldermaston who specialized in the study of DNA. By comparing the DNA found in these scant remains with that of known relatives of the Romanovs – such as Prince Philip, whose grandmother was the Tsarina's sister – the scientists were able to prove that, because the DNA profiles were such an exact match, the bones were definitely those of an aristocratic family, and most probably those of the Romanovs.

Aware that these bones might be in themselves a hoax, the scientists were very cautious about their findings. Yet they argued most persuasively in defence of their case, pointing out that, if the bones were fakes, they had still come from bodies maternally related to the Romanovs, that they were the correct age and sex and that they were of aristocratic origin, because of the gold and platinum fillings in their teeth. In July 1993 the scientists held a press conference. Here are their findings as reported by the *Guardian* of 10 July: "It has been 'proved virtually beyond doubt' that five of the nine skeletons unearthed in a pit in Ekaterinberg, Eastern Russia, were those of the last Tsar, Tsarina and three other members of the Russian Imperial Family." These are impressive results, even if not quite conclusive. After all, there were nine bodies in the pit, four of which remained unidentified. And when pressed about the real riddle, Anastasia, the scientists had to admit that they did not know whether she had perished with her family or had escaped. However, if another grave were found, with bones intact, then even this most mysterious of puzzles might be solved.

But before science proves the case one way or the other, one can attempt a summing up. Anna Anderson had gained the support of surprisingly few members of the Romanov family and its close friends. She did not state her claim until prompted by a fellow inmate of a lunatic asylum. She was clearly mentally unstable, not just during the 1920s, so much of which she spent in institutions, but throughout her life. Her knowledge of Russian was non-existent and the few intimate details which she recounted could have been picked up from other sources. In short, all the evidence points to her being a misguided fraud and this is backed up by her own comments in 1979 that her whole story was nonsense and that it should be consigned to a litter bin.

PART 4: SCANDALS

SEX SCANDALS

Sex Scandals have occurred throughout the ages and no one is immune. A colonel attempts to rape a girl who has rebuffed him, a star who believes he is irresistible thinks any woman will want to be with him, and a "prophet" endorses free love – who has significantly more women in the congregation than men . . .

Colonel Valentine Baker – Attempted Rape on a Train

The attempt of Colonel Valentine Baker to rape a young lady on a train was one of the most widely publicized scandals of the 1870s.

On the afternoon of 17 June 1875, a 21-year-old girl named Rebecca Kate Dickinson boarded the Portsmouth to London train at Midhurst, in Sussex. She was alone in the compartment when 49-year-old Colonel Valentine Baker, until recently commanding officer of the 10th Hussars, entered the train at Liphook. Miss Dickinson was a pretty, self-possessed young lady who was on her way to Switzerland for a holiday. Colonel Baker was Assistant Quartermaster-General at Aldershot, a highly distinguished soldier who was an intimate friend of the Prince of Wales. He was also a married man, with two young daughters.

Baker made polite conversation for the first fifty minutes of the journey, apparently the ultra-respectable English gentleman exchanging commonplaces with a girl young enough to be his daughter or even granddaughter. But when the train pulled out of Woking, and London was half an hour away, he suddenly asked her if she often travelled alone. When she said she didn't, he asked her if they could meet on the train at some future time. She said no. He asked her name and she declined to tell him. He asked if he could write to her and she said no. He then closed the window and sat down next to her. When she asked him to sit further away he said, "Don't be cross", and put his arm round her waist. "You must kiss me, darling." She struggled to her feet but he forced her down again and held her down with his weight while he kissed her again and again on the lips. "If I give you my name will you get off?" she asked. Instead of replying he sank in front of her, thrust one hand up her dress and began to fumble with his flies with the other.

She struggled to her feet and tried to smash the window with her elbow; then she lowered it and screamed. Baker pulled her back so violently that she was half suffocated. She twisted the door handle and began to climb out backwards. "Get in, dear!" said the Colonel in great alarm. And he offered to get out of the other door in an effort to calm her. But she knew the other door was locked.

She could see two men looking out of the window of the next compartment as she balanced on the running board and she shouted, "How long before the train stops?" But their answer was carried away by the roar of the engine and the wind.

At 4.45 the train passed through Walton station and a brick-layer called William Burrowes saw a young lady standing on the running board, clinging to the handle of the door; someone inside the compartment seemed to be preventing her from falling by holding on to her other arm. The stationmaster signalled to Esher and there the train stopped. As it began to slow down, Baker said urgently, "Don't say anything – you don't know what trouble you'll get me into. Say you were frightened."

Railway officials at Esher wanted to know what had happened but she was too upset and exhausted to say much. Baker was told to go into another compartment. A clergyman named Baldwin Brown got in with Miss Dickinson and travelled with her to London.

At Waterloo, Miss Dickinson, Colonel Baker and the Reverend Brown were taken to the Inspector's office. Baker must have been relieved when she declined to go into details about her complaint. She gave her name and address; so did Baker. And then the Reverend Brown escorted her to her brother's house – he was a doctor living in Chesterfield Street. At this point, Rebecca Dickinson apparently wanted to forget the whole thing but her brother pointed out that Baker might do the same thing to other girls. So, reluctantly, she agreed to report the matter to the police.

The news items about the case caused widespread interest and astonishment. Valentine Baker was the kind of soldier who had created the British Empire; he was also the author of a number of books on cavalry tactics. He was the younger brother of the explorer Sir Samuel Baker, who had journeyed to the source of the Nile. It was true that he was the son of a merchant, not a "gentleman", but the Victorian era was the age of opportunity, and no one held this against him, least of all the future King Edward VII, his close friend. Surely there must be some mistake? Why should such a man risk his career and reputation to assault a girl on a train?

Three days after the assault, Baker was arrested at Guildford. His trial took place at Croydon Assizes on 2 August 1875, a Bank Holiday Monday. Huge crowds gathered outside the courtroom long before the trial was due to start at 10.30 a.m. Two well-dressed ladies even tried to get in through a window. Many peers were in court, including Lord Lucan and the Marquess of Tavistock. A rumour was going about that those in "high places" had arranged for the whole thing to be dropped, so there was some relief when the Grand Jury found a True Bill and Mr Justice Brett refused to postpone the trial. There was so much noise coming from the crowds outside – disappointed at being unable to get in – that the case had to be adjourned for ten minutes while the police tried to restore order. Then Mr Sergeant Parry, QC, for the prosecution, called Miss Dickinson into the witness box. But he declined to increase her distress by asking her a single question. So the defence lawyer, Henry Hawkins, cross-examined her. He elicited the interesting fact that part of the conversation between Liphook and Woking had been about hypnotism and that Colonel Baker had told Miss Dickinson that he thought she could be mesmerized. She also detailed other topics they had discussed, including the murder of a certain Mr Walker. The defence was obviously trying to establish that Miss Dickinson's openness, her willingness to engage in animated conversation,

had probably convinced the Colonel that a kiss might not be
rejected.

But the evidence against the Colonel was serious. He had fairly
certainly intended rape – otherwise, why had he unbuttoned
his flies? The guard had noticed that they were undone at
Esher. And so had the two gentlemen in the carriage that
Baker transferred into. He had also put his hand up her skirt,
although it had apparently gone no further than above the top
of her boot.

The judge's summing up emphasized that Baker's chief concern had apparently been to save Miss Dickinson from falling
from the running board and he indicated that he could see
no evidence that there was "intent to ravish". This was on
the grounds that Baker had hoped to win the girl's consent
to intercourse by "exciting her passions". The jury took the
hint. Baker was found not guilty of intent to ravish but guilty
of indecent assault and common assault. The judge then told
Baker sternly that, "Of all the people who travelled in the train
that day, you were the most bound to stand by and defend a
defenceless woman. Your crime is as bad as it could be." And
he sentenced Baker to a year in jail – without hard labour – and
a fine of £500.

The Press, on the whole, felt it was a just verdict – most people
had believed that this friend of royalty would be acquitted. But
the general public seemed to feel that Baker had got off too
easily – a mere year in "honourable detention", then back to
the old life.

But Baker was disgraced. He tried to resign his commission
and was told that he was to be cashiered. It was widely believed
that this was due to Queen Victoria's intervention. (The Queen
was not fond of her rakish son – or his friends.) It is true
that, in Horsemonger Lane jail, Baker was treated with due
consideration, allowed to wear his own clothes, to send out for
his food and to receive his friends more or less as he wished.
But the knowledge that he had involved his family in the most
degrading kind of public scandal was enough to turn him into
a psychological wreck. Three months after his imprisonment,
it was reported that he was critically ill. *The Times* published
a letter from his wife assuring his "many friends" that he was
no longer in danger of his life but admitting that his condition
caused her much distress.

He served his full term; then, with his wife and two young
daughters he left England. He became a lieutenant-general in
the Ottoman army and fought bravely during the Russo-Turkish

war. Then he went to Egypt and accepted an appointment
as a commander of police. He attempted unsuccessfully to
relieve Tokar during the Sudan war but his poorly trained
force was destroyed. He himself was seriously wounded in
a later action. When he came back to London to recuperate,
a cheering crowd greeted him at Victoria Station. His friends
tried hard to get him reinstated in the British army. But their
efforts were a failure – almost certainly due to Queen Victoria's determination that the would-be rapist would never
again become a soldier of the queen. Baker died of heart
failure, after an attack of typhoid, on 12 November 1887, twelve
years after the Dickinson case. The Queen finally relented and
cabled that Baker was to be buried in Cairo with full military
honours.

The mystery remains: why did Baker do it? In court he swore
solemnly that the facts were not as Miss Dickinson represented
them. His supporters took this to mean that she had given him
some encouragement. He also spoke of her "exaggerated fear".
Did he mean that he believed she had been willing to be kissed
but had become alarmed when he had shown signs of being
carried away?

But the theory that Baker gave way to an "irresistible impulse"
will not hold water. He was a highly disciplined soldier and
discipline means the ability to resist "impulses". Yet this in
itself suggests another explanation. Baker was a close friend
of the Prince of Wales who spent much of his time bedding
attractive women. So it is easy to understand that Baker may
have regarded Rebecca Dickinson as a challenge, the natural
prey of a dashing cavalry officer. But when he asked her if
he might see her again, he was promptly rebuffed. For a man
who is accustomed to giving orders and having them obeyed
– and probably dominating his own wife and daughters with
the natural authority of a sultan – this must have seemed an
intolerable humiliation. He might have withdrawn stiffly into
his shell and passed the rest of the journey to London in
sulky silence. But he was not that kind of a man; he was
used to pressing on in the face of odds. He asked her name
and again was rebuffed. The distinguished soldier, the friend
of royalty, was being snubbed by a mere "chit of a girl".
By this time he was probably burning with humiliation –
and with the feeling that perhaps, after all, he was making
a fool of himself. The author of a book on cavalry tactics
had mistimed his charge. If he drew back now, he would
remember this for the rest of his life with a shock of outraged

vanity. The soldier had to act. He stood up and closed the window . . .

Cleveland Street Scandal – The "Sex-for-Sale" Telegraph Boys

In early July 1889, there was a theft of money from a room in the General Post Office in St Martin's-Le-Grand, in the City of London. A telegraph messenger boy named Charles Thomas Swinscow came under suspicion and when he was searched, he proved to have eighteen shillings on him – a far larger sum than he was likely to save up from his wages. On 4 July 1889, a police constable named Hanks questioned the boy, who told him that he had obtained the money for doing some "private work" for a gentleman named Hammond, who lived at 19 Cleveland Street, just north of Soho. Finally, he admitted that he had been taken to the house by a post office clerk named Henry Newlove – who, like Swinscow, was fifteen. Newlove, it seemed, had earlier persuaded Swinscow to go with him to a lavatory in the basement of the Post Office where he had "behaved indecently". Then Newlove had suggested that Swinscow might like to earn a little money by doing the same thing with a gentleman. At the house in Cleveland Street, Swinscow had got into bed with a gentleman who, in the language of the police report, "put

---

Georges Simenon, the creator of Inspector Maigret, caused wide-spread consternation in 1974 when he told a Swiss journalist during an interview that he had had sex with ten thousand women. He expanded on this in his book *Intimate Memoirs*, explaining that about eight thousand of these had been prostitutes. In his biography of Simenon, Fenton Bresler describes how Simenon had his first sexual encounter at the age of twelve – with a girl of sixteen – and how, in later life, he obsessively sought out prostitutes in every place he visited. Yet Bresler admits that Simenon's claim is probably exaggerated. Even at a rate of a woman a day, ten thousand would require thirty years, without a day off . . .

his person between my legs and an emission took place". The gentleman then gave him half a sovereign, which Swinscow handed to the landlord of the house, Hammond. Hammond had given him back four shillings. The same thing had apparently happened on a subsequent occasion.

Swinscow mentioned two other telegraph boys who had gone to Cleveland Street: seventeen-year-olds George Wright and Charles Thickbroom. Wright admitted that he and Newlove had gone to the basement lavatory and "Newlove put his person into me . . . and something came away from him." Wright went with Newlove to the Cleveland Street house where he went to a bedroom with a "foreign looking chap". They undressed and got into bed. He had a go between my legs and that was all." Wright also received four shillings. Thickbroom told how Newlove had persuaded him to go to Cleveland Street, where he went to bed with a gentleman and they "played with one another. He did not put his person into me." He also received four shillings.

Newlove admitted the truth of the statements. The next morning he hastened to 19 Cleveland Street and warned Hammond. Charles Hammond, a 32-year-old male prostitute, married to a French prostitute known as "Madame Caroline" – on whom he had fathered two sons – lost no time in fleeing. So did another homosexual, George Veck, who liked to pose as a clergyman. Veck moved to lodgings nearby under a false name, while Hammond fled to France.

Chief Inspector Frederick Abberline of the CID applied for warrants for the arrest of Hammond and Newlove on a charge of criminal conspiracy. But when the police arrived at Cleveland Street the next day the house was shut up.

On his way to the police station, Newlove commented that it was hard that he should be arrested when men in high positions should be allowed to walk free. Asked what he meant, he replied, "Lord Arthur Somerset goes regularly to the house in Cleveland Street. So does the Earl of Euston and Colonel Jervois."

Lord Arthur Somerset, the son of the Duke of Beaufort, was a major in the Royal Horse Guards, and superintendent of the stables of the Prince of Wales, Queen Victoria's son, whose name was to be associated with many scandals (including the Tranby Croft card scandal). When Lord Arthur – known as "Podge" – was identified by the two telegraph boys Swinscow and Thickbroom as the man who had climbed into bed with them, "Podge" hastily obtained four months' leave of absence and vanished to the Continent. His elder brother Henry had been deserted by his wife because of his homosexual inclinations.

Veck was also arrested and he and Newlove were committed for trial at the Old Bailey. But by that time, the press had got hold of the story. The *Pall Mall Gazette* published a paragraph deploring the "disgraceful nature" of the charge against Veck and Newlove and asking whether the "two noble lords and other notable persons in society" were going to be allowed to get away with it. It obviously had the makings of a first-class scandal. It may have been at this point that Arthur Newton, "Podge's" solicitor, breathed another name that made the Director of Public Prosecutions raise his eyebrows: that of "Eddy", the Duke of Clarence, son of the Prince of Wales. Eddy, according to rumour, had also visited the Cleveland Street brothel. Meanwhile, "Podge" was in more trouble; another teenager, Algernon Allies, had been interviewed by the police and admitted that he had been intimately involved with Lord Arthur Somerset, whom he called "Mr Brown". "The prosecution wishes to avoid putting any witness in the box who refers to 'Mr Brown'," wrote the Director of Public Prosecutions, Sir Augustus Stephenson to the Attorney-General.

It was no surprise to anyone when the case came up at Bow Street on 18 September 1889 and lasted a mere half hour. Veck and Newlove both pleaded guilty and were both given light sentences. Veck nine months' hard labour and Newlove four months'. That, it seemed, was the end of the case.

But the Press was not willing to allow it to rest there. There were many crusading editors in London, like W.T. Stead of the *Pall Mall Gazette*, Henry Labouchere of *Truth*, and Ernest Parke of the *North London Press*. It was Parke who put the cat among the pigeons. On 16 November 1889 Parke identified the aristocrats whose names had been so carefully suppressed at the time of the trial: Lord Arthur Somerset and the Earl of Euston. (These names, we may recall, had been mentioned to Abberline by Newlove when he was arrested.) Parke also commented that "a far more distinguished and more highly placed personage . . . was inculpated in these disgusting crimes."

The Earl of Euston, Henry James Fitzroy, was thirty-eight years old at the time of the Cleveland Street trial. He immediately instructed his solicitor to sue for libel. Parke's trial opened at the Old Bailey on 15 January 1890. One of the most serious points against Parke was his allegation that the Earl of Euston had fled to Peru; Euston had done nothing of the sort. (It had been unnecessary, for his name had never entered the case after Newlove mentioned it to Abberline.)

Euston admitted that he had been to 19 Cleveland Street. But, he said, it had been a misunderstanding. He had, he said, been in Piccadilly in May or June 1889, when someone had put an advertising card into his hand. It said *"Poses plastiques"*, and gave the address of 19 Cleveland Street. *Poses plastiques* meant naked girls posing in Grecian attitudes. So, according to Lord Euston, he hurried to 19 Cleveland Street. He was admitted by a man who told him there were no women there but left no doubt about what the house had to offer. "You infernal scoundrel, if you don't let me out I'll knock you down," said Lord Euston and rushed out.

The defence called several witnesses who said they had seen Lord Euston going in or out of Cleveland Street. The final defence witness was a male prostitute named John Saul. He claimed to have been picked up by Lord Euston and took him back to Cleveland Street where they went to bed. *The Times* declined to report what Saul claimed then took place but we can reconstruct what he said from a comment Saul had made to Ernest Parke about Euston: "He is not an actual sodomite. He likes to play with you and then 'spend' on your belly."

The judge emphasized the contradictions in the statements of witnesses, and described Saul as a "loathsome object". The strongest point against Parke was his statement that Euston had fled to Peru. The jury found Parke guilty of libel without justification. He was sentenced to a year in prison without hard labour. The sentence was not regarded as severe by the Press.

The case was still not quite over. In December 1889, "Podge's" solicitor, Arthur Newton, was accused of conspiring to defeat the course of justice. The charges said that he had tried to get an interview with Algernon Allies – the youth who had admitted being "Podge's" lover – and had collected three of the accused telegraph boys after they had left police custody and sent them to a lodging house while he arranged for them to leave the country. Newton's defence was that his clerk Frederick Taylorson, who was charged with him, had met Allies by accident and exchanged a few words with him. And as to the second charge, it was true that he had sent the three boys to a lodging house overnight, telling them that they ought to go abroad, but that this was because "Podge's" father, the Duke of Beaufort, wanted to interview them to see if they had been bullied by the police. The Duke had subsequently changed his mind. Newton was, he admitted, therefore technically guilty of conspiracy. The judge took a light view of it and sentenced him to six weeks in prison. Taylorson, who pleaded not guilty, was acquitted.

Hammond, the man who ran the brothel, had fled from France to America and was never tried. "Podge" spent the rest of his life living abroad, under an assumed name, and died in Hyères, on the French Riviera, in 1926. The scandal undoubtedly ruined his life. In his book *The Cleveland Street Scandal*, H. Montgomery Hyde suggests that he would have been wise to return and "face the music"; a good solicitor could also certainly have secured his acquittal, as in the case of Lord Euston. (The evidence suggests that Euston was a regular visitor at Cleveland Street.) Euston's trial certainly did him no harm; at the time of the Cleveland Street case he was a prominent Freemason, the Provincial Grand Master of Northamptonshire and Huntingdonshire, and subsequently became Grand Master of the Mark Masons. He was also appointed an aide de camp by King Edward VII in the coronation year, 1901. He died of dropsy in 1912.

Ernest Parke became a Justice of the Peace after he retired as a newspaper editor. But the subsequent career of Arthur Newton, who went to prison for conspiracy, was less fortunate. In 1910 he defended the murderer Crippen and received much favourable publicity. But he then conceived the idea of forging a Crippen "confession" and selling it to a newspaper: *The Evening Times* bought it for £500, the writer Edgar Wallace acting as a go-between. Although Newton got cold feet at the last moment, the newspaper forced him to deliver the promised confession and sold a million copies as a result. Newton was suspended from practice by the Law Society for unprofessional conduct. In 1913 he was charged with being involved in a Canadian timber fraud, sentenced to three years in jail, and struck off the rolls as a solicitor.

Henry Ward Beecher – The Preacher and the Adoring Disciples

Beecher was one of the most celebrated preachers of the nineteenth century. He was almost ruined by a scandal in which he was accused of adultery with one of his flock.

Henry Ward was born in Litchfield, Connecticut, USA in June

The Reverend Horatio Alger was one of the most popular of American authors in the late nineteenth century; his "rags to riches" success stories, with titles like *Dan the Newsboy* and *Paul the Peddler*, sold in vast numbers. He was also widely respected as the devoted head of the Newsboys' Lodging House in New York. What no one knew at the time was that Alger was a pederast, and that in 1864 (when he was thirty) he had been forced to hastily resign his position as pastor of the Unitarian Church of Brewster (Cape Cod) when the church committee learned that he had been buggering the choirboys. Alger left town before he could be arrested, and the committee was too embarrassed to publicize the matter.

Two years later he was made chaplain of Newsboys', and devoted the rest of his life to the care of young boys . . .

1813, the eighth of thirteen children of the Reverend Lyman Beecher. He had been a shy child with a stammer and his scholastic performance had been abysmal until he went to Amherst College at the age of seventeen. At twenty-four he became minister to a small congregation at Lawrenceburg, Indiana, and began to develop his preaching talent. He was fundamentally an actor: he preferred to stand or sit on a platform rather than in a pulpit and told anecdotes with a wealth of gesture and facial expression that made his audience feel they were in a theatre. On one occasion, he mimed catching a fish so perfectly that a man in the front row jumped up crying, "By God, he's got him!" Physically speaking, Beecher was not unusually attractive, with a round face, thick lips, a fleshy nose and shoulder-length hair. But his congregation found him magnetic and women adored him. A book of his called *Seven Lectures to Young Men* appeared in 1844 and became something of a bestseller. Yet for many years he was regarded simply as one of the preacher-sons of the far more famous Lyman Beecher. In 1847, he was persuaded to move east by Henry C. Bowen, a Brooklyn businessman, whose young wife was an admirer of Beecher. Within three years, his sermons were attracting audiences of more than 2,000, and he had the largest congregation in America.

As he grew older, Beecher gradually changed his stance from that of a narrow, hell-fire revivalist preacher to a liberal who advocated women's rights and Darwinian evolutionism, and opposed slavery. In 1861, Bowen made Beecher the editor of his newspaper *The Independent*. A young man named Theodore

Tilton, who passionately admired Beecher, had been given the job of managing editor, largely due to Beecher's insistence. In 1855, Beecher had married Theodore Tilton to a pretty, dark-eyed young woman named Elizabeth Richards who like her husband regarded Beecher with adoration. *The Independent* became one of America's most widely read newspapers, largely due to Beecher's regular contribution, "The Star Papers". It was partly through the influence of Theodore Tilton that Beecher preached liberal doctrines.

In 1862, the attractive and popular Lucy Bowen died at the age of thirty-eight; she had borne ten children. On her death bed she beckoned her husband to move closer and whispered into his ear a confession that stunned him. She had been committing adultery with Henry Ward Beecher. Henry Bowen was in a difficult position. He was convulsed by jealousy and resentment: the man he had brought from Indiana and made editor of his newspaper had been his wife's lover. Beecher's column ceased to appear in *The Independent* and not long after Beecher himself left for England to preach the doctrines of anti-slavery. It was many years before he and Bowen renewed their friendship. When Beecher returned from England, Tilton insisted that he should become a regular visitor at his house; he wanted to share his friend with his wife. If anyone had told him that this would one day involve sharing his wife with his friend, he would have been furiously indignant; no one believed more deeply than Tilton in Beecher's total honesty and integrity.

Theodore Tilton, like Henry Ward Beecher, had started life as a highly orthodox young man who would "rather have had my right hand cut off than have written a letter on the Sabbath." Yet when he had met the seventeen-year-old Elizabeth Richards – known to all as Libby – their passion had been so intense that they consummated their love before Beecher joined them in wedlock. Ten years after their marriage, Tilton began to experience "doubts" – about Christ's divinity, the absolute authority of the Bible, and other such weighty matters. Libby was horrified and Beecher had to comfort and soothe her. While her husband was away lecturing, Libby wrote him long letters in which she spoke freely of her love for Beecher. Neither she nor her husband experienced any misgivings; both believed implicitly that the highest form of love is wholly spiritual, and that such love casts out carnal desire. So Libby went on playing with fire, assuring herself that she was part of a "blessed trinity" rather than an eternal triangle. In 1867, Beecher signed a contract to write a novel for which he was to receive the record sum of

Rev. Henry Ward Beecher

$24,000. (His sister was Harriet Beecher Stowe, author of *Uncle Tom's Cabin*.) He would bring the novel – *Norwood* – to Libby's house to ask her advice.

In August 1868, the Tiltons' baby son, Paul, died of cholera. Soon afterwards, Theodore Tilton set out on another of his lecture trips. On 9 October Libby went to hear Beecher deliver a speech at the Brooklyn Academy of Music and was overwhelmed with admiration. On the following day, Libby called on him at his home. That afternoon the inevitable happened: Libby became his mistress. It seems to have been Beecher who took the lead, since she later explained that she had "yielded to him" in gratitude for the sympathy he gave her on the death of her child. Beecher had apparently assured her that their love was divine and that having sexual intercourse was its proper and valid expression, like a handshake or a kiss. He insisted that she should guard their secret – he called it "nest hiding", borrowing the terminology from bird-watching. Not long after this, Beecher called on Libby at her home at 174 Livingston Street in Brooklyn, and once again they made love. After that, they made love on a number of occasions, at their respective homes, and in "various other places."

But the delicate, romantic Libby was not made for adultery. It began to prey on her mind. Beecher enjoyed sex much more than she did and wanted to make love every time they were alone. He obviously enjoyed it so much that Libby began to wonder whether it could be true that their relationship was blessed by God. In the summer of 1870, Libby went to pass the hot months – as was her custom – at Schoharie, New York. But on 3 July tormented by conscience, she returned to Brooklyn and confessed everything to her husband.

Tilton was deeply shaken. His initial reaction, understandably, was to denounce the "whited sepulchre", but his wife had preceded her confession with the demand that he would not harm the person implicated. His mind was still in confusion the next day when he went to his office. He admitted later that his chief desire was to find some excuse for his wife. He decided that ". . . she sinned as one in a trance. I don't think she was a free agent. I think she would have done his bidding if, like the heathen-priest in the Hindoo-land, he had bade her fling her child into the Ganges . . ." In this he showed a great deal of insight – there can be no doubt that Lib Tilton regarded herself as Beecher's slave, to do with as he would. Tilton then decided that he would not denounce Beecher, but that his punishment would be that Lib herself would go and tell him that she had confessed to her husband. Having decided "in my secret self to be a conqueror", Tilton experienced a kind of ecstasy; for the next two weeks, "I walked the streets as if I scarcely touched the ground." Then human nature asserted itself. He had to tell somebody. One evening three prominent figures in the feminist movement came to the house and Tilton unburdened himself about the "lecherous scoundrel who has defiled my bed". When he came back from seeing two of the ladies home, the third – a woman named Sue Anthony – had to interpose herself between Tilton and his wife as he railed at her. She was later to allege that Libby Tilton then confessed in detail to her adultery with Beecher.

Libby then made the immense mistake of telling her mother – a psychotic and an impossible lady named Mrs Nathan B. Morse – about her affair. Mrs Morse had separated from her second husband after trying to strangle him to death. She hated Tilton and adored Beecher. Now she glimpsed the marvellous possibility that Libby might divorce Tilton and marry Beecher; she set about promoting this end by gossiping all over Brooklyn about the scandal, writing abusive letters to her son-in-law, and insinuating letters to Beecher that began "My dear son . . ."

On Christmas Eve that year, Lib Tilton suffered a miscarriage; she later referred to it as "a love babe" and there seems no doubt that she believed the child to be Beecher's. She was in a state of agonized misery. Her husband hardly ever spoke to her – he spent much of his time at the house of a friend called Frank Moulton, who became his confidant – and on one occasion, she went to the graveyard and lay down on the grave of her two dead children until a keeper made her move on.

Mrs Morse's gossip finally reached the ears of Henry Bowen, the other man Beecher had cuckolded. He immediately saw it as a marvellous opportunity to get his own back on Beecher without compromising the reputation of his dead wife (he had now remarried). Bowen asked Tilton to go and see him and then proceeded to accuse Beecher of being an inveterate seducer. According to Bowen, Beecher was even a rapist – he had thrown down a well-known authoress on the sofa and taken her by force. The story of Beecher's seduction of the former Mrs Bowen was repeated. Finally, Tilton was persuaded to write a letter to Beecher, ordering him to renounce his ministry and quit Brooklyn "for reasons he well understood". Bowen promised to deliver this. But Bowen was playing a double game. He was too much of a coward to want to confront Beecher openly. What he wanted to do was to pretend he was the friend of both parties, while setting them at one another's throats. He went to Beecher, gave him the letter, then assured him that he was on his side and that Tilton was himself a seducer of many women. (This seems to be true – Tilton apparently admitted to one of Bowen's employees, Oliver Johnson, that he had even slept with one of his mistresses in his own home.) Meanwhile, Tilton decided to use Frank Moulton as a go-between; he made his wife write a confession of her adultery, then sent Moulton to tell Beecher about it. This was the first Beecher knew about Libby's confession of adultery.

Beecher now went to see Libby, who was still in bed after her miscarriage. And he succeeded in persuading her to write a letter in which she declared that her confession had been untrue, wrung out of her by her husband's jealousy. There followed more to-ing and fro-ing between the various parties which ended finally in an uneasy truce between Beecher and the wronged husband. Beecher heaved a sigh of relief; it looked as if his sins would not find him out after all.

But he had reckoned without an extraordinary lady named Victoria Woodhull, an ardent "women's libber" of the period, who became known as "Mrs Satan" because she preached the doctrine of "free love". Victoria Woodhull was, in her way, as remarkable a character as Beecher himself. She was the daughter of a riverboat gambler and maidservant, and as a child she discovered she was psychic. She became a clairvoyant and spirit medium. At fifteen she married an alcoholic doctor named Woodhull, to whom she bore a child. She divorced him when she met a spiritualist named Colonel Blood but allowed Woodhull to continue living in the household. Then she made her greatest conquest: she and her equally remarkable sister Tennessee Claflin persuaded one of America's richest men, old Commodore Vanderbilt, that they could heal his various ailments with "magnetism". Vanderbilt fell in love with Tennessee (or Tennie C, as Victoria's younger sister preferred to spell it). He set them up in a brokerage business and financed a magazine called *Woodhull and Claflin's Weekly*, in which Victoria preached her doctrines of free love, attacked the rich (though not, of course, Vanderbilt) and espoused Marxism.

On 22 May 1871, Victoria published in the *World* a letter in which she praised free love "in its highest, purest sense as the only cure for immorality", and stated that people who attacked her were hypocrites. "I know of one man, a public teacher of eminence, who lives in concubinage with the wife of another public teacher." And she sent Theodore Tilton a

message asking him to come and see her. Tilton had by
now been sacked by Bowen, but with the help of Beecher,
had started another magazine called *The Golden Age*. He was
curious to see the notorious "free lover" and hurried round to
her office. He found her to be a highly attractive woman in her
early thirties who seemed far less formidable than he expected
– even when she showed him her letter in the newspaper. Soon
he and Victoria became good friends – in fact, Victoria was later
to declare that they became lovers. Tilton no doubt told himself
that he was only trying to prevent a scandal by keeping Victoria
friendly. Victoria Woodhull also met Beecher and admitted that
she found him a magnetic and attractive personality. But when
Beecher declined to introduce Victoria at a suffragette meeting
(where he knew she was going to preach free love), Tilton
stepped into the gap. It did his reputation no good at all to be
publicly associated with "Mrs Satan" and her scandalous doctrines. Unfortunately, Victoria was so carried away by her new
popularity with the women's movement (which had formerly
regarded her as a crank) that she allowed herself to denounce
her former protector Commodore Vanderbilt as a capitalist; he
promptly dropped her. In May 1872, Victoria announced that
she was standing as the first woman president of the United
States, with a Negro reform leader as her running mate. She
was infuriated when Tilton declined to support her cause and
instead declared his support for Horace Greeley. (Because of the
bad reputation he was acquiring, Tilton's support did Greeley
no good at all.) Victoria Woodhull became increasingly angry
and embittered. And finally she did what Beecher had always
feared she would do: she told the whole story of his affair with
Libby Tilton and the subsequent "cover up", in her magazine.
The result was as sensational as she had hoped. The magazine
sold 100,000 copies and could have sold many times that number
– copies began to change hands for as much as $40. A young
man named Anthony Comstock, the vice warden for the Young
Men's Christian Association, saw the story, was outraged at this
smear on the saintly Henry Ward Beecher, and was responsible
for the arrest of the Claflin sisters for sending indecent material
through the United States mails. Victoria and Tennessee went
to jail. But the damage was done. The whole country was now
gossiping about the Beecher-Tilton scandal. Six months later,
when Victoria and her sister were acquitted (on the grounds that
their accusations did not constitute pornography), everyone in
the country wanted to know whether Tilton was a cuckold and
Beecher was a seducer.

Beecher's own congregation increased his problems by insisting on expelling Tilton from the church. If, as Beecher insisted, he was innocent of adultery, then Tilton was a wicked traducer. Tilton, who had so far been more-or-less on Beecher's side (at least in wanting to suppress the scandal) now began to smoulder with resentment. This was not assuaged when Beecher decided to air the scandal by holding a "trial" in his own church and Libby was persuaded to leave her husband and take Beecher's side. The church committee, predictably, decided that Beecher was not guilty. Tilton was branded as a liar. On 24 August 1874, Tilton swore out a complaint against Beecher, charging him with having wilfully alienated his wife's affections.

The Beecher-Tilton trial began on 11 January 1875, and lasted until 2 July. The whole nation was agog. Beecher spent much of his time in court; so did his sour-faced wife Eunice (known locally as "the Griffin"). Beecher took the line that he had never, at any time, sinned with Libby Tilton, but that he fully acknowledged his guilt in having allowed her to idolize him to the exclusion of her husband – this, he claimed, was the meaning of some of the letters he had written admitting his guilt.

During those six months, the American public had more than its fill of scandal. It learned that Beecher was accused of seducing Lucy Bowen as well as Lib Tilton. One newspaper cartoon showed a Brooklyn businessman locking his wife in a huge safe with a notice on the door Proof Against Fire And Clergymen, while another showed a hatter who sold the "new style of Brooklyn hat" – with horns on it. The public also learned that the wronged husband was not entirely innocent. He was alleged to have seduced the seventeen-year-old daughter of a congressman named Lovejoy in Winsted, Connecticut, and to have made an unsuccessful attempt to seduce a young girl who formed part of his household; this girl, Elizabeth Turner, told how Tilton had laid on her bed, kissed her, and put his hand "down her neck" (i.e. on her breast). On another occasion he had come into her bedroom when she was fast asleep and carried her out; if he had failed to seduce her, it was plainly not for want of trying. The story of Tilton's "affair" with Victoria Woodhull was also raked up. On the other hand, various servants testified to having seen Beecher in situations of intimacy with Libby Tilton; even her own brother reluctantly admitted that he had walked into the room and seen Beecher and Libby separating with obvious embarrassment. Libby herself, like Beecher, denied any misconduct.

The jury was out for eight days; it was unable to reach

> The philosopher A.J. Ayer was a notorious seducer. One of his mistresses, the stage designer Jocelyn Rickard, records in her autobiography *The Painted Banquet* that she broke off her affair with him when he had acquired seven more mistresses – not because she was jealous, but because there were not enough nights in the week.

a unanimous verdict but voted nine to three against Tilton. Beecher's supporters regarded this as a triumph and he left the court like a conquering hero. His trials were not quite over, however. Frank Moulton sued Beecher for malicious prosecution but the suit was dismissed. Then Henry Bowen demanded that the Plymouth Church Committee should try Beecher for adultery with Lucy Bowen. The Committee disbelieved him and Bowen, like the Moultons, was expelled from the church. Beecher made a lecture tour of the country and although he was booed in many places, he never failed to draw enormous crowds. When he died, thirteen years later (in 1887) his popularity with his own congregation was as great as ever.

Theodore Tilton also continued to lecture but his fortunes declined. He left the country in 1883, to settle finally in Paris, where he wrote novels and romantic poetry, and spent his days in a café playing chess. Libby, deserted by her husband and her lover, became a schoolteacher; she remains the most pathetic figure in the case. The Woodhull sisters both married rich men, and Victoria died in 1927, at the age of eighty-nine.

In retrospect, it is difficult not to agree with the reporter who wrote: "Mankind fell in Adam and has been falling ever since, but never touched bottom until it got to Henry Ward Beecher."

John Hugh Smyth Pigott – The "Abode of Love" Scandal

The Reverend John Hugh Smyth Pigott threw his congregation into noisy disarray when he announced, during a Sunday evening service in 1902, that he was the Lord Jesus Christ arisen. The several hundred worshippers, gathered in the Agapemonite

'Ark of the Covenant' church in Clapton, North London, did not react as orthodox Christians might have expected. Not a soul dissented; instead the whole congregation fell to their knees weeping and praising the Lord who stood before them.

The Agapemonites believed with absolute certainty that they were living in the last days before the Final Judgement and many had fostered the hope that their leader might be the Lord of Hosts. For the fifty-six years since it's founding the Church of the Agapemone, meaning 'Abode of Love', had caused controversy, but never as much as it did that day in Clapton. So, while the Reverend Pigott's disciples rejoiced, their enemies delighted in what they saw as the Agapemonites' greatest folly and, they hoped, their ultimate downfall.

The sect was founded in 1846 by a thirty-five-year-old ren- egade Church of England curate, Henry James Prince. It began as a small religious commune of divinity students at the village of Spaxton, near Bridgewater in Somerset. The community, housed in a single large building, was named Agapemone by its founder and gave its name to the the developing sect.

Reverend Prince built the 'Abode of Love' with a sizable legacy he had received from his wife and from the start the community prospered both spiritually and financially. All the adherents and their loved ones lived together at the Abode, gladly sharing all their worldly possessions under the eyes of the Lord, as they called Reverend Prince.

Outsiders soon noted that there were significantly more women than men in the commune and it soon got about that Reverend Prince encouraged free love. Lawsuits pressed by the families of several of the unmarried women who had joined the community successfully regained some of the money taken into the community coffers and a Chancery Court in 1860 noted that 'breaches of decorum and manners' had taken place at Agapemone.

Yet, despite the antagonism, the Agapemonites prospered and grew. The donation of all worldly goods made by fresh converts enabled the members of the sect to live quite comfortably and ensured that they were never short of cash. When a wealthy London businessman joined the faith he gladly pooled his entire fortune with the rest; as a sign of special favour "the Lord" made him his personal butler.

Prince was convinced that the Second Coming was at hand and saw himself as the new John the Baptist. He did not how- ever, adopt the original Baptist's spartan way of life, preferring to live more like a rich aristocrat. For example, he travelled widely

at home and abroad in a magnificent coach-and-six with liveried
outriders and a pack of hounds always at hand. Since they were
living well themselves, his followers did not begrudge him his
little pleasures, keeping in mind his words: 'The time of prayer
is past and the time of grace has come.'

In 1896, fifty years after the founding of the sect, the eighty-
five-year-old Reverend Prince decided that expansion was in
order. With commune money he commissioned the building of
an impressively large church with an attached mansion in the
London Borough of Clapton. He named the church the 'Ark
of the Covenant', and had the words 'Love in Judgement and
Judgement unto Victory' inscribed over the entrance. The new
church attracted many people to join the sect and it seemed the
Agapemonites had reached a new pinnacle.

Unfortunately, a major blow came just three years later.
Prince, as the new John the Baptist was considered literally
immortal by both his followers and himself; it seemed incon-
ceivable that he should die before the Final Judgement, after
which the chosen would live for ever. His death at the age of
eighty-eight deeply shook his followers.

Into the spiritual breach stepped the Reverend John Hugh
Smyth Pigott, a Church of England curate like Prince and the
Lord's favoured disciple. At fifty-years-old Reverend Pigott
was an imposing man, tall and lean with intense eyes and a
resounding voice. Under his new leadership the Agapemonites
overcame the loss of the Lord and continued to prosper.

Then three years later, in 1902, Reverend Pigott announced his
assumption of Godhead. His faithful flock took this in their stride
– for decades they had lived with a benign leader to whom they
had ascribed virtual deification and this simply seemed the next
step towards Judgement Day – but other Londoners were less
enthusiastic. A large crowd gathered to view the new Messiah
the following Sunday, very few of them friendly.

As Pigott and his retinue arrived for the evening service the
police had to hold the angry mob back. When he entered the
Ark of the Covenant many of the crowd managed to climb the
iron railings surrounding the church grounds and thronged the
pews. Pigott's sermon was drowned-out by their cat-calls and
as he left he had to dodge a shower of stones and bricks hurled
by indignant unbelievers. One local paper noted that, "this
self-styled Messiah would probably have been thrown into the
pond at Clapton Common but for the protection of the mounted
police."

In the face of this unchristian behaviour Pigott retired with his wife Kathie and disciples to the Abode of Love in Somerset. Once there he clearly decided to refrain from making any more public claims to divinity and the local people seemed glad to leave the sect in peace. Reverend Pigott settled down to a quieter life with his family which now included his "spiritual bride", Ruth Preece.

At this time the Church of England still considered him to be a member of the Anglican clergy, as did Pigott himself. That he had claimed to be Christ the Redeemer did not stir his bishop to action, but the fact that he subsequently begot two boys, whom he called Power and Glory, on a merely "spiritual bride" brought-about an immediate charge of immoral behaviour from the Bishop of Bath-and-Wells. Pigott was defrocked on the floor of Wells Cathedral in 1909.

This, of course, had no effect on his standing as a spiritual leader with the Agapemonites, but their numbers were now on the wane. At the time of his defrocking the movement consisted of only about a hundred women and a handful of men, but despite the hopes of their enemies the Agapemonites soldiered on. Pigott died in 1927, at the age of seventy-eight, leaving only a few followers.

His spiritual bride, Sister Ruth, who had borne him another child, carried on the faith until her death in 1956. The old woman was mourned by the fifteen remaining members of the Agapemonite church. Shortly thereafter another fringe sect took over the Ark of the Covenant church in Clapton and the Abode of Love was sold and converted into council flats.

Fatty Arbuckle – A Star's Disgrace

The scandal that wrecked the career of film comic "Fatty" Roscoe Arbuckle – and tarnished the image of Hollywood – occurred after a three-day drinking party in 1921.

Arbuckle was born on 24 March 1887 in Smith Center, Kansas, USA and named Roscoe Conklin Arbuckle. He worked as a plumber's assistant, then became a performer in carnivals and vaudeville – for all his enormous weight (303 lb or 21 stone) he was incredibly agile. At the age of twenty-one he was hired as an extra by the Selig Polyscope Company and he made his first one-reel comedy – *The Sanitarium* – in 1910. He was hired by

Mack Sennett and made a dozen films in 1913 including *Fatty's Day Off* and *Fatty's Flirtation*. His attraction lay in his cherubic innocence – the good nature that he radiated was obviously genuine. Neither, for a Hollywood star, was he unusually sex-oriented; the girls he worked with found him protective and "big brotherly". His reputation was a great deal better, for example, than that of his co-star Charlie Chaplin. In 1917, he moved with Sennett to Jesse Lasky's Artcraft, and wrote and directed most of his own films. He gave Buster Keaton a start in life. When he made a film for Paramount, a banner over the gate read: Welcome To The Prince Of Whales. But an all-night party laid on in his honour by Jesse Lasky in Boston on 6 March in 1917, almost led to scandal. Twelve party girls were paid over $1,000 for their night's work. But some Boston resident who peered through the transom and saw Fatty stripping on a table with several girls called the police. It is alleged that Lasky, Adolph Zukor and Joseph Schenck ended by paying the district attorney and mayor $10,000 to overlook the incident.

In 1921, Arbuckle signed a contract worth $3 million and he decided to celebrate with a party in the St Francis Hotel in San Francisco. He arrived from Bay City on the evening of Saturday, 3 September 1921, and took a suite, as well as three rooms on the twelfth floor, in the unlikely event that anyone should want to sleep. By the following afternoon, the party was in full swing, with about fifty guests, including such Hollywood cronies as Lowell Sherman and Freddy Fishback, and a number of pretty actresses. Arbuckle, separated from his wife, had asked his friend Bambina Maude Delmont to invite a girl he particularly admired – the starlet Virginia Rappe. The two women were staying at the nearby Palace Hotel, together with Virginia's agent.

Twenty-five-year-old Virginia Rappe was a model from Chicago, who had achieved public notice when her face appeared on the sheet music of "Let Me Call You Sweetheart". She was a pretty, fresh-faced girl, the type Hollywood liked to cast as a milkmaid – dressed in a check frock and sunbonnet she looked the essence of female innocence. According to film-maker Kenneth Anger (in *Hollywood Babylon*) this appearance was misleading. "An offer came from Sennett, and she went to work on his lot, taking minor parts. She also did her share of sleeping around, and gave half the company crabs. This epidemic so shocked Sennett that he closed down his studio and had it fumigated." Arbuckle had been pursuing Virginia – without success – for five years. She found him unattractive

Fatty Arbuckle with Virginia Rappe, the girl he was accused of raping

and was later quoted as having said: "I'd sooner go to bed with a jungle ape than have that fat octopus groping at me." But since Arbuckle was now an influential figure in the film world and Virginia was still an unknown starlet, she was willing to make certain compromises to advance her career.

On Labour Day, Monday, 5 September 1921, the party was still going, and Virginia had come from the Palace Hotel, accompanied by a "bodyguard". Arbuckle was still dressed in pyjamas, carpet slippers and a bathrobe. Most of the other guests were in a similar state of *déshabillé*. Virginia refused champagne and accepted a gin and orange. She was drinking her third – and was anxious to get to the bathroom, which seemed to be constantly occupied – when Arbuckle grabbed her and steered her into a bedroom, winking at his friends and commenting: "This is what I've been waiting for."

A few minutes later, there were screams from the bedroom. Suddenly, the party noises died away. Maude Delmont went and tried the bedroom handle, calling, "Virginia, what's happening?" There were more screams. Maude Delmont picked up the telephone and called down for the manager. The assistant manager, H.J. Boyle, rushed into the suite just as the door of bedroom 1219 burst open and Arbuckle appeared with Virginia's hat perched on his head at an absurd angle. He gave an innocent smile and did a little dance on the carpet. Back in the room, Virginia was making groaning sounds. Fatty's good temper seemed to slip and he said to Maude Delmont, "Get her dressed and take her back to the Palace." And when Virginia started to scream again he yelled, "Shut up, or I'll throw you out of the window."

Virginia was lying on the bed, almost nude, with her clothes scattered around her. She was moaning, "I'm dying, I'm dying. He hurt me." They tried to dress her, but her blouse was badly torn – it had obviously been ripped from her by force.

The house doctor was sent for and Virginia was moved to another room, still moaning. Arbuckle seemed to feel she was "putting it on", perhaps to blackmail him into offering her a part, and snapped, "Shut up. You were always a lousy actress."

She was in pain for the next three days, often becoming unconscious. She was transferred to a nursing home, where she died. The doctor who performed the autopsy discovered that her bladder was ruptured. The result was death from peritonitis. What had happened seemed clear. Arbuckle had flung himself on her with his full weight when she had a full bladder and it had ruptured like a balloon. When it was reported to the coroner, police interviewed hospital staff to find out who was behind the accident. The next morning newspaper headlines all over the country talked about the orgy that had ended in rape and death.

An inquest found that Arbuckle was "criminally responsible" for Virginia's death and recommended that he should be charged with manslaughter. Even before he went on trial in November, his career was in ruins. The fat, innocent man who made everybody laugh was really a "sex fiend". Rumours had it that his penis was so enormous that it had ruptured her bladder. But Arbuckle's friend Al Seminacher introduced a note of horror when he told people that Arbuckle had used a large piece of ice from the ice bucket to penetrate Virginia. Rumour added that he had first assaulted her by introducing a champagne bottle.

Church groups and women's clubs demanded that his films should be withdrawn from circulation, and that unreleased films should never be shown. It was hardly necessary. No one could laugh at Arbuckle when they remembered that this innocent, babylike character had torn off a girl's clothes and raped her. A "Fatty lynching" mood swept the country: in Wyoming, cowboys shot up the screen of a cinema showing an Arbuckle short; in Hartford, Connecticut, women tore down the screen.

Arbuckle was released on bail. His trial began in November; he denied doing any harm to Virginia and his lawyers did their best to suggest that she was little better than a prostitute. After forty-three hours deliberation, a jury was in favour of acquitting Arbuckle by ten to two but a majority verdict was not good enough and a mis-trial was declared. At his second trial, the jury found him guilty by ten to two and again they were dismissed. On 12 April 1922, a third jury found him innocent, and the foreman added: "Acquittal is not enough. We feel a grave injustice has been done him and there is not the slightest proof to connect him in any way with the commission of a crime." Outside the court, Arbuckle told newsmen, "My innocence of the hideous charge preferred against me has been proved." But it made no difference. Comedy depends upon a make-believe world in which no one does any real harm and everything is a joke. Fatty's "rape" had introduced a brutal element of reality. This was the real reason why he remained unforgiven.

The $3 million contract was cancelled and his unreleased films were suppressed. It cost the studio $1 million. His friend Buster Keaton suggested he should change his name to Will B. Good. In fact, he directed a few comedy shorts under the name of William Goodrich. He toured America's backwoods in second-rate farces, but some of them were booed off the stage. In 1931 he pleaded in *Photoplay*: "Just let me work . . . I think I can entertain and gladden the people that see me." He seemed incapable of grasping that the case had somehow undermined the public's willingness to laugh at him.

He began to drink heavily: in 1931 he was arrested in Hollywood for drunken driving. Yet in 1933, his luck seemed to be turning. Warner Brothers took the risk of hiring him to make several short comedies. But after a celebration party in a New York hotel on 28 June 1933, he returned to his room and died of a heart attack. He was forty-six years old.

> Towards the end of his life, the French novelist Henri Murger, author of *La Bohéme*, was seen standing in a urinal groping inside his trousers and muttering: "Come on out, you little devil. It's only to pee."

FINANCIAL SCANDALS

*B*ribery is a dirty word and when it involves policemen it becomes
even dirtier. In 1877 Scotland Yard was at the centre of a large
cover-up scandal that involved several high-ranking policemen. And
even to this day, people will often offer a bribe to get out of a sticky
situation that is of their own making.

Scotland Yard – The Great Bribery Scandal

Harry Benson, one of the most ingenious swindlers of all time,
is remembered chiefly for his leading role in the great Scotland
Yard scandal of 1877.

Benson was the son of a well-to-do Jewish merchant with
offices in the Faubourg St Honoré in Paris. He had charming
manners, spoke several languages, and liked to represent himself as a member of the nobility. Soon after the Franco-Prussian
war of 1870–71, he approached the Lord Mayor of London,
calling himself the Comte de Montague, Mayor of Châteaudun,
seeking a subscription for the relief of citizens made destitute by
the war. He collected £1,000 but his forged receipt gave him away
and he was sentenced to a year in prison. He found prison life so
intolerable that he attempted suicide by trying to burn himself

to death on his prison mattress. He was crippled by it and had to walk with crutches thereafter.

When he came out of prison, Benson advertised for a secretarial position, mentioning that he spoke several languages. The man who answered his advertisement was a certain William Kurr, who specialized in swindles connected with racing. His crude method was to decamp hastily with his customers' winnings. The ingenious Benson soon convinced him that there were better and less risky ways of making a fortune. Members of the French aristocracy were the chosen victims. Kurr and Benson issued a newspaper called *Le Sport* which contained articles about racing translated from British newspapers. It also contained many references to a wealthy Mr G. H. Yonge, who was so incredibly successful in backing horses that British bookmakers always shortened their odds when they dealt with him. *Le Sport* was sent out, free, to dozens of French aristocrats interested in racing; they had no earthly reason for suspecting a prospective swindle.

One of the aristocrats who became a victim was a certain Comtesse de Goncourt. She received a letter from Mr Yonge of Shanklin, Isle of Wight, asking her if she would agree to act as his agent in laying bets. All she had to do was to send the cheque he would send her to a certain bookmaker; if the horse won, she would receive his winnings, which she would forward to Mr Yonge, and would receive a 5 per cent commission. Madame de Goncourt agreed to this arrangement and received a cheque for a few hundred pounds, which she posted off to the bookmaker in her own name. In due course, she received a cheque for more than a thousand pounds in "winnings" and after she had sent this off to Mr Yonge, she received her £50 or so commission. It seemed a marvellously easy way of earning £50. What she did not realize was that the "bookmaker" to whom she forwarded the cheque was simply another of Mr Yonge's aliases. When she had sent Mr Yonge several more lots of winnings and received several more lots of commission, she decided that he was obviously a financial genius and entrusted him with £10,000 of her own money to invest on her behalf. That was the last she saw of it.

Although Scotland Yard was a relatively new institution in the 1870s (it was established in 1829), its methods of crime-fighting depended a great deal on underworld "narks" who betrayed fellow criminals. Police officers, then as now, were forced to cultivate the acquaintance of many criminals. It also meant that an underpaid police officer – in those days the salary of a detective was a mere £5 6s. 2d. a week – might be subjected to the temptation of accepting presents, favours and open bribes for protecting his own "narks". This may well be how a certain detective officer named John Meiklejohn became friendly with William Kurr and then began to accept money from him in exchange for not pressing his investigations into Kurr's earlier swindles. When Chief Inspector Nathaniel Druscovich, a naturalized Pole, confided to Chief Inspector Meiklejohn that he was in financial difficulties, Meiklejohn told him he knew a "businessman" who could help him. The businessman was Benson and all he wanted in return for the £60 he "lent" Druscovich was a little information – prior warning if the Yard intended to arrest him. Soon a third detective had been drawn into the net – Chief Inspector William Palmer. Not long after this, Meiklejohn warned Kurr and Benson that the Yard was getting close. Meiklejohn's superior, Chief Inspector Clarke, had been tracking down sham betting offices and was hot on the trail of Gardner and Co., the name under which Kurr and his confederates had been operating.

Among these confederates was a man called Walters who belonged to a gang that Clarke had recently broken up. Now Benson wrote to Clarke from his pleasant home in the Isle of Wight – he kept a carriage, and had an excellent cook and many servants – saying that he had some interesting information about Walters. Unfortunately, he explained, he was crippled and could not come to Scotland Yard but if Clarke would be kind enough to come down to Shanklin . . . In those days, policemen stood in awe of the aristocracy and were likely to treat a wealthy suspect with obsequious respect. So Clarke hurried down to Shanklin and was duly overawed by Mr Yonge's magnificent home. He was worried when Mr Yonge told him that Walters was going about saying that he had bribed Clarke and that he had in his possession a letter to prove it. Indeed Clarke had written Walters a letter; he was not a very literate man and he might easily have expressed himself in a way that could be open to false interpretation. Mr Yonge promised to try to get hold of the letter and he and Clarke parted on friendly terms. But Clarke than reported to his own superior that Yonge was a scoundrel. They had some correspondence and Yonge addressed Clarke as "My Dear Sir and Brother" for they were both freemasons. They met several times and "Yonge" later claimed he had given Clarke £50.

With this network of "police spies", the Benson-Kurr gang should have been untouchable. But Benson now overstepped himself. He wrote to the Comtesse de Goncourt saying that he had a marvellous and unique opportunity to invest a further large sum for her. The Comtesse had no more ready cash and she called on her lawyer, a Mr Abrahams, to ask him to turn certain securities into cash. Mr Abrahams took the precaution of contacting Scotland Yard and asking whether they knew anything about a certain Mr Yonge of "Rose Bank", Shanklin. Druscovich, who was in charge of frauds connected with the Continent received the message and hastened to warn Benson that trouble was brewing. Scotland Yard had been asked by the Paris police to intercept letters containing money from various dupes – but the telegram containing this request was pocketed by Druscovich. Druscovich could see that he was playing a dangerous game; he would be expected to make an arrest soon. He begged the swindlers to remove themselves beyond his reach as soon as possible.

The gang, which included Kurr's brother Frederick, and two men named Murray and Bale, had put most of its ill-gotten gains into the safest place, the Bank of England. They could, of course, withdraw it without difficulty. The only problem about that was that English bank notes are numbered and for such a large sum of money, they would be numbered consecutively and would, therefore, be easy to trace. If the gang escaped to the Continent, they would be leaving a trail of bank notes behind them like a paperchase. Benson withdrew about £16,000 from the bank and hastened up to Scotland where he opened an account in the Bank of Clydesdale in Greenock; he also withdrew £13,000 in Bank of Clydesdale £100 notes. These had the advantage of bearing no number but they were still easily traceable. Benson was eating dinner with the manager of the Clydesdale Bank when he received a telegram from Druscovich warning him that he was on his way to arrest him. Benson fled, forfeiting the £3,000 still in his account at Greenock.

The detectives were rewarded with about £500 each (although Clarke does not seem to have been included). Meiklejohn immediately made the mistake of cashing one of his £100 notes and giving an office of the gang as his address. A week later he cashed another note with a Leeds wine merchant. The Leeds Police discovered this and since they were on the lookout for the gang sent a telegram to Scotland Yard. Druscovich intercepted the telegram and burned it.

Scotland Yard found it baffling that, in spite of all their efforts, the Benson gang had slipped through their fingers. The bribed detectives were still not suspected. Clarke's superior Williamson set it all down to sheer bad luck. In fact, most of the gang was now in hiding at Bridge of Allan in Scotland. When the Comtesse's lawyer Abrahams traced them to Scotland, Detective Officer William Palmer sent them a letter warning them to scatter.

It was Druscovich who was made responsible for rushing around the country to trap the swindlers. He met Kurr at the Caledonian Station in Edinburgh and was offered £1,000 by him if he did not go to Bridge of Allan. Druscovich had to decline for he had been ordered to go to Bridge of Allan to collect certain letters that had been addressed to one "Mr Giffard" at the Queen's Hotel. Mr Giffard was William Kurr.

Inevitably, the birds had flown by the time Druscovich reached Bridge of Allan. Williamson was understandably disappointed. He was astounded to learn that his subordinate Meiklejohn had been seen in the company of the swindlers at Bridge of Allan. This was surely the point when Scotland Yard had to smell a rat . . . But Meiklejohn explained that he had no idea he had been wining and dining with crooks. He had met Yonge by chance and believed him to be a perfectly respectable gentleman. Williamson accepted his story.

Now the gang found themselves with thousands of pounds in uncashable £100 notes and with no ready cash. Murray was sent off to cash a cheque at one of the banks in Scotland where they had opened an account; the police were waiting for him. Benson went to Rotterdam and tried to cash a note at his hotel but Scotland Yard had alerted the Dutch police and he was arrested. Druscovich passed on the news to Kurr who persuaded a crooked attorney named Froggatt to send the Dutch police a telegram signed "Scotland Yard", ordering them to release Benson on the grounds that his arrest had been a mistake. It almost succeeded but the Dutch police decided to wait for a letter confirming the telegram, and this never came.

It was Druscovich, the expert on Continental crime, who was sent to Rotterdam to bring back Benson – and Bale, who had also been arrested there. There was nothing he could do about it except to look at them sternly and mutter under his breath that he would do his best. There was no opportunity to allow them to escape. Besides, his own position was now in danger. Williamson had now heard about the letter from the Leeds Police, telling them that Meiklejohn had cashed a £100 note there. He wanted to know if Druscovich had seen it. Druscovich denied all knowledge of it and he realized that any attempt to allow Benson to escape was now out of the question.

The swindlers finally stood in the dock and were found guilty. Benson received fifteen years and Kurr received ten. As soon as they reached Millbank Prison, they asked to see the governor and told the story of the corrupt detectives. A short time afterwards, Druscovich, Meiklejohn, Palmer and Clarke all stood in the dock – and, for good measure, the police had also arrested the crooked attorney Froggatt. Many letters from the detectives were produced, warning the crooks of the activities of Scotland Yard. Druscovich had also been seen talking to Benson and Kurr at St Pancras Station, London.

All except Clarke were convicted – the evidence against Clarke was inconclusive. Druscovich, Meiklejohn and Palmer all received two years' hard labour, the maximum sentence for conspiring to defeat the ends of justice.

Clarke was retired on a pension. Meiklejohn became a private detective. Palmer used his savings to become a publican. What happened to Druscovich is not known but he disappeared from sight; while Froggatt died in a workhouse.

The two principal swindlers still had many successful years before them. Benson and Kurr both received a remission of sentence for good conduct. They teamed up again and slipped across the Atlantic where they became mining company promoters. Benson returned to Belgium and continued in business selling stock in non-existent mines. The Belgian Police found out more about him from Scotland Yard and arrested him. Huge quantities of postal orders and cheques, apparently sent to him by gullible investors were found in his lodgings. He spent another two years in jail then moved to Switzerland. There he again set out to give the impression he was a wealthy stockbroker. He met a girl in his hotel, whose father was a retired general and surgeon of the Indian army. He persuaded the girl to marry him and induced the father to sell his shares and hand over the proceeds of £7,000 for "investment". Then he tried to disappear to America. His father-in-law managed to have him arrested at Bremen but decided not to prosecute when Benson gave back £5,000. Jewellery that Benson had given his fiancée proved to be made of paste.

His last great coup was in America. The singer Adelina Patti was arriving in New York for a tour. Benson, calling himself Abbey, bribed Customs officials to let him on the boat ahead of the Patti Reception Committee. He introduced himself to her as the head of the committee. When the committee arrived, he was deep in conversation with her and they assumed he was her manager. She left the boat on his arm. He then went to Mexico

> One of the greatest financial scandals in history was the notorious "South Sea Bubble", a scheme thought up by novelist Daniel Defoe and launched by Robert Harley, the Earl of Oxford, in 1720. The idea was to import African slaves to work plantations in South America. But the shares sold so well that this part of the plan was never put into operation – no one then understood the idea of "credit". After taking 8½ million pounds, confidence began to flag, shareholders began to sell, and the company collapsed. Thousands were ruined and scores committed suicide. The company's directors were heavily fined. The scandal put the Whig Opposition in power for the next four decades.

and sold thousands of bogus tickets of Patti concerts. He was arrested when he went back into the States and committed to the Tombs. Apparently, unable to face the prospect of another long period in prison, he leapt from a high gallery and fell 50 feet snapping his spine. At the time of his death he was little more than forty years of age.

Teapot Dome Scandal – The Ohio Gang Hijacks America

Warren Gamaliel Harding was probably the worst President the United States has ever had. The best that can be said of him is that the Teapot Dome scandal that erupted after his death was none of his doing; it was simply the result of his failure to do anything except play poker and make love to his mistress in a room behind the Oval office.

Warren Harding's only asset was a ruggedly handsome face and a square jaw that made him look like a president. He was born in the small town of Corsica, Ohio, in 1865. He made half-hearted attempts to become a schoolteacher and a lawyer, and finally acquired a newspaper on the verge of bankruptcy. At about this time he met Florence Kling de Wolfe, the daughter of a leading citizen, who married him in spite of her father's bitter opposition. She was the driving force in their marriage for Harding was lazy, good natured and easy going. It was largely due to her hard work that the Marion *Star* became a successful newspaper.

As editor, Harding met many politicians, including Harry Daugherty, who lacked the personality to achieve the political ambitions he dreamed about. But Harding looked like a politician and with Daugherty as his campaign manager, he soon became a Republican State senator, then Lieutenant-Governor of Ohio. That was as far as Harding wanted to go, but his wife and Daugherty continued to push him until, to his bewilderment, he found himself elected to the United States Senate with a large majority.

Harding had no real interest in politics. He spent more time on the golf course or attending baseball games than in the Senate. He also took a mistress. A schoolgirl named Nan Britton had fallen hopelessly in love with him back in Marion and when she moved to New York they began meeting secretly. Soon she was pregnant and bore him a daughter.

In 1920, a presidential election was due; Woodrow Wilson had suffered a breakdown in 1919 and had no intention of running again. The Republicans had no clear favourite among their candidates. At the Convention in Chicago in June, none of the three main contenders was able to command a clear majority. Harding, a "dark horse", seemed an acceptable alternative. He was asked if there was any scandal in his life that might cause the party embarrassment; he emphatically denied this and was nominated on the tenth ballot. In November, he beat the Democratic candidate James M. Cox and became twenty-ninth President of the United States. At the Convention, his wife had been heard to mutter, "I can see only one word written above his head if they make him President, and that word is 'Tragedy'."

It was not quite as bad as that; rather something closer to farce. Presidents do not need to be intellectual giants but Harding was barely an intellectual gnat. He was bewildered by all the tasks he ought to be tackling: post-war disarmament, world monetary problems, tariffs, tax proposals; he was like a schoolboy faced with a page of quantum equations. He invited all his cronies to the White House where they drank and played poker in his study. When Nan Britton arrived, they retired to a private room. Harding liked to sit with his waistcoat unbuttoned, his feet on the desk and a spitoon by his side, in a room thick with tobacco smoke.

Meanwhile, all his old political cronies – "the Ohio gang" – had moved to Washington and set up a kind of alternative White House on K Street. Harry Daugherty, now Attorney-General, sold government jobs and other favours, using a jobber named Jesse W. Smith as a go-between with the men who wanted to buy favours. Smith, a coarse, genial man used to love to sing: "My God, how the money rolls in."

Another member of the Ohio gang was the Secretary of the Interior, Albert Fall. Fall itched to get his hands on an enormous oil reserve known as Teapot Dome, an area of land in Wyoming, north of the town of Caspar. Woodrow Wilson had decided that Teapot Dome should be held in reserve in case of future national emergencies and it was under the control of the Naval Department. Fall persuaded the Secretary of the Navy, then the President, to transfer the lease to his Department of the Interior. Then it was secretly leased to Harry F. Sinclair, president of the Mammoth Oil Company, for more than $14 million. Another oil reserve at Elk Hills, California, was leased to another friend, Edward Doheny, for $100,000. Fall was soon able to pay nine years of back-taxes that he owed on a New Mexico ranch, and to stock it with prize cattle. Another Harding crony, Charles R. Forbes, was head of the Veterans' Bureau, and was in charge of purchasing supplies for hospitals for ex-servicemen and awarding contracts for new hospitals. Hospital supplies bought with public money were promptly sold as government surplus – a million towels that had cost 34 cents each were sold at 36 cents a dozen; sheets costing $1.35 a pair were sold at 27 cents a pair. Vast sums were paid to him in exchange for hospital contracts. He also received "kickbacks" from real estate dealers from whom he bought land for the hospitals at far more than its value.

Sooner or later, this empire of corruption had to collapse under its own weight. Washington journalists began to hint more and more openly at what was going on. The Attorney-General's office under Daugherty became known as the Department of Easy Virtue. Finally, the rumours reached Harding's ear. His health was breaking down – no doubt due to his intake of Bourbon – and now his nerve began to crack. A visitor to the White House took the wrong turning and was startled to come upon Harding grasping a man by the throat and shouting, "You yellow rat! You double crossing bastard!" The man was Charles Forbes, head of the Veterans' Bureau. Soon after, Forbes took a trip to Paris and sent in his resignation "for health reasons".

Jesse Smith, the go-between who liked to sing "My God, how the money rolls in", had been sent back to Ohio by Daugherty because he talked too openly. Harding summoned him to the White House and listened, aghast, as Smith told him the extent of the skulduggery. When he had finished, he asked the President what would happen now. "Go home. Tomorrow you will be arrested." Smith went back to his hotel and shot himself.

Harding was due to make a trip to Alaska and he decided that this might be an opportune moment to escape from Washington. There was talk of a Congressional Enquiry; Charles Cramer, Forbes' right-hand man, also shot himself; there was an increasing number of resignations. As Harding returned from the Alaskan trip, down the Pacific coast, he fell ill, his doctor diagnosed food poisoning from crab meat. On 2 August 1923, he died of pneumonia. His wife died in the following year. The Teapot Dome scandal now erupted and Nan Britton added to it by writing a bestselling book about her affair with Harding called *The President's Daughter*.

When a Harding Memorial Association raised $700,000 for a monument in Marion, Ohio (where the President was buried), it was decided that it should take the form of a huge marble cylinder with colonnades. Others greatly preferred a design that was closer to a sphere. This idea was dropped when someone pointed out that it only needed a spout and a handle to look like a teapot.

The "Suicide" of Roberto Calvi

On the morning of Friday, 18 June 1982, a postal clerk walking across Blackfriars Bridge in London looked down and saw a body dangling by its neck from the scaffolding. When the police arrived they cut down the body of a paunchy man of about sixty, with large red bricks stuffed into his pockets, and about $15,000, in various currencies, in his wallet. His passport identified him as Gian Roberto Calvini, but a check with Italian authorities revealed that he was, in fact, Roberto Calvi, chairman and managing director of the Banco Ambrosiano in Milan.

In the previous year Calvi had been sentenced to four years in prison for illegally exporting $20 million in lire; he had been released pending appeal. A week before his body was found Calvi had disappeared from his Rome apartment.

On 23 July, the London coroner decided that Calvi's death had been a suicide. By that time, however, a great deal of information about Calvi's financial associates had been unearthed, and the coroner's verdict began to seem less and less likely . . .

Calvi had joined the Banco Ambrosiano at the age of twenty-six. He was an excellent linguist, and assisted in the closing of international deals. Some of Calvi's schemes netted the bank a great deal of money, and his promotion was fast: he rose from easing international transactions to becoming the bank's "central manager" in twenty years. Many people saw him as a cold and ruthless character – his wife maintained that he was merely shy. He was obsessed with the idea of *sottogoverno*, the secret interaction of hidden agencies and apparent political power. He carried a copy of Mario Puzo's *"The Godfather"* in his briefcase at all times, like a Bible.

Calvi was also ambitious, and despite his success he realized that he could not make the amount of money his ambition demanded managing a Catholic bank. He needed to deal in shares. The only problem was that Italian law did not allow banks to own shares, it being assumed that the temptation to siphon off other people's money into the bank's holdings would be too great. Calvi seemed to have reached a dead-end in his career.

In the late sixties Calvi met Michele Sindona, one of Italy's most successful financiers. Sindona had based a fortune upon Black Market trading during World War II. In the late fifties Mafia families in New York approached Sindona to launder some of their drug profits through investments in Italy. Sindona also had financial contacts in the Vatican. He had been made main financial adviser to the Vatican Bank, *uomo di fiducia*, when a friend, Cardinal Montini, became Pope in 1963.

Sindona was very useful to the Vatican Bank, as he could deal with matters that might appear too secular for the financial wing of a religious body. If any anti-religious groups, such as the communists, were to transact business with the Vatican, Sindona would be the negotiator, a secular frontman. He would attempt to disconnect inappropriate links and put the money into innocuous overseas holdings. A Vatican-owned company built the Watergate complex.

Sindona's closest link with the Vatican was Bishop Paul Marcinkus, secretary of the Vatican bank and bodyguard to the Pope. Marcinkus was a large American, born in Al Capone's Cicero. His association with Sindona profited both the Church and its adviser enormously.

When Sindona met Calvi in the late sixties he immediately recognized a man of ambition. He also correctly guessed that he

Roberto Calvi, Italian banker and alleged member of the secret masonic lodge "P-2"

would not mind becoming involved in transactions that were not one hundred per cent above board. Sindona, who owned many banks, had overcome the prohibition on his owning shares by setting up companies in "fiscal paradises" like Liechtenstein or Luxembourg and using these as a front for his own share deals. Now Calvi, in association with Sindona, began to avoid the Italian authorities' scrutiny in the same way. When Calvi opened a bank in South America the Italian banking overseers only found out about it through the newspapers.

Both Calvi and Sindona made a great deal of money through overseas share-holdings. The Bank of Italy seemed unwilling to interfere with their business. Only the oil crisis of 1973 brought an end to Sindona's world-spanning financial colonialism. He had planned to buy several extremely large banking institutions within Italy and merge them into the biggest single financial powerblock in the country. The worldwide crisis of confidence created by oil prices going up hit Sindona badly. The Franklin Bank, which Sindona owned, crashed in the biggest banking failure in American history. Sindona was charged with breaking American financial laws. The Vatican was rumoured to have lost $60 million in the crash. Marcinkus hastily declared that he hardly knew Sindona.

Calvi meanwhile was flourishing. He owned many banks and insurance companies. He had replaced Sindona as *uomo di fiducia* with the Vatican bank, and even bought a bank from them, the Banca Cattolico del Veneto. He planned to buy the bank that employed him, Banco Ambrosiano, through his foreign puppet companies. By 1975 he had became chairman and effectively owner of Banco Ambrosiano.

It was at this point that Calvi became involved with the Italian Freemason's lodge P2. The head of the lodge, Licio Gelli, offered Calvi membership, and on 23 August 1975 Calvi joined. P2 or Propaganda Two was an extremely powerful affiliation of members of government, businessmen and other people of influence. Gelli, a mysterious figure, was a kind of super-Mafia boss, in a position to grant favours to even the most powerful in the land. Calvi, with his prior interest in *sottogoverno* naturally saw membership of P2 as an essential accessory of power.

As Calvi was in the ascendant, Sindona's fortunes foundered. Calvi was reluctant to financially re-establish his old partner – he had provided the $40 million with which Sindona had bought the Franklin bank – and did not want to throw good money after bad. Sindona anonymously informed the Bank of Italy of certain "questionable" deals struck between the Vatican

Bank and Calvi. Spurred by these revelations, the Bank of Italy
opened an investigation into Calvi's finances.

A greater problem was also about to assail Calvi. In August
1978 Pope Paul VI died. He was replaced by Albino Luciano,
Pope John Paul I. Luciano had objected to Calvi's purchase of
the Veneto Bank in 1974 and fully intended, now that he had the
power, to investigate the Vatican Bank's dealings with Calvi and
Sindona. However, Pope John Paul I died after only thirty-three
days in the office. The medicines that he had been using during
his sudden sickness were removed from his bedside table just
after he died by Cardinal Villot, a member of P2. Calls for
an autopsy were ignored and his body was hastily embalmed
and interred. It has been argued that Luciano was poisoned.
Whatever the case, the death must have been a great relief
to Calvi.

The Bank of Italy's investigation soon foundered as well, as
both the governor of the bank and the chief investigator into
Calvi's accounts were arrested. Ironically, the charge was that
they had not sufficiently investigated criminal actions of banks
under their jurisdiction. Thus Calvi was saved any embarrassing
results of the investigation becoming public.

At the same time a lawyer who was in charge of liquidating
one of Sindona's Italian banks made some interesting discoveries
regarding Calvi and the Vatican Bank. He found that the sale
of the Veneto bank had involved a $6.5 million brokerage fee
being paid to Marcinkus and Calvi. The day after he told
writer Gianfranco Modolo his findings, he was shot dead in
the street.

Sindona meanwhile had faced charges in the United States.
He was found guilty on sixty-five counts of fraud and sentenced
to twenty-five years in jail. Although Sindona was a member of
P2, there was little that they could do for him in America. Also,
P2 had problems of their own . . .

Mino Pecorelli, a member of P2 had published articles hinting
at a tax fraud perpetrated by Gelli and an oil magnate involving
diesel. Gelli had found a way to sell domestic heating diesel,
which is taxed at a low rate, as fuel for vehicles, which is heavily
taxed. The money made had been laundered through Sindona
and the Vatican Bank. Pecorelli did not realize the full extent of
the scandal. When a fellow member of P2 tried to buy his silence,
it became clear to Pecorelli that there was a great deal of money
to be made blackmailing the Masons. He published an article
revealing that Gelli had spied for the Communists during the
war, and also that hinted at the extent of P2's influence. Within

hours of the article hitting the newsstands, Pecorelli was dead, shot twice in the mouth while climbing into his car.

The hidden organization was beginning to become visible. In 1981, two magistrates investigating Sindona's connection with the Mafia came upon the name Licio Gelli. They ordered that his house be searched. In a safe was a list of P2's members. At first the investigator's thought that P2 was the plan for a *coup d'etat*. It soon dawned on them that P2 *was* a *coup d'etat*, it already controlled the actions of the state.

Gelli fled from Italy. The scandal brought down the Prime Minister Arnoldo Forlani. Calvi, whose name had been in the P2 file, was arrested.

Two share deals that Calvi had been involved in had led to the illegal export of billions of lire. Calvi struggled to keep Banco Ambrosiano from crashing, obtaining legitimate outside investment and himself investing in Italian business, but all avenues seemed closed. The Bank of Italy, for so long intimidated whenever it inquired into Calvi's funds, scented blood and demanded details of Calvi's foreign puppet companies. When the board of Banco Ambrosiano asked Calvi if they could see details of these companies themselves he flatly refused, and for the first time Calvi's board voted him down four to ten. On the morning of 11 June, Calvi disappeared.

Why he disappeared, and what he hoped to achieve are not known. It seems likely that he hoped to accumulate materials for his defence. What is known is that he drove halfway across Europe during the last week of his life. He had contacted an associate called Silvano Vittor and obtained a false passport in the name of Gian Roberto Calvini. A Swiss businessman, Hans Kunz, organized low-key accommodation for Calvi in London at a block of serviced flats called the Chelsea Cloisters. Vittor and Calvi flew to London and checked into the hostel. From there Calvi telephoned his wife and seemed hopeful, saying that something had turned up that would help his defence. However, Calvi was still extremely nervous, refusing to leave his room and insisting that Vittor knocked in a pre-arranged fashion before he tried to enter.

On Thursday, 17 June 1982, a business associate of Calvi's called Carboni arrived at the Chelsea Cloisters and asked to speak to him. Calvi refused, and sent Vittor in his place. When Vittor returned, Calvi had gone. A few hours later he was found hanging under Blackfriars bridge.

A BBC team investigating the death established that Carboni's brother booked into a hotel in Geneva the previous night. On the evening after Calvi's death a private plane flew from Geneva to Gatwick, where it stayed only ninety minutes. On its return journey it had a briefcase on board. Calvi never travelled without his briefcase, but it was not found in the hotel room or at the scene of his "suicide". It contained, according to the BBC, papers detailing Calvi's dealings with the Vatican and P2. It has never been found.

In June 1983, a second inquest on Calvi in London preferred to return an open verdict on his death. That decision paid Calvi's widow $3 million in insurance money.

If Calvi was murdered who, then, was responsible? The question is difficult to answer, as so many people would have been pleased to see him out of the way. Calvi's wife believes that the Vatican was behind his murder. Italian Prime Minister Bettino Craxi has gone on the record as saying that Calvi was murdered by criminals associated with P2. It is certain that if Calvi had been prosecuted, the trial would have uncovered many details of Italy's huge *sottogoverno*. That, rather than Calvi's murder, is the real scandal.

When one examines the extent of the covert influence that moved the events of this story, it becomes easy to understand Calvi's fixation with *"The Godfather"*.

LITERARY FRAUD

It is amazing how a brilliant writers often resort to untruths to get noticed. They sensationalize the contents of their books to get accepted, and then find themselves in a dilemma when they realize that a follow-up book is wanted, and they have to embellish even more to continue the story.

Mikhail Sholokhov – The Quiet Flows the Don Plagiarism Scandal

The most eminent Russian author to emerge since the Revolution in 1917 is undoubtedly Mikhail Alexandrovitch Sholokhov, born in the hamlet of Kruzhlino, on the banks of the Don, in 1905. Like Gorky, Sholokhov led a varied life – soldier, handyman, statistician, food inspector, goods handler, mason, book-keeper and finally journalist – before he hurtled to literary fame at the age of twenty-three with the first volume of *Tikhi Don*, *The Quiet Don* (translated into English as *Quiet Flows the Don*). When compared with the great Russian novels of the nineteenth century, it seems full of "shock tactics" of the kind associated with cheap popular novels in England and the United States. The book begins with a scene in which the Turkish wife of a Cossack is trampled by a mob who believe her to be a witch. As a result she dies in premature childbirth. Shortly thereafter there is a description of how a seventeen-year-old girl is raped by her father and how her brother and mother then beat and kick him to death. Seductions, rapes and various forms of violence follow at regular intervals. But the nature writing is as fine as anything in the work of the novelist Turgenev.

Sholokhov's first book *Tales of the Don* appeared when he was only twenty. It is interesting to note in these tales of the civil war and shortly after that the village leaders are portrayed as isolated from the people; later, as he learned communist conformity, Sholokhov showed them integrated with the people.

Sholokhov began work on *Tikhi Don* when he was twenty-one. When it appeared two years later – and became an instant bestseller – critics were amazed that anyone so young could write so powerfully; it eventually sold four and a half million copies before its fourth and final volume appeared fourteen years later. The later volumes are generally admitted to be inferior to the first. *Virgin Soil Upturned* (1932), about a collective farm, was a success in Russia but it is considered inferior to the earlier parts of *Tikhi Don*.

Soon after the first volume of *Tikhi Don* appeared in 1925, rumours began to spread around Moscow literary circles to the effect that Sholokhov was not the true author and that he had found the manuscript or a diary on which he based the book. In 1929, *Pravda* published a letter from a number of proletarian writers denouncing the "malicious slander". It even threatened prosecution. Nevertheless, Sholokhov was generally regarded as Russia's most important writer. In 1965 he was given the Nobel Prize for literature. By then, Sholokhov had become spokesman for the Soviet literary establishment, denouncing writers like Pasternak and Solzhenitsyn and taking an aggressively anti-intellectual stand that has caused young writers to regard him with distaste. This may be fuelled by envy for his life style on a large estate at Rostov-on-Don, where he has a private aeroplane and theatre, and hunts regularly.

Alexander Solzhenitsyn, who was forced into exile in Zurich in 1974, brought out of Russia a number of documents about Sholokhov's work by a friend whom he identifies simply as "D". "D", according to Solzhenitsyn, engaged in painstaking literary analysis of *Tikhi Don* but died before he could complete it. Solzhenitsyn explained that he could not reveal "D's" real name for fear of reprisals against his family but he published the manuscript and appealed to Western scholars to help complete the research.

In December 1926, the novelist Agatha Christie disappeared from her home in Sunningdale, Berkshire. Twelve days later her husband tracked her down to an hotel in Harrogate – a waiter had recognized her. The press was told that she had suffered a loss of memory – it was true that her husband was having an affair with another woman at the time, and she was under considerable emotional pressure. But from then on, her detective novels – so far hardly noticed – began to enjoy increasing sales. Was her disappearance a deliberate publicity stunt, as many have alleged? For the rest of her life, Agatha Christie flatly refused to discuss the matter.

"D's" textual analysis revealed two different authors of *Tikhi Don*: some 95 per cent of its first two volumes belong to the "original author", while less than 70 per cent of the second two are his work. "D's" scepticism was apparently aroused by the fact that the first two volumes which showed intimate acquaintance with pre-Revolutionary society in the Don region and described World War I and the Civil War were allegedly written by a young man between the ages of twenty-one and twenty-three. Sholokhov was too young to have witnessed either war. Even the speed of composition seems incredible – a novel of well over a quarter of a million words had been written in two years. Yet it took another fourteen years to complete the remaining two volumes and the first part of *Virgin Soil Upturned*. Sholokhov seemed to have "dried up". His collected works, issued in honour of his seventy-fifth birthday in 1980, amounted to a mere eight volumes.

According to Solzhenitsyn, (introducing "D's" book *The Mainstream of the Quiet Don*) the true author of *Tikhi Don* was a historian of the Don region, one Fyodor Dmitrievitch Kryukov, born in 1870, the son of a local "ataman" (village leader). By the end of the nineteenth century he had achieved great popularity as a recorder of Cossack life and was elected to the state parliament (Duma). Solzhenitsyn believes he began writing his major work, *Tikhi Don*, in Petrograd during World War I. As a Cossack, he was opposed to the Bolsheviks who seized power in 1917 and fought with the army of the Don. When this collapsed, he retired to the Kuban and died there of typhoid at the age of fifty. "D's" analysis of Kryukov's earlier works, which were never reprinted by the Soviet regime, convinced him that he was the true author of *Tikhi Don* and that as a journalist Sholokhov somehow came across Kryukov's manuscript and used it as a basis for his own book, deleting whole chapters where they did not suit his purpose and inserting material of his own. This, according to "D", explains the unevenness of the style and various internal contradictions.

Understandably, the Soviet view is that Solzhenitsyn is merely concerned with slandering and undermining the greatest Soviet novelist. But if this is so, at least he has presented his evidence in full so it can be studied by literary scholars and experts who can decide on its merits.

Lobsang Rampa – The "Third Eye" Hoax

Some time in 1955, a man arrived at the office of the publisher Secker and Warburg in Great Russell Street, London, and managed to persuade its chairman, Fred Warburg, to see him. The man, who wore a tonsure, introduced himself as Dr T. Lobsang Rampa, and explained that he had written his autobiography and wanted Mr Warburg to publish it. He declared he was a medical doctor and produced a document, in English, which he said was issued by the University of Chungking. Mr Warburg agreed to look at the manuscript, which thereafter arrived in sections. It was a fascinating document describing how the young Rampa, child of wealthy parents, had been singled out by astrologers at the age of seven to become a monk and how he had trained in a monastery. At the age of eight, he had submitted to a brain operation to open the "third eye" – the source of man's psychic powers. A hole was drilled in his forehead, then a sliver of very hard wood poked into this brain, so he saw "spirals of colour and globules of incandescent smoke". "For the rest of your life you will see people as they are and not as they pretend to be." And Rampa saw, to his astonishment, that all the men in the room were surrounded by a luminous golden flame, the vital aura.

Warburg had his doubts; the details seemed authentic, but the style was curiously English and colloquial. "I really did not think so much of kite-flying. Stupid idea, I thought. Dangerous. What a way to end a promising career. This is where I go back to prayers and herbs . . ." It didn't sound Tibetan. Various experts expressed contradictory opinions. But Rampa stood by his story of being a Tibetan. Warburg submitted him to a test: a few words of Tibetan. Rampa agreed that he could not understand it but explained that there was a perfectly good reason. During World War II he had been a prisoner of the Japanese, who had tortured him for information about his country; he had used his psychic powers to blot out all his knowledge of Tibetan.

Warburg swallowed his doubts and published, and the results vindicated his commercial sense. The book became a bestseller. It went into many languages and made Rampa a rich man.

A body of "Tibetan scholars" was doubtful about its authenticity and hired a private detective, Clifford Burgess, to find out about Lobsang Rampa. What he discovered was that Rampa was in reality Cyril Henry Hoskins, a Devon man who now lived in Thames Ditton. Hoskins had been born in Plympton, near Plymouth, in 1911, and entered his father's plumbing business. He was apparently deeply interested in psychic matters and claimed to have been taken to China as a child. It seemed that Hoskins was given to fantasizing about China and things Chinese; a journalist on *Psychic News*, John Pitt, tracked down a couple who had known him when he was a clerk in Weybridge and was told that Hoskins had claimed to be a flying instructor in the Chinese air force and had had an accident when his parachute failed to open. Later still, Hoskins changed his name to Carl Kuon Suo, called himself Dr Kuon, and claimed to have been born in Tibet.

Fred Warburg was understandably dismayed by these revelations but pointed out that he had published a note in the book saying that the author took full responsibility for all statements made in it. And he hinted at an alternative theory. "But is the truth, the whole truth, out? . . . Did he believe his own fantasies? Was he, perhaps, the mouthpiece of a true Lama, as some have alleged?" Rampa/Hoskins was tracked down to a house outside Dublin, where he was living with a lady whom he had, apparently, seduced away from her Old Etonian husband. Rampa declined to be interviewed; so did the Old Etonian husband.

Quite undeterred by the furore, Rampa went on to write a second book, *Doctor From Lhasa* (1959), which was accepted by Souvenir Press. The publisher's note in this book acknowledged that *The Third Eye* had caused great contention but went on to state that the author's explanation was that he had been "possessed" by the Tibetan lama Rampa since a blow on the head had caused mild concussion, and that Rampa now wrote his books through the author. Whatever the truth of the matter, the publisher added diplomatically, it is right that the book should be available to the public . . . *Doctor From Lhasa* continued the story where *The Third Eye* left off but is even more incredible. There is, for example, a chapter describing how Rampa jumped into an aircraft and, without any flying lessons, flew around for an hour or so, then brought the plane in to land.

Doctor From Lhasa revealed that Rampa had an audience who would believe anything he said. In a third book, *The Rampa Story*, he continued Rampa's autobiography from the point where he had left off at the end of the previous book – where Rampa was a prisoner of the Japanese and narrowly escaped execution – and described how he crossed into Russian territory, was imprisoned in the Lubianka prison in Moscow, then escaped, via Europe, to America. But the high point of the book is its seventh chapter, where Rampa described leaving his body and soaring to the astral plane, where his old teacher, the Lama Mingyar Dondup, was awaiting him. Dondup tells him: "Your present body has suffered too much and will shortly fail. We have established a contact in the Land of England. This person wants to leave his body. We took him to the astral plane and discussed matters with him. He is *most* anxious to leave, and will do all we require . . ." Later, in London, Rampa is able to study the history of this Englishman in the Akashic record – the record on the "psychic ether" of everything that has ever happened (Madame Blavatsky invented the phrase). Then Rampa goes to the Englishman's bedroom – in his astral body – and converses with the English-man's astral body, agreeing to the swap. The Englishman tells him how he fell on his head and stood up to find himself stand-ing by his physical body, connected to it by a silver cord. Then he saw a Tibetan walking towards him. "I have come to you because I want your body . . ." And, after thinking it over, the unselfish Mr Hoskins decided that he had had enough of life anyway, and that he might as well hand over his body to someone who could make better use of it. The lama instructs him to climb the tree again and fall on his head in order to loosen the cord. Then a lama takes Hoskins by the arm and floats away with him to heaven, while Lobsang Rampa squeezes himself into the vacated body with a sensation of suffocating. Rampa finds himself confronted with such problems as riding a bicycle and claiming unemployment benefit. Life was difficult and painful until he met a literary agent and outlined the story of *The Third Eye* . . .

The book should end there, but there is more to tell. After finishing *The Third Eye* he has a heart attack, and he and his wife move to Ireland. (It is not clear why the climate of Ireland should be better for heart ailments than England.) There he wrote *Doctor*

From Lhasa. But the task was still not completed; he had to go on and tell *The Rampa Story*. Driven out of Ireland by income tax problems, he moves to Canada. There he receives a telepathic message: he must go on writing and tell the *Truth*. "Write it down, Lobsang, and also write of what *could* be in Tibet." And he continues to tell a story of how Truth found it difficult to obtain an audience until he borrowed the coloured garments of Parable. After that, Truth was welcome everywhere . . . (This, presumably, is intended as a reply to people who claim that Rampa's Tibet is unlike the real place; he can always claim he is talking in parables.) The book ends with a nasty vision of an atomic rocket, launched from Tibet by the Chinese. "Is it fantasy?" he asks. "It could be fact." The placing of the quotation suggests that it could refer to the whole Rampa story.

Rampa's explanations about his body swap must have convinced a fair number of readers, for he has gone on to produce several more books: *Cave of the Ancients*, *Living With a Lama*, *You-Forever*, *Wisdom of the Ancients*, and a book called *My Visit to Venus* in which he describes how he was taken to Venus in a flying saucer and spent some time studying the history of Atlantis and Lemuria in its skyscraper cities. (Space probes have since shown that Venus is too hot to support any form of life.)

It seems that Hoskins has constructed a story that cannot be disproved by the sceptics, since he has an answer to every objection. Yet there still remain a few matters that need explaining. Why did Hoskins tell his neighbours, a Mr and Mrs Boxall, in 1943 or 1944 that he had been a pilot in the Chinese air force? This was some years before his first "meeting" with Lobsang Rampa. And why, in 1948, did he change his name to Dr Carl Kuon Suo, rather than to Lobsang Rampa? Of one thing we can be sure: Rampa would have no difficulty providing answers that would satisfy the faithful.

Carlos Castaneda – The Don Juan Hoax

In 1968, the University of California Press published a book called *The Teachings of Don Juan: A Yacqui Way of Knowledge*, by Carlos Castaneda. Castaneda had entered the University of California – UCLA – as an undergraduate in 1959, and had received a BA in anthropology in 1962. The University of California Press accepted *The Teachings of Don Juan* as an authentic account of Castaneda's 'field work' in Mexico. The book told how, when he was an anthropology student, in 1960, Castaneda made several trips to the southwest to collect information on medicinal plants used by the Indians. At a Greyhound bus station, he was introduced to a white-haired old Indian who apparently knew all about peyote, the hallucinogenic plant. Although this first meeting was abortive – Castaneda tells with touching honesty how he "talked nonsense" to Don Juan – Castaneda made a point of finding out where Don Juan lived and was finally accepted by the old *brujo* (medicine man or magician) as a pupil, a sorcerer's apprentice. The teaching begins with an episode in which Don Juan tells Castaneda to look for his "spot", a place where he will feel more comfortable and at ease than anywhere else; he told Castaneda that there was such a spot within the confines of the porch. Castaneda describes how he spent all night trying different spots, lying in them, but felt no difference. Don Juan told him he ought to use his eyes. After this, he began to distinguish various colours in the darkness: purple, green and verdigris. When he finally chose one of these, he felt sick and had a sensation of panic. Exhausted, he lay by the wall and fell asleep. When he woke up, Don Juan told him that he had found his "spot" – where he had fallen asleep. The other spot was bad for him, the "enemy".

This episode helps to explain the subsequent popularity of the book which was published in paperback by Ballantine Books and sold 300,000 copies. Don Juan is a teacher, a man of knowledge – the kind of person that every undergraduate dreams of finding – and he introduces Castaneda to the most astonishing experiences. When Castaneda first eats a peyote button, he experiences amazing sensations and plays with a mescalito god whose mind he can read. On a later occasion he sees the mescalito god himself as a green man with a pointed head. When Don Juan teaches him how to make a paste from the *datura* plant – Jimson weed – he anoints himself with it and has a sensation of flying through the air at a great speed. (In their book *The Search for Abraxas*, Stephen Skinner and Neville Drury speculate that witches of the Middle Ages used a similar concoction and that this explains how they "flew" to Witches' Sabbaths.) He wakes up to find himself half a mile from Don Juan's house.

During the period when the book was published every young

American was smoking pot and experimenting with "psyche-delic drugs" like mescalin and LSD, and Timothy Leary was advising American youth to "Turn on, tune in, drop out." This apparently factual account of semi-magical experiences became as popular as Tolkien's *Lord of the Rings* and for much the same reason: it was escapist literature, but, more important, it claimed to be true.

Reviews were excellent. Anthropologists and scientists took the book seriously – the psychologist Carl Rogers called it "one of the most vividly convincing documents I have read". The philosopher Joseph Margolis said that either Castaneda was recording an encounter with a master or he was himself a master.

This was clearly a success that had to be followed up. *A Separate Reality* described how Castaneda had returned to Don Juan in 1968. A giant gnat, 100 feet high, circles round him; he rides on a bubble; he has a semi-mystical experience in which he hears extraordinary sounds and sees the sorcerer's "ally", who shows him a "spirit catcher".

The demand for more about Don Juan remained strong but Castaneda had a problem. *A Separate Reality* came to an end in 1970 and was published in 1971; for the time being he had used up his Don Juan material. But not quite. He explained in his next book, *Journey to Ixtlan* (1973) that he had made the erroneous assumption that the glimpses of reality that Don Juan had given him could only be obtained through drugs. Now he realized he was mistaken. In fact, Don Juan had told him many other things during his years as a sorcerer's apprentice, but although he had written these non-drug revelations in his "field notes", he had failed to see their significance. Now, looking back over his notes, he realized that he had a vast amount of material that showed that drugs were not necessary for achieving unusual states of consciousness. So *Journey to Ixtlan* goes back to 1960 and recounts still more astonishing adventures: he has strange visions, mountains move, and Castaneda describes his encoun-ter with a sinister but beautiful sorceress named Catalina.

In retrospect, it seems that Castaneda made his first major error in writing *Ixtlan* (although it was one that, according to his agent, made him $1 million). The "lost" field notes sound just a little too convenient. Yet, oddly enough, scholars continued to take him seriously. Mary Douglas, a professor of social anthropology, wrote an article about the first three books called "The Authenticity of Castaneda", which concluded: "From these ideas we are likely to get advances in anthropology." Moreover,

UCLA granted Castaneda his Ph.D for *Ixtlan* and he lectured on anthropology on the Irvine campus.

If reviewers would swallow Ixtlan they would clearly swallow anything. Now that enough time had elapsed since his last visit to Sonora, Castaneda could renew his acquaintance with Don Juan and bring his revelations up to date. But *Tales of Power* (1974) seems to indicate that either Castaneda or his publisher felt that the game would soon be up. The dust jacket declares that this is the "culmination of Castaneda's extraordinary initiation into the mysteries of sorcery". At last, it declares, Castaneda completes his long journey into the world of magic and the book ends with a "deeply moving farewell". In many ways *Tales of Power* – covering a period of a few days in 1971 – is more rewarding than the earlier Don Juan books because it attempts to present a philosophical theory about reality, in terms of two concepts which Don Juan calls the *tonal* and the *nagual*. The *tonal* is "everything we are", while the *nagual* is pure potentiality. The *tonal* is the pair of Kantian spectacles through which we see the world and impose meaning on it; it consists mainly of linguistic concepts and preconceptions. These conceptions are illustrated with the usual tales of magical experiences: Don Juan shows him a squirrel wearing spectacles which swells until it is enormous and then disappears; Carlos walks a few steps and finds he has travelled one and a half miles.

It was at this point, after publication of *Tales of Power*, that a teacher of psychology named Richard de Mille was persuaded by his niece to read all four Don Juan books one after the other. ("You have to take the whole trip.") *The Teachings* struck him as authentic and factual. *A Separate Reality* raised doubts; it was better written but somehow not so "factual". And the character of Don Juan had changed; he seemed more "joky", while in the first book he had been grimly serious. Of course, Castaneda himself had already mentioned this. "He clowned during the truly crucial moments of the second cycle." But when he came to *Ixtlan*, De Mille was puzzled to find that the Don Juan of the notes made as early as 1960 was as much of a humorist and a clown as the later Don Juan. Made suspicious by this inconsistency, he began to study the books more closely and soon found contradictions that confirmed his feeling that he was dealing with fiction rather than fact. A friend pointed out one obvious inconsistency: in October 1968 Castaneda leaves his car and walks for two days to the shack of Don Juan's fellow sorcerer Don Genaro but when they walk out of the shack they climb straight into the car. De Mille discovered a similar contradiction. In *Ixtlan*, Castaneda goes looking for a certain bush on Don Juan's instructions and finds it has vanished; then Don Juan leads him to the far side of the hill, where he finds the bush he thought he had seen earlier on the other side. Later Don Juan tells him, "This morning you *saw*", giving the word special emphasis. Yet six years later, in 1968, Castaneda is represented (in *A Separate Reality*) as asking Don Juan what is *seeing* and Don Juan tells him that in order to find out, Castaneda must *see* for himself. He seems to have forgotten that Castaneda had an experience of *seeing* six years earlier. And while it is understandable that Don Juan should forget, it is quite incomprehensible that Castaneda should.

These and many similar inconsistencies convinced De Mille that one of the two books had to be fiction, or that, more probably, they both were. He published his results in a book called *Castaneda's Journey* in 1976 and it led many anthropologists who had taken Don Juan seriously to change their views. Joseph K. Long felt "betrayed by Castaneda". Marcello Truzzi, on the other hand, admitted that he had felt aghast at the initial reactions of the scientific community to Castaneda's books and that he was equally outraged by the lack of serious reaction now De Mille had exposed them as frauds.

Castaneda's admirers were mostly infuriated. Their feeling was that even if Castaneda had invented Don Juan, the books were full of genuine knowledge and wisdom, and should be gratefully accepted as works of genius. One lady wrote to De Mille saying she was convinced he didn't exist and asking him to prove it. De Mille had, in fact, accepted that the Don Juan books had a certain merit, both as literature and as "occult teaching". But when, in 1980, he edited a large volume of essays on the "Castaneda hoax" called *The Don Juan Papers* his admiration had visibly dwindled. Some of the essays present an even more devastating exposure of Castaneda than De Mille's original volume: for example, Hans Sebald, an anthropologist who had spent a great deal of time in the southwestern desert, pointed out that it was so hot from June to September that no one with any sense ventures into it; dehydration and exhaustion follow within hours. Yet according to Castaneda, he and Don Juan wandered around the desert for days, engaged in conversation and ignoring the heat. Sebald goes on to demolish Castaneda's animal lore: "Where . . . are the nine-inch centipedes, the tarantulas big as saucers? Where are the king snakes, scarlet racers, chuckawallas, horned toads, gila monsters . . ." A lengthy appendix to *The Don Juan Papers* cites hundreds of parallel passages from the Castaneda books and from other works on anthropology and mysticism that bear a close resemblance. The book establishes, beyond all possible doubt, that the Castaneda books are a fraud.

Richard De Mille's own researches revealed that Carlos Arana was born in 1925 (not 1935, as he has told an interviewer) in Cajamarca, Peru, and came to San Francisco in 1951, leaving behind a Chinese-Peruvian wife who was pregnant. In 1955 he met Damon Runyon's distant cousin Margaret and married her; they separated after six months. In 1959 he became an undergraduate at UCLA and the Don Juan story begins . . .

Castaneda himself has proved to be an extremely elusive individual, as *Time* discovered when it sent a reporter to interview him in 1973. In the light of De Mille's discoveries this is easy to understand. Castaneda's career can be compared to that of the Shakespeare forger, William Ireland who began by forging a few Shakespeare signatures to gain his father's attention and found himself forced to continue until he had concocted a whole new Shakespeare play, which brought about his discovery and downfall. Castaneda presumably produced the original *Teachings of Don Juan* as a mild form of hoax. The publication by Ballantine launched him, whether he liked it or not, on the career of a trickster and confidence man. It would, perhaps, have been wiser to stop after *Ixtlan*, or possibly *Tales of Power*. But the demand for more Don Juan books has presumably overcome his caution. In fact, the fifth, *The Second Ring of Power*, reads so obviously as fiction that it raises the suspicion that Castaneda wanted to explode his own legend. But he shows caution in offering no dates, no doubt to escape De Mille's vigilant eye. Castaneda tells how he went back to Mexico looking for Don Juan and instead encountered one of his disciples, a sorceress named Madame Solitude. Last time he saw her she was fat and ugly and in her fifties; now she is young, slim and vital, and within a few pages, she has torn off her skirt and invited him to make love to her – an invitation he wisely resists. Then Castaneda somehow invokes his own double out of his head – not a mild-mannered scholar but a super-male authority figure who hits Madame Solitude on the head and almost kills her. Then four lady disciples arrive and make more assaults on Castaneda, which he overcomes, and after which they all encounter other-worldly beings . . .

In his sixth book, *The Eagle's Nest*, Castaneda returns to Mexico as "a sorcerous leader and figure in his own right" (as the blurb says) and enters into a closer relationship with one of the female sorcerers of the previous book, La Gorda. The two of them develop the ability to dream in unison. It is clear that, since writing the earlier book, Castaneda has come across split-brain physiology and now we hear a great deal about the right and left sides of a human being, the left being the *nagual* and the right the *tonal*. De Mille had pointed out that the Don Juan books seem to chart Castaneda's literary and philosophical discoveries over the years and this book confirms it. For those who read it with the certainty that the previous books were a hoax, it seems an insult to the intelligence. But it seems to demonstrate that Castaneda can continue indefinitely spinning fantasies for those who regard him as the greatest of modern gurus.

HOW HAVE THE MIGHTY FALLEN

They may be famous but it doesn't mean they can get away with anything – even if they may think so. A rail ticket scandal, where a "professor" was found not to have a ticket for his journey and then tried to buy one from the ticket collector for only part of his journey; or the famous actor who tried to swindle more petrol rations from the government for his Rolls-Royce during the war. Because they were in the public eye, they thought they were above the law.

Heinrich Schliemann – The Great Troy Hoax

During his lifetime and for more than eighty years after his death, in 1890, the name of Heinrich Schliemann – "the man who found Troy" – remained untainted by the slightest breath of scandal. The discovery in the late 1970s that he was, in fact, a pathological liar and a crook caused tremendous reverberations in the world of archaeology.

Heinrich Schliemann, the man who was to be described as "the creator of prehistoric Greek archaeology", was born on 6 January 1822 at Neu-Buckow, Germany, the son of a country parson. It was from his father that young Heinrich first heard about ancient history. In his autobiography, he tells of the crucial event of his childhood: how, at the age of seven, he received for Christmas a copy of Jerrer's *Universal History*, with an illustration showing Troy in flames. Surely, reasoned the young Heinrich, walls so mighty could not have been destroyed? They must still be there . . .

His childhood was not happy. One of seven children, he was shattered by the death of his mother and by the scandal when his father took a maidservant as a mistress, and later when his father was accused of misappropriating church funds and dismissed (he was later exonerated). Heinrich and his father had many bitter arguments. At the age of fourteen, Heinrich became a grocer's assistant and had to work fourteen hours a day. Suffering from tuberculosis, he gave up his job and became a cabin boy on a boat sailing for South America; it was shipwrecked and he found himself eventually in Amsterdam. There he became a clerk, taught himself English and went on to learn nine foreign languages in six years. At the age of twenty-four, he was sent to Russia as the chief agent of an Amsterdam merchant. In 1850, he sailed for America to claim the estate of his brother Louis, who had died in California. He records in his diary that he called on the President of the United States, Zachary Taylor, and had an hour-and-a-half's conversation with him, meeting his family and being treated with great kindness. Then he went on to Sacramento, where he set up an office to buy gold dust from the miners for the gold rush was at its height at that time. He amassed a fortune of $350,000 as a result. He noted in his diary that he was in San Francisco during the great fire of 1851. Back in Europe, he married a Russian beauty but she did not care for archaeology or travel and they eventually divorced. Schliemann visited Greece for the first time at the age of thirty-seven. Four years later, he was rich enough to realize the ambition of a lifetime and to become an archaeologist. He studied archaeology in Paris and travelled extensively in the Mediterranean area. In 1868 he visited Mycenae, in Greece – the home of Agamemnon – and propounded a startling theory that the royal tombs would be found within the ruined walls of the citadel, and not, as the Greek geographer Pausanias stated, outside the walls. Soon after this he was awarded his doctorate by the University of Rostock, writing his thesis, according to his autobiography, in classical Greek.

An old friend, Archbishop Theoclitus Vimbos of Athens, helped him find a Greek wife. A sixteen-year-old schoolgirl, Sophia Engastromenos, was selected for him; her parents agreed, and the couple were married. Her parents were much impressed by his tales, particularly the story about the fire of San Francisco.

Schliemann was convinced that Troy really existed and that it was no legend, as many scholars believed. Those scholars who accepted the existence of Troy – ancient Ilion – thought that it was situated three hours from the sea near Bunarbashi, on the Balidagh, in a mountain fastness. On the evidence of Homer, Schliemann disagreed – Homer's heroes had ridden between Troy and the coast several times a day. He decided that the site of Troy was probably a mound at a place called Hissarlik, an hour from the sea. He obtained permission from the Turkish authorities to dig there and started in 1871, with a gang of eighty men.

It must be admitted that, as an archaeologist, Schliemann does not rate very highly. His method was as subtle as a bulldozer. He simply ordered his men to cut a deep trench through the mound. He soon discovered that the mound contained several cities, one on top of the other. Convinced that ancient Troy must be the lowest, he ordered his workmen to dig straight down to it, destroying all the ruins above, including those of the city archaeologists now know to be the Troy of Homer. The city Schliemann thought was the Troy of King Priam was in reality many centuries earlier.

In the following year, Schliemann's workmen sliced the top off the mound. Many discoveries came to light, but so far, there was no sign of the gold that Homer talked about. At least he found structures he identified as the royal palace, the wall of the gods, and the ramp leading to the Scaean Gate.

By the spring of 1883 he was becoming worried; he had still found no gold and he had agreed to end the excavations in June. Then, one day in May he thought he glimpsed a copper vessel through a hole in a wall. What followed has been told in breathless detail by more than twenty biographers of Schliemann. Afraid that his workmen would make off with part of his find, he waited until they were eating, then asked Sophia to help him remove the "treasure". Indifferent to his danger for the wall above was made of loose masonry, he tore out the stones, aided by a large knife and, piece by piece, handed the marvellous gold objects – drinking vessels and jewellery – to his wife, who wrapped them in her shawl. Later, behind closed doors, Sophie was dressed in the jewels of Helen of Troy – Schliemann was later to take a photograph of her draped in the gold ornaments. In June he returned to Athens and finally announced his discovery of the treasure. It made him world

famous. He was later to excavate Mycenae, where his guess
about the situation of the tombs proved correct. He died in 1890,
at the age of sixty-eight. Sophia survived him by forty years.

That is the story of Heinrich Schliemann, and it has been retold
many times. Guides at Hissarlik still show fascinated tourists the
spot where Schliemann discovered the treasure of Priam, only a
few weeks before he was due to leave Troy for ever.

In 1972 William Calder, Professor of Classics at the University of Colorado, was asked to go to Schliemann's birthplace,
Neu-Buckow, to give a lecture on the hundred-and-fiftieth anni-
versary of his birth. Studying the various biographies of the great
man, he realized that about 90 per cent of their material came
from Schliemann himself. As soon as he began to check source
material, he discovered that Schliemann was rather less trust-
worthy than his admirers had assumed. Checking at the University of Rostock, Calder discovered that the doctoral thesis was
not, as Schliemann had declared, written in classical Greek; it
only had a short section in classical Greek and this was atrocious.
Calder checked on the story about calling on the President of the
United States and being kindly received; the reception at which
Schliemann claimed he was presented to six hundred guests
would certainly be mentioned in Washington newspapers. There
was nothing whatever – Schliemann had invented it.

Calder's lecture about these saddening discoveries was read
by David Trail, a classics professor at the University of California.
In San Francisco, he was able to check the records of the bankers
who had stored the gold dust that Schliemann had bought
from the miners in Sacramento and found suggestions that
Schliemann had systematically cheated them by sending them
short-weight consignments. Checking Schliemann's account of
the great fire of San Francisco, Trail discovered that Schliemann
had quoted the wrong date – he gave it as 4 June 1851 when it had
taken place on 4 May. Schliemann's papers are stored in Athens,
and Trail checked the diary. The page with the account of the fire
proved to have been glued in later. The page preceding it has
an entry in Spanish, which continues on the following page.
The account proved to have been culled from newspapers of
the time.

Calder's opinion was that Schliemann was a pathological liar
– a liar so convinced of his own romances that a lie-detector test
would probably have indicated he was telling the truth. Even
the story about seeing the pictures of Troy in a book he was
given for Christmas proved to be an invention, fabricated later
for Schliemann's book *Ilion*.

The diaries also revealed that there were doubts about the finding of the treasure. There was no entry for the discovery of the treasure; he speaks about it for the first time in an entry dated 17 June. In the published account, this entry is datelined from Troy. In the diary, "Athens" has been crossed out and "Troy" substituted. An entry that was a draft-account of the discovery for his German publishers fails to describe the treasure, with the exception of one gold cup, noted as having large handles and being shaped like a champagne glass, with a rounded bottom (the shape we would now describe as a hock glass). There is no such vessel among the treasure. The nearest to it is a kind of gold sauce boat with handles and the descriptions do not correspond. But Schliemann had unearthed many terracotta vessels that looked exactly like the "champagne glass" he described. It seems that he simply invented the item in order to give his publisher a foretaste of the treasure.

Further investigation revealed that Sophia was not present at the time Schliemann claims he found the treasure. She was in mourning for her father in Athens and did not return to Troy. And although excavations continued for two weeks after Schliemann claimed to have found the treasure – giving him plenty of time to describe it – there is nevertheless not a single description in his diary. The inference is that he did not find any treasure – at least, not in the manner he described.

But where did the treasure come from? Trail's conclusion was that the "treasure" was already back in Athens at the time Schliemann claims he discovered it. He was obliged by contract to share anything he found with the owners of the site, a Pasha and an American named Frank Calvert. What almost certainly happened is that Schliemann systematically cheated them, claiming he had found nothing, and smuggling his finds back to Athens – his letters often refer to objects that he failed to show to Calvert. In March, before the "finding" of the treasure,

---

Foremost American author William Faulkner was virtually a pathological liar. "You never knew when he was telling the truth" said his cousin. When he came back from World War I in 1918, he was wearing an officer's uniform, and walked with a limp, which he claimed had been caused in a plane crash in France. In fact, he had been a private in the Canadian Royal Air Force (in which he impersonated an Englishman) for less than six months, had never flown a plane and had not been out of the United States.

a letter mentions sixty gold rings – precisely the number of rings in the treasure.

That Schliemann found something is proved by the testimony of his trusted overseer, Nicolaos Yannakis, who later told an English antiquarian, William Borlase, that he had been with Schliemann at the time of the find and not Sophia. And the find contained no gold or jewellery – only a quantity of bronze objects, found in a stone enclosure outside the city wall.

So why did Schliemann do it? Psychoanalysts who have considered the problem have talked about his relationship with his father – the admiration combined with fear and dislike that compelled him to seek fame so that he could finally feel he had outstripped his father. This may or may not be true. All that is certain is that Schliemann craved fame and applause – his lie about the meeting with the President reveals the desire to impress. "We all bid for admiration with no intention of earning it," says Shaw. In his own devious way, Schliemann set out to earn it. He wanted to believe that he had found Homer's Troy; to complete the triumph he needed to find King Priam's treasure. And if the treasure did not exist, then it had to be made to exist. Only in this way could Schliemann achieve the kind of celebrity he craved.

But although these revelations reveal Schliemann as a crook and a liar, they leave one part of his reputation untouched: that strange, intuitive genius that led him to dig in exactly the right place, first at Hissarlik and later at Mycenae. He may have been a confidence man, but he was still, in spite of everything, "the creator of prehistoric Greek archaeology".

Oscar Wilde – "One must seek out what is most tragic"

Oscar Wilde's father, Sir William Wilde, was a constant subject of Dublin gossip and scandal. Known as "the Wilde knight", he was reputed to be the father of many illegitimate children – Bernard Shaw said he had a child in every farmhouse. In 1864 (when Oscar was ten), a libel case against his wife, Lady Jane Francesca Wilde, turned into a trial of Sir William, a leading physician, on a charge of raping a female patient.

Lady Jane had written a furious letter to a Dr Travers, Professor of Medical Jurisprudence at Trinity College, accusing his daughter of blackmailing Sir William and disseminating a pamphlet accusing him of "an intrigue" with her. The daughter, Miss Mary Josephine Travers, decided to sue; she wanted £2,000 damages.

When the case came up on 12 December 1864, the prosecution lost no time in informing the jury that "the particulars . . . are of so shocking a description that I wish to God it had devolved upon some other counsel to present them . . ." Having cured Miss Travers of ear trouble, Sir William had lent her books and money, bought her bonnets and dresses, taken her to lectures and exhibitions, and finally raped her in his consulting room. (One lady fainted and had to be carried out of the courtroom.) She had gone to him to be treated for a burn on her neck and in the course of the treatment had fainted. She had awakened to realize that, alas, she was no longer a maid. Sir William had urged her to keep this quiet. Miss Travers had gone to Lady Wilde to complain but had been treated with scorn. She had attempted suicide with a dose of laudanum (opium) but had recovered. To redress her wrongs, she had printed the pamphlet accusing Sir William of taking advantage of her. When Miss Travers was called to the witness box, the judge told the ladies in the gallery that any who wished to do so might leave; no one did. Then the prosecution asked the question, "When you were unconscious was your person – er – violated?" and Miss Travers replied, "It was."

But the cross-examination was damaging. Why, Miss Travers was asked, did she accuse Sir William of violating her after administering chloroform? Miss Travers agreed that it had not happened like that but could give no excuse for printing a false version. Then Sergeant Sullivan, in Sir William's defence, went in for the kill. Had the alleged assault happened on other occasions? Blushing, Miss Travers admitted that it had. She explained that Sir William had led up to it with "rudeness and roughness". But the jury must have found it a little odd that a girl who had been raped while unconscious should give the rapist the opportunity to do it several times more – even with rudeness and roughness. The jury returned to say that they found Lady Wilde's letter libellous, which implied that her husband was guilty, but they awarded Miss Travers only one farthing in damages. The Wildes had to pay the considerable costs. Oscar should have learned from the example of Miss

Travers that it can be dangerous to accuse someone of libel; it can lead to embarrassing counterclaims.

Oscar Wilde was born on 16 October 1854. At seventeen he won a scholarship to Trinity College, Dublin. There he came under the influence of the remarkable Professor of Ancient History, the Reverend John Pentland Mahaffy. It was from Mahaffy that Wilde picked up his passionate love of the classics, particularly those of ancient Greece. At this time, Wilde's sexual inclinations were basically heterosexual, with a mild touch of ambivalence, such as may also be noted in Lord Byron. And, as with Byron, his intellectual and emotional appreciation of Mediterranean pederasty laid the foundations for his later development.

At Trinity, and later at Oxford, Wilde was brilliant rather than hardworking. He had the typical charm of those born under Libra. At Oxford he came under the influence of John Ruskin, who taught him to appreciate painting and architecture, and Walter Pater, who taught that the basic aim of life is to live with "a hard, gem-like flame" and who revived Victor Cousin's phrase "Art for art's sake". Pater confirmed Wilde in that intellectual elitism he had picked up from Mahaffy, the feeling that the true aristocrats of this world are the men of brilliance and imagination. And when, at the age of twenty-three, he accompanied Mahaffy on a tour of Greece, the experience confirmed his conviction that beauty is the only ultimate value.

In his last year at Oxford, Wilde wrote to a friend: "I'll be famous, and if not famous, I'll be notorious." And when he went to join his mother in London – his father had died – he decided to become both at once. His elder brother Willie, who had become a journalist, introduced him to editors, and Wilde published some poems. He fell in love with the famous beauty Lily Langtry, mistress of the Prince of Wales, and wrote her a number of poems. When a volume of verse failed to bring him fame, he announced that a revolution in dress was more important than a revolution in morals, and began to call attention to himself with a velvet coat edged with braid, knee breeches and black silk stockings. He was one of the first great modern experts in the art of self-publicity. By 1880, he was being regularly satirized in *Punch*. In the following years, W.S. Gilbert portrayed him in *Patience* as the mediocre poet Bunthorne. Gilbert no doubt thought he was being cruel but Wilde was delighted with the notoriety it brought him. This led to a request to go on a lecture tour of America. Wilde arrived in New York with the typical comment, "I have nothing to declare but my genius." He was not particularly fond of America. Later, when he heard that Rossetti had given someone the money to go to America he commented, "Of course, if one had enough money to go to America, one wouldn't go."

In 1833, after a lecture tour of Scotland, he announced his engagement to Constance Lloyd, daughter of an Irish barrister, a beautiful and sweet-natured girl. They were deeply in love and on the morning after his wedding night, Wilde strolled in Paris with his friend Robert Sherard and described his sexual pleasures with embarrassing detail. Two sons were born of the marriage.

It was about two years after his marriage that Wilde made a shattering discovery. At Oxford he had contracted syphilis from a prostitute and had been "cured" with mercury treatment (which had discoloured his teeth). Now he learned that the spirochetes were still in his bloodstream. With modern treatment he would have been cured in a weekend. As it was, he felt that he had to give up sex with Constance. At about this time he met a seventeen-year-old youth named Robert ("Robbie") Ross, who was amusing, cultivated and amiable. Ross later claimed that he was the first male Wilde had been to bed with.

Success was slow in arriving; early plays like *Vera, or the Nihilists* and *The Duchess of Padua* failed to make an impression. He was literary critic for the *Pall Mall Gazette*, and he became the editor of a magazine called *The Lady's World* (renamed *Woman's World*). He wrote short stories, children's stories, poems and essays. Finally, in 1891, when he was thirty-seven, *The Picture of Dorian Gray* appeared and caused a degree of public outrage that he must have found highly satisfying. In the following year, *Lady Windermere's Fan* went on at the St James's Theatre and finally made Wilde rich as well as famous.

In the year of *Dorian Gray*, Wilde met a handsome young aristocrat of twenty-two, Lord Alfred Douglas, son of the Marquess of Queensberry (responsible for the Queensberry Rules in boxing). Soon they were inseparable, dining in expensive restaurants, spending weekends at country houses, attending art exhibitions and first nights. Inevitably, they slept together, although Douglas later insisted that there was no sodomy – only mutual masturbation and a certain amount of oral sex. "Bosie" (as Wilde called Lord Alfred) was himself a pederast and preferred boys to older men. The French novelist André Gide has described how Wilde and Douglas were responsible for his own downfall. For years he had been struggling against his homosexuality. In Algiers, he discovered that Wilde and

Douglas were staying in the same hotel – he had met Wilde
in Paris. Before they set out for the evening, Douglas remarked
to Gide, "I hope you are like me. I have a horror of women. I
only like boys." Wilde told the "vile procurer who came to pilot
us through the town" that he wanted to see some Arab boys
and added "as beautiful as bronze statues". But a brawl broke
out in the café the procurer took them to and they went home
disappointed. Soon after, Douglas went off to Blidah, where
he was hoping to buy an Arab boy from his family (in fact,
the boy ran away with a woman). Wilde took Gide out for
another evening in the Casbah, and in a little café, a beautiful
Arab youth came and played on a flute for them. Then Wilde
led Gide outside and whispered in his ear, "Dear, would you
like the little musician?" and Gide, his voice choking, answered,
"Yes." Later, the youth came to a hotel room and Gide wrote:
"My joy was unbounded, and I cannot imagine it greater even
if love had been added."

Back in London, Wilde met Alfred Taylor, an upper-class
young man who had spent his way through a fortune. Taylor
was a homosexual who liked to dress as a woman; he burned
incense in his dimly lit apartment and spent his days picking
up young men – many of them telegraph boys of the kind who
figured in the Cleveland Street scandal – and taking them back to
his room for sex. The first youth Taylor picked up for Wilde was a
twenty-year-old named Sidney Mavor – known in his own circle
as Jenny. The following evening, Wilde took Taylor, Douglas
and "Jenny" to dinner at Kettner's and afterwards Wilde and
Mavor went to a hotel room together. It emerged later that
Wilde's idea of sex was to have the boy seated on his knee, while
he fondled his genitals and occasionally indulged in oral sex.
Wilde would tell them to imagine they were women and that he
was their lover, which suggests that his role was fundamentally
masculine and dominant. He disliked obviously feminine youths
– he commented once that having sex with coarse, masculine
types gave him a feeling of "dining with panthers". His appetite
seems to have been enormous – he told Beardsley once that he
had had five messenger boys in one evening and had kissed
them all over their bodies. "They were all dirty and appealed
to me for that reason."

Some time in 1893, Douglas gave a suit of clothes to an
unemployed clerk, who found in the pockets a number of letters
from Wilde. The result was an attempt to blackmail Wilde. "A
very curious construction can be put on that letter," said the
blackmailer, to which Wilde replied, "Art is rarely intelligible

to the criminal classes." When the blackmailer said he could get £60 for the letter from a certain man, Wilde advised him to go and sell it immediately. The astonished blackmailer relented and gave Wilde the letter back for nothing – an example of Wilde's extraordinary charm, which was based upon a fundamental kindliness.

Unfortunately, a copy of the letter fell into the hands of the Marquess of Queensberry who was particularly outraged by the sentence: "it is a marvel that those rose-red lips of yours should have been made no less for music of song than for the madness of kisses." Queensberry was an eccentric Scottish aristocrat – in *The Trial of Oscar Wilde* Montgomery Hyde calls him "arrogant, vain, conceited and ill tempered", and says that he was probably mentally unbalanced. One day when Queensberry saw Wilde and his son dining together at the Café Royal, he allowed himself to be persuaded to join them, and was dazzled by Wilde's charm, and told "Bosie" afterwards that he could understand why he loved him. The "rose-red lips" letter seems to have changed his mind and he wrote a furious letter ordering Douglas never to see Wilde again. Douglas replied with a telegram: "What a funny little man you are." Queensberry began to haunt the restaurants where Wilde and Douglas dined, threatening to thrash Wilde. One afternoon, the Marquess came to Wilde's house to order him to stop seeing his son. Wilde ordered him, and his bodyguard, out. Queensberry continued to persecute Wilde. He tried to get into the theatre on the first night of *The Importance of Being Earnest*, but was kept out by police. On 18 February 1895, he left his card at Wilde's club, the Albemarle, with a note written on it: "To Oscar Wilde, posing as a sodomite" [*sic*]. When he received it two weeks later, Wilde decided to sue. He went to see a solicitor, Charles Humphries, and assured him that the accusation of being a sodomite was untrue. (He may well have felt he was being honest – he was not, as we know, inclined to sodomy.) Humphries agreed to prosecute.

The first trial proved a disaster for Wilde. His old schoolfellow Edward Carson was defending. Wilde was brilliant and amusing in the witness box but when Carson declared in court that he would prove that Wilde brought boys to the Savoy Hotel, it was obvious that Queensberry had done his homework – or paid private detectives to do it – and the prosecution realized it would have to withdraw or suffer defeat. The Marquess was acquitted.

Now Wilde's friends begged him to flee the country. Homosexuality was a criminal offence. Wilde refused and there was undoubtedly a touch of masochism in his refusal. In fact, he seemed to identify himself with Christ and to believe that he had to live out a tragic destiny. ("One must always seek what is most tragic", Wilde had told Gide.) On the day the Marquess was acquitted, a warrant was issued for Wilde's arrest, on a charge of committing acts of indecency with various male persons. Taylor, who had refused to betray Wilde, was also charged with him. This, Montgomery Hyde insists, was unfair to Wilde, since the case against Taylor was a great deal stronger than that against Wilde. The second trial lasted from 6 April to 19 April 1895. The judge's summing up was in Wilde's favour – at least, he urged the jury to take into account every possible doubt of Wilde's guilt. The jury failed to reach an agreement. For the next three weeks Wilde was out on bail.

The third trial began on 20 May 1895, and this time, Taylor was tried separately. He was soon found guilty of indecent acts with males. Then Wilde stepped into the dock. Again, a succession of working-class young men described being taken back to Wilde's room. Sodomy sometimes took place; more often, mutual masturbation and fellatio. Wilde was again brilliant and amusing in the box but seldom convincing. Finally, as everyone by now expected, Wilde was found guilty on every count but one. He and Taylor were sentenced to two years' imprisonment with hard labour.

Wilde was taken to Reading jail. Standing around on the station platform he remarked to the guard, "If this is the way Her Majesty treats her prisoners, she doesn't deserve to have any." But the old sparkle had gone. The experience of prison almost drove Wilde insane. He wallowed in self-pity and wrote a long letter – in fact, a short book – to Alfred Douglas, accusing him of his ruin. It was later published, in an expurgated version, as *De Profundis*. His hard labour consisted in picking oakum (that is unpicking old ropes for caulking boats). He served every day of his sentence and was finally released on 19 May 1897.

The desire to write had vanished. "Something is killed in me", he told Robbie Ross. Constance Wilde died in a nursing home in Genoa after an operation to correct a spinal injury, soon after reading Wilde's long poem *The Ballad of Reading Gaol*. Wilde went to Dieppe, where he bumped into the poet Ernest Dowson, who persuaded him to go to a brothel. Wilde did not enjoy it. "The first in these ten years – and it will be the last," he told Dowson. "It was like cold mutton." He lived in Paris under the name of Sebastian Melmoth – borrowing the name from the Gothic novel *Melmoth the Wanderer* by Maturin – and died in poverty in a cheap

> The poet Algernon Charles Swinburne scandalized the Victorians by writing poetry that was frankly sensuous. But he himself had little or no interest in normal sex; he was obsessed by flogging, and regularly attended a brothel in St John's wood to be flogged by prostitutes dressed up as governesses. The American actress Ada Mencken accepted a fee of £10 to seduce him from his friend Rossetti, but returned the money with a confession of failure; she said she had been unable to persuade Swinburne that biting was no substitute for intercourse.

hotel on the Left Bank on 30 November 1900, telling a friend who came to see him, "I am dying beyond my means."

Ivor Novello – The Red Rolls-Royce Scandal

In April 1944, a year before the end of World War II, newspapers all over England carried headlines: Famous Actor Jailed For Petrol Offence. Ivor Novello, Britain's most famous matinée idol, had been sentenced to two months' imprisonment for an offence that amounted to fraud.

Ivor Novello was born David Ivor Davies in Cardiff, Wales, the son of an accountant and a music teacher. He was taught singing by his mother and proved to be brilliantly gifted. At the age of ten he took first prize for singing at a National Eisteddfod and his soprano voice won him a singing scholarship to Magdalen College, Oxford. He wanted to become a composer and conductor. His first song was published when he was sixteen, and was performed – without much success – at the Royal Albert Hall in London with Novello as accompanist. His first successful song, "The Little Damozel", appeared when he was seventeen, and was soon being sung by every soprano in the country. At this time, he also moved to London, supported by a modest income from his songs. He became famous at twenty-one, in 1914, with the song "Keep the Home Fires Burning", which became almost a second national anthem during World War I.

The singer, John McCormick, earned £20,000 from his recording of this song alone.

During the war Novello served in the Royal Naval Air Service but after two crashes he was transferred to the Air Ministry. There, in 1916, he wrote half the music for a show called *Theodore and Co.* produced by the actor George Grossmith. His fellow composer was Jerome Kern. The show ran for eighteen months at the Gaiety.

After the war, Novello was asked if he would act in a film *The Call of the Blood* which was filmed in Rome. It was an immense success. Novello had exactly the right kind of romantic good looks for a silent screen star and acting ability was hardly required – although he had his share of that too. In the 1920s he was a film star, an actor-manager, a composer and a playwright. People argued whether he or John Barrymore had "the world's most handsome profile". He starred in Hitchcock's "first true film" *The Lodger* in 1926 – it has become a classic of the silent cinema. But it was in 1935 that he achieved a new dimension of fame with *Glamorous Night,* a combination of drama and musical with lavish spectacle. His formula was escapist romance and it was exactly what the audiences of the 1930s craved. *Careless Rapture* (1936) and *The Dancing Years* (1939) repeated the success. When World War II broke out in 1939, he had a luxurious flat in the Aldwych and a country home near Maidenhead. He was driven around in a red Rolls-Royce inscribed with his initials in black.

As the petrol shortage increased, it became increasingly difficult for Novello to travel from London to his country home for the weekend. His secretary wrote to the Regional Transport Commissioner's office to request extra petrol for him to drive to Maidenhead on the grounds that he needed to spend the weekends there writing his plays. The application was twice turned down. Just before Christmas 1942, Novello went into his dressing room where there was a crowd of admirers and asked despondently, "Anyone want a Rolls? Mine's no good to me."

Among the admirers in the room was a dumpy, middle-aged woman who had adored Novello from afar for years and gradually managed to get herself accepted among his retinue. He knew her as Grace Walton but her real name was Dora Constable. She now told Novello that she might be able to solve his problem. She was, she said, the secretary of the managing director of a firm with an office at Reading. She suggested that she might be able to apply for a special licence if the car was transferred to her firm for "war work". All this was arranged by Novello's secretary.

Ivor Novello as the mysterious stranger in the film "The Lodger"

The car was formally transferred into the firm's name; the firm even took over the insurance policy. Then Dora Constable wrote to the Regional Transport Commissioner to ask for a licence to "facilitate speedier transport by the managing director and his staff between our many works and factories". A few weeks later she collected the permit and handed it to Novello. He was effusively grateful and gave her a pair of earrings that had belonged to his mother, who had recently died.

Whether the firm actually made use of the initialled Rolls-Royce is not clear. Novello's biographer Peter Noble implies that it did, and that Novello then simply used the car "from time to time" to take him from London to Maidenhead. But if this is so, then it is difficult to see why the firm was shocked to discover that it was supposed to be the owner of Ivor Novello's Rolls-Royce. For this is what happened in October 1943, almost two years after Novello had received his permit. The managing director of the firm rang Novello and asked him to come to his office. On arrival, he learned that his admirer was not called Grace Walton but Dora Constable, and that she was not the managing director's secretary but a filing clerk. The firm knew nothing whatever about the deal with the Rolls-Royce.

Novello realized that he could be in serious trouble. Not long before, the bandleader Jack Hylton had been fined £155 and sentenced to two weeks in jail for a similar petrol-rationing offence. (In the event the jail sentence was quashed.)

Novello decided against a cover-up – he felt it was not his fault. He informed the authorities what had happened and so did the firm. An inspector from the Fuel Ministry came to see him and Novello rather ungallantly put all the blame on Dora Constable, saying it was her idea and that he had no suspicion that he was doing anything illegal. This, of course, was nonsense; he knew he was using a false permit for his petrol. His waspishness backfired. When his remarks were repeated to Dora Constable, she replied indignantly that Novello was being unfair. He had known exactly what he was doing and even made various suggestions about the transfer. "He was willing to do anything crooked as long as he had the use of the car."

With a statement like that, the authorities had to act. On 24 March 1944, Novello was summoned to appear at Bow Street Court. He went to pieces and protested, "The suggestion of my conspiring with a person of this woman's type is repugnant." But it was too late. On 24 April 1944, he stood in the dock at Bow Street alongside Dora Constable. His self-pitying remarks were quoted to the magistrate. The managing director of the firm went into the witness box and admitted, "Novello was deceived as completely as I was."

Novello gave one of his worst performances in the witness box. He was muddled and panic-stricken, and he gave the unfortunate impression that he was trying to unload the blame on to Dora Constable. The judge was an old-fashioned gentleman and there can be no doubt that Novello's attempt to dodge the blame revolted him. Dora Constable was fined £50 with £25 costs. Novello was fined £100. But, added Mr Justice McKenna, "that would obviously be no punishment for a man like you, so I sentence you to eight weeks' imprisonment." Novello was granted bail, pending an appeal. Shattered and stricken, he staggered from the court.

Two months later, on 16 May 1944, the appeal was heard at the London Sessions courthouse. The Chairman of the appeals committee was Mr Eustace Fulton who had quashed Jack Hylton's prison sentence. This time he was not in such a lenient mood. When Novello's secretary Fred Allen said that he had no suspicion there was anything wrong about the car transaction, "otherwise I wouldn't have touched the damn thing", Fulton rebuked him for the use of "damn". Allen stammered nervously and Fulton snapped, "Oh, get on!" The defending solicitor said, "I am sorry your Lordship shows signs of impatience." The judge snorted, "I have shown every patience." It did not bode well for Novello. And in spite of some distinguished character witnesses – Sir Lewis Casson, Dame Sybil Thorndike, Sir Edward Marsh – the most Fulton would concede was that Novello's sentence was perhaps too long and halved it to four weeks. As Novello left the court he turned and flung open his arms "in a gesture of infinite despair".

Novello was not a good prisoner. Although the authorities at Wormwood Scrubs leaned over backwards to treat him kindly – he was placed in charge of the prison choir – he almost went insane with despair and he plunged into extravagant self-pity. When he was released on 13 June 1944 he looked thin and haggard. A week later, he returned to the stage in *The Dancing Years* and was cheered by a sympathetic audience who delayed the start of the show by ten minutes. His biographer Peter Noble is nevertheless convinced that the jail sentence should be regarded as a tragedy. Novello died seven years later of a heart attack at the age of fifty-eight. He was to write three more successes after his prison sentence: *Perchance to Dream, King's Rhapsody* and *Gay's the Word*. Noble believes the sentence shortened his life. In *Scales of Justice*, Fenton Bresler speculates that the prison sentence also cost Novello the knighthood that crowned the careers of most of his successful theatrical contemporaries.

Yet for the objective observer, it is hard to feel too much pity for Novello. His own behaviour was almost certainly responsible for the prison sentence. The obvious self-pity, the attempt to lay the blame on his admirer, who showed altogether more dignity when she decided not to testify, undoubtedly produced a mood of impatience in both judges. They probably felt that he was a spoiled brat who deserved a rap on the knuckles. Novello's real problem was that his life had been an almost unbroken run of success and until he was middle aged he always had his adored mother to give him approval and moral support. The result was that he never really grew up. And, like a certain type of homosexual, he was prone to self-pity and self-dramatization. He once told Peter Noble, "I have a suspicion that Fate has a sense of humour, and a rather malicious one. Fate says, 'Ah, that boy's had a success. He is getting a bit above himself. Now for a few slips!'" A little more of this attitude might have averted the prison sentence or at least made it more bearable.

"Professor" C.E.M. Joad – The Rail-Ticket Scandal

When "Professor" Joad was caught out trying to dodge paying his rail fare in January 1948, he was a famous public figure, a writer and broadcaster whose favourite expression "It depends what you mean by . . ." had become a popular catch-phrase. The incident of the rail ticket brought his career to a premature close.

Cyril Edward Mitchinson Joad was born in Durham on 12 August 1891, the son of a school inspector. He was educated at Blundell's, the famous public school, and at Balliol College, Oxford. At twenty-three he was awarded the John Locke scholarship in mental philosophy and on coming down from Oxford, he became a civil servant in the Board of Trade. He later declared that he used his sixteen years as a civil servant mainly to write his books. By 1924, his *Introduction to Modern Philosophy* had underneath his name: "Author of *Essays in Common Sense Philosophy, Common Sense Ethics, Common Sense Theology,* etc." In his book on Shaw, Joad tells how he came to Oxford in 1910 and read simultaneously Wells's *Tono Bungay* and Shaw's *Candida*, and of the "heady exhilaration" of this "intoxicating intellectual brew". A meeting with Shaw soon after that turned him into a "Shaw-worshipper". Joad himself had something in common both with Shaw and Wells: like Shaw, he was an incorrigible "performer" who loved to propagate the myth of himself – even his titles reveal his obsessive self-preoccupation: *The Book of Joad, The Testament of Joad, The Pleasure of Being Oneself*; like Wells, he was an incurable philanderer. He once said that at the age of eleven he thought all women were solid from the waist down; his discovery that they were, so to speak, accessible seems to have resulted in a lifelong desire to prove that there were no exceptions to the rule. He also said once that he had no interest in speaking with a woman unless she was willing to sleep with him. He called all his mistresses Maureen, in case he made a slip of the tongue in addressing them. His wife, whom he married in 1915, seemed to accept his *affaires*.

Joad was one of the great popularizers; his *Guide to Philosophy* (1936) was as influential, in its way, as Wells's *Outline of History* or Hogben's *Mathematics for the Million*. But Joad was by no means an intellectual lightweight; his *Matter, Life and Value* (1929) is a brilliant and original exposition of the philosophy of "vitalism". He believed firmly in the reality of objective values and had no sympathy with the tendency of the logical positivists to dismiss metaphysics. He was, in his way, a religious man. But he was inclined to model himself on Shaw and to waste a great deal of his time in controversy to the detriment of his serious work. From the age of thirty-nine, he became head of the department of philosophy at Birkbeck College, London; but he was never, strictly speaking, a "professor".

In 1941, the British Broadcasting Corporation started a programme called "The Brains Trust", broadcast on its "Forces" wavelength. It was so popular that it was soon repeated on the Home Service. Soon it had become – together with Tommy Handley's comedy show ITMA – one of the most successful programmes of the war years. Joad had a rather precise, high-pitched voice, and sounded exactly like the popular idea of a university professor. *Punch* carried a cartoon of him saying to a waiter: "It all depends on what you mean by (a) thick, and (b) clear." He became so popular that police had to escort him through the crowds at public meetings, and the Ministry of Food launched a dish called "Joad-in-the-Hole". He loved his notoriety. "He was an immensely vain individual", his BBC

"Professor" C.E.M. Joad

producer told Fenton Bresler, who devoted a chapter to Joad in his book *Scales of Justice*. The least suggestion of a snub could throw him into a towering rage but a soft answer – particularly if it was mixed with a judicious dose of flattery – had him cooing like a dove. He was not much liked at the BBC, partly because of a pathological meanness that made him dodge paying for his round of drinks whenever possible.

At 10.50 on the morning of 5 January 1948, Joad boarded the Atlantic Coast Express at Paddington, bound for Exeter in Devon; his secretary was with him. Both booked for the second sitting at lunch. When the ticket collector came to their table at lunch, his secretary held out her ticket but Joad explained: "I haven't got one. I was late and the collector let me through. I got on at Salisbury." The ticket collector gave him a return from Exeter to Salisbury. But the dining car attendant, who overheard the exchange, told the collector that there was something odd going on; Joad and his secretary had booked for lunch before the train reached Salisbury. The inspector went back to question Joad, who persisted in saying that he had boarded at Salisbury. It was only when the train stopped at Exeter that Joad admitted: "I made a mistake. I did come from Paddington . . ." He had indeed made a mistake to admit his guilt. If Joad had kept silent, he would undoubtedly have heard the last of it. He made a further mistake by writing to the railway authorities and explaining that the problem had been a "misunderstanding".

Ernst Roehm – the leader of the two and a half million strong Brown Shirt Storm Troopers, the street-fighting arm of the Nazi Party – was a brutal, working-class demagogue with undisguised homosexual tendencies, but had been with Hitler from the beginning and was one of his closest colleagues. The aristocratic Prussian Military High Command loathed him instinctively and wanted him destroyed at any cost. One general later said of the Brown Shirts, "[Germany's] rearmament was too serious and difficult a business to permit the participation of peculators, drunkards and homosexuals."

Hitler also felt Roehm was becoming too powerful. In the early morning of 30th June, 1934, he ordered the entire Brown Shirt Command arrested for treason. Roehm and many of his colleagues were found in the Hanslbaur Hotel at Weissee, most asleep in one another's beds or with teenage boys. All were taken to the yard and shot.

What decided the authorities to take Joad to court was undoubtedly their discovery that this was not the first time and that he had made a habit of travelling without a ticket for years. On 12 April 1948, counsel on his behalf pleaded guilty at the Tower Bridge magistrates' court to "unlawfully travelling on the railway without having previously paid his fare and with intent to avoid payment." Joad was fined £2, with 25 guineas costs. That evening a newspaper carried the headline: Joad Fined For Common Ticket Fraud. Joad had tried to save himself 17s. 1d. On the same evening, Joad was on "The Brains Trust" and seemed as jaunty and confident as ever. But in Parliament the following Friday, a Tory MP said, "In the last week a public figure was convicted for telling lies and defrauding the public and he was hired the same evening by the BBC to entertain people." On the evening of Joad's next scheduled appearance, he was dropped in favour of Commander King-Hall. He never again appeared on "The Brains Trust".

Joad continued to write books but he knew that, as a moral philosopher, his authority was gone. He became a practising Christian and wrote books about his new religious belief. In 1953, at the age of sixty-two, he died of cancer.

Why did Joad do it? When he was asked this question by the "Brains Trust" question master, Donald McCullough, he replied: *"Hubris"* – the Greek word for pride or conceit. Another motive was clearly his meanness. But his friend Hugh Schonfield, the Biblical scholar, has a different explanation. He told the present writer (CW) that Joad always had a need to "kick over the traces". Rebellion was a basic necessity of his nature – thumbing his nose at authority. So although he was "Britain's foremost philosopher" (as he claimed at the head of his newspaper column) and a famous public figure, there was a need to reassure himself that he was still a rebel at heart by small acts of antisocial defiance.

POLITICAL SCANDALS

*S*candals *of the political nature scream into the headlines when a politician has put himself (or herself) into an embarrassing position that leaves nothing to the imagination. President John Kennedy openly had numerous women attend to him, even though he was married, and didn't seem to worry, or care, what effect this would have on his political career. In 1906 Wilhelm Voigt impersonated a captain in the German army and "arrested" the mayor of a town, taking his cash box with all its money and then disappearing. The story caused great hilarity in Germany at the time.*

Wilhelm Voigt – "The Captain of Kopenick"

The story of the bogus "Captain of Kopenick" made all Kaiser Wilhelm's Germany rock with laughter. On the morning of 17 October 1906, a troop of ten soldiers, headed by a sergeant, was marching through Tegel (in Berlin). Suddenly, a man in a captain's uniform stepped in front of them and roared, "Halt!" The captain was a plump man with a drooping moustache, in his late fifties. He inspected the squad, then ordered the sergeant to accompany him to Kopenick, a dozen or so miles away, where he had official business at the town hall. Being Prussians, they obeyed without question. When they arrived at Kopenick, the captain gave them a mark each and told them to fall out for the midday meal. After their meal, he lined them up outside the town hall and set guards at the doors, ordering them to keep callers from entering. Then he marched the remaining seven men into the building, set some of them as guards on stairs and in corridors, and marched into the mayor's office. The captain informed the mayor that he was under arrest. Then he demanded to be shown the cash box with the municipal funds. It contained 4,000 marks which he confiscated, after carefully counting them.

The captain ordered his men to lead the prisoner away, while a soldier was told to requisition three vehicles. Into the first two of these, the soldiers and the mayor were ordered; their destination was a police station some fifteen miles away. The captain and the cash box entered the other cab. It was this cab that failed to arrive at the police station. It took more than two hours of confusion and mutual recriminations before it dawned on the police and the mayor that they were victims of a hoax.

The "captain" was an old lag named Wilhelm Voigt, who had spent twenty-seven of his fifty-seven years in jail. He had walked into a pawn shop, shortly after his release from his latest spell in prison, and purchased the second-hand captain's uniform. It is not clear whether the robbery was planned, or whether it was a spur of the moment decision as he saw the soldiers marching through Tegel.

The news of the comic-opera robbery spread round the world. Even the kaiser is said to have roared with laughter when he heard about it and said, "Such a thing could only happen in Germany." From the description, it didn't take the police long to identify the captain as Voigt. While all the Berlin police searched for him, the city was flooded with picture postcards of the exploit showing the trembling mayor standing before the ferocious captain, while another showed Voigt winking and smoking a fat cigar. The newspaper *Berliner Tageblat* said that he ought to be rewarded, not punished, for teaching the Germans a lesson.

Voigt was arrested ten days later in his room in a Berlin slum. Most of the 4,000 marks were still unspent. He was sentenced to four years in jail but this was later reduced to twenty months – on the direct intervention of the kaiser, it was whispered.

Voigt came out of prison in 1908 and discovered that a dramatist called Kalnberg had written a successful play called

The Captain of Kopenick. Voigt requested, and received, a free seat for a performance of the play.

The case had political echoes. In 1910, Herr von Oldenburg-Januschau, a fire-eating right winger, defended Prussian militarism against the dangerous liberalism that seemed to be undermining the country. He declared, "It must always be possible for the German Emperor and King of Prussia to tell the nearest lieutenant: take ten men and close down the Reichstag (parliament)." This sentiment backfired as comedians all over Germany parodied the statement. After the exploit of Wilhelm Voigt, Prussian authoritarianism was no longer treated with quite the same respect.

President John F. Kennedy – All the President's Women

During his political career – spanning the late 1940s, the prudish fifties and the pre-hippy years of the sixties – John F. Kennedy pursued a sex-life that would make most of us dizzy to contemplate.

Protected and covered-up for by friends and colleagues, tactfully ignored by a more gentlemanly (not to say timorous) media, and almost unassailably popular with his supporters, he indulged himself with almost every attractive woman who showed willing – and there were plenty of those for the glamorous Jack Kennedy. Nobody has ever tried to put a figure to his conquests, but these must have been well into the upper hundreds.

In his book, *"Kennedy and His Women"*, Tony Sciacca records numerous accounts of Kennedy's philandering from those close to him throughout his political career. Reading the anecdotes one soon forms an impression that Jack Kennedy must have viewed attractive women in the same light that a voracious reader might consider paperbacks. He clearly needed a continuous and ever-changing supply of lovers, yet he seems to have viewed sex more as a relaxing and necessary pastime than the driving force of his life.

However, this did not stop him from allowing his sex-drive to occasionally impinge on his political life. He often spent pleasant afternoons (when his wife Jackie was away) bathing naked in the Whitehouse swimming pool with whatever young lady or ladies he presently had attached to his entourage. Hassled presidential aides had a lively time stopping uninitiated ministers and diplomats wandering round to the pool to have a quick word with Mr President.

During the 1962 Nassau conference he shocked the British Prime Minister, Harold Macmillan, by offhandedly saying: "You know, I get very severe headaches if I go too long without a woman." He then excused himself and left with two attractive members of his personal staff, who up to then had seemed to fulfil no specific purpose. An hour later he returned alone, looking much refreshed. Smiling, he told the mildly indignant Prime Minister: "My headache's gone."

Life as a Kennedy Whitehouse staffer could be both hectic and demanding. The secret service men seconded to protect the President were given the additional duty of unobtrusively sneaking-in his girlfriends on demand. Presidential aides often had to rush about tidying-up the evidence of the President's visitors when Mrs Kennedy's pending arrival was unexpectedly announced. Possible hairpins were searched for in thick carpets, beds were rapidly remade and the odd female garment swiftly relocated.

On one occasion they were a bit lax in their efforts and Jackie Kennedy found a pair of women's panties stuffed in a pillow case. She calmly handed them to her husband saying, "Would you please shop around and see who these belong to? They're not my size."

It seems clear that Jackie knew about at least some of the other women, but aside from creating a slight distancing from her husband, she did not let it spoil her marriage. One must respect her fortitude; she not only had to put-up with the arduous life of the First Lady, but had also to contend with the fact that her husband was totally incapable of being faithful to her.

In contrast to contemporary politicians, Kennedy seems to have been totally unconcerned that his enemies might use his private life to wreck his career. In 1952, during his first campaign to enter the Senate, a photograph of Kennedy and a young lady lying naked on a sun drenched beach came into the hands of his Republican opponent, Henry Cabot Lodge. Instead of handing it straight to the media, Lodge had a copy of the photograph sent to Kennedy's campaign headquarters, where it caused quite a stir.

Kennedy's campaign strategists examined the photograph and despaired; it looked like the end of his electoral chances and possibly his entire political career. It was decided that Kennedy must be informed of the situation and several unhappy aides took the photograph to his office. One later said that Kennedy "just looked at the picture a long time and then told us about all the great times he had with the girl and how fond he'd been of her. He put it in his desk and told us not to worry about it." Lodge did not publish the photograph, perhaps merely hoping to shake his opponent's confidence, and Kennedy won the election easily.

Another example of Jack Kennedy's rakish attitude to women is related by a fellow congressman who attended an informal dinner party thrown by Kennedy at his Washington house in 1948. Also present were several of Kennedy's Navy friends from his war service days and an attractive red-head from an airline ticket office that Kennedy had casually asked along.

She noticed that he was not eating and asked him why. Kennedy replied: "How can I eat when all I'm thinking about is taking you upstairs?" She replied that she wasn't hungry either and they excused themselves and went upstairs.

Later they all went to the movies after which Kennedy packed his date off in a cab. As soon as she was gone he called another young lady. He said he had met her a few weeks before at Palm Beach, and had offered to show her the sights of Washington. They picked her up at her hotel and drove back to Kennedy's house. After a brandy the Congressman and his date tactfully left.

The next day the Congressman met Kennedy on Capitol Hill and asked how things had gone. Kennedy said he had a terrible time. His new date seems to have thought that "after one screw with Jack Kennedy she was going to marry him." She had finally stormed out at about two in the morning. "Then he turned and waved toward some real luscious woman sitting up in the House gallery. And he stage whispered to me: 'She's the one I spent the night with.' Jack wasn't bragging. To him, it was all very casual, something that a bachelor had coming to him . . . I tell you, I was awfully jealous of that man. The women seemed to be coming out of the woodwork . . ."

This playboyish detachment seems to have characterized Kennedy's dealings with women. Yet, despite the modern view of Don Juanism, his womanizing almost certainly did not spring from a contempt for the female sex. Even his detractors admit that he invariably behaved with courtesy and tact in his love affairs and, as can be seen above, he was at pains to avoid giving the impression that he wanted anything other than a casual commitment.

Although most of Kennedy's affairs were short term – as little as a couple of hours in some cases – he also maintained a few longer lasting relationships – the most notorious perhaps being with the icon goddesses, Marilyn Monroe and Jayne Mansfield. His basic good nature was again illustrated by his conduct in these affairs. He would go to elaborate lengths to ensure that the lady was protected from difficulties while being almost cavalier with his own reputation.

At the beginning of World War II Kennedy was stationed in Washington, working in the ONI, the Office of Navy Intelligence. Captain Alan Kirk, director of the ONI, was an old family friend, and Jack's father, Joe Kennedy, – then Ambassador to Great Britain – had pulled strings to get his boy into a plum job. Yet by January 1942, Jack had been kicked-out of Naval Intelligence and sent to a minor desk job in South Carolina. The reason was one Inga Arvad, a gorgeous Danish journalist whom Adolf Hitler had once described as "a perfect Nordic beauty".

Inga had come from Europe with her pro-Nazi husband, had left him for a suspected pro-Nazi and had eventually ended-up working on *The Washington Times-Herald* on a society column, through which she met Jack. The FBI already saw her as a potential Mata-Hari and her involvement with a young intelligence officer in a key position decided them. They bugged her telephone and had her kept under surveillance.

Great pressure was placed on Jack, by the Navy and his father, to break with Inga, but he remained intransigent. His lover was not, he insisted, a Nazi spy. Eventually he pulled enough strings to receive an interview with FBI director J. Edgar Hoover himself. Hoover was forced to admit that there was absolutely no evidence against Inga and apologized on behalf of the Bureau. Jack Kennedy at the age of twenty-five, with the mere rank of Navy Ensign, had faced down one of the most powerful men in the country to protect the reputation of his lover.

J. Edgar Hoover must have recalled the Inga Arvad incident with some irony when he was handed a report, late in 1961, on one Judith Campbell. It seemed that Judy, as she was known to her friends, had been ringing the White House to speak with the President. Hoover was, of course, well aware of Jack Kennedy's affairs – the prudish bureau chief was obsessed by the need to gather information about the sex-lives of the famous and powerful – and can have

had little doubt what the attractive Miss Campbell's connection was with the President's office. The trouble was that
the FBI also had information that she was a lover of Sam
Giancana, one of the most powerful Mafia bosses in the United
States.

Kennedy had met Judy in February 1960, at a party thrown by
his close friend Frank Sinatra. She was one of Hollywood's many
aspiring actresses and was also known as something of a "party
girl"; a facet that endeared her to the hard-playing Sinatra and
his circle.

Jack and Judy became lovers and saw each other fairly
frequently over the next two years. Judy later claimed that
he rang her often and that she had visited him at the White
House at least twenty times for intimate lunches. She called
him quite often as well. The White House telephone logs
recorded seventy calls from Judy Campbell during a fifty-four
week period in 1961 and early 1962. Some of those calls were
made from a house in Oak Park, Illinois; the home of mobster
Sam Giancana.

Whether Giancana was using Judy to get a blackmail angle on
Kennedy has never been made clear, but he certainly must have
known that he was sharing his girlfriend with the President.
Once, when Judy was staying with Giancana in the luxurious
Miami Beach Hotel, Kennedy got word to her that he was
vacationing alone at Palm Springs and would appreciate a little
female company. Apparently with Giancana's blessings she left
to join the President immediately.

Hoover contacted Bobby Kennedy, Jack's younger brother,
then serving as Attorney General. Bobby Kennedy had a particular hatred for organized crime and had personally insisted on
the multi-level FBI surveillance on Sam Giancana. First Bobby,
then J. Edgar Hoover remonstrated with the President and he
was finally persuaded to stop Judy ringing him at the White
House. Even so, he continued to see Judy until the summer
of 1962.

It may seem insanely foolish of Kennedy to have continued
such a dangerous affair once he had been appraised of the
facts, but on closer inspection one realizes that it was yet
another illustration of his cool political insight. He had no
intention of breaking-off an enjoyable relationship and he knew
that Giancana could not harm him; in fact, quite the opposite.

One of his former aides later commented on the affair: "Back
in those days no reporter in the country would have touched

the Judy Campbell story, no one would have believed Jack was screwing around and certainly not with a mobster's woman. If it got out in any way, we would have just said that it's a vicious tale spread by a murderer from Chicago named Giancana because the Kennedy Administration is seriously damaging the mob. We could have easily turned it into a plus for Jack. And Jack knew it."

Various psychological explanations for Jack Kennedy's womanizing have been suggested over the years. Not the most infrequent is the theory that he was trying to live up to his father. Old Joe Kennedy Snr was one of the great American entrepreneurs in every sense of the word. He made a huge fortune from the stock market, from the movie business and, it is alleged, the bootlegging trade during prohibition. Joe Kennedy nursed a life-long chip on his shoulder over his family's exclusion from the East Coast "Brahmin" upper class circles, due to their Irish background. As a result he was as aggressive in his sexual affairs and home life as he was in the business and political worlds, and encouraged his boys to behave in the same way. Jack Kennedy, always a sickly person, is known to have felt inadequate to his father's demands and spent much of his youth fighting with his father's favourite, his older brother Joe Jnr.

During World War II, two events seem to have deeply marked Jack. The first was his own near death when a Japanese destroyer rammed his small "PT" patrol boat (Kennedy was cited for conspicuous bravery in his efforts to get himself and his crew rescued afterwards). The second was the death of Joe Jnr on a volunteer-only bomber mission against a German V–1 missile base in France. Afterwards Jack Kennedy seems to have been driven by the certainty of his own death and a determination to live life to its fullest before he died. His very poor state of health throughout his life reinforced this drive. He once admitted to a colleague, "The doctors say I've got a sort of slow-motion leukaemia, but they tell me I'll probably last until I'm forty-five."

In this light one can see that Kennedy's hyperactive sex-life was only part of the picture. Everything he did, including his successful run for the presidency, was part of his need to enjoy and excel in life. In his eulogy to his brother, Bobby Kennedy pointed out that at least half of Jack's days had been spent in agony due to his poor health, yet he was one of the most fulfilled people that he had ever known. Jack

> The American President Calvin Coolidge and his wife were visiting a government farm and were taken on separate tours. As she passed the chicken pen, Mrs Coolidge asked the man in charge how many times a day the rooster mounted the hens. "Dozens of times." "Please tell that to the President" said Mrs Coolidge. When the President visited the pen, the man passed on the message. "And does the rooster choose the same hen each time?" "Oh no – a different one." "Please tell that to Mrs Coolidge."

Kennedy was forty-six-years-old when he was assassinated in Dallas in 1963.

The Profumo Scandal

The recent Palace Pictures film about the Profumo affair was called simply *"Scandal!"* reflecting how much this particular fall from grace seems to represent the whole idea of scandalous behaviour. Many people maintain that it was the publicity surrounding the scandal that lost the Conservatives the election in October 1964. In the general outrage, it was difficult to evaluate who the victims of this scandal actually were.

Britain's population in the early sixties had an abnormally low average age. The post-war baby boomers were attaining their majority, and the staid attitudes of the fifties were slowly giving way to a more casual view of sex and morality. In London, prostitution was booming and nightclubs offered a useful marriage of brothel and bar. The economy was in a healthy state, and people were prepared to spend money on leisure. As Prime Minister Macmillan put it: "Our people have never had it so good." Following the Profumo scandal the satirical magazine *Private Eye* was to alter the quote to "We've never had it so often."

John Dennis Profumo had been the Minister for War in Macmillan's cabinet since July 1960. He had married a popular British actress, Valerie Hobson in 1954. His appearance was grimly respectable: balding, solemn-faced and neatly dressed. It was perhaps his very respectability, his conservative appearance that made his fall from grace so very shocking to the public at large.

For the weekend of 8 July Profumo and his wife were invited by Lord Astor to a party at his country estate, Cliveden, near Maidstone in Kent. More than twenty rich and influential people were to attend. Another party was taking place at Cliveden that weekend, at the cottage of Dr Stephen Ward in the grounds of the estate. He rented the cottage from his friend Astor for the token amount of £1 a year.

Stephen Ward was an osteopath. His charming and refined manner and his habit of name-dropping had gained him a roster of celebrities as both patients and friends. His acquaintance with much of the aristocracy left him perfectly placed to make introductions; he had set up many society marriages. He would allow attractive young women to stay at his flat free of charge, never behaving in a less than gentlemanly fashion with them, simply in order to look at them and to have beautiful escorts when he went out. The spirit of growing sexual freedom in Britain at the time was not limited to the lower reaches of society, and Ward attended and organized expensive parties where group sex was an accepted after-dinner pastime. It was perhaps because his circle of friends encompassed both influential men and poor but attractive women, that he gained a reputation as a procurer.

Among those at Ward's house party this particular weekend was Christine Keeler, a nineteen-year-old nightclub hostess whom Ward had taken under his wing. Keeler had left home at sixteen, after a self-induced abortion, and came to London to be a model. She found work as a topless dancer at Murray's Cabaret Club, mingling with the customers between numbers and sometimes accepting money for sex. Ward found her in Murray's and offered her a room in his flat. She became Ward's confidante.

Ward had permission from Lord Astor to use the swimming pool in the grounds of the Cliveden estate. On this night Ward had told Keeler that she should swim in the pool naked, as her borrowed costume did not fit her. As she was swimming Lord Astor and John Profumo, who were taking the air in the garden, happened upon the party. Keeler tried to make a grab for her discarded costume, but Ward got to it first and threw it into the bushes. The embarrassed swimmer tried to get out of the pool while covering herself with an inadequately small towel. Lord Astor and Profumo decided to chase her, and it was as

Christine Keeler as a showgirl at Murray's Cabaret Club

the aristocrat and elder statesman were trying to tackle the effectively naked Keeler that the rest of Astor's guests including Mrs Profumo, reached the swimming pool. The two groups of guests mingled and got on well, so much so that the Ward party was invited to meet the other guests at the swimming pool the next night.

This next night Eugene Ivanov, a naval attaché at the Soviet embassy attended the party around the pool. Ward had met him through his illustrious circle of friends and, always keen to develop important acquaintances, he had invited him to the cottage for the weekend. During the evening Profumo tried to get Keeler's phone number from her. The same night Keeler had sex with Ivanov.

This was the beginning of a period during which the British Minister for War and a Soviet naval attaché shared the same lover. Profumo was not particularly careful to conceal his affair, driving with Keeler in his government car, and having sex with her in his own house when his wife was away. He would meet her at Ward's flat in Wimpole Mews, as would Ivanov. However, there is no evidence to suggest that Profumo and Ivanov ever met there, although according to Keeler there were a few near misses. During this period Ward was twice visited by MI5, who advised him to dissociate himself from Ivanov. This, in retrospect was a bad mistake on the intelligence agency's part, as it gave Ward the impression that he had some effect on the exercise of international political power, a delusion that he had secretly fostered anyway. He felt immersed in a world of espionage, and jokingly asked Keeler to learn from Profumo when the Americans intended to site nuclear weapons in Germany. At the time the Soviets were deploying weapons in Cuba, and the information would have been immensely valuable to them.

MI5 soon received information from a defecting Soviet that Ivanov was a spy, and discreetly informed Profumo that he should not have contact with him. The intelligence agency apparently did not know about both men's association with Keeler despite tentative gossip column items in the press mentioning a certain London flat where a Government car no sooner pulled away than a Soviet diplomatic vehicle pulled up. Profumo's indiscretion had also created a wealth of verbal rumours. Impressed by the gravity of the situation, Profumo wrote Keeler a goodbye letter and broke contact with her.

Keeler then went through a succession of boyfriends, moving

Christine Keeler

in and out of Stephen Ward's flat depending on the state of her relationships. She went to America with Mandy Rice-Davies, a friend from her time at Murray's.

All this time Christine Keeler was being harassed by ex-lover "Lucky" Gordon, a West Indian drug dealer and underworld figure. On two occasions "Lucky" held Keeler at knife point for days on end, refusing to let her leave his presence and repeatedly raping her. He had been prosecuted for an assault that involved inserting a knife into a woman's vagina. Gordon would find out where Keeler was living and make nuisance calls or hang around outside waiting for her to leave. For a short time he and Keeler were reconciled and they lived together, but Gordon was obsessively jealous and repeatedly violent.

After Gordon had attacked Keeler she would usually return to Stephen Ward's flat, for comfort and protection. Eventually she became sick of living in fear and bought an illegal handgun and two magazines. In her autobiography *"Nothing But . . ."* Keeler admits that she had every intention of killing Gordon if he attacked her again.

Keeler became the lover of Johnny Edgecombe, a West Indian

associate of "Lucky" Gordon's. After Gordon had again attacked Keeler in public Edgecombe insisted upon confronting Gordon with the fact that Keeler did not love him, and that she did not want to see him again. When the three of them met in a club, Gordon tried to hit Edgecombe with a chair, and the ensuing fight ended with Edgecombe slashing Gordon's face from forehead to chin. Keeler went into hiding at Stephen Ward's flat, severing all contacts with Gordon and Edgecombe.

Eugene Ivanov was still a close friend of Ward's, visiting him regularly. During the week of the Cuban missile crisis, Ivanov told Ward that his superiors had authorized him to negotiate an unofficial solution with the British Government and asked Ward to use his contacts to get Ivanov meetings with British MPs. Ward had little luck, but managed to get Conservative back-bencher William Shepherd to meet Ivanov at the flat in Wimpole Mews. Nothing came of the meeting but Shepherd became suspicious of the set-up at Ward's flat and conducted his own investigations. He even interviewed Percival Murrays proprietor of Christine Keeler's old place of work. He then passed his findings on to MI5.

Meanwhile Johnny Edgecombe had tired of waiting for Keeler to come out of hiding. He arrived at Ward's home in a minicab, carrying Keeler's gun. When Mandy Rice-Davies had refused him entry he tried to shoot the lock off the door. When this failed he took a shot at Keeler through a window, missing. The police arrived and Edgecombe was arrested.

Keeler's name in the headlines revived the rumours of the previous year concerning Profumo. George Wigg, the Labour Shadow Spokesman on Defence, who had clashed with Profumo in the commons over the Vassall Spying case received an anonymous phonecall: "Forget about Vassall. You want to look at Profumo."

Keeler took legal advice over her role in the Edgecombe/Gordon attacks, and realized that if she testified in Edgecombe's trial she would have to admit that she had bought the gun, and that she was the basis for the antagonism between the two men. She also realized the potentially scandalous nature of her joint affairs with Ivanov and Profumo. Ward disassociated himself from her, making a statement to the police suggesting that he was put upon by Keeler, who was always smoking drugs and having sex with West Indians in his flat without his approval. Keeler responded with a statement that portrayed Ward as little better than a perverse, down-market pimp and then sold her story to the *Sunday Pictorial*.

However they did not publish. The facts were known to many people, yet the press were afraid to print them as truth; Profumo's solicitors had cowed them into silence. MI5 knew of the affair by this time also, but they decided that it was best to leave the facts secret, and instructed the police to leave certain avenues of investigation untrodden. Profumo seemed to have escaped once again from the consequences of his ill-considered affair.

A few days before Edgecombe's trial Keeler escaped to Spain. Her absence was a major news story, and the newspapers took the opportunity to insinuate all they dared about Profumo's connections with the missing witness. Finally Labour's George Wigg voiced the question that the newspapers had avoided. During a Parliamentary debate on Press freedom, and thus in a situation immune to threats from Profumo'solicitors, he said: "There is not an Honourable Member in this House . . . who in the last few days has not heard rumour upon rumour involving a member of the Government Front Bench. The Press has got as near as it can – it has shown itself willing to wound, but afraid to strike . . . I rightly use the privilege of the House of Commons to ask the Home Secretary to go to the Dispatch Box – he knows that the rumour to which I refer relates to Miss Christine Keeler and Miss Davies and a shooting by a West Indian – and on the behalf of the Government, categorically deny the truth of these rumours. On the other hand if there is anything in them, I urge the Prime Minister to set up a select committee, so that these things can be dissipated and the honour of the Minister concerned freed from the imputations and innuendoes that are being spread at the present time."

Profumo was not in the House at the time, but when he heard of Wigg's question he prepared a personal statement to be read to the House. Traditionally personal statements to the House are not questioned by other Members, thus it is a matter of honour that they are wholly true. His statement conclusively denied any impropriety in his relationship with Christine Keeler. He admitted meeting both her and Ivanov through Ward, a mutual friend. He threatened libel writs against anyone mentioning the rumours outside the protection of Parliamentary privilege. The Press, that had held back partly out of fear but also because of respect for high office was enraged by such an obvious lie. Yet they were gagged by Profumo's threats of libel action. They dropped as many damaging hints as they could, but it seemed that

Profumo had escaped a possible scandal through sheer nerve and dishonesty.

However, Dr Stephen Ward knew the true facts, and he seemed unwilling to keep them to himself. He was sure that his knowledge would lead to his being framed. He affirmed that Profumo had shared Christine Keeler's favours with Ivanov to both George Wigg and MI5. He wrote to the Home Secretary with the same message. At the same time the CID were receiving anonymous messages suggesting that Ward was a pimp. A substantial power-group wanted Profumo's lie revealed; another group wanted it concealed. Stephen Ward, through his innate urge to be at the hub of important events was setting himself up as a target.

Keeler returned to Britain after being tracked down by the newspapers. Mandy Rice-Davies was arrested for possession of a forged driving license, a charge that a judge later admitted was created merely to prevent her from leaving the country. She spent two weeks in Holloway.

Profumo had gone on holiday to Venice. There, he confessed

Christine Keeler with her friend Paula Hamilton Marshal on their way to court

to his wife that he had lied to the Commons, and that the rumours were true. His letter of resignation and Macmillan's acceptance were published in all newspapers. A vote of no confidence was entered by the Labour Party, and the general feeling was that Macmillan would have to resign. However he succeeded in hanging on, buying time by appointing Lord Denning to investigate the affair.

The police interviewed one hundred and forty people in relation to the allegations about Ward's immoral earnings. Eventually they felt they had enough evidence and Ward was arrested for charges under the Sexual Offences Act. At the Committal Hearing a key police witness, Margaret Richardson lied about Ward's status as her pimp. She admitted at the later trial that it was due to "police pressure". It was clear that there was a great deal of pressure for justice to appear to be done to Ward, Keeler and Rice-Davies. Keeler was sent to prison for nine months for perjury in "Lucky" Gordon's trial. Rice-Davies spent time in Holloway so that she could be a witness against Ward. Ward himself could not bear the feeling of persecution that the police investigations and his trial had brought to him. He overdosed on Nembutal on the night before his trial reached verdict. In his suicide note he wrote: "It's not only fear, it's a wish not to let them get me. I'd rather get myself."

Macmillan finally did resign after some disastrous by-election results in late 1963. Sir Alec Douglas-Hume took over, and was defeated by Harold Wilson in September 1964.

John Profumo was at fault, both for allowing his affair to be noticed and in lying to Parliament about it. He lost his job, but saved his marriage, and his wife remains with him to this day. Christine Keeler had to live with being labelled a tart who could not keep quiet. Although one would imagine her story would guarantee her livelihood, she is by no means wealthy and relies upon social security. Stephen Ward was hounded to death. Keeler recalls that in his heyday Ward attended orgies with the Prosecutors of the "Lady Chatterley's Lover" pornography trial. These friends showed no hurry to help him later on. Eugene Ivanov flew back to the Soviet Union two days after Keeler was first interviewed by the police.

A mystery still remains as to why the police needed one hundred and forty interviews to bring charges of living off immoral earnings. It seems clear that Ward was set up by the authorities as a figure of malign influence in order to explain Profumo's fall. Only his suicide spoilt that manufactured image.

Jeremy Thorpe – Did the Liberal Leader hire a Hitman?

The trial of Jeremy Thorpe, the leader of the British Liberal Party on a charge of conspiracy to murder was the single greatest political scandal in the UK since the Profumo affair. The details of the charge were that Thorpe had incited three men – who stood in the dock beside him – to murder the former male model Norman Scott, with whom Thorpe was alleged to have had a homosexual affair.

The publicity surrounding the charge destroyed what had been an incredibly successful political career. The son of a Conservative MP, Thorpe had been educated at Eton College and Oxford University. At University he had headed many Liberal political groups, finally becoming president of the prestigious Oxford Union Society. He was called to the bar in 1954, and stood for election as Liberal candidate for North Devon in the same year. At the first attempt he lost, but he cut the Tory majority in half. He contested the seat again in 1959, and won by 362 votes. He immediately made a great impression in the House of Commons with his wit and oratory. Only one potential problem existed: in March 1960 a routine security check into Thorpe's background revealed that he had homosexual tendencies. At this time homosexual activity was still a criminal offence. It was also in 1960, on a visit to an Oxfordshire riding stable, that Thorpe met the man who was to precipitate his downfall, Norman Josiffe, later known as Norman Scott.

Josiffe, eleven years Thorpe's junior, was the child of a broken marriage. He had a history of emotional problems and was on probation for larceny. He also claimed that both his parents were dead. Thorpe obviously took a liking to him as he offered him help if ever he needed it. A year later, after an unsuccessful suicide attempt Josiffe remembered the offer and got in contact with Thorpe. He went to meet him at the House of Commons on 8 November 1961. Afterwards, they went to Thorpe's mother's house in Oxted, Surrey. There, according to Josiffe, their homosexual affair began.

Thorpe allegedly instructed Josiffe to assume the identity of a member of a TV crew in order to allay any suspicions that Thorpe's mother may have had. That night Thorpe went to Josiffe's room with a copy of James Baldwin's homosexual novel *Giovanni's Room*. Later he returned in his dressing gown. According to Josiffe: "He said I looked like a frightened rabbit . . . he just hugged me and called me 'poor bunny' . . . he got into bed with me." Thorpe then sodomized Josiffe. Josiffe denied that he found the experience pleasurable: "I just bit the pillow and tried not to scream." Despite this the affair did continue, Josiffe being given a job on the staff of Len Smith, a Liberal Party official. He accompanied Thorpe on visits to his mother's in Devon and they met in Josiffe's flat near the House of Commons. A problem arose however when Josiffe was accused of stealing the coat of a Mrs Ann Gray. Thorpe basically fixed the trouble for Josiffe, insisting that the police interview take place in his room in the House of Commons, claiming that he was Josiffe's guardian. Shortly afterwards Josiffe moved to work on a farm in Somerset and Thorpe sent him a letter: "take the Ann Gray incident as over and done with". The letter ended: "Bunnies can (and will) go to France."

Josiffe stayed put however, and was soon thrown off the farm when his dog killed some ducks. He tried confessing his "sins" to a Catholic priest, but was denied absolution unless he broke off his relationship with Thorpe. Josiffe was becoming very bitter, and openly discussed a plan to kill Thorpe and then commit suicide. The result was that Josiffe was interviewed by the police. He told them all about his relationship with Thorpe, handing over the "Bunnies can (and will) go to France" letter to confirm his story. The police, not unsurprisingly, did nothing.

Meanwhile, Thorpe had been investigating Josiffe's background, and had discovered that his parents were not dead. This seems to have prompted Thorpe to break off the affair. When Gieves Ltd, a West End outfitter demanded payment for a pair of silk pyjamas that Josiffe had ordered on Thorpe's account, Thorpe told them he would not pay, and that he had no idea of Josiffe's present whereabouts.

In fact Josiffe was in Ireland, once again working with horses. Soon he tried to contact Thorpe again, asking him to lend money for a trip to the Continent. Thorpe provided the money and Josiffe went to Switzerland. However he disliked his job and surroundings and promptly returned without his luggage. With exemplary patience Thorpe offered to try and recover the lost cases. He enlisted the help of fellow Liberal MP Peter Bessel, member for Bodmin. Bessel flew to Dublin to see Josiffe, and found him on the whole likeable. However he told Josiffe that he did not believe the allegations of homosexuality against Thorpe, and demanded proof. Josiffe told him that the luggage in Switzerland contained compromising letters from Thorpe. Bessel agreed to recover them. When the cases finally reached Josiffe, the letters had gone . . .

The cycle of Thorpe casting him off and Josiffe returning when he was broke continued. Undoubtedly some element of blackmail kept Thorpe ready to provide help. In January 1967 Thorpe became head of the Liberal Party. The information Josiffe held now became proportionately more important, and in 1968, according to the prosecution case, Thorpe began to consider killing Josiffe, who had now changed his name to Scott. In a conversation with Bessel over what was to be done with Josiffe/Scott, Thorpe said, "We have got to get rid of him". Bessel asked, "Are you suggesting killing him off?" "Yes," Thorpe replied.

Nothing proceeded immediately. Scott once again threatened Thorpe with revelation, this time of the compromising letters that Bessel had written to him on Thorpe's behalf. He received £2,500 in exchange for the "Bessel File". With the money he moved to a cottage on Exmoor and began to drink heavily and take drugs. Eventually he was contacted by a man who called himself Peter Keene, who told him that his life was in danger, that a hired killer was on his way from Canada to assassinate him. Keene maintained that he had been sent by an "unknown benefactor" to warn Scott. He asked Scott to come with him in order to meet this unknown figure. Scott refused, but agreed to meet him in the centre of the local town, Combe Martin on 24 October 1975. Scott decided to take his Great Dane along.

"Keene", whose real name was Andrew Newton, met Scott and put him at his ease with his friendly manner. They drove off to the rendezvous. Newton began driving very badly, saying that he was tired. Scott offered to drive. They stopped, and as Scott approached the driver's door he saw that Newton was pointing a Mauser handgun at him. "This is it," said Newton and shot the Great Dane, Rinka, through the head. "It's your turn now," said Newton, but the gun seemed to jam. He jumped into the car and drove away. Scott succeeded in flagging down a car and calling the police.

Newton had not put much effort into concealing his movements, and was arrested soon afterwards. He told the police that Scott had been blackmailing him, and that he had shot his dog in order to scare him. He received two years imprisonment, of which he served slightly more than a year.

Scott did not take this incident as a warning, and in January 1976, when charged with defrauding the DHSS, he did what he had been threatening to do for a long time, he blurted the details of his affair with Thorpe. He told the court that he had been hounded for many years because he had had a homosexual relationship with a Jeremy Thorpe.

Now the story was out, Thorpe immediately denied the allegation. He told Cyril Smith, the Liberal chief whip, that Scott was a blackmailer, extorting money not from him but from Peter Bessel. Thorpe said that Scott knew of an extra-marital affair of Bessel's. Now Thorpe actually had corroboration for this, Bessel had written him a letter to that effect as a last-ditch line of defence. When Thorpe leaked the letter to ease pressure on himself, Bessel prepared to deny it. Thorpe desperately asked him to wait: "Peter, I'm begging for time."

Inevitably however, the press forced Thorpe to resign. Newton, now freed, sold a sensational story to the *London Evening News*. When Bessel, who was by now disillusioned with Thorpe, commented in print, Thorpe declared war on him, attacking his integrity and honesty. The press meanwhile had found a connection between Newton and Thorpe in the form of three South Wales small businessmen, John Le Mesurier, David Holmes and George Deakin. These men had hired Newton to frighten Scott into leaving Thorpe alone. The Director of Public Prosecutions was less sure, and charged Thorpe, Deakin, Le Mesurier and Holmes with conspiracy to murder.

The case opened at the Old Bailey on 8 May 1979. Soon Peter Bessel was called by the prosecution and seemed to provide damning evidence. He told the court of the 1968 conversation in which Thorpe had first brought up the idea of murder. He also said that he had been the contact between Holmes and Thorpe and described long conversations between the three of them discussing possible ways of disposing of Scott's body. When Bessel had questioned the morality of killing Scott, Thorpe allegedly replied, "It's no worse than shooting a sick dog."

Bessel also suggested that Thorpe had paid Newton with money embezzled from Liberal Party funds. Taken as a whole the evidence seemed damning. However George Carman QC cross-examined Bessel skilfully, establishing that he had a deal with a newspaper to buy his story. The price would be £50,000 if Thorpe was convicted and only £25,000 if he was not. The

Jeremy Thorpe leaving the Old Bailey

suggestion, of course, was that Bessel had a vested interest in seeing Thorpe convicted.

Scott appeared in the witness box, and made a terrible impression on the court. Carman managed to establish that Scott had been boasting about having a homosexual relationship with Thorpe before he went to meet him in the House of Commons for the very first time. This completely undermined Scott's account of his unwillingness on that first night at Thorpe's mother's house.

In his summing-up the judge described Scott as a fraud, a whinger, a whiner and a parasite. On the basis of these remarks and the generally poor performance of prosecution witnesses Thorpe and his alleged accomplices were acquitted.

It is difficult to say exactly where the truth lies in the complex web of contradictory evidence surrounding the Thorpe trial. There was strong feeling at the time that the judge's summing-up contained too much conjecture and personal comment about Scott. All that seems clear is that although Scott was torn apart in court and Thorpe was acquitted, it was Thorpe who fell furthest. By the time a verdict was reached, the scandal had destroyed him.

President Richard Milhous Nixon – The Watergate Break-in Scandal

No scandal has shaken the American public as much as the Watergate affair. Indeed, subsequent political scandals have tended to carry the word "gate" as a suffix (i.e. Irangate, Contragate, etc) as if to pay tribute to the grandfather of them all.

At 1 a.m. on the night of 17 June 1972, twenty-four-year-old security guard Frank Mills noticed something odd as he was completing his patrol around the Watergate shopping/office complex in downtown Washington DC. A piece of tape had been placed over the spring catch of a door to the garage basement, preventing it from locking. Unperturbed, he removed the tape and went off to buy a cheeseburger. Forty-five minutes later he returned and found the door had been re-taped. At last

realizing that the building was being burgled he rushed to phone
the authorities.

Three plain clothes policemen responded to the call and
proceeded to search the building. Across the street a look-out in
a Howard Johnson motel spotted the armed officers and started
to make some desperate telephone calls. He was too late, the
officers were already searching the complex's third floor and
his accomplices were trapped. Five burglars were found hiding
behind desks in the Democratic National Committee offices—the
Democrat's election headquarters. All of them were wearing neat
suits and blue rubber gloves. They were carrying cameras, rolls
of film, equipment suitable for setting-up electronic surveillance
(i.e. telephone taps), and around $2,000 in hundred dollar bills.
The officers quickly realized that their suspects were hardly run
of the mill petty crooks.

At first the burglars gave false names to the police and tried
to brazen it out. But, when the police found keys to rooms
in the Watergate Hotel on two of them they rapidly changed
their minds and gave their true names. The five burglars were:
James McCord, Bernard Barker, Virgilio Gonzalez – a locksmith
– Eugenio Martinez and Frank Sturgi. McCord had been an
FBI agent and an officer in the CIA. Barker was also a CIA
agent. Gonzalez and Martinez were Cuban exiles, and Sturgis
was a "soldier of fortune". In court they gave their professions
as "anti-communists".

The Democrats were naturally delighted with these events.
With a presidential election in the offing, they hoped to discredit Nixon, and if possible prove that he had ordered the
bugging of the democratic headquarters. The American public
in general was not deeply interested in the scandal; few people
seemed to feel that bugging the Democratic headquarters was a
particularly serious crime. Understandably, the Democrats, who
smelt blood, were determined to alter that opinion – perhaps
even to indict the President himself.

The subsequent story of Watergate is a tale of Nixon's attempts
to play down the scandal, and of his opponents' determination
to play it up and make the utmost political capital out of it.
The struggle went on for two years, and culminated in the
resignation of Richard Nixon in August 1974. By the time it
was all over, most Americans – and in fact, most of the rest
of the world – were utterly bored with Watergate, and a full
account of all the twists and turns of those two years would
probably be equally boring for the reader. In summary, the story
is as follows.

Nixon's campaign manager, Attorney General John Mitchell, lost no time in disowning the burglars and insisting that they had acted alone. Nixon quickly confirmed this. But things began to go wrong for Nixon when Press investigators – particularly from the *Washington Post* – learned that $114,000 had been paid into Barker's bank account in Miami two months before the break-in. It was soon established that a large part of this money represented "campaign contributions" for the Campaign for the Re-election of President Nixon, called CRP for short, and known to the press as Creep. It seemed that Creep used some of the money to finance a "dirty tricks" squad known as "The Plumbers" (or White House Special Investigations Unit), and that this included the five burglars. So a link with the Republican party was now established beyond all doubt. The Plumbers also included a former District Attorney, G. Gordon Liddy, and a novelist and CIA agent called Howard Hunt. Orders were passed on to the Plumbers via the President's chief domestic adviser John Ehrlichman.

By August 1972 Nixon was fighting an action in damage limitation; on 29 August he announced that White House counsel John Dean had conducted an investigation that proved that no one on the White House staff knew anything about the burglary. Two weeks later the five "burglars" were charged, and their trial was set for the following January.

The American public was not particularly interested in Watergate, and Nixon was voted back into office by a landslide. Meanwhile, the *Washington Post* was determined to make his second term of office as difficult as possible, and continued to "dig". They struck gold when some anonymous White House informant who called himself "Deep Throat" (and whose identity is still unknown) provided all kinds of inside information about Creep and the Plumbers, and their campaign to discredit the Democrats – if necessary, through "dirty tricks". Nixon's supporters reacted by mounting an attempt to damage the *Post*; its ownership of two Florida TV stations was challenged, and the value of *Post* stock dropped by 50 per cent

The "burglar" trial opened on 8 January, 1973, with two additional defendants, Liddy and Hunt. All seven pleaded – and were found – guilty. Inevitably, the press felt that the guilty plea was simply a method of hushing up the whole affair as soon as possible, and this seemed to be confirmed when the *Post* learned that the defendants had received promises that their families would be taken care of if they went to jail. The sentencing was deferred for two months.

Meanwhile, a Senate Investigation Committee was set up under Democrat Sam J. Ervin. Great embarrassment was caused to Nixon when Patrick Gray, J. Edgar Hoover's successor as head of the FBI, revealed that a great deal of phone tapping had gone on for the four years up to 1972, when the Supreme Court ruled it illegal.

The sentences, when they came, were wildly out of proportion to the offence: twenty years for Liddy, thirty for Hunt, forty each for Barker, Gonzalez, Martinez and Sturgis. McCord was released on bail. He had written a letter to Judge Sirica admitting that there was a cover-up and that higher-ups in the conspiracy had not been named. The Democrats had achieved their aim. By imposing patently outrageous sentences – the equivalent of mediaeval torture – Sirica had cracked the "conspiracy of silence". McCord subsequently told the Senate Committee that both presidential aide John Dean and Jeb Magruder, Deputy Director of Creep, had known about the burglary in advance.

On the same day, 15 April, Nixon summoned Dean to his office and proceeded to ask him a number of leading questions – which led Dean to the correct conclusion that his words were being taped, with a view to being used in the President's defense at some later date.

On 30 April, 1973, Nixon appeared on television to admit that there had been a cover-up – of which he himself had been ignorant – and that Ehrlichman and Bob Haldeman, his chief of staff, had resigned. John Dean also "resigned". So did Richard Kleindienst, John Mitchell's successor as Attorney General. Patrick Gray also resigned as head of the FBI.

The President was obviously involved in a landslide which he could do nothing to prevent; there was nothing he could now do but watch helplessly while the Democrats undermined his administration. In Los Angeles, a man named Daniel Elsberg was on trial for handing to the press secret Pentagon papers about America's involvement in the Vietnam war. He was patently guilty of publishing secrets that could damage his country, but the powerful anti-Vietnam movement chose to regard him as a hero. The case against Elsberg collapsed when the judge, Matthew Byrne, revealed that he had been offered Patrick Gray's job as head of the FBI – obviously as a bribe to make sure of a guilty verdict.

On 13 July, 1973, the last phase of Nixon's downfall began when Alexander Butterfield, a Haldeman aide, revealed the existence of tapes of the President's conversations over the past two years – the implication again being that Nixon had taped conversations to use as evidence in his favour if the necessity arose. Instantly, the chairman of the Committee, Sam Ervin, wrote to Nixon demanding the tapes. Nixon declined, claiming executive privilege. On 22 July, a subpoena was served on him demanding that he produce the tapes.

Ehrlichman and Haldeman were quizzed by the Committee; both pleaded ignorance of the break-in. Now everyone was hitting harder. Nixon offered a summary of the tapes, and when Prosecutor Archibald Cox refused to halt the judicial process, Nixon ordered his dismissal. Attorney General Richardson, who had succeeded Kleindienst, also refused, and resigned; so did his deputy William D. Ruckelshaus. But Nixon got his own way and Cox was finally dismissed.

This undemocratic procedure – which became known as the Saturday Night Massacre – caused such uproar that Nixon was forced to hand over some the tapes – seven of them. One of these proved to contain an eighteen and a half minute gap that could not have been caused accidentally. Nixon finally handed over another fourteen tapes. Then he went on a public relations tour of the country, assuring voters: "I am no crook".

On 1 March, 1974, Haldeman, Ehrlichman and five others were indicted for the Watergate break-in. Nixon was named as an "unindicted conspirator", although this fact was not immediately released.

Now the Committee was demanding a further sixty-four tapes. Nixon released a 1,254 page transcript which he claimed to be complete. Even this contained some damning evidence of Nixon's knowledge of the cover-up. The Committee put out its own transcript of nineteen tapes that revealed that Nixon had been highly selective. Moreover passages described in the Nixon transcript as inaudible or irrelevant turned out to be both audible and relevant. When the Committee demanded two more tapes, Nixon flatly refused.

Finally, the Supreme Court stepped in and ordered him to hand them over. If he refused, he would be impeached – i.e. charged as a criminal. Reluctantly, Nixon handed over a recording that had become known as the "smoking gun tape". It proved beyond all doubt that Nixon had known about the cover-up from the beginning. As the Committee began its debate on impeachment, Nixon stated: "Whatever mistakes I made . . . the basic fact remains that when the facts were brought to my attention I insisted on a full investigation . . ." It was patently untrue.

Nixon was plainly overwrought – he was reliably reported to

be wandering the corridors of the White House at night, making speeches to pictures of dead presidents. The Defense Secretary issued a directive to the armed forces that any orders Nixon gave were to be ignored. He was afraid that, in his desperation, Nixon might attempt a military coup.

On 7 August, 1974, Barry Goldwater, perhaps the staunchest of Nixon's conservative supporters, told Nixon he would vote against him in the impeachment proceedings; so did other senior Republicans. That day, Nixon went on his yacht down the Potomac, and startled his adviser Henry Kissinger by bursting into tears and beating his head against the carpet. The following day Nixon went on television and resigned. But he did so unapologetically, without confessions of guilt. If he is sorry for anything, it was clearly that the burglars had been caught. The following day, as he took his leave of the White House, he raised his fingers in a V for Victory salute.

On 8 September, 1974, the new President, Gerald Ford, issued a pardon for Nixon. A suggestion that all the conspirators should be pardoned was dropped in the face of hostile reaction from Congress.

All the indicted men served short terms in prison. Haldeman served eighteen months, then wrote a best-selling book called *The Ends of Power* in which he admitted that Nixon had been involved in Watergate from the start. John Dean served four months, and his book *Blind Ambition* made him a millionaire. Jeb Magruder served seven months and became a born again Christian. John Mitchell served nineteen months. The terms of the original "burglars" were all commuted to similar short periods. Gordon Liddy served the longest of all – fifty-two months.

Nixon remained unrepentant, and is on record as saying that the whole thing was a storm in a teacup. There is a sense in which he is obviously correct. It was in the interests of the Democrats to represent a mild misdemeanour, worth at most a few months in jail, into a major crime. It has been argued that the real crime was the cover-up, but unless Nixon had simply capitulated to the hysteria at an early stage, it is hard to see what else he could have done. In the last analysis, Watergate reflects little credit on anybody – least of all on the "investigative" journalists who were hailed as the heroes of the affair.

Perhaps the final irony of the whole scandal was that historians are now looking on the Nixon presidency as one of the most successful of the twentieth-century. His ability to adjust foreign policy with the long-term in view led to warmer relations with the Soviet Union. The first Strategic Arms Limitation Treaty (SALT I), arguably the first tangible step towards the end of the cold war, was only made possible by Nixon's efforts. His recognition of communist China and his personal meeting with Chairman Mao Tse-Tung stands as one of the great diplomatic coups in American history. Even his ignominious departure from the White House arguably served an important purpose.

ROYAL EMBARRASSMENTS

*R*oyals are not immune to the scandals that happen around them – in the past some were even to blame for them. It is very difficult for the royals to maintain a low profile because they are in the public eye the whole time. Queen Caroline decided that as her husband no longer seemed interested in her, she would look elsewhere, without being discreet about it. In the case of Michael Fagin, who was found by the Queen to be sitting on her bed, he had only wanted to chat to her about her security arrangements, or lack of them, when he broke into the Palace.

Queen Caroline – The Only British Queen to be Tried for Adultery

It is something of a mystery why the Prince of Wales, the son of King George III, agreed to marry the fat, ugly and tactless Caroline of Brunswick. It is true that he did it largely to persuade parliament to pay his enormous debts. But he could have married the queen's niece, the beautiful and talented Louise of Mecklenburg-Strelitz. His marriage to Caroline was a disaster for everyone.

George Augustus Frederick, the Prince of Wales, was born in August 1762. Determined that his son would grow up virtuous and serious-minded, George III had him brought up far from the court, according to a strict academic and physical regimen. It had the opposite effect: the prince became a rebel, a spendthrift and a waster. At the age of seventeen he embarked on an affair with an actress, Mary Robinson, and his letters to her had to be bought back eventually for £5,000. The prince became a member of a hard-drinking, hard-gambling set, which included the Whig politician Charles James Fox – one of his father's chief enemies – and the playwright Sheridan. He began to run up vast debts. He voted for Fox – and against his father – when Fox's India Bill came before parliament but the Whig politician lost and was dismissed. When he was twenty-three, the prince fell in love with the beautiful Catholic, Mrs Fitzherbert, and although she fled to France to escape his attentions, he finally persuaded her to go through a secret marriage. But constancy was not one of his strong points and he soon took another mistress, Lady Jersey.

By the time he was thirty, the prince was an embarrassment to his father and intensely unpopular with the British public. His debts now amounted to £630,000 – many millions in present-day terms – and Pitt's administration showed no eagerness to find the money. So when it was suggested by his father that he should marry and furnish an heir, he agreed on condition that parliament paid his debts.

Caroline of Brunswick was short, plump and ugly, and she suffered from body odour – probably as a result of infrequent washing. Lady Jersey, the prince's current mistress, may have pushed him into marrying Caroline rather than the beautiful Louise of Mecklenburg-Strelitz as she would be less of a rival. On 5 April 1795, at St James's Palace, the prince was introduced to Caroline; he was shattered. He staggered to the far end of the room and called for a brandy. He went on drinking brandy for three days until the marriage ceremony. On the honeymoon – with Lady Jersey also in attendance – he seems to have done his duty as a husband for Caroline discovered she was pregnant soon thereafter. But the prince found her unbearable and stayed as far away from her as possible; in the following year he wrote her a letter saying that, "our inclinations are not in our power", but that being polite to one another was. When she received the letter, Queen Caroline was with the politician George Canning and asked him what he thought it meant; Canning replied that it seemed to give her permission to do as she liked. Whereupon Queen Caroline proceeded to do just that with Canning.

What no one realized at the time was that the royal line of

Hanover suffered from the disease known as porphyria, the "royal disease", a genetic disorder in which, due to an enzyme defect, the body accumulates large quantities of porphyrins (precursors of red blood pigment). The disease affects the digestive tract, the nervous system, the circulatory system and the skin; it causes psychotic disorders and epilepsy. George III had several attacks of it and died insane. The Prince of Wales was also subject to it and so was Caroline – two of her brothers were imbeciles, probably due to porphyria. It may explain Caroline's utter lack of self-control and her tendency to behave outrageously which led many to suspect she was insane.

Rejected by her husband she retired to a house in Blackheath and behaved in a manner that led Lady Hester Stanhope to call her "a downright whore". She had a Chinese clockwork figure in her room which, when wound up, performed gross sexual movements; she was also given to dancing around in a manner that exposed a great deal of her person.

In 1806, rumours that a four-year-old child in her entourage, William Austin, was her illegitimate son, led to what became known as "the Delicate Investigation". A Royal Commission repudiated the charge and found Lady Douglas, who had started the rumour, guilty of perjury. But years later, Caroline told her lawyer's brother that the child was the natural son of Prince Louis Ferdinand of Prussia, who had always been her love. Mrs Fitzherbert was to state later that Caroline had secretly married Prince Louis before she married the Prince of Wales.

Finally, in August 1814, Caroline decided to leave England. In Geneva, at a ball given in her honour, she shocked her hosts by dancing naked to the waist. In Naples she became the mistress of King Joachim, Napoleon's brother-in-law. When she left Naples – at the time Napoleon escaped from Elba – she had with her Napoleon's courier, a coarsely handsome Italian named Bartolomeo Bergami, a former quartermaster in a regiment of hussars. This swarthy, bearded, intensely masculine character looked like a brigand from a Drury Lane play. He travelled with her to Munich, Tunis, Athens, Constantinople and Jerusalem, and when they settled in her villa near Pesaro they behaved as man and wife.

James Brougham, her lawyer's brother, now wrote to England suggesting that the prince – he was now Prince Regent (his father having become insane) – should obtain a legal separation from Caroline so she could never become queen of England. But the prince wanted divorce or nothing. So nothing came of this suggestion.

George III finally died in January 1820 and his son became George IV. Caroline of Brunswick was now Queen Caroline. The government quickly offered her £50,000 a year if she would agree not to return to England. In a fury, Caroline hurried across the Channel. Her husband was one of the most unpopular men in the country and on that count many people espoused her cause. To the intense embarrassment of the government, she settled at Brandenburg House, in Hammersmith. And on 17 August the government took the offensive by hauling her in front of the House of Lords. Its aim was to dissolve the marriage on the grounds that Caroline had engaged in "a most unbecoming and degrading intimacy" with Bergami, "a foreigner of low station". But the government had bitten off more than it could chew. Noisy mobs demonstrated in favour of Caroline and the House of Lords had to be surrounded by two strong timber fences. The queen's coach was always surrounded by a cheering crowd. After fifty-two days the divorce clause was carried. But the oratory of Henry Brougham caused a turn in the tide and when the Bill was given its final reading, it had only a pathetic majority of nine. The Lords decided to drop it.

The coronation was scheduled for 29 April 1821. The queen wrote to the Prime Minister, Lord Liverpool, to ask what kind of a dress she ought to wear for the coronation. He replied that she could "form no part of that ceremony". But when George was crowned, Caroline arrived at the Abbey dressed in a muslin slip and demanded to be admitted. When she shouted, "The queen – open!", pages opened the doors. She continued with "I am the queen of England." An official roared, "Do your duty, shut the Hall door", and the door was slammed in her face. Undaunted, Caroline drove back to Brandenburg House and sent a note to the king asking for a coronation "next Monday".

She died two weeks later, on 7 August 1821 – so suddenly that it was widely rumoured that she had been poisoned. When her body was on its way to the ship that would take it back to Brunswick, there were riots at Kensington Church, bricks were thrown, and two men were shot by the Life Guards. Caroline was buried in Brunswick Cathedral, with an inscription on her coffin: The Injured Queen Of England.

George IV remained intensely unpopular. He lived on for only nine years after the death of Caroline. The major issue of the time was Roman Catholic emancipation (England had been anti-Catholic since the time of Elizabeth I and George I had come to the throne of England from Hanover because of the Act that prevented a Catholic from becoming king of England.)

As Prince of Wales, George had been in favour of Wellington who, as prime minister, carried the act of parliament that finally achieved Catholic emancipation (although Wellington was himself basically opposed to it, believing it would finally destroy English rule in Ireland – as it did.) George IV became hysterical about the issue and threatened to use the royal veto. But the throne no longer held the political power it had under George III, and he was reluctantly forced to accept Catholic emancipation. After that, the king's health deteriorated swiftly and he died on 26 June 1830. He had a portrait of Mrs Fitzherbert round his neck on his death bed. But the two had been estranged for many years – ever since, at a dinner in honour of Louis XVIII in 1803, he had made sure there was no fixed place for her at table, so she must sit "according to her rank". After that insult, she had retired from the court.

The Baccarat Scandal – The Tranby Croft Case

His Highness Albert Edward, Prince of Wales – the son of Queen Victoria – seems to have been in many ways a rather unsavoury character. He was an incorrigible seducer of women, who spent most of his time drinking, playing cards, and indulging in slightly sadistic forms of horseplay. At least one of his friends – Christopher Sykes – ruined himself trying to keep up with the Prince's extravagant way of life. Another, Sir William Gordon Gordon Cumming, Bart., a Scottish landowner, also owed his ruin – although in a slightly less direct manner – to his spoiled and unreliable friend.

Gordon Cumming seems to have been rather a disagreeable character, noted for his rudeness and boorishness; the *Sporting Times* described him as "possibly the handsomest man in London, and certainly the rudest". On meeting a medical acquaintance in the courtyard of Buckingham Palace he is said to have enquired: "Hello, is one of the servants sick?"

On 8 September 1890, the Prince of Wales was a guest at Tranby Croft, the house of Arthur Wilson, a rich Hull shipowner. By his special request, Gordon Cumming had also been invited to Tranby Croft. Cumming was at the time a lieutenant-colonel in the Scots Guards.

After a late dinner, the guests listened to some music, then settled down to play baccarat – a card game which has something in common with both roulette and bingo. A dealer hands out a card, face downwards, to two sets of players who sit on either side of him. The aim is to get eight or nine. The dealer looks at his own two cards, and he may "declare". Or he may offer another card to the two lots of players. When either a player or the dealer has eight or nine, he has won. It is a game of chance. The players may stake what they like on the game, and the dealer, like the croupier in roulette, either wins or loses.

The players must sit with their money – or counters representing money – in front of them. The cheating of which Gordon Cumming was accused consisted in quietly adding a few counters to his stake after the cards had been declared in his favour. It was the son of the house, Arthur Stanley Wilson, who thought he saw Gordon Cumming doing this. He quietly drew the attention of another guest, Berkeley Levett, to this. Levett watched carefully and was soon convinced that he had also seen Gordon Cumming add to his stake after he had won, so increasing his winnings. Later that evening, when the game was finished, he told his mother, and his brother-in-law, Lycett Green, what he had seen. It was decided that the best thing to do was to watch Gordon Cumming carefully the next evening to see if he cheated again.

They did this on the evening of 9 September and five of them – Lycett Green and his wife, and the two Wilson parents and their son – were all convinced they saw Gordon Cumming cheating.

Now this was a serious business – not because of the money involved – for Gordon Cumming had only won £228 in two nights' play but because he was there at the invitation of the Prince of Wales. Albert Edward – later Edward VII – already had a bad reputation as a gambler and ladies' man, and was often pilloried in the Press. The first thought of his hosts – and they seem to have been social climbers – was to save the Prince from scandal.

Other guests were let into the secret, including Lord Coventry and his assistant General Owen Williams, a close friend of Gordon Cumming. The Prince was told by Coventry that Gordon Cumming had been seen cheating at baccarat, then Coventry and General Williams went to Gordon Cumming, who was in the smoking room, and told him that he had been accused by Lycett Green and young Wilson of cheating at baccarat. Gordon Cumming was indignant and said, "Do you believe the statements of a parcel of inexperienced boys?" After dinner, Coventry, Williams and the Prince of Wales all confronted Gordon Cumming, who continued to insist on his innocence. And later, a document was presented to Gordon Cumming, which he was asked to sign. It declared that, in exchange for the silence of the witnesses against him, Gordon Cumming would solemnly undertake never again to play cards. If he did not sign it, he was told, he would have to leave the house immediately and be proclaimed a cheat on every racecourse in England. Gordon Cumming decided to sign.

Far from "hushing up" the scandal, all this secrecy only made it a better subject for gossip. By the next day it was being openly discussed on Doncaster Racecourse. And three months later, on 27 December 1890, Gordon Cumming received an anonymous letter from Paris saying that the scandal was being discussed in Paris and Monte Carlo. Belatedly, he decided to sue. He was demanding an apology from the Wilsons, the Lycett Greens, and Berkeley Levett. Understandably, they refused. Gordon Cumming's solicitors issued a writ for slander.

Sir Edward Clarke was briefed for the prosecution and Sir Charles Russell for the defence – Russell had a reputation of being quite as rude and arrogant as Gordon Cumming. The judge was the Lord Chief Justice himself, the Right Honourable John Duke Bevan Coleridge, a close friend of Russell.

The case opened on 1 June 1891. The defence was one of justification – that Gordon Cumming had not been slandered because he really had cheated. There were no spectacular revelations and no dramatic surprises. The Prince of Wales appeared in the witness box but his evidence was neither for nor against Gordon Cumming. The prosecution failed to shake the witnesses who thought they had seen Gordon Cumming cheat, although he scored a few good points. Gordon Cumming explained that he signed the paper "because it was the only way to avoid a terrible scandal". Clarke's final speech was so brilliant that it looked for a while as if Gordon Cumming had won after all. But the judge's summing up was against Gordon Cumming, his central point being that surely an innocent man would not have signed a paper virtually admitting his guilt. One writer on the case has described the summing up as "polished, skilful and fiendishly unfair". The jury took only thirteen minutes to find the defendants not guilty. They were awarded their costs. Gordon Cumming – now a socially ruined man – slipped out of court immediately after the verdict. The crowd hissed the jurors, and even tried to attack the defendants as they left the court; this was probably due less to a conviction that Gordon Cumming was innocent than to an intense dislike of the Prince of Wales.

The following day, Gordon Cumming married his 21-year-old fiancée, an American heiress named Florence Garner, who had stuck to him throughout his ordeal. She remained convinced to the end of her life that her husband had been deliberately "framed" by the Prince of Wales because of a disagreement about a lady. It is true that "Bertie" (as the Prince was known) was a petty and vindictive man – he continued to persecute Gordon Cumming for the rest of his life – but there seems to be no evidence for Lady Gordon Cumming's assertion. The Gordon Cummings spent most of their lives on their Scottish estate and seem to have been reasonably happy together.

The Buckingham Palace Security Scandal

House break-ins have become so common in London that it has become a genuine oddity to see one reported in the media. Yet in the summer of 1982 one particular break-in caused such a furore that questions were asked in the House of Commons and calls were made for the resignations of both the Chief of the Metropolitan Police and the Home Secretary. Oddly enough, the cause of so much fuss was not a burglar or a spy, but an unemployed labourer trying to do Queen Elizabeth a favour.

Thirty-two-year-old Michael Fagan broke into Buckingham Palace *twice* in the months of June and July 1982 and might have gone undetected both times if he had not felt it was his duty to tell Her Majesty that her palace security was shockingly poor.

Fagan later claimed that he had noticed that Buckingham Palace's security was "a bit lax" during a sightseeing trip with his two young children. He became increasingly disturbed by this risk to the Royal family – for whom he had great admiration – and eventually decided to break into the palace as an act of public-spiritedness. "I wanted to prove the Queen was not too safe," he said later.

Fagan must also have been inspired by the fact that a year

before, in the summer of 1981, three West Germans had been
found peacefully camping in the palace grounds. When questioned by police they said that they had arrived in London late
at night and had climbed over the palace railings in the belief
they were entering a public park. They had camped there totally
undisturbed until the next morning. A rueful palace spokesman
later admitted that this was not the first time that this sort of
thing had happened.

   On the night of 7 June 1982, Fagan clambered over the iron
railings that surround the palace and wandered into Ambassa-
dors Court. Here he found a sturdy drain pipe and proceeded
to shin his way up to the roof. On the way he paused to
look in at a lighted window. The occupant, housemaid Sarah
Jane Carter, was reading in bed and happened to look up
when Fagan was looking in. He moved on quickly and the
housemaid, shaken and partially convinced that she had been

Michael Fagan, the Buckingham Palace intruder – the Queen awoke to find
him sitting on the end of her bed

seeing things, called security. They decided not to investigate.

After climbing fifty feet – no small feat in the dark – Fagan reached a flat roof that adjoined the royal apartments. He opened a window and climbed in. Over the next half hour he wandered about quite freely, crossing several infra-red security beams as he did so. These had been fitted incorrectly, like the window alarm, and failed to go off.

During his walk-about he paused to admire the various royal portraits and had a brief rest on the throne. He also came across some royal bedrooms – those of Mark Phillips and the Duke of Edinburgh – the first he decided not to bother and the second turned out to be elsewhere. He then entered the Post Room and found a fridge containing a bottle of Californian white wine. Expecting to be arrested at any moment he decided to relax a bit first. He had drunk half the bottle by the time he realized that nobody was coming to get him, so he put it down and left by the risky way he had entered.

Just over a month later, on the night of 9 July, he drank a fair amount of whisky and set out to repeat his performance. Once again he entered the palace with no difficulties. This time though, he was clearly suffering from stress and too much booze. He smashed a royal ash-tray with the intent of cutting his wrists with the jagged edge, but in doing so cut his hand. Thus, looking for a suitable place to kill himself and dripping blood on the carpet, he came across a door that pronounced itself to be the entry to the Queen's bedroom.

Her Majesty awoke to find Michael Fagan sitting on the edge of her bed, nursing his wounded hand and mumbling in a quiet voice. Speaking reassuringly to him she quietly reached for the alarm button by her bed, but unfortunately it had been incorrectly wired and failed to work. When she realized that nobody was coming she marshalled considerable courage and picked up the bedside telephone – this apparently didn't bother Fagan in the least. The telephone connected her directly to the palace switchboard and she asked them to put her through to security. Unfortunately the police guard had already knocked-off for the night and nobody else in the vicinity could be raised. Her footman was out in the grounds walking the royal corgis and the nightmaid was working in a room out of earshot of a telephone. The Queen kept a brave face in what must have been a nightmare situation and kept on chatting with the intruder.

Eventually Fagan asked for a cigarette and the Queen, pointing out she was a non-smoker, said she would go and get one from a member of staff. By this time the footman, Paul Whybrew, had returned from walking the dogs and quickly went in to confront the intruder. Fagan quietly insisted that all he wanted to do was talk with *his* Queen. Whybrew said that was fine, but in all fairness he should let her get dressed first. Fagan agreed and went with the footman and a maid to a nearby pantry. He waited there quietly until the police eventually arrived and arrested him.

Despite the fact that Michael Fagan gave a full and detailed confession of both break-ins the police and crown prosecution faced a difficult problem. It is a peculiarity of English law that entering another person's property is not a criminal offence unless it can be proved that it was done with an intent to commit a crime (Fagan could have been charged with trespassing, but that would have merely been a civil offence). Thus, rather ridiculously, Fagan was tried in the Old Bailey for the theft of half a bottle of wine (valued by the court at £3) that was technically owned by the Prince and Princess of Wales.

The trial contained some farcical scenes. When Mrs Barbra Mills, acting for the prosecution asked Fagan: "It wasn't your drink was it?" he replied: "It wasn't my palace either." "It was not your right to drink it," she insisted, to which Fagan countered: "Well, I'd done a hard day's work for the Queen, showing her how to break her security." He went on to point out that Her Majesty was lucky that somebody as public-spirited as himself had broken into her apartments; "I mean, I could have been a rapist or something!"

The jury acquitted Fagan of the crime of theft, but he was held in custody on an unconnected charge of taking and driving away a car without the owners permission, to which he had also admitted. His second trial took place that October and after he had pleaded guilty the judge ordered him to be placed in the care of a high security mental hospital. Despite the fact that it was pressed by several doctors that he should be held without time limit he was given the right to appeal.

In January of the following year the psychiatric review board found that he was "not fully recovered", but on the grounds that he offered no threat to the community allowed his release. Perhaps predictably, angry questions were asked in the House of Commons.

The mortified police officers in charge of palace security might have hoped for a bit of peace and quiet in which to put their house in order, but this was not to be. Fagan's break-in indirectly sparked-off another, if unconnected, scandal involving one of their most senior officers.

Commander Michael Trestrail, MVO, was the Queen's personal bodyguard and a man of impeccable reputation. He had served in the Royal Protection Group for sixteen years and had been awarded membership of the Royal Victorian Order. Four months before the arrest of Fagan he had successfully passed the infamous "positive vetting" process; a rigorous investigation of all aspects of an individual's life, designed to weed-out security risks. Yet it took only one telephone call to wreck his career.

Trestrail was a closet homosexual and had indulged in frequent liaisons with male prostitutes over the years. On reading the press reports of the Fagan break-in an ex-lover of Trestrail's, male prostitute Michael Rauch, decided to try to sell his story to the Fleet Street papers. The newspaper he contacted turned him down and decided to report the matter to the Palace. Rauch was taken in by Scotland Yard for questioning and Trestrail resigned immediately. During his interrogation, Rauch admitted to the police that he had tried to blackmail Trestrail some time before; an event that had, not surprisingly, marked the end of their relationship. This disclosure worked an increasingly ugly media mob into a frenzy.

By indulging in a promiscuous, homosexual secret life, Trestrail, it was argued, had left himself open to blackmail by *anybody*, including those who might wish to assassinate the Queen. This belief was refuted by a subsequent official enquiry into the affair. It was found that Trestrail had know he was homosexual since his teens, and though generally attempting to suppress this aspect of himself, he often found it impossible to do so; especially when drunk. Even so, the Commission reported that he had carried out his duties in an exemplary fashion and his private practices had not breached palace security in any way; in fact, only Rauch and another male lover had known of his position at the palace.

Even so, the damage was done. The media trial, which had concentrated on the Commander's homosexuality rather than on his promiscuity, had ruined any chance of his being reinstated. Trestrail took early retirement on a reduced pension.

Later that month, as if to bring everyone back down to earth, the Irish Republican Army (IRA) provided a genuine example of breached security. On 20 July, a car bomb exploded in Hyde Park, killing three members of the Household Cavalry as they rode from their barracks to the changing of the guard ceremony at Whitehall. Twenty-three people were injured and a number of horses were killed or injured so badly they had to be put down. Two hours later a second bomb went off under a bandstand in Regent's Park during a lunchtime concert by the band of the Royal Greenjackets. Six bandsmen were killed in the blast and twenty-eight people were injured. The Queen, although visibly shaken by the events of the last month, continued with all of her official engagements, although under rigorously tightened security.